UNSTABLE RELATIONS

UNSTABLE RELATIONS

INDIGENOUS PEOPLE AND ENVIRONMENTALISM IN CONTEMPORARY AUSTRALIA

EDITED BY EVE VINCENT AND TIMOTHY NEALE

First published in 2017

UWA Publishing
Crawley, Western Australia 6009
www.uwap.uwa.edu.au
UWAP is an imprint of UWA Publishing

THE UNIVERSITY OF
WESTERN AUSTRALIA

a division of The University of Western Australia

National Library of Australia Cataloguing-in-Publication entry
Title: Unstable relations : indigenous people and environmentalism in contemporary Australia / Eve Vincent, Timothy Neale, editors.
ISBN: 9781742588780 (paperback)

Subjects: Aboriginal Australians—Land tenure.
Aboriginal Australians—Attitudes.
Land tenure—Environmental aspects.
Land use—Australia.
Green movement—Australia.
Environmentalism—Australia—Attitudes.
Other Creators/Contributors:
Vincent, Eve, editor.
Neale, Timothy, editor.
Dewey Number: 333.730899915

Typeset by J & M Typesetting

Warning: This book contains the names and images of Aboriginal people now deceased.

CONTENTS

ACKNOWLEDGEMENTS

This book is the product of a long-term collaboration between the editors, which began with a panel on the theme of 'Environmentalists' Worlds' at the Australian Anthropological Society annual conference in 2013. The ideas driving this panel, featuring contributions by Stephen Muecke, Catherine Wohlan, Fern Thompsett, Heidi Norman, Jeremy Walker, James Goodman, Simon Foale, Rosita Henry and the editors, went through several transformations in the years that followed. The result was a workshop, held in September 2015 at Macquarie University, on the specific theme of this collection. This workshop drew together the authors in this book with discussants – Leah Lui-Chivizhe, Tim Rowse, Juan Francisco Salazar, and Lisa Slater – to discuss draft chapters. We thank all of those listed above, as well as Jacky Green, Sean Kerins, Jane Lydon and Karrina Nolan, for their assistance. In helping us make the workshop and book happen, we would like to acknowledge the support of a Macquarie University Faculty of Arts Themed Research Workshop grant, a grant from the Heritage and Environment group at Western Sydney University's Institute for Culture and a Macquarie University Faculty of Arts publication subsidy.

Map of Australia showing key regions and sites discussed in this collection.
Map: Francis Markham.

AUTHOR BIOGRAPHIES

Jon Altman is an economist and anthropologist who has collaborated in research with Kuninjku-speaking communities in west Arnhem Land since 1979. From 1990 to 2010 he was the foundation director of the Centre for Aboriginal Economic Policy Research at the Australian National University where he is an emeritus professor in anthropology. He is currently a Research Professor at the Alfred Deakin Institute for Citizenship and Globalisation at Deakin University, Melbourne. As a foundation company director of Karrkad-Kanjdji Limited he works closely with the Djelk and Warddeken Rangers in their overlapping Indigenous Protected Areas, but the views in this chapter are his alone.

Tony Birch is a fiction writer, poet and academic. His books include *Shadowboxing* (2006), *Father's Day* (2009), *Blood* (2011), *The Promise* (2014), *Ghost River* (2015) and *Broken Teeth* (2016). He is currently the inaugural Dr Bruce MacGuinness Research Fellow in the Moondani Balluk Academic Unit at Victoria University.

Anthony Esposito has been an activist for over three decades, working in multiple environmental organisations and with traditional owner organisations. He ran the Native Title and Protected Areas project under the auspices of the Queensland Conservation Council, before becoming the manager of the National Indigenous Conservation Program for The Wilderness Society. Through his roles in these organisations he was engaged in major campaigns and collaborations in northern and south-west Australia. For the past several years, Anthony has been involved in strategic efforts to prevent the opening up of the Galilee Basin to coal mining, and works with the Wangan and Jagalingou Traditional Owners Family Council in their opposition to the proposed Carmichael mega-coalmine and in their 'defence of country'.

Robert Levitus is an anthropologist currently working in the School of Culture, History and Languages at the Australian National University. He has conducted research in the Alligator Rivers region of the Northern Territory since 1981, focusing on the social history of intercultural relations in the buffalo industry, and on a range of topics associated with the modern era of large-scale mining and national park management. He has also carried out applied research in the East Kimberley and south-west Queensland, and into Aboriginal policy issues. He is currently documenting the career and views of Dave Lindner, a conservationist of long experience in Kakadu National Park.

Richard J. Martin is a Research Fellow at The University of Queensland. His research is focused on the politics of land and identity, with a particularly interest in the Gulf Country of northern Australia. In addition to his academic studies, he has carried out extensive applied research, including work on multiple native title claims and cultural heritage matters around Queensland.

Monica Morgan is a Yorta Yorta woman living on Cummeragunja lands. She was co-founder and facilitator of the Murray Lower Darling Rivers Indigenous Nations, an advocacy body on culture and water. Monica has a long history in advocacy and activism for First Nations rights to land and water. She has represented her people at both the state, national and international level and is currently the director of a number of Aboriginal Community-Controlled organisations. Monica has authored and co-authored a number of publications on native title and water rights, was a member of the UNESCO Panel Cultural Diversity in Water and contributed to an anthology entitled *Water, Cultural Diversity, and Global Environmental Change: Emerging Trends, Sustainable Futures?* (Springer, 2012).

Stephen Muecke is Professor of Ethnography at the University of New South Wales, Sydney, where he is part of the Environmental Humanities program. He has written extensively on Indigenous Australia, especially in the Kimberley, and on the Indian Ocean. He is a Fellow of the Australian Academy of the Humanities. Recent books are *The Mother's Day Protest and Other Fictocritical Essays* (Rowman and Littlefield International, 2016) and a new edition of Paddy Roe's, *Gularabulu: Stories from the West Kimberley* (University of Western Australia Publishing, 2016).

Timothy Neale is currently a Research Fellow at Deakin University's Alfred Deakin Institute for Citizenship and Globalisation. He is the co-editor, with Crystal McKinnon and Eve Vincent, of *History, Power, Text: Cultural Studies and Indigenous Studies* (UTS E-Press, 2014) and, with Stephen Turner, of *Other People's Country: Law, Water and Entitlement in Settler Colonial Sites* (Routledge, 2016). He is also the author of *Wild Articulations: environmentalism and indigeneity in Northern Australia* (University of Hawaii Press, forthcoming).

Michaela Spencer works as a Postdoctoral Fellow in the Contemporary Indigenous Knowledges and Governance Group at the Northern Institute, Charles Darwin University. Drawing on both environmental science and STS, her past research has focused on multiple natures and differing practices of knowledge making within changing regimes of environmental management. Her current research involves working collaboratively with Indigenous researchers, government and service providers in remote Indigenous communities, carrying out projects focused on governance, disaster management, community engagement, and health and wellbeing.

Dave Sweeney has been active in the uranium mining and nuclear debate for three decades through his work with the media, trade unions and environment groups on nuclear, resource and Indigenous issues. With a background in political science and journalism he has been closely involved with Australia's major campaigns against uranium mining and nuclear-waste dumping, presented in national and international political and media forums and been involved in events ranging from protests at remote mine sites to presentations in the boardrooms of some of the biggest resource companies. Dave works as a national nuclear campaigner for the Australian Conservation Foundation and holds a vision of a nuclear-free Australia that is positive about its future and honest about its past.

David Trigger is Professor of Anthropology at The University of Queensland. His research interests encompass the different meanings attributed to land and nature across diverse sectors of society. He has carried out more than thirty-five years of anthropological study on Indigenous Australian systems of land tenure, including applied research on resource development negotiations and native title. He is the author of *Whitefella Comin': Aboriginal Responses to Colonialism in Northern Australia* (CUP, 1992).

Eve Vincent is a Lecturer in the Department of Anthropology, Macquarie University. She is the co-editor, with Timothy Neale and Crystal McKinnon, of *History, Power, Text: Cultural Studies and Indigenous Studies* (UTS E-Press, 2014).

Jessica K. Weir is a Senior Research Fellow at Western Sydney University's Institute for Culture and Society and Visiting Fellow at The ANU's Fenner School. Her research is part of the critical intellectual work of the Environmental Humanities to resituate humans within their environments, and more-than-humans within cultural and ethical domains, as part of responding to ecological devastation and climate change. She is the author of *Murray River Country* (Aboriginal Studies Press, 2009) and editor of *Country, Native Title and Ecology* (ANU E-Press, 2012).

1

INSTABILITIES AND INEQUALITIES: RELATIONS BETWEEN INDIGENOUS PEOPLE AND ENVIRONMENTALISM IN AUSTRALIA TODAY

Timothy Neale and Eve Vincent

From Affinity to Conflict? Introducing 'Green-Black' Relations Today

In 2014, David Ritter, former native title lawyer and current Chief Executive Officer of Greenpeace Australia Pacific, provided his assessment of the state of 'green-black' relations in contemporary Australia. Ritter began by establishing the fact that news media stories increasingly report the relationship as fractious and proceeded to argue against the assumption that there exists 'an essential and irreconcilable *conflict* between the values underpinning Indigenous land rights and aspirations on the one hand and environmental imperatives on the other'.[1] The emphasis is ours – we are struck by 'conflict' assuming centre stage as the popular assumption characterising this time period, to the point that Ritter was compelled to counter it.

In previous decades, critical assessments of 'green-black' (or environmentalist–Indigenous) relationships cautioned against the assumption that there existed an essential *affinity* between Indigenous interests in and relations to land and water, on the one hand, and environmental objectives, on the other.[2] Over recent decades, in Australia, an inversion of the underlying assumption about the status of relations between Indigenous people and environmentalist groups seems to have taken place. In the past five years especially, such relations have been subjected to renewed public attention, driven, in part, by strident criticisms of environmentalist groups advanced by both Indigenous and non-Indigenous public figures. Prime ministers, politicians, journalists, academics, community leaders and others have variously accused 'greenies' of being an obstructive or stifling influence on resource extraction and, thereby, the improvement of Indigenous lives.[3]

The message has been consistent. As Warren Mundine, chair of the Abbott-Turnbull government's Indigenous Advisory Council, wrote in 2014: 'The only way for Indigenous people to rise out of poverty is through commercial and economic develop-ment'.[4] When environmentalist groups' objections to commercial industrial activity on Indigenous people's country are sustained, this prospect is imperilled. And yet, productive and new alliances continued to be forged in this same time period. In this volume, for example, Stephen Muecke characterises the relationship between those Goolarabooloo people who sought to protect Walmadany (James Price Point) in Western Australia from a major liquid-gas processing plant and port, and their green supporters, as the most 'successful, Indigenous-green alliance in Australia's history'.[5] This campaign culminated in proponents Woodside Petroleum aban-doning the project in 2013. Elsewhere, Heidi Norman highlights that Gomeroi people in north-western New South Wales are in the process of forging new relationships with both green groups and local farmers in the midst of a massive expansion of coal mining and coal seam gas exploration in Gomeroi country.[6] How do we make sense of these simultaneous changes?

Ritter notes, and we agree, that the current moment does not in fact mark a rupture from a past history of mutually reconciled interests. In Ritter's terms, 'relations between environmentalists and Indigenous people have always been complicated and taken multiple forms'.[7] In this volume, we prefer to suggest that they have long been 'unstable'. Further, Indigenous–environmentalist relations are not only unstable but also they take ever more diverse forms under the influence of two conditions. First, the definitions and meanings of 'environmentalism' or 'greenness' have diffused. Second, and more importantly, Indigenous interests in land are increasingly shaped by coercive and complex legal mechanisms, such as the *Native Title Act 1993* (Cth) (NTA), which serves to facilitate ongoing resource extraction from Indigenous lands through the agreement–making processes it mandates.

Focusing in

This volume takes the present, persistently unstable situation as a stimulant to further inquiry. We seek, first, to learn more about the current status of environmentalist–Indigenous relations through the use of specific, empirically grounded case studies. As is to be expected, the authors of these case studies arrive at different conclusions; the anthropologists, geographers, historians and writers collected in this work do not hold a uniform perspective on this topic. While some search for a way forward for this unstable alliance, others develop the implications of Professor Marcia Langton's trenchant critique of environmentalists' involvement in Indigenous communities, delivered in the nationally broadcast Boyer Lectures in 2012. All submit the interrelationships between the environment movement, environmental organisations, 'greenies', Indigenous people – as well as images of, ideas about and investments in indigeneity – to rigorous analysis.

Second, we note that as recent critiques of 'greenies' gained ground, the social worlds and workings of environmentalists have been only crudely characterised before being lampooned. In seeking to shed light on the relationship, we deemed it a priority to subject actual environmentalists to analytic scrutiny

3

and rich description. Robert Levitus takes up this task in honing in on Dave Lindner's approach to conservation. Lindner has long worked on the wetlands of the South Alligator River in Kakadu National Park: he is not a 'greenie' or environmentalist as such, but an individual who has dedicated himself to landscape restoration. Levitus carefully details Lindner's sometimes politically unpopular conceptualisations of wilderness, land 'management', modernity and Aboriginal practices that inform Lindner's undertakings and thinking.[8] Non-Indigenous citizen scientists are a major focus of Stephen Muecke's account of the dispute over Walmadany. Muecke's interviewees explain the ways their survey work was directed by Goolarabooloo people who had long 'paid attention' to the movements and preferences of turtles, whales and bilbies. In Eve Vincent's essay 'environmental culturalists' are the primary subject of an inquiry into the exchanges that unfold between them and a small group of Aboriginal greenies. While elsewhere Vincent has stressed the possibilities offered by this engagement, here the sticky problems of fostering relationships across racialised difference in a settler colonial setting are foregrounded.[9] As Vincent writes, 'non-Indigenous desires for contact with Aboriginal people, reification of cultural otherness, and postcolonial guilt combine to shape, constrain and sometimes wreck these relations'.

Third, the authors here are not content to simply represent Indigenous and environmental groups as separate and pre-formed entities, although hard distinctions are unavoidable at times. What emerges across the volume is that all the scenarios the authors describe are not just understood as shared worlds, structured by historic and ongoing inequities, and characterised by com-plex entanglements and the co-constitution of Indigenous and non-Indigenous identities. A major objective of this volume is to begin to account, analytically, for Indigenous 'greenies', be they protestors, rangers, residents or others. And we are just as interested in the ways in which greenies might seek to become indigenised, often through involvement in an environmental issue or scene. Perhaps the language of 'alliances' and 'allies' limits our understanding of the ways in which social groups such as 'greenies' or 'Aboriginal spokespeople' – and even entities such as 'a mine' – come into being and are rendered coherent in relation to each other?[10] Such language may be altogether too tidy and deceptively realist for the messiness of the world. Further, as our contributors bring to light, encounters between environmentalists and Indigenous people might prove profoundly transformative for all involved. The instability we reference in the book's title then is not just a quality of the relationships between Indigenous people, environmentalists, and environmentalism, but also internal to each of these realms.

Finally, we add to these case studies a series of interviews with Indigenous and non-Indigenous 'practitioners', whom we have asked to reflect on their experience of working at the interface between environmentalist and Indigenous groups. Here we establish a dialogue between some of the ideas presented in the scholarly work and the insights of those whose analysis is derived primarily through involvement.

In the remainder of this brief essay, we first backtrack to summarise the history of environmentalist-Indigenous relations and recent legislative developments affecting them,[11] before highlighting three themes common to the contributions – proximity, governmentality and indigeneity.

A History of Unstable Meetings

In the 1970s, a new protest-based social movement gained prominence in Australia, as it did globally. Its broad focus was 'protecting
the environment or improving its condition'.[12] The prominence
of this movement grew to the point that, today, multinational
corporations and political parties alike lay claim (however cyni-
cally) to the language of environmental awareness, 'greenness' and
sustainability. A cursory survey of the history of environmentalist-
Indigenous engagements over this same period helps illustrate the
various sources of both affinity and conflict within specific meetings of these groups' concerns. For example, revisiting the Franklin
Dam controversy (1978–83) recalls the environment movement's
early history of circulating and reproducing problematic images
of people-less landscapes: here the colonial overtures of 'wilderness' discourse are starkly in evidence.[13] The dispute over the
road in the Daintree Rainforest (1983–84) reveals the tendency
of environmentalists to interpret pro-development Indigenous
positions as a symptom of 'cultural loss'. On the other hand at
Noonkanbah in 1979, as at Coronation Hill (1984–91) and other
places, Indigenous peoples' notions of sacredness were articulated
to make arguments for conservation against the large-scale designs
of extractive industries. These notions came to be incorporated in
various ways into the environmental movement's understanding
of the value of Australia's undeveloped landscapes and its frequent
support for campaigns and legislation protecting Indigenous heritage and sacred sites. While these cases point to the variability of
the meeting of Indigenous people and environmentalism over
time, these relations, as already stated, have become ever more
unstable in recent years.

One established account proposes that environmentalists
and mining companies have traded places. Marcia Langton and

others suggest that mining and other forms of resource extraction present a unique opportunity for sustaining remote and regional Indigenous communities.[14] As environmentalists or the 'green left' cannot offer forms of development that compare to those allegedly offered by multimillion dollar mining operations, those who object to the mineral sectors' proposals – including against new fossil fuel projects that accelerate global climate change – are taken to constitute a threat to Indigenous peoples' present and future prosperity. Where environmentalist campaigns ostensibly align with the positions of local Indigenous people, the former are criticised as opportunistic agents sowing discord or exploiting 'misfits' to the latter's ultimate detriment. There are several problems with this account.[15]

One is the assumption of Indigenous passivity, whereby Indigenous people are represented as being freely manipulated by outsiders' ideological agendas. Anyone can be manipulated, but it is untenable to assume members of a given ethnic group are *necessarily* being manipulated, especially when they say that they are not. Second, this argument assumes that the economic benefits associated with land use agreements are transformative of social conditions, which we do not deny are often dire. Third, this celebratory account redirects our attention away from broader systemic developments within the nation, in which neoliberal economic restructuring has produced a situation in which mining companies are depended upon to provide what are essentially state services. 'Resource frontiers', to use anthropologist Anna Tsing's term, are spaces that engender 'revitalization and renewal, as well as inequality, exploitation, and displacement', whether located in regional and remote Australia or elsewhere.[16]

The realignment between Indigenous and extractive interests has been produced in part by the NTA, the legislative response to the High Court's famous 1992 *Mabo* decision, and the resulting 'native title market'. Like state-based land rights legislation, the federal NTA recognises the reality of Indigenous land title and places a statutory obligation on resource companies (and others) to enter into negotiations with Indigenous claimants or owners prior to development.[17] The new era of agreement-making, Langton and others argue, promises to deliver real economic benefits to communities proximate to mine sites. We argue that policy analyst Ciaran O'Faircheallaigh's point is crucial: it 'is necessary to examine and assess the actual outcomes of agreements before reaching any conclusions about their role and significance', particularly as close examination of high-profile agreements reveals a mixed picture.[18]

Employment opportunities at mines are often unavailable to Indigenous people for reasons of health or education levels, while some find themselves precluded because they have a criminal record or substance abuse problem.[19] Deeper problems are common to many agreements, which see minimal amelioration of Indigenous poverty through the payment of compensatory and/or consent monies, and often engender conflict and differentiation between Indigenous groups drawn into involvement in complex organisational landscapes. Furthermore, with Australia's recent and richest mining boom now over, those Indigenous communities that have become integrated with mining economies are left exposed to their market volatility; wages, like agreement benefits, stop and start in relation to production. As such, the end of the boom is especially concerning in remote and regional areas where state service provision is minimal and where mining companies have come, often reluctantly, to assume a 'state-like' role. As in comparable settler colonial countries, such as Canada, politicians routinely describe remote Indigenous communities without major projects as 'unviable' or 'unsustainable'. In late 2014, for example, the Western Australian Barnett administration suggested it would defund or forcefully close up to 150 out of the state's 274 remote communities precisely on these grounds. Asked to respond to this plan, then prime minister Tony Abbott insisted: 'What [governments] can't do is endlessly subsidise lifestyle choices'.[20]

Proximity

One of the abiding criticisms of environmentalists, in Australia as elsewhere, has been their apparent disconnection from the places they seek to 'defend'. That is, they are seen to campaign in the name of sites that they do not reside in and whose inhabitants they do not personally know. This is both paternalistic and hypocritical, critics add: paternalistic in its presumption to speak for others' places; and, hypocritical in that environmentalists are often urbanites seeking to preclude further industrialisation. Having singularly benefited from economies of resource exploitation, while externalising their costs, urban greenies now want to prevent its expansion. Underlying this criticism is the more general idea that we are most sympathetic with and understanding of those people we live with, or are proximate to. However, as the above suggests, the mining and environmentalist sectors have in fact each been in proximity to Indigenous lands and people for several decades.

Garawa elder Jacky Green's paintings – such as *Lots of Money Moving around over Aboriginal Heads* (2012) and *One Eye on the Money* (2016) – visually illustrate this, connecting past and present proximities as part of a criticism of, in Green's words, 'the absurdity of what's being offered to us' by mining companies today (see Figure 1.1 and Figure 1.2). Green's artworks speak to his concern about Glencore's thirty-year-old McArthur River zinc mine, the poor environmental record of which has attracted considerable attention of late.[21] Green explains that the presence of mining and government interests in their midst does not guarantee that the financial benefits stay. In *Lots of Money*, 'The road-train with the dollar signs represents the wealth being taken away from us, from our country'.[22] The criticism of dislocation, then, does not help us to either account for or understand the nature of the manifold proximities that clearly exist. Over 60 per cent of Australia's mines neighbour an Indigenous community, producing everyday interactions and structural entanglements that seem incompatible with the familiar image of mining as a definitively 'whitefella' project. Environmentalists, similarly, can no longer be thought of as a simple externality to Indigenous worlds. Where 'greenies' become conscious of their lived separation from Indigenous people, they might actively travel or work to bridge this difference.

Figure 1.1: Lots of Money Moving around over Aboriginal Heads (*Jacky Green, 2012*).

Figure 1.2: One eye on the Money *(Jacky Green, 2016).*

This is not to suggest proximities are intentional or beneficial. It is rather that their existence would be hard to believe, let alone conceptualise, given the ways in which environmentalists are typically discussed. While it is clear that environmentalist organisations of various kinds draw significant authority and resources from non-Indigenous populations, in cities and elsewhere, it is also clear that environmentalists of various kinds have been, and remain, intimately engaged with Indigenous people in urban, remote and rural areas. To draw upon an example from this book, the campaign against the gas hub at Walmadany (James Price Point) in northern Western Australia over the past decade was based in long-term collaborations between Goolarabooloo people and white environmentalists. This joining together in common cause was shaped by years, if not decades, of association and allegiance, based around the Lurujarri Heritage Trail, just as it was shaped by a lack of relation between the environmentalists and Jabirr Jabirr people who, ostensibly, hoped for the hub to go ahead. Alternately, as Timothy Neale reminds us in his chapter, engagement can turn to enmity, as in the case of the recent *Wild Rivers Act* controversy in Cape York Peninsula, Queensland. During the controversy, environmentalist organisations and peak Indigenous bodies raged against one another in the nation's news media, though these same groups had worked explicitly as a 'green-black alliance' to acquire land for conservation in the mid-1990s and continued to engage in negotiated outcomes together. Proximate relations do not equate to stable relations over time. In other situations, as Richard Martin and David Trigger's chapter suggests, proximity can be highly ambivalent. Taking the example of the Australian Wildlife Conservancy's Pungalina-Seven Emu sanctuary in Queensland's Gulf Country, they detail the emergent relations between Garawa people and whitefellas in the context of a conservationist land and water use project. The groups' proximity to one another, country, and their respective 'intimacies with country' both unite and differentiate them as they negotiate the governance and care of this remote space. Further, Martin and Trigger show that groups who have long lived in the same geographic place can sustain certain kinds of disengagement. Pastoralists who have been intimately acquainted with Garawa people for many generations profess ignorance of Garawa attachments to and knowledge of country.

As these examples suggest, proximities spawn complex interactions, exchanges or disengagements, whether between organisations or individuals. One way of accounting for these dimensions is to attend to the types of institutions involved and their structural positioning. For Indigenous groups, any interest in working with environmentalist organisations and drawing upon their resources likely depends upon their own limitations and affordances. The potential gains are undoubtedly different for Indigenous land councils, particular traditional owner groups, or community-based groups, for example, as each is able to draw upon different procedural rights in their encounters with developers and state and federal government agencies.

Another analysis of the various meetings of Indigenous and environmentalist groups would attend to the principles that explicitly underwrite their respective positions, pointing out overlaps and divergences in their commitments to conservation, environmental sustainability, sovereignty, and so on. But the necessary companion to any legal and philosophical account of interactions is, we suggest, ethnographic attention. Too frequently, the people caught up in the events and sites addressed in this book have been discussed as agents of institutional forces, cleansed of their personal and interpersonal details. Instead, authors in this book ask after the social textures of campaigns and negotiations. How are these events founded in, and foundational of, exchanges between people? Are indigeneity and environmentalism the primary coordinates within such spaces? How are these concepts 'at large' in these collaborative spaces? Such inquiries are all the more pressing as anthropogenic climate change, like global warming before it, continues to cut across established political lines as an issue of urgent public concern. Organisations such as Seed (http:// www.seedmob.org.au) and anti-fracking and anti-coal groups (e.g. Protect Arnhem Land, Frack-Free NT Alliance) are a few examples of recent Indigenous mobilisations to end or prevent fossil fuel projects in collaboration with environmentalist groups.

Governmentality

In this book, we seek to pair the context of such environmental campaigns with another set of interactions and proximities. Over the past decade, Indigenous people have become increasingly engaged in conservation and payment for ecosystem services (PES) projects. This engagement is extensive and occurs across a variety of contexts, including through direct employment, advisory roles, and entrepreneurial enterprises.[23] Having been previously excluded from environmental management, such changes have been viewed positively by many as offering opportunities for both culturally appropriate employment and community development. As advocates note, not only have Indigenous people long expressed a desire to look after their country, conservation and PES projects can be empowering and are closely associated with positive health outcomes.[24] However, while Indigenous engagements with such projects are often glossed as a 'propitious niche' – founded on 'a congenial or favourable match' between people and their cultural and economic needs[25] – this book offers a more circumspect appraisal. As Lee Godden summarises, 'When agreements are implemented in contractually-oriented policy settings, there is the potential for them to act as powerful agents of settler colonial administration'.[26] For all their avowed fit with Indigenous culture, such projects are necessarily influenced and, in some cases, directed by other agents, discourses and processes. In her contribution to this volume Michaela Spencer, for example, wrestles with her role in mediating between state directives and Indigenous priorities in Arnhem Land, a political dilemma that resonates with earlier fieldwork experiences. Spencer was already familiar with the ways in which environmentalist groups might come to participate in marketised environmental projects, assisting the Tasmanian forestry industry offset their environmental impact.

The larger point is this: whatever their effects, conservation projects are necessarily transformative; they bring with them ideas and practices of environmental care, accountability and accountancy that, to varying degrees, require the reordering of local ideas and practices. Environmental management is, as political scientist Arjun Agrawal suggests, a form of governmentality comparable to others, in that it mandates certain ways of going about things.[27] Other arrangements and other practices persist, but in the context of new norms and sanctions. A recent essay by Ute Eickelkamp confirms this point. Writing about Anangu – Pitjantjatjara-speakers in northern South Australia – Eickelkamp argues that imposed conceptual shifts have recently turned *kuka wiru* (good meat) into 'endangered species'. While this new framework might be endorsed, scepticism is another possible response, as is re-indigenisation either within or against a colonising conservation framework.[28]

A concrete example from the Northern Territory helps ground these Foucauldian points. As anthropologist Sean Kerins writes, the widely praised initiative 'Caring for Country' began in 1995 as a 'social movement' managed by the Northern Land Council, working towards environmental and employment objectives while maintaining relations to country. However, this program eventually morphed into a federally funded program in 2007 called 'Working on Country,' which centralised power, reduced budgets and focused on technical outputs.[29] Political empowerment had been turned, as Kerins suggests, into a narrowly defined employment program aimed at 'normalising' how people work and behave.[30] Yet, as Jon Altman shows, these governmental aims are not neatly transposed. Altman's essay in this collection draws on his long association with Kuninjku people to consider the place of buffalo in the Kuninjku imaginary. A younger generation has, as Jon Altman writes, been 'bestowed with a great deal of power through the Working on Country program'. Rangers enjoy wages, the opportunity to acquire new skills and access to resources including high-quality work vehicles and high-powered rifles. But their involvement in this scheme also 'lumbers them with more and more relational responsibility to deliver meat to their families in Maningrida and at outstations'.[31] In the process of becoming individuated wage-earners, kin-based demands make their presence keenly felt. Just as we should question the professed benevolence of mining projects, we should remain critical of the manifold effects of conservation projects, whether directed by Indigenous people or not.

Indigeneity

For all our efforts to redirect scholarly attention towards environmentalists and environmentalism, indigeneity remains a major theme of the contributions. This is, in part, because Australian environmentalists make themselves and their environmentalism through their relationships with and understandings of indigeneity.

Many of the essays take us to places seen in Indigenous terms, whereby ancestral beings created landscapes, waterways and other features in a creative epoch and continue to manifest their lively presence in country. In Muecke's essay, Goolarabooloo protestors, non-Indigenous supporters and non-human species are bound to reproduce the powerful institution of the *Bugarrigarra* or Dreaming. Martin and Trigger travel with their companions into Emu Dreaming country; Vincent visits powerful Seven Sisters

Dreaming sites tended by Kokatha people today. Monica Morgan argues that when Yorta Yorta people explain that the Murray cod is sacred, they face incomprehension. But, she notes, 'If you say to [whitefellas] that it has a financial means, because we catch cod to have a feed, it sustains our family: they understand that'. Jessica Weir shows that Indigenous conceptions of country condition the basis and content of claims to the Murray-Darling Basin, disrupting techno-rationalist views of water as a resource. Altman illustrates that Indigenous understandings of country might encompass species that conservationists categorise as introduced and an environmental threat, such as buffalo or *nganabbarru*. This builds on earlier work, such as that of Lesley Head, which argues that the persistent use of 1788 as marker between 'native' and 'exotic' species is scientifically arbitrary,[32] and that Indigenous responses to introduced species are characterised by their intellectual flexibility.[33]

In the essays in this volume, environmentalists of various ilk explicitly and implicitly express that there is much to 'learn' from Indigenous ways of relating to an interconnected whole. Non-Indigenous people are invited to take tutelage from contact, often assiduously sought, with Indigenous land-based cosmologies, in the process of these precepts being lived out, retrieved and revived, or redirected into new ends such as conservation projects or protests. Autochthony can of course also be laid claim to by pastoralists and settlers, as several key works from Australia and elsewhere have recently made clear.[34]

However, the closing contribution by Tony Birch urges us to proceed with caution. Where does this association of Indigenous people with nature leave the majority of Indigenous Australians, who live in urban settings? '*Where we are* has a negative impact on how outsiders perceive *who we are*', writes Birch. Indeed, we are conscious of reproducing the focus on the north in this volume, at the expense of analysis of south-eastern settings. As Birch is keenly aware, Indigenous knowledge has never been posited as more 'valuable' than these during times of global environmental crisis, first in the 1970s and 1980s and, more recently, in the context of discussions of the Anthropocene and catastrophic climate change. For Birch this offers the prospect of engaged and respectful dialogue amid the persistence of colonial denial and cultural ignorance in Australia. But, Birch says, these conversations cannot take place without also maintaining a commitment to its consequences: the valuing of ecological wisdom also 'impacts directly on the legitimacy of the intellectual and cultural knowledge held in urban Indigenous communities'. An anti-essentialist position would, we conclude, see ecological knowledge as socialised, or even learned (potentially by non-Indigenous people), rather than intrinsic and a requisite aspect of an Indigenous identity. Are the perspectives Birch holds in a productive tension to be reconciled? Further research is needed to determine future directions.

Conclusion

We do not seek to stabilise the terms of engagement, these categories or these sets of relations. This volume aims to identify and give terms to the nature of the problems present in these spaces. Further, our contributors do not hold uniform political commitments to environmental agendas, and variously engage with our themes in order to critique, challenge or advance agendas that might be described as environmentalist. Certainly, colonialism – historical and contemporary – remains a fundamental analytical touchstone throughout this volume. Colonial categories, frontier violence and racialised dynamics are everywhere apparent in our authors' analyses of contemporary meeting points. The encounters, scenes and spaces analysed here must be understood as both unequal and unstable.

Nonetheless, this volume is also an effort to trouble the binaries we have listed and sideline the bipartisan politics through which discussions of the 'green' and 'black' are usually framed and analysed; to continue talking simply of the 'left' or 'right', for example, is both poor a descriptive technique and a circular method. Our hope is that this volume provides grounds for different kinds of conversations *about* indigeneity and environmentalism, and *with* Indigenous people and environmentalists (and Indigenous environmentalists), that take account of the proximities and governmentalities that condition the lives of many in contemporary Australia. We argue that it is untenable for analysts to proceed as though non-Indigenous political agendas and intentions are the determining aspect of Indigenous-environmentalists engagements. Conversely, it is untenable for environmentalists to proceed as if Indigenous actors are either naturally conservationist in their orientation, or if they are not, that their cultural difference has been somehow corrupted or diluted. Both approaches deny the presence and agency of Indigenous people in shaping these relations with environmentalists.

We hope this volume proves a useful critical intervention into important public debates, and stimulates further empirical research into the meeting of environmentalist and Indigenous worlds, as well as anthropological analysis of the cultures of Australian environmentalism.

Bibliography

Agrawal, A., *Environmentality: Technologies of Government and the Making of Subjects*, Duke University Press, Durham, 2005.

Altman, J. & Kerins, S. (eds), *People on Country: Vital Landscapes, Indigenous Futures*, Federation Press, Sydney, 2012.

Altman, J. & Martin, D. F. (eds), *Power, Culture, Economy: Indigenous Australians and Mining*, CAEPR Research Monograph No. 30, ANU E-Press, Canberra, ACT, 2009.

Bomberg, E. & Schlosberg, D., *Environmentalism in the United States: Changing Conceptions of Activism*, Routledge, 2013, p. 1.

Burgess, C. P., Johnston, F., Berry, H., McDonnell, J., Yibarbuk, D., Gunabarra, C., Mileran, A. & Bailie, R., 'Healthy Country, Healthy People: the relationship between Indigenous health status and "caring for country"', *Medical Journal of Australia*, vol. 190, no. 10, 2009, pp. 567–72.

Cleary, P., *Minefield: the Dark Side of Australia's Resource Rush*, Black Inc, Melbourne, 2012.

Dominy, M. D., *Calling the Station Home: Place and Identity in New Zealand's High Country*, Rowman & Littlefield Publishers, Lanham, 2001.

'EDO NT points finger at McArthur River Mine over potential contamination of more than 400 cattle', *ABC News*, 24 August 2015.

Eickelkamp, U., 'From good meat to endangered species', in J. Marshall & L. Connor (eds), *Environmental Change and the World's Futures: Ecologies, Ontologies and Mythologies*. London and New York: Routledge, 2016, pp. 160–77.

Fache, E., 'Caring for Country, a Form of Bureaucratic Participation: Conservation, Development, and Neoliberalism in Indigenous Australia', *Anthropological Forum*, vol. 24, no. 3, 2014, pp. 267–86.

Godden, L., 2012, 'Native Title and Ecology: Agreement-making in an Era of Market Environmentalism', in J.K. Weir (ed.), *Country, Native Title and Ecology*, ANU EPress, Canberra, pp. 105–34.

Golub, A., *Leviathans at the Gold Mine: Creating Indigenous and Corporate Actors in Papua New Guinea*, Duke University Press, Durham, NC, 2014.

Gressier, C., *At Home in the Okavango: White Batswana Narratives of Emplacement and Belonging*, Berghahn Books, 2015.

Haynes, C., 'Seeking Control: disentangling the difficult sociality of Kakadu National Park's joint management', *Journal of Sociology*, vol. 151, no. 2-3, 2013, pp. 194–209.

Head, L., 'Decentring 1788: Beyond Biotic Nativeness', *Geographical Research*, vol. 50, no. 2, 2011, pp. 166–78.

Hill, R., Grant, C., George, M., Robinson, C. J., Jackson, S. & Abel, N., 'A typology of indigenous engagement in Australian environmental management: implications for knowledge integration and social-ecological system sustainability', *Ecology and Society*, vol. 17, 2012, pp. 1-17.

Langton, M., 'The "Wild," the Market and the Native: indigenous people face new forms of global colonization', in S. Vertovec & D. Posey (eds),

Globlization, Globalism, Environments, Environmentalisms, Oxford University Press, Oxford, UK, 2003, pp. 141–70.

Langton, M., *The Quiet Revolution: Indigenous People and the Resources Boom*, Boyer Lectures, ABC Books, Sydney, NSW, 2013.

Lydon, J., 'Resource Frontiers in the Pilbara: Lifestyle Choices?', Hot Spots, *Cultural Anthropology*, 2015 <http://www.culanth.org/fieldsights/773-resource-frontiers-in-the-pilbara-lifestyle-choices>.

Moorcroft, H., 'Paradigms, paradoxes and a propitious niche: conservation and Indigenous social justice policy in Australia', *Local Environment*, 2015, pp. 1–24.

Mundine, W., 'Green groups keep Aboriginal people in poverty', *Australian Financial Review*, 2 July 2014.

Neale, T., *Wild Articulations: Environmentalism and Indigeneity in Northern Australia*, University of Hawaii Press, Honolulu, HI, forthcoming.

Norman, H., 'Mining Gomeroi country: sacred lands, economic futures and shifting alliances', *Energy Policy*, In Press, <http://dx.doi.org/10.1016/j.enpol.2016.06.006>.

O'Faircheallaigh, C., 'Evaluating Agreements between Indigenous Peoples and Resource Developers', in M. Langton, M. Tehan, L. Palmer & K. Shain (eds), *Honour Among Nations?*, Melbourne University Press, Melbourne, 2004, pp. 303–28.

Ritter, D., *Contesting Native Title*, Allen & Unwin, Crows Nest, NSW, 2009.

Ritter, D., 'Black and green revisited: Understanding the relationship between Indigenous and environmental political formations', *Land, Rights, Laws: Issues of Native Title*, vol. 6, no. 2, 2014.

Robins, L. & Kanowski, P., '"Crying for our Country": eight ways in which "Caring for our Country" has undermined Australia's regional model for natural resource management', *Australasian Journal of Environmental Management*, vol. 18, no. 2, 2011, pp. 88–108.

Sackett, L., 'Promoting Primitivism: conservationist depictions of Aboriginal Australians', *The Australian Journal of Anthropology*, vol. 2, no. 2, 1991, pp. 233–46.

Scambary, B., *My Country, Mine Country: Indigenous People, Mining and Development Contestation in Remote Australia*, Centre for Aboriginal Economic Policy Research, ANU, Canberra, ACT, 2013.

Social Ventures Australia, *Social Return on Investment: Consolidated Report on Indigenous Protected Areas*, Department of the Prime Minister & Cabinet, Canberra, ACT, 2016.

Taylor, J. & Scambary, B., *Indigenous People and the Pibara Mining Boom: A Baseline for Regional Participation*, CAEPR, ANU, Canberra, 2005.

Trigger, D., 'Indigeneity, Ferality, and What "Belongs" in the Australian Bush: Aboriginal responses to "introduced" animals and plants in a settler-descendant society', *Journal of the Royal Anthropological Institute*, vol. 14, no. 3, 2008, pp. 628–46.

Tsing, A. L., *Friction: an Ethnography of Global Connection*, Princeton University Press, Princeton, 2005.

Vincent, E., 'Hosts and Guests: Interpreting Rockhole Recovery Trips', *Australian Humanities Review*, vol. 53, 2012.

Vincent, E. & Neale, T., 'Unstable Relations: a critical appraisal of indigeneity and environmentalism in contemporary Australia', *The Australian Journal of Anthropology*, In Press <http://onlinelibrary.wiley.com/doi/10.1111/taja.12186/abstract>.

Notes

1   D. Ritter, 'Black and green revisited: Understanding the relationship between Indigenous and environmental political formations', *Land, Rights, Laws: Issues of Native Title*, vol. 6, no. 2, 2014.

2   M. Langton, 'The "Wild," the Market and the Native: indigenous people face new forms of global colonization', in S. Vertovec & D. Posey (eds), *Globlization, Globalism, Environments, Environmentalisms*, Oxford University Press, Oxford, UK, 2003, pp. 141–70; L. Sackett, 'Promoting Primitivism: conservationist depictions of Aboriginal Australians', *The Australian Journal of Anthropology*, vol. 2, no. 2, 1991, pp. 233–46.

3   See T. Neale, this volume; T. Neale, *Wild Articulations: Environmentalism and Indigeneity in Northern Australia*, University of Hawaii Press, Honolulu, HI, forthcoming; M. Langton, *The Quiet Revolution: Indigenous People and the Resources Boom*, Boyer Lectures, ABC Books, Sydney, NSW, 2013.

4   W. Mundine, 'Green groups keep Aboriginal people in poverty', *Australian Financial Review*, 2 July 2014.

5   See S. Muecke, this volume.

6   H. Norman, 'Mining Gomeroi country: sacred lands, economic futures and shifting alliances', *Energy Policy*, In Press, http://dx.doi.org/10.1016/j.enpol.2016.06.006.

7   D. Ritter, *Land, Rights, Laws: Issues of Native Title*.

8   See R. Levitus, this volume.

9   E. Vincent, 'Hosts and Guests: Interpreting Rockhole Recovery Trips.' *Australian Humanities Review*, vol. 53, 2012.

10   A. Golub, *Leviathans at the Gold Mine: Creating Indigenous and Corporate Actors in Papua New Guinea*, Duke University Press, Durham, NC, 2014.

11   For a longer version of this history and the arguments made here see

E. Vincent & T. Neale, 'Unstable relations: a critical appraisal of indigeneity and environmentalism in contemporary Australia', *The Australian Journal of Anthropology*, In Press <http://onlinelibrary.wiley.com/doi/10.1111/taja.12186/abstract>.

12 E. Bomberg & D. Schlosberg, *Environmentalism in the United States: Changing Conceptions of Activism*, Routledge, 2013, p. 1.

13 See R. Levitus, this volume, for a fulsome consideration of wilderness discourse.

14 Langton, *The Quiet Revolution*.

15 See Vincent & Neale, *The Australian Journal of Anthropology*.

16 A. L. Tsing, *Friction: an Ethnography of Global Connection*, Princeton University Press, Princeton, 2005; J. Lydon, 'Resource Frontiers in the Pilbara: Lifestyle Choices?', Hot Spots, *Cultural Anthropology*, 2015 <http://www.culanth.org/fieldsights/773-resource-frontiers-in-the-pilbara-lifestyle-choices>.

17 D. Ritter, *Contesting Native Title*, Allen & Unwin, Crows Nest, NSW, 2009.

18 C. O'Faircheallaigh, 'Evaluating Agreements between Indigenous Peoples and Resource Developers', in M. Langton, M. Tehan, L. Palmer & K. Shain (eds), *Honour Among Nations?*, Melbourne University Press, Melbourne, 2004, p. 304. See also: J. Altman & D. Martin (eds), *Power, Culture, Economy: Indigenous Australians and Mining*, CAEPR Research Monograph No. 30, ANU E-Press, Canberra, ACT, 2009; B. Scambary, *My Country, Mine Country: Indigenous People, Mining and Development Contestation in Remote Australia*, Centre for Aboriginal Economic Policy Research, ANU, Canberra, ACT, 2013.

19 J. Taylor & B. Scambary, *Indigenous People and the Pilbara Mining Boom: A Baseline for Regional Participation*, CAEPR, ANU, Canberra, 2005.

20 S. Medhora, 'Remote communities are "lifestyle choices", says Tony Abbott'. *The Guardian*, 10 March 2015.

21 See: P. Cleary, *Minefield: the Dark Side of Australia's resource Rush*, Black Inc, Melbourne, 2012, pp. 86–8; 'EDO NT points finger at McArthur River Mine over potential contamination of more than 400 cattle', *ABC News*, 24 August 2015.

22 Sean Kerins, personal communication, 26 February 2016.

23 R. Hill, C. Grant, M. George, C. J. Robinson, S. Jackson & N. Abel, 'A typology of indigenous engagement in Australian environmental management: implications for knowledge integration and social-ecological system sustainability', *Ecology and Society*, vol. 17, 2012, pp. 1–17.

24 C. P. Burgess, F. Johnston, H. Berry, J. McDonnell, D. Yibarbuk, C. Gunabarra, A. Mileran & R. Bailie, 'Healthy Country, Healthy People:

the relationship between Indigenous health status and "caring for country"', *Medical Journal of Australia*, vol. 190, no. 10, 2009, pp. 567–72; J. Altman & S. Kerins (eds), *People on Country: Vital Landscapes, Indigenous Futures*, Federation Press, Sydney, 2012; Social Ventures Australia, *Social Return on Investment: Consolidated Report on Indigenous Protected Areas*, Department of the Prime Minister & Cabinet, Canberra, ACT, 2016.

25 H. Moorcroft, 'Paradigms, paradoxes and a propitious niche: conservation and Indigenous social justice policy in Australia', *Local Environment*, 2015, pp. 1–24.

26 L. Godden, 'Native Title and Ecology: Agreement-making in an Era of Market Environmentalism', in J. K. Weir (ed), *Country, Native Title and Ecology*, ANU EPress, Canberra, 2012, p. 116.

27 A. Agrawal, *Environmentality: Technologies of Government and the Making of Subjects*, Duke University Press, Durham, 2005.

28 U. Eickelkamp, 'From good meat to endangered species', in J. Marshall & L. Connor (eds), *Environmental Change and the World's Futures: Ecologies, Ontologies and Mythologies*. London and New York: Routledge, 2016, pp. 160–77.

29 L. Robins & P. Kanowski, '"Crying for our Country": Eight ways in which "Caring for our Country" has undermined Australia's regional model for natural resource management', *Australasian Journal of Environmental Management*, vol. 18, no. 2, 2011, pp. 88–108.

30 E. Fache, 'Caring for Country, a Form of Bureaucratic Participation: Conservation, Development, and Neoliberalism in Indigenous Australia', *Anthropological Forum*, vol. 24, no. 3, 2014, pp. 267–86; C. Haynes, 'Seeking Control: disentangling the difficult sociality of Kakadu National Park's joint management', *Journal of Sociology*, vol. 151, no. 2–3, 2013, pp. 194–209.

31 See J. Altman, this volume.

32 L. Head, 'Decentring 1788: Beyond Biotic Nativeness', *Geographical Research*, vol. 50, no. 2, 2011, pp. 166–78.

33 D. Trigger, 'Indigeneity, Ferality, and What "Belongs" in the Australian Bush: Aboriginal responses to "introduced" animals and plants in a settler-descendant society', *Journal of the Royal Anthropological Institute*, vol. 14, no. 3, 2008, pp. 628–46.

34 H. Norman, *Energy Policy*; C. Gressier, *At Home in the Okavango: White Batswana Narratives of Emplacement and Belonging*, Berghahn Books, 2015; M. Dominy, *Calling the Station Home: Place and Identity in New Zealand's High Country*, Rowman & Littlefield Publishers, Lanham, MD, 2001.

2

RE-READING *THE WILD RIVERS* ACT CONTROVERSY

Timothy Neale

Introduction

On my first night in Cooktown, my host asked what brought me to Cape York Peninsula in Queensland's tropical far north. Founded in the mid-1870s to service a short-lived gold rush, Cooktown today is the political and social hub of whitefella life in a region predominantly populated by Aboriginal people; a starting point for the platoons of 'grey nomads' and sunburnt fishermen who relay through northern Australia in the dry season. When I told my host I was interviewing people about the controversy over an environmental regulation – the *Wild Rivers Act 2005* (Qld) ('the Act') – she blanched a little. 'That stops recreational fishing doesn't it?' she said. She remained unconvinced when I assured her that was not the case; for my part, I should have anticipated this response. I had heard the same misinformation from the mouths of stakeholders at one of the three federal parliamentary inquiries conducted on the issue the previous year. Did the *Wild Rivers Act* stop Aboriginal people from exercising hunting rights protected by native title legislation? No. Did it stop grazing? No. At one inquiry hearing, such dry clarifications prompted an activist central to one campaign against the Act to finally state: 'Who the hell knows? We do not know. Who the hell is going to tell us?'[1] At session after session, it became clear that while what the Act achieved legally was uncertain to many, its effects extended far beyond the regulation of land use within certain 'wild' river catchments. It was, as I have written elsewhere, *first a law but foremost an event* that both revealed and altered the politics of conservation, development and indigeneity.[2]

This is what the Act, as an actor, *did*. It put things in motion. It revived established grievances and minted new ones. It attracted the disinterested and solicited deeper investigation. Rich and insightful as the various accounts of the Act have been – between its passage into law in 2005 and its demise in 2014 – none have captured this agentive quality.[3] A technical legal answer of 'what the Act did', for example, would simply state that it provided for the declaration of 'Wild River areas', meaning spaces deemed to have sufficient environmental value as to require new developments to comply with a 'Wild Rivers code'. This code prescribed select zones with different planning restrictions, the most constricting being a one-kilometre buffer zone – or 'High Preservation Area' – either side of the given river and its major tributaries within which major alterations to the landscape, such as broad-acre clearing or strip mining, were forbidden.[4] As such, the Act was one law out of twelve (or more) laws in the complex architecture introduced by federal and state administrations to govern what any titleholder could do with their land. When critics of the Act appeared before the aforementioned inquiries to speak about forestalled developments, the cause was typically revealed to be rumour or another law. The controversial Act was almost never the primary culprit.

This is not to suggest that the Act was not restrictive, particularly in relation to future development, or that perceived limits are not important, but to suggest that debating the legal effect of the thirteen Wild River areas that were declared in Queensland only gets us so far. What is perhaps more significant – and certainly more revealing of present encounters between Aboriginal people and environmentalists – is to attend to how the controversy over the Act brought together a diverse and divided collective of interested parties to debate the present and future of these 'wild' waterways. It made the rivers 'public', in the sense that it forced hard questions about the political and economic life of remote places into diverse public forums: scientific reports, newspapers, television broadcasts, parliamentary inquiries, protests, courts, and so on. I suggest that this event was one in which different actors pursued given ends using the tools and discourses available to them, producing both novel and uncanny articulations of indigeneity and environmentalism. In the absence of robust procedural rights, the politics of Indigenous land have become entwined with diverse invocations of past activism, present poverty, future prosperity and traditional authority.

This essay, like much of the literature on the *Wild Rivers Act*, centres on the controversy in relation to Cape York Peninsula (see Figure 2.1). While the first Wild River areas were not in 'the Cape', as it's commonly known, much of the resistance to the regime began there, and was sustained through several years by the efforts of key figures from the region such as public intellectual Noel Pearson, head of the Cape York Land Council (CYLC) Richie Ah Mat, and Gerhardt Pearson, head of the CYLC-affiliated development corporation Balkanu. Other Wild River declarations, such as those declared in the Lake Eyre basin in the state's south-west, were received and debated differently, in part because they attracted significant support across stakeholder groups. The reasons for this differential reception are complex, though, for brevity's sake, they can be glossed from three interlinked idiosyncrasies. First, as historian Noel Loos states, the Cape's history has been one of 'uncompleted colonisation'; unlike most of Australia, settler industries and populations have maintained a tenuous and marginal presence.[5] Second, this marginality has (unintentionally) led to the creation of a space with both significant ecological value and Indigenous groups living on or close to their ancestral country. Today, the Cape is a site of both large national parks and extensive native title claims and determinations. Third, as geographer John Holmes suggests, approaching the Cape's stakeholders as stable blocs of 'conventionally identifiable power groups' is to misinterpret a situation 'characterised by flux in alliances'.[6] Pastoralists, environmental groups, different Indigenous organisations, state agencies and others have, in fact, been engaged in an antagonistic series of disputes for several decades. Following this interpretation, we might regard each as engaged in strategic manoeuvres within a shared social field.

I do not want to overemphasise the Cape's idiosyncrasy, particularly as my intention in this chapter is to draw attention to aspects of the Act controversy that are relevant to understanding other contexts. As much as the region is peculiar, many of its peculiarities derive from differences of degree rather than kind. Whereas recognised or registered Indigenous land rights cover approximately a third of Australia's landmass, for instance, they cover over two-thirds of the Cape. At the same time, these Indigenous lands are all subject to the same settler legal regimes which, as others have established, are coercive, inequitable, and give rights-holders no formal rights to refuse mining, environmental regulation, or any other changes in water or land use.[7] Similarly, just as Noel Pearson is often regarded as the most influential Indigenous person engaged in Indigenous policy today, he is not without compare; there are many other unelected advocates with strong political ties one could also discuss.[8] In light of these differences of degree, the following sections survey several aspects of the *Wild Rivers Act* controversy in order to illustrate emergent aspects of the broader situation in Australia.

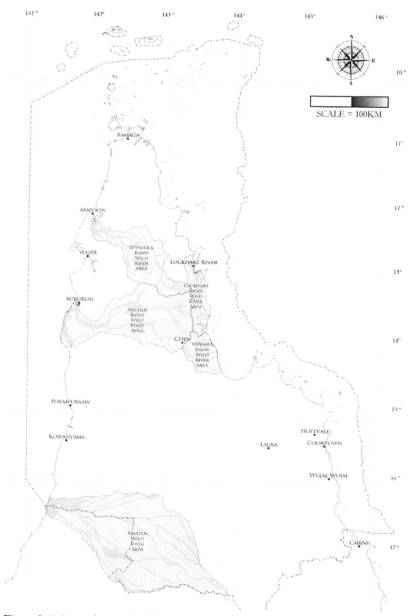

Figure 2.1: Map of Cape York Peninsula showing the Cook electorate, major locations and Wild River declaration areas. Map: Timothy Neale.

Fighting in Public

The *Wild Rivers Act* controversy occurred, to a significant degree, through the publicity of the nation's news media. But very little was written about the policy when premier Beattie announced, in January 2004, that he would introduce legislation to ensure that 'our wild rivers will run free', just as few paid attention when it passed through the state parliament with bipartisan support in May 2005. Only another eight months later did national broadsheet *The Australian* begin reporting concerns regarding the 'discriminatory' effects of the legislation, initiating a sequence in which campaigns for and against the Act routinely centred far more around press conferences and op–eds than protests or other community actions. For example, when, in January 2010, Tony Abbott decided to launch a federal Bill to 'overturn' the Queensland Act, he marked the occasion with a press event on the Cairns beachfront, flanked by Noel Pearson and others. Later, Abbott journeyed north in the company of several journalists to visit Carpentaria Land Council chairman Murrandoo Yanner, only to play a supporting role in an orchestrated humiliation; Yanner handed the Coalition leader a swimsuit emblazoned with the words 'Wild Rivers Ranger' before presenting his frank assessment to the press that Abbott's 'shonky Bill' was 'a dog's breakfast'.[9] Alongside such events, the mediatisation of the issue was also influenced by the intense and partial interest of particular outlets. To give a statistical illustration, between 2004 and 2012 *The Australian* quoted those critical of the Act twice as often as its supporters, its preference becoming exaggerated in 2009 and 2010 when Noel Pearson was directly quoted in approximately half of its stories on the issue, compared to a tenth in Queensland tabloid *The Courier-Mail*.[10]

Sifting through this coverage reveals the frames through which different actors mobilised for and against the Act. My initial task is not to assess their coherence (nor should it be), but rather to survey the basis on which different actors tried to establish publicly what the controversy was 'about' and, thereby, why their own position was defensible. For example, Noel Pearson's contributions in news media capture several key aspects of the arguments used against the Act. He and others frequently drew connections between the environmental policies of successive Labor governments and the treatment of Indigenous people under past (infamous) conservative governments. Wild Rivers declarations were, on this account, 'much worse than even [Joh] Bjelke-Petersen would have done', or 'doing to our people what Bjelke-Petersen did 25 years ago'.[11] Additionally, the government's actions were also described as a 'new wave of colonialism', in that they avowedly overrode peoples' interests and reinstated *terra nullius*, the colonial doctrine through which dispossession was justified, as '*wilder nullius*'.[12] Until the Act's instantiation, Pearson said at one point, 'the whole rights fight for Indigenous Australians was over'.[13] Another trope of the opposition stemmed from the supposition that the regulation's alleged effects on development would harm populations already coded as vulnerable, particularly Indigenous children. In the words of Pearson and others, the regulation was 'choking' and 'suffocating' Indigenous prosperity: a 'foot on our throats', or 'death by a thousand lashes' that would 'rip the future out from under Indigenous children's feet'.[14] By pairing these concerns with discussions of regulation as 'red tape', the metaphors of market liberalisation were connected to metaphors of humanitarian care. Finally, the regulation was also illegitimate because Indigenous people, and traditional owners in particular, had not been consulted prior to its passage into law. As such, it was said to violate both native title principles and (like most Australian laws) the principles of consent outlined in the United Nations Declaration on the

Rights of Indigenous People.[15] Collectively, these themes drawn from Pearson and others emphatically framed the Wild Rivers regime as consistent with an established history: the oppression of Indigenous people by a malicious and authoritarian government.

Act opponents paired this genealogy of state actions with a history of actions against the state by Indigenous people. Over the past several decades, legal challenges have been a major form of political action by claimants and activists. Legal recognition has been the basis of many substantial and celebrated gains, both in the Cape and elsewhere, leading to a determined focus on the law as an effective domain of action and achievement. As such, statements by Act opponents that they would 'go back to the barricades', in Pearson's words,[16] were made alongside direct references to nationally famous litigations by Cape groups such as the 1982 *Koowarta* decision and the 1996 *Wik* decision. In *Koowarta*, the High Court found that the Bjelke-Petersen government's attempts to preclude the acquisition of pastoral land by several Aboriginal claimants – led by a Mungkanhu man from Aurukun named John Koowarta – was racially discriminatory and therefore illegal.[17] *Wik*, as is well known, established that native title rights could coexist with pastoral titles, increasing the area of Australia over which native title rights (for all their limits) might be legally recognised.[18] In various reports, opponents to the *Wild Rivers Act* positioned their efforts as an attempt 'to refight *Wik*' and continue the 'Wik people's battle' by again confronting the government directly.[19] When the CYLC began its legal challenge to the Act in 2009, and when the Federal Court ruled in their favour in June 2014, the news was publicised in these terms; the role of people involved in *Wik* was foregrounded and Martha Koowarta, John Koowarta's widow, was the lead claimant.[20] By putting the Act in this context, opponents implicitly endorsed the authority of the settler legal order while also invoking a familiar history of adversarial and heroic contests against an established rival.

As in the inquiries noted earlier, the two abiding confusions in the coverage of the Act were what it achieved and what it precluded. Journalists and politicians sought evidence of harm, and while some disputed this was a relevant consideration, stories nonetheless appeared invoking (and dismissing) various victims of the Act: community housing, a toilet block, a fence, a biodiesel plantation and so on. By far the most feted casualty was Cape Alumina's proposed Pisolite Hills bauxite mine near Mapoon, on the north-west coast. According to the company, a significant amount of the bauxite that it hoped to extract was within the Wenlock River area's buffer zone, overlapping also with a reserve named and managed in honour of the late khaki-clad television conservationist Steve Irwin. When the area was declared in 2010, the company suggested that the project had become unfeasible, and in the months that followed it, and others, explained this as a loss to Indigenous 'prosperity'. It was reported that the mine would provide '250 permanent, full-time jobs' during its fifteen-year lifespan, then 950 'full-time and indirect jobs', then '1,000 jobs' in construction and '350 permanent jobs', then '1,700 jobs', and finally 'more than 1,300 jobs for unemployed Indigenous people' and 'up to $2 million a year' in direct payments.[21] The circulation of such grossly inflated figures is not itself unusual, given how closely the mining sector's social licence to operate in countries such as Australia has become bound to (forecasted) economic growth and Indigenous employment.[22] What was distinctive was that this discussion was accompanied by public support by Indigenous people. As Pargan traditional owner Lily York stated, 'through this company...we will have a future'. Without the mine, York continued, 'What wild rivers gonna do for us? It's nothing'.[23] Mining sector lobbyists, journalists and state governments typically position specific projects as beneficial, with Indigenous groups – at most – expressing support for the *processes and outcomes* of prescribed negotiations. But perspectives were arranged differently here. For several Indigenous stakeholders, this involved not only public enthusiasm for a mine but also treating a mining company and government as similar 'state-like' actors.

Whereas critics of the Act worked to maintain its image as variously constraining, Act supporters did not present a comparably coherent narrative. One countervailing story, presented by the state government and environmentalist NGOs, was to allege that these critics were, as premier Bligh argued, spreading 'terrible lies'.[24] From 2007 onwards, these supporters often stated that there was 'a lot of misinformation' and 'outlandish claims' in the far north regarding the regulation.[25] Of course, the presence of such 'misinformation' did not itself make this regulation worthy or defensible. In other environmental reforms the Queensland government had been acting to preclude an existing threat such as rampant land clearance and the depletion of water resources. Here, precautionary action not only seemed less warranted (if not unwarranted), but its predominant focus on Indigenous lands suggested that Indigenous landholders needed regulation. Attempts to justify the Act in the name of national heritage and natural values did little to dispel this implicit slight, as assertions that a given river was 'one of *our* most precious environmental jewels',[26] for example, could rightly be read as a co-optation of Indigenous property. Overall, when representatives of the government and environmentalists did appear in reportage, they were typically positioned as respondents. Their common role was to dispute narratives rather than generate them. Perhaps the most interesting aspect of this was the relative absence of explanations for the existence of misinformation. The Wilderness Society (TWS) and others speculated that the former was part of a pro-development campaign 'waged by Tony Abbott and Noel Pearson'; however, this angle received little coverage.[27] Second, Act supporters rarely explicitly explained the need to regulate Indigenous lands. While Act supporters and opponents alike averred that Indigenous people had been custodians of these waterways for millennia, regulation implied that it was at least possible for Indigenous people to also deplete or harm them. Very rarely were the state government or environmentalists willing to say this publicly.

The final drivers of Act coverage were the eleven traditional owners who publicly supported the Act, including Donald De Busch (Southern Kaanju), David Claudie (Kuuku I'yu Northern Kaanju), Gina Castelain (Wik-Waya), and Murrandoo Yanner (Gangalidda), amongst others. In September 2010, as Abbott rallied federal politicians against the Act, these individuals travelled to Canberra specifically to make two things clear to the nation's political journalists. First, as Claudie stated, 'Noel Pearson doesn't speak for us'.[28] Pearson's lack of either a democratic or traditional mandate meant, in their terms, that he lacked a legitimate basis for involvement. Such criticisms of Pearson's willingness to act as a representative were hardly unprecedented; however, Cape traditional owners had never said it so explicitly. Second, these traditional owners said they supported the Act. The primary reasons given for their support were that it prevented further mining and 'unrestrained development' while, as several noted, encouraging sustainable Indigenous projects and employment opportunities. 'From our point of view', Castelain stated, 'we don't see any way in which [a] Wild Rivers [declaration] is going to cost any jobs, and we actually see ways in which it can create jobs'.[29] This support did not waver throughout the controversy, though some news outlets, such as *The Courier-Mail*, paid significantly more attention to it than others. As on other occasions, reports in *The Australian* lead me to conclude that its staff were generally incredulous about the very idea that Indigenous people in the Cape could disagree with Pearson.

Moving across the media coverage, opponents of the Act described it as a singularly powerful actor that could be explained with reference to an established history of antagonistic resistance to (settler) state control. Reading through what I will call an 'oppositional' frame, a familiar cast of representatives were once again striving to defend Indigenous peoples' rights against the deprivations of the settler colonial state. Those non-Indigenous groups who supported the Act could not piece together such a clear narrative, describing these opponents as too misinformed or mendacious to see the 'light touch' regulation for what it was. For these stakeholders the precautionary protection of 'our' rivers was justified, foremost, by a 'conservational' frame which privileged the wealth of natural values. This differed from the 'culturalist' frame presented by certain traditional owners, who insisted that the Cape was being misrepresented and that their own development aspirations were, if anything, being fostered by the *Wild Rivers Act*.

Proximate Entanglements

Decades of engagement and negotiation between the parties described above compromised the routine descriptions and self-descriptions of them as distinct or stable blocs. In speaking to the 'oppositional', 'conservational', and 'culturalist' frames, stakeholders often had to speak against their cultivated proximities in ways that reveal critical fissures in the contemporary politics of indigeneity and environmentalism. During the 1990s, for example, the CYLC and environmentalist groups such as TWS and the Australian Conservation Foundation had actively campaigned together to have lands targeted for tourist development returned to traditional owner groups in the name of what Pearson called, at the time, 'a conservation strategy based on Aboriginal land ownership and management'.[30] A formal 'green–black alliance' was announced in 1995, followed by the signing of a hard-fought Heads of Agreement in 1996 with pastoralist interests and others that ostensibly paved the way for sustainable land-use planning, World Heritage listing, and Indigenous rights of access. This moment, just prior to the turbulence of the *Wik* decision, has been the focus of attention by others already.[31] Did it represent 'a real possibility of reconciliation' for others to emulate, for instance, or was it largely symbolic? What happened to the mutual commitment to conservation? My own suggestion is that the importance of such moments as this – in which one might also include *Wik* and 1998 native title reforms – are the longer-term processes and expectations they established. For while the Heads of Agreement became a kind of curio or novelty, it was one step in a sequence of legal and political shifts that secured new forms of proximity between Indigenous groups, governments and third parties; shifts in which the future of native title-claimed areas became more an object of negotiation than disputation. In order to enact the public controversy of the *Wild Rivers Act*, though, these proximities tended to be denied or backgrounded.

Perhaps the foremost obstacle for several key Act opponents was their practical involvement in organisations engaged closely with state agencies. In short, how can you maintain an 'oppositional' separation from settler government when you are on the inside of the Indigenous governance sector (or what Emma Kowal calls the 'Indigenous governance machine')?[32] To use Noel

Pearson as an example, his rise to prominence over the past two decades has been founded upon assurances that engagement with government is more prudent than opposition. This has led to his involvement in negotiations towards multiple pieces of state and federal legislation and the founding of a network of allied, publicly funded, service provision NGOs. A strategic advantage of this network, as I have argued elsewhere, is that it is able to cooperate, but it is also able to survive the collapse of a single funding source, the criticism of a single organ, or the 'reform' of a single sector.[33] But while this network operates at a distance from both government and Pearson himself, its existence and public prominence mean that it is difficult for him to in turn dissociate from the settler state. I do not mean this simply in terms of economics, as criticising government means criticising his patron, but also politics. In Pearson's case, he has consistently worked with politicians and environmentalists alike at different points to negotiate solutions. Talk of heading 'back to the barricades' appears incompatible with his position as the figurehead of a government-sponsored reform program and high-level policy consultant.

The CYLC and its development subsidiary Balkanu present a parallel set of entanglements. Each fulfils key functions within the governance machine. The CYLC is a Native Title Representative Body (NTRB), a corporate entity with both statutory and non-statutory roles in the administration of native title rights that render it a medium between native title claimants and holders (or traditional owners) and third parties. NTRBs play an important role in providing legal advice and coordinating negotiations, for example, with mining companies. But while NTRBs are thoroughly bureaucratised, as Ritter notes, many also persist in acting as activists and 'guardians of Aboriginal interests', as they did prior to the formalisation of native title law.[34] Many have also acquired associated bodies, such as Balkanu, to provide services and coordinate service delivery in native title areas. As such, it is unsurprising that when the Queensland government sought to consult with traditional owners over several Wild Rivers declarations in Cape York, they contracted Balkanu as a facilitator.

This, from several stakeholders' perspective, was a strategic error. First, it was an error on the part of government representatives because both the CYLC and Balkanu were openly campaigning against the declarations. Balkanu had been put 'in a position to totally scuttle negotiations', TWS's Glenn Walker said in an interview, 'which [in his view] is what they deliberately did'.[35] Second, it was an error on the part of government representatives because some traditional owners were hostile to Balkanu. '[As] we consulted through the Cape', the state director of Wild Rivers Scott Buchanan explained to me, 'that Cape York Land Council and Balkanu do not represent "us" – that was a very consistent message'.[36] Third, it was an error on the part of Balkanu because it compromised the oppositional narrative. As Balkanu's Chief Operating Officer Terry Piper said, '[Though] we'd gone out on a limb and spent our own money to help the government with its consultation...that $63,000 [paid to Balkanu to facilitate consultations] was used by government to hit us across the head'.[37] While Balkanu representatives, amongst others, would argue that there had been no consent to the river regulations, it was incongruous for them to criticise a consultation process they had supported logistically.

Let us concentrate on proximities. Part of what agents such as NTRBs offer to state governments and developers is access – or proximity – to Indigenous authorisation. In this instance, these corporate agents facilitated consultations between the state and its Indigenous clients while taking a position that, according to

Claudie and others, contradicted that of their clients. When I put this conflict to Piper he restated that 'our job' is not just to provide logistical support 'but also to advocate for Indigenous people so that they get a good deal out of it'. The result of their dual role, from his perspective, was that the Queensland Government had subsequently given less funding to Balkanu and established its own reference groups of traditional owners to consult in the future. These groups, Piper suggested:

> ...are just means that the government then use to bypass us...the [reference groups] may not be a bad thing, but they should be entitled to get proper and independent advice that the land council and ourselves can provide.

According to this view, select state government and Indigenous agents, in order to achieve certain aims, found ways to reduce the influence of troublesome advocates searching for 'a good deal'. What is instructive about this series of events, more generally, is that it illustrates the proximities that corporate actors within the governance machine – such as Pearson, the CYLC, and Balkanu – must manage. Their own independence and strategic interests are in tension with the robust forms of attachment, if not entanglement, that they maintain with state, private, and Indigenous parties. The Act controversy suggests that while this situation empowers such actors, their influence still derives at least as much from the settler state as it does from traditional owners.

Other stakeholders had their own entanglements to manage also: TWS, for instance, was widely criticised as being too 'close' to government. For Act opponents, the fact that TWS was involved in high-level consultations and had, in past elections, directed its supporters to vote for Labor party candidates were proof enough of a secret 'deal' or 'pact' wedding the environmentalists to the Labor party.[38] This was compounded by evidence of relationships between TWS and several of the traditional owners mentioned above, particularly Claudie, whose country is in the eastern reaches of the Wenlock River. In 2005, as CEO of Chuulangun Aboriginal Corporation, Claudie had signed a cooperative agreement with TWS which committed both to support conservation on the Chuulangun homeland (also known as Kaanju Ngaachi). This led to accusations, aired at several parliamentary inquiries, that Claudie was ethically compromised and that TWS was overriding the interests of other traditional owners if not, as one politician suggested, impugning their commitment to care for country.[39] As TWS's Indigenous Conservation Program manager Anthony Esposito told one inquiry:

> The view we hold is that in traditional Aboriginal society there is a conservation ethic – there is no question about that. There is certainly strong evidence of deep connection to country and deep desire to protect and manage country...We look to and support *Indigenous conservationists*.[40]

One way of rephrasing this, then, is that TWS representatives make differentiations, refuting the idea – presented in these inquiries and elsewhere – that Indigenous land uses do not need to be regulated because they 'would not do anything to harm [their] cultural heritage'.[41] 'The extension of [the traditional conservation ethic] to assume that Aboriginal people left entirely unregulated are simply going to pursue a path of conservation is a contemporary nonsense', Esposito said, 'to be honest'.[42] The explicit position of environmentalist organisations on the relative importance of conservation and Indigenous autonomy is often hard to delineate, though this comment makes clear an aspect implied in the legal focus of policy documents and campaigns. In short, the conservational frame used by TWS relies on the (unremarkably colonial) assumption that Indigenous people are necessarily governed subjects within the settler state.

Throughout the Wild Rivers controversy, talk of what 'traditional owners' thought was a consistent focus, whether it was in claims that 'Cape traditional owners' had not been consulted about the laws, that it was 'clear to Cape York traditional owners' that environmentalists were trying to prevent development, that Pearson enjoyed the 'near-unanimous support from traditional owners', or that 'many traditional owners' backed further conservation.[43] Therefore, before turning to Claudie and others supportive of the Act, it is worth briefly explaining the singular emphasis on traditional owners (or 'TOs') as representative figures. Many anthropologists have addressed the social and political roles of traditional owners, which have changed significantly in the wake of the progressive 'recognition, translation, [and] coexistence' of Indigenous land rights.[44] These rights have hinged, to a distinctive degree, on the detection and recognition (or not) of particular groups as in possession of pre-colonial 'normative properties', 'institutions and authority roles', or 'traditional laws and customs'; 'tradition', as Francesca Merlan states, is the coin of the settler state's 'currency of indigeneity'.[45] Only rarely are land rights allotted on another basis, such as in recognition of past injustice or a local population's present need. Of course, traditional owner authority derives from Indigenous law, and is therefore external to processes of settler recognition. At the same time, such forms of recognition have led to the sedimentation of traditional owner authority throughout the Indigenous governance machine, its form becoming central to land rights administration, development planning, service provision, and so on. As anthropologist James Weiner has argued, traditional owners often paradoxically possess (increasing) access to processes and resource rights that are actually inconsistent with their (increasingly) minimal legal rights.[46] There are further knots and inconsistencies to detail; although here I want to focus only upon the representative function of traditional owners.

In an immediate sense, summary statements like those above about 'traditional owners' are incoherent. That is, much like a Wild Rivers declaration, the authority of traditional owners is geographically specific. A traditional owner speaks for their country, to the exclusion of all others, meaning that their positions are not simply synthesisable or quantifiable in terms of aggregated majorities or regions; one individual or grouping is neither convertible nor comparable with another. Visiting Claudie at Chuulangun, I repeated this misstep by asking him what other Northern Kaanju people thought of the Act. His answer was that:

> I can't speak for them...These are the questions that white men ask Indigenous people. 'What do you reckon about that other mob there?' They're only going by numbers. And *we don't play the number game here.*[47]

Claudie's substantive point was that, outside of settler law, the Cape is not an electorate and it does not have a representative democratic structure. What such an account leaves out, however, is that traditional owner authority is nonetheless frequently made to perform for other audiences in proportional and geographically generalising ways. Discussing his decision to advocate for the Act, Don De Busch explained to me that:

43

The whole Wild Rivers debate and issue was a real opportunity to negotiate strongly with government. Those [Wild Rivers] rangers and management systems, we took advantage of the opportunity to strongly negotiate those…it strengthened our position to negotiate for the benefit of our people.[48]

Similarly, 'we were strong Wild Rivers supporters', Claudie told me, because 'the state government then – like [former premier] Anna Bligh and all them – came straight directly to us. Here, in Chuulangun'. In short, the Queensland government's need for public Indigenous support was actually a rare opportunity to achieve greater proximity to government institutions and, thereby, gain some much-wanted financial and political independence. In their terms, consistent with the 'culturalist' frame, it was appropriate that support or disapproval for anything relating to country come from relevant traditional owners, as opposed to the CYLC, Pearson, Indigenous mayors, or Indigenous residents. At the same time, part of the value of the traditional owners to the Queensland government was a social licence to operate. It was a licence to say, as they did in a full-page advertisement in *The Australian*, that (some) 'Traditional Owners support Wild Rivers'.[49]

Reading across this section, the Act controversy is illustrative of the ways in which contemporary relations between settler institutions – whether they are state governments, federal inquiries, environmentalist NGOs, or mining companies – are conditioned by a deficit of authorisation and a surfeit of authorising processes. However limited or nominal their efforts may be (and often are), these institutions regularly seek acceptance and endorsement of their actions from Indigenous parties. Public advocacy, negotiation, formal contracts, and native title proceedings are a few of the many ways in which settler institutions seek to justify their involvement in Indigenous territory; or, alternately, seek to mediate their illegitimacy. The correlate of this is that, in a country where Indigenous governance and land claims have been dealt with in a paltry and piecemeal manner, there are many conflicting sources from which to seek acceptance and endorsement, including Indigenous-elected national and local bodies, Indigenous politicians, Indigenous public intellectuals, NTRBs, prescribed bodies corporate, traditional owners, and community members. To take an example from the controversy, we need only look at Abbott's Bill, which ostensibly endeavoured to secure 'consent' from Indigenous people over Wild River declarations. In its first incarnation, the Bill stipulated only that the consent of native title holders was required, while in its third incarnation it required the consent of up to eight types of 'owner' in relation to seven types of Indigenous land.[50] In interpreting the controversy over the Act, journalists, politicians, and others demonstrated their absolute uncertainty about the politics of indigeneity in the region and, in turn, the authority of different actors. Just as Noel Pearson was regularly presented as a 'Cape York leader', though he has no elected or inherited mandate, specific traditional owners were conflated with the whole region as 'Cape York traditional owners'. While, from one perspective, this sometimes allowed different parties to pick and choose representative voices, it also meant that each performance of Indigenous authority was then troubled by several others. The controversy shows, to rework Weiner's phrase, the conventionality of inconsistency in the contemporary elicitation of Indigenous authority.[51]

Conclusion

It has been several years since Queensland's *Wild Rivers Act* was an object of national controversy, catching the attention of national news media, politicians, and parliamentary inquiries. The legislation was repealed in 2014 with little fanfare, in part because, after years of trenchantly criticising it, the right-wing Liberal National Party (LNP) administration led by Campbell Newman replaced it with a regional plan that retained many of the Wild Rivers provisions while deregulating land clearance elsewhere.[52] Certainly, key actors moved on to other concerns after the LNP took power in March 2012. Tony Abbott, who used the Act controversy to rally for Indigenous people's right to consent to regulation, became prime minister in September 2013 and – much like his colleagues in Queensland – subsequently abandoned any and all mention of Indigenous consent upon taking office. Noel Pearson, perhaps out of political necessity, had himself migrated to issues of constitutional recognition. Meanwhile, the mining and development projects avowedly 'suffocated' by the Act had either collapsed on their own accord, been ruled out by the Newman government, or continued to be 'warehoused' – as they have been for decades – by multinational companies. One would be justified in suspecting that the dire warnings and moral stands that surrounded the Act between 2005 and 2012 were not to be taken at face value.

The legacy of the Act, I suggest, is that it presents insights into the contemporary politics of indigeneity and environmentalism in Australia. This is illustrated if, in light of the analysis above, we pose the question: who is able to speak for a river? There is little question that various settler political institutions speak for the interests of rivers constantly – through the implementation of planning laws, management plans, water leases, and so on – often in the name of the state or nation and its present and future citizens.

Environmental planning law is the banal infrastructure of settler political authority over freshwater and saltwater country. Similarly, environmentalist NGOs also derive their avowed right to speak about water from an electorate (their members) alongside, often, ideas of environmental aesthetics and the interests of biodiversity and non-human others. But while environmentalists and settler governments alike might once have freely made authoritative claims about rivers, it has become impossible to ignore Indigenous peoples' immanent right to articulate, and have an interest in, these same rivers. This is not to suggest such rights are addressed well or equitably when, evidently, they are not. But it is inevitable that the diverse institutions of Australian public life, from news media to government departments, make decisions about which of the diverse forms of Indigenous authority can, or should, speak for rivers. What is clear, re-reading the *Wild Rivers Act* controversy, is that contemporary Australian politics lacks any common criteria or coordinates for making such decisions. An individual elected by the residents of a community whose lives are materially bound up with the wellbeing of the river? An individual who inherits authority from their ancestors and totemic relations to place? An unelected individual entitled by their contributions to public debates and influential political networks? An elected national body selected by urban, rural and remote voters? The Act controversy suggests an emergent preference for the traditional owner as the arbiter of both Indigenous interests in rivers and Indigenous interests more generally. It is not an innocent or inconsequential development, I suggest, that the interests of traditional owners are so often rendered equivalent to the interests of all Indigenous people.

Acknowledgements

My thanks to Eve Vincent and Leah Lui–Chivizhe for their comments on earlier drafts of this chapter. I would also like to thank those I interviewed concerning the *Wild Rivers Act* in 2011–12 for offering their time and insight.

References

ABC, 'A River Divides', *Landline*, 17 October 2010.

Ah Mat, R., 'Greenies use "wilder nullius" to get their way in Cape York', *The Australian*, 19 April 2010.

Akerman, P., 'Pearson to sue on wild rivers threat to jobs', *The Australian*, 7 May 2009.

Altman, J., *Wild Rivers and Indigenous Economic Development In Queensland*, CAEPR Topical Issue No. 6, Centre for Aboriginal Economic Policy Research, Australian National University, Canberra, ACT, 2011.

Brennan, F., *The Wik Debate: Its Impact on Aborigines, Pastoralists and Miners*, UNSW Press, Sydney, 1998.

Brown, A. J., *Keeping the Land Alive: Aboriginal People and Wilderness Protection in Australia*, The Wilderness Society and the Environmental Defenders Office, Sydney, NSW, 1992.

Carter, D., 'Wild rivers deja vu', *The Cairns Post*, 19 September 2009.

Dixon, N., *A Framework to Protect Wild Rivers in Queensland: the Wild Rivers Bill 2005 (Qld)*, Queensland Parliamentary Library, Brisbane, Qld, 2005.

Elks, S., 'Cape York traditional owner Bernie Hart to challenge Aust-Pac Capital mine plan', *The Australian*, 22 November 2011.

Elks, S. & Barrett, R., 'Wild Rivers Act crushes Aborigines: Pearson', *The Australian*, 5 November 2011.

Fraser, A., 'East and west at odds as Cape confronts wild rivers reform', *The Australian*, 9 June 2009.

Holmes, J., 'Contesting the Future of Cape York Peninsula', *Australian Geographer*, vol. 42, no. 1, 2011, pp. 53–68.

Holmes, J., 'Cape York Peninsula, Australia: a frontier region undergoing a multifunctional transition with indigenous engagement', *Journal of Rural Studies*, vol. 28, 2012, pp. 252–65.

Koch, T., 'Noel Pearson slams Anna Bligh on Wild Rivers Deal', *The Australian*, 4 April 2009.

Koch, T., 'Noel Pearson's Last Stand: Cape York's Wild Rivers Run Dry', *The Australian*, 7 April 2009.

Koch, T., '*Wik* lawyer takes on rivers battle', *The Australian*, 17 September 2009.

Kowal, E., 'Postcolonial Friction: the Indigenous governance machine', in G. Hage & E. Kowal (eds), *Force, Movement, Intensity*, Melbourne University Press, Carlton, 2011, pp. 136–50.

L&C, *Committee Hansard: Cairns 13 April 2010*, Senate Legal and Constitutional Affairs Legislation Committee, Commonwealth of Australia, Canberra, ACT, 2010.

Langton, M., 'Koowarta: A Warrior for Justice: A Brief History of Queensland's Racially Discriminatory Legislation and the Aboriginal Litigants Who Fought It', *Griffith Law Review*, vol. 23, no. 1, 2014, pp. 16–34.

Loos, N., *Invasion and Resistance: Aboriginal–European relations on the North Queensland Frontier 1861–1897*, ANU Press, Canberra, ACT, 1982.

Ludwick, H., 'Your Say', *Cairns Post*, 6 February 2010.

Maddison, S., *Black Politics*, Allen & Unwin, Crows Nest, NSW, 2009.

Madigan, M., 'Consensus washes away', *The Courier-Mail*, 2 October 2010.

Merlan, F., 'Beyond Tradition', *The Asia Pacific Journal of Anthropology*, vol. 7, no. 1, 2006, pp. 85–104.

Michael, P., 'Wild Rivers push runs dry', *The Courier-Mail*, 11 November 2010.

Neale, T., 'Duplicity of Meaning: wildness, indigeneity and recognition in the *Wild Rivers Act* debate', *Griffith Law Review*, vol. 20, no. 2, 2011, pp. 310–23.

Neale, T., 'Contest and Consent: the legacy of the *Wild Rivers Act 2005* (Qld)', *Indigenous Law Bulletin*, vol. 8, no. 3, 2012, pp. 6–9.

Neale, T., *A Stake in the Game*, Sydney Review of Books, 2014 <http://www.sydneyreviewofbooks.com/noel-pearson-rightful-place/>.

Neale, T., *Wild Articulations: Environmentalism and Indigeneity in Northern Australia*, University of Hawaii Press, Honolulu, HI, forthcoming.

O'Faircheallaigh, C., 'Aborigines, mining companies and the state in Contemporary Australia: a new political economy or "business as usual"?', *Australian Journal of Political Science*, vol. 41, no. 1, 2006, pp. 1–22.

Parnell, S., 'We won't stop, warn wild river protestors', *The Australian*, 3 April 2007.

Pearson, N., 'Abbott's bill would reverse the injustice of Wild Rivers laws', *The Australian*, 3 April 2010.

Ritter, D., *Contesting Native Title*, Allen & Unwin, Crows Nest, NSW, 2009.

Ritter, D., *The Native Title Market*, UWA Press, Crawley, WA, 2009.

Roberts, G., 'Aboriginal leaders divided on wild rivers as Wilderness Society denies veto', *The Australian*, April 13 2009.

SCE, *Committee Hansard: Weipa 30 November 2010*, House of Representatives

Standing Committee on Economics, Commonwealth of Australia, Canberra, ACT, 2010.

SCE, *Committee Hansard: Brisbane 9 March 2011*, House of Representatives Standing Committee on Economics, Commonwealth of Australia, Canberra, ACT, 2011.

Skilton, N., Adams, M. & Gibbs, L. M., 'Conflict in Common: Heritage-making in Cape York', *Australian Geographer*, vol. 45, no. 2, 2014, pp. 147–66.

Slater, L., '"Wild Rivers, Wild Ideas": emerging political ecologies of Cape York Wild Rivers', *Environment and Planning D: Society and Space*, vol. 31, no. 5, 2013, pp. 763–78.

Smith, B. R., 'Differences and Opinions: Aboriginal people, pastoralism and national parks in Central Cape York Peninsula', *Spinifex*, June 2002.

Smith, B. R. & Morphy, F., 'The Social Effects of Native Title: Recognition, Translation, Coexistence', in B. R. Smith & F. Morphy (eds), *The Social Effects of Native Title*, ANU E-Press, Canberra, ACT, 2007, pp. 1–30.

State of Queensland, *Cape York Regional Plan*, Department of State Development, Infrastructure and Planning, 2014.

Stevenson, B., *Cape York Land Use Heads of Agreement*, Queensland Parliamentary Library, Brisbane, 1998.

Tan, P-L. & Jackson, S., 'Impossible dreaming: does Australia's water law and policy fulfil Indigenous aspirations?', *Environment and Planning Law Journal*, vol. 30, 2013, pp. 132–49.

Walker, G., 'Let the river run free in our "most beautiful place"', *The Courier-Mail*, 12 April 2010.

Walker, J., 'Tony Abbott vows to turn back Wild Rivers legislation', *The Australian*, 12 January 2010.

Weiner, J. F., 'Conflict in the Statutory Elicitation of Aboriginal Culture in Australia', *Anthropological Forum*, vol. 21, no. 3, 2011, pp. 257–67.

Williams, B., 'Wild outcry at Abbott's plan', *The Courier-Mail*, 2 October 2010.

Williams, B., 'World Heritage talks back on for Cape York', *The Courier-Mail*, 1 March 2013.

Wilson, L., 'Pearson opts out of wild rivers inquiry', *The Australian*, 2 October 2010.

Notes

1   SCE, *Committee Hansard: Weipa 30 November 2010*, House of Representatives Standing Committee on Economics, Commonwealth of Australia, Canberra, ACT, 2010, p. 27.

2   T. Neale, *Wild Articulations: Environmentalism and Indigeneity in Northern Australia,* University of Hawaii Press, Honolulu, HI, forthcoming.

3   J. Altman, *Wild Rivers and Indigenous Economic Development In Queensland*,
     CAEPR Topical Issue No. 6, Centre for Aboriginal Economic Policy
     Research, Australian National University, Canberra, 2011; T. Neale,
     'Duplicity of Meaning: wildness, indigeneity and recognition in the *Wild
     Rivers Act* debate', *Griffith Law Review*, vol. 20, no. 2, 2011, pp. 310–23;
     T. Neale, 'Contest and Consent: the legacy of the *Wild Rivers Act 2005*
     (Qld)', *Indigenous Law Bulletin*, vol. 8, no. 3, 2012, pp. 6–9; N. Skilton,
     M. Adams, & L. M. Gibbs, 'Conflict in Common: Heritage-making in
     Cape York', *Australian Geographer*, vol. 45, no. 2, 2014, pp. 147–66; L. Slater,
     '"Wild Rivers, Wild Ideas": emerging political ecologies of Cape York Wild
     Rivers', *Environment and Planning D: Society and Space*, vol. 31, no. 5, 2013,
     pp. 763–78.

4   N. Dixon, *A Framework to Protect Wild Rivers in Queensland: the Wild Rivers
     Bill 2005 (Qld)*, Queensland Parliamentary Library, Brisbane, 2005.

5   N. Loos, *Invasion and Resistance: Aboriginal–European relations on the North
     Queensland Frontier 1861–1897*, ANU Press, Canberra, 1982, p. xvii.

6   J. Holmes, 'Contesting the Future of Cape York Peninsula', *Australian
     Geographer*, vol. 42, no. 1, 2011, pp. 54–5.

7   D. Ritter, *Contesting Native Title*, Allen & Unwin, Crows Nest, NSW, 2009;
     P-L. Tan, & S. Jackson, 'Impossible dreaming: does Australia's water law and
     policy fulfil Indigenous aspirations?', *Environment and Planning Law Journal*,
     vol. 30, 2013, pp. 132–49.

8   S. Maddison, *Black Politics*, Allen & Unwin, Crows Nest, NSW, 2009.

9   P. Michael, 'Wild Rivers push runs dry', *The Courier-Mail*, 11 November
     2010.

10   Neale, *Wild Articulations*.

11   D. Carter, 'Wild rivers deja vu', *The Cairns Post*, 19 September 2009;
     T. Koch, 'Noel Pearson slams Anna Bligh on Wild Rivers Deal', *The
     Australian*, 4 April 2009.

12   R. Ah Mat, 'Greenies use "wilder nullius" to get their way in Cape York',
     The Australian, 19 April 2010.

13   T. Koch, 'Noel Pearson's Last Stand: Cape York's Wild Rivers Run Dry',
     The Australian, 7 April 2009.

14   P. Akerman, 'Pearson to sue on wild rivers threat to jobs', *The Australian*,
     7 May 2009; S. Elks & R. Barrett, 'Wild Rivers Act crushes Aborigines:
     Pearson', *The Australian*, 5 November 2011.

15   N. Pearson, 'Abbott's bill would reverse the injustice of Wild Rivers laws',
     The Australian, 3 April 2010.

16   Koch, 'Noel Pearson's Last Stand'.

17   M. Langton, 'Koowarta: A Warrior for Justice: A Brief History of

Queensland's Racially Discriminatory Legislation and the Aboriginal Litigants Who Fought It', *Griffith Law Review*, vol. 23, no. 1, 2014, pp. 16–34.

18 F. Brennan, *The Wik Debate: Its Impact on Aborigines, Pastoralists and Miners*, UNSW Press, Sydney, 1998.

19 T. Koch, '*Wik* lawyer takes on rivers battle', *The Australian*, 17 September 2009.

20 To give another example, a Pearson-allied organisation staged a rally against the Act in Aurukun on 9 December 2009, locally known as 'John Koowarta Day'.

21 Neale, *Wild Articulations*.

22 C. O'Faircheallaigh, 'Aborigines, mining companies and the state in Contemporary Australia: a new political economy or "business as usual"?', *Australian Journal of Political Science*, vol. 41, no. 1, 2006, pp. 1–22.

23 ABC, 'A River Divides', *Landline*, 17 October 2010.

24 J. Walker, 'Tony Abbott vows to turn back Wild Rivers legislation', *The Australian*, 12 January 2010.

25 M. Madigan, 'Consensus washes away', *The Courier-Mail*, 2 October 2010; S. Parnell, 'We won't stop, warn wild river protestors', *The Australian*, 3 April 2007.

26 G. Walker, 'Let the river run free in our "most beautiful place"', *The Courier-Mail*, 12 April 2010.

27 L. Wilson, 'Pearson opts out of wild rivers inquiry', *The Australian*, 2 October 2010.

28 B. Williams, 'Wild outcry at Abbott's plan', *The Courier Mail*, 2 October 2010.

29 A. Fraser, 'East and west at odds as Cape confronts wild rivers reform', *The Australian*, 9 June 2009.

30 Noel Pearson in A. J. Brown, *Keeping the Land Alive: Aboriginal People and Wilderness Protection in Australia*, The Wilderness Society and the Environmental Defender's Office, Sydney, NSW, 1992, p. iii.

31 J. Holmes, 'Cape York Peninsula, Australia: a frontier region undergoing a multifunctional transition with indigenous engagement', *Journal of Rural Studies*, vol. 28, 2012, pp. 252–65; B. R. Smith, 'Differences and Opinions: Aboriginal people, pastoralism and national parks in Central Cape York Peninsula', *Spinifex*, June 2002; B. Stevenson, *Cape York Land Use Heads of Agreement*, Queensland Parliamentary Library, Brisbane, 1998.

32 E. Kowal, 'Postcolonial Friction: the Indigenous governance machine', in G. Hage & E. Kowal (eds), *Force, Movement, Intensity*, Melbourne University Press, Carlton, 2011, pp. 136–50.

33 T. Neale, *A Stake in the Game*, Sydney Review of Books, 2014 <http://www.sydneyreviewofbooks.com/noel-pearson-rightful-place/>.

34 D. Ritter, *The Native Title Market*, UWA Press, Crawley, WA, 2009.

35 Glenn Walker, interview with author, November 2011.

36 Scott Buchanan, interview with author, December 2011.

37 Terry Piper, interview with author, November 2011.

38 S. Elks & R. Barrett, 'Wild Rivers Act crushes Aborigines: Pearson'.

39 L&C, *Committee Hansard: Cairns 13 April 2010*, Senate Legal and Constitutional Affairs Legislation Committee, Commonwealth of Australia, Canberra, ACT, 2010.

40 SCE, *Committee Hansard: Brisbane 9 March 2011*, House of Representatives Standing Committee on Economics, Commonwealth of Australia, Canberra, ACT, 2011, pp. 17–18. My emphasis.

41 S. Elks, 'Cape York traditional owner Bernie Hart to challenge Aust-Pac Capital mine plan', *The Australian*, 22 November 2011.

42 SCE, *Committee Hansard: Brisbane 9 March 2011*, p. 18.

43 H. Ludwick, 'Your Say', *Cairns Post*, 6 February 2010; G. Roberts, 'Aboriginal leaders divided on wild rivers as Wilderness Society denies veto', *The Australian*, 13 April 2009; B. Williams, 'World Heritage talks back on for Cape York', *Courier-Mail*, 1 March 2013.

44 B. R. Smith, & F. Morphy, 'The Social Effects of Native Title: Recognition, Translation, Coexistence', in B. R. Smith & F. Morphy (eds), *The Social Effects of Native Title*, ANU EPress, Canberra, ACT, 2007, pp. 1–30.

45 F. Merlan, 'Beyond Tradition', *The Asia Pacific Journal of Anthropology*, vol. 7, no. 1, p. 101.

46 J. F. Weiner, 2011, 'Conflict in the Statutory Elicitation of Aboriginal Culture in Australia', *Anthropological Forum*, vol. 21, no. 3, 2011, pp. 257–67.

47 David Claudie, interview with author, September 2012. My emphasis.

48 Don De Busch, interview with author, September 2012.

49 State of Queensland's 'Traditional Owners support Wild Rivers' advertisement was printed in *The Australian*, 14 May 2011.

50 See: Wild Rivers (Environmental Management) Bill 2010 and Wild Rivers (Environmental Management) Bill 2011 (No. 2).

51 Weiner, *Anthropological Forum*.

52 State of Queensland, *Cape York Regional Plan*, Department of State Development, Infrastructure and Planning, 2014.

3

KUNINJKU PEOPLE, BUFFALO, AND CONSERVATION IN ARNHEM LAND: 'IT'S A CONTRADICTION THAT FRUSTRATES US'

Jon Altman

On Tuesday 20 May 2014 I was escorting two philanthropists to rock art galleries at Dukaladjarranj on the edge of the Arnhem Land escarpment. I was there in a corporate capacity, as a director of the Karrkad-Kanjdji Trust, seeking to raise funds to assist the Djelk and Warddeken Indigenous Protected Areas (IPAs) in their work tackling the conservation challenges of maintaining the environmental and cultural values of 20,000 square kilometres of western Arnhem Land. We were flying low in a Robinson R44 helicopter over the Tomkinson River flood plains – Bulkay – wetlands renowned for their biodiversity. The experienced pilot, nicknamed 'Batman', flew very low, pointing out to my guests herds of wild buffalo and their highly visible criss-cross tracks etched in the landscape. He remarked over the intercom: 'This is supposed to be an IPA but those feral buffalo are trashing this country, they should be eliminated, shot out like up at Warddeken'. His remarks were hardly helpful to me, but he had a point that I could not easily challenge mid-air; buffalo damage in an iconic wetland within an IPA looked bad. Later I tried to explain to the guests in a quieter setting that this was precisely why the Djelk Rangers needed the extra philanthropic support that the Karrkad-Kanjdji Trust was seeking to raise.

★ ★ ★

This opening vignette highlights a contradiction that I want to explore from a variety of perspectives in this chapter – abundant populations of environmentally destructive wild buffalo roam widely in an Indigenous Protected Area (IPA) declared for its natural and cultural values of global significance, according to International Union for the Conservation of Nature criteria. The buffalo has been very effectively incorporated into the transforming domestic economy of the Kuninjku-speaking people with whom I work, and yet it is also causing environmental damage and impacting significantly on biodiversity.[1] I set out here to explore the tensions created by this contradiction for a number of key stakeholders in the Djelk IPA, which covers much of the Maningrida region in Arnhem Land: land owners (including conservation rangers who are also land owners), regional organisations, the Australian government and environmental philanthropies.

I begin by providing some background and an historical account of the rapid growth in the number of buffalo in the IPA. I then share my observations of conservation planning meetings, aimed to develop a strategy to deal with this environmental threat, held in early 2015. Using the idiom of 'unstable relations', I then analyse some of the political contestations that emerge in competing proposals to cull buffalo numbers at the regional scale; and, at a broader scale, consider some of the emerging tensions in north Australia in attempting to reconcile sustainable use of resources with conservation objectives in an IPA. I end with some broader reflections about livelihood opportunity for Indigenous people seeking to negotiate a pathway through the complexities generated by entanglements with the customary, the market and the state in remote Australia.

Kuninjku Country and the Beginning of the Djelk Rangers

I have worked in the Maningrida region as an academic researcher since 1979 and using the analytic lenses of economics and anthropology I have documented economic transformations in the region, especially among members of the Kuninjku community. I have also politically championed the rights of Kuninjku people to pursue their chosen way of life, one which has evolved into a hybrid form of economy informed by a complex mix of Kuninjku and *Balanda* (their term for European or Western) values.[2] This championing has involved representing Kuninjku perspectives, as I understand them, to politicians and officials as well as wider publics.

In more recent times, I have become conscious of my deep emotional entanglements both with my Kuninjku friends – who actively adopted me into their relational world decades ago – and with particular meaningful places on Kuninjku country that I have frequently visited, with Bulkay being one. I am also conscious of my changing perspectives on buffalo, who I once viewed simply as game to be hunted and consumed when I lived with Kuninjku people. Now I see buffalo more sympathetically as a majestic animal that has adapted very successfully to the tropical savanna of northern Australia.

Reading Hage's *Alter-Politics* has assisted me to recognise and come to terms with the tensions of being an academic researcher and a political advocate for both *Bininj* (the Kuninjku term for themselves as black people in contrast to *Balanda*) and the environment.[3] As a personal friend of many Kuninjku people, I have been deeply moved by their current precarious circumstances which, as I argue elsewhere, have resulted from thoughtless policy shifts and changes in global circumstances.[4] By my observations, Kuninjku people are currently more impoverished and, at times, hungrier than at any other time over the last 37 years. I sense a growing nostalgia amongst Kuninjku people for earlier, better times that I also share. These emotional entanglements extend, as will become apparent, to the buffalo; like my interlocutors, I have a growing antipathy towards culling due to its wastefulness.

When, in the 1980s, I first camped out on the Bulkay flood plains with Kuninjku at a seasonal camp called Mankodbe Kayo – or, the place where the bush potato rests – there were few buffalo. There were also no feral pigs or cane toads on these resource-rich wetlands where Kuninjku people gathered regularly to feast on seasonal surpluses of game, aquatic birdlife, barramundi, catfish, goannas and wallabies. We drank fresh water from the clear billabongs and waded in creeks relatively free of estuarine crocodiles to fish with spears for barramundi. When I flew low over Bulkay in a light plane for the first time in May 1980 there were no herds of buffalo to be seen, no wallows in billabongs, no pugmarks in the black soil plains, no criss-crossing trails etched into the landscape.

In 1979 and 1980, when I resided at Mumeka outstation (see Figure 3.1 for location) and a number of related seasonal camps, I described Kuninjku as 'hunter–gatherers today'.[5] I did not think of them as environmentalists or conservationists, but rather as people who hunted and fished and gathered, managed the landscape with fire, and produced art for sale, while belatedly, from 1980, gaining access to their welfare entitlements as Australian citizens. At that time the relatively sparse buffalo population on Kuninjku country was eagerly exploited as a source of protein super-abundance. Buffalo did not then constitute what is now regarded as an environmental threat.

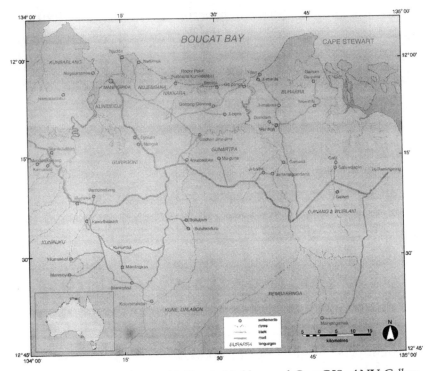

Figure 3.1: Map: Jon Altman with Francis Markham and CartoGIS, ANU College of Asia and the Pacific

In 1981, in one of my early acts of advocacy for Kuninjku people I defended their right to harvest buffalo to an Inquiry by the Feral Animals Committee Buffalo Working Party; during my time living with a group at Mumeka outstation buffalo meat was an important part of our dietary intake.[6] I was concerned that the federal government's Brucellosis and Tuberculosis Eradication Campaign (BTEC) to eliminate wild buffalo and feral cattle, regarded as a threat to the export trade, might extend into Arnhem Land.

I recently found my submission from that time in the archives of the Australian Institute of Aboriginal and Torres Strait Islander Studies. I am sure it made little impact on the Inquiry, as financial costs and political complexities were likely higher order considerations than the rights of Aboriginal people to buffalo as hunted game. Nevertheless, parts of my submission remain apposite today. I noted that Aboriginal people in western Arnhem Land were unconcerned about the environmental impact of buffalo regarded by them as posing a low-grade environmental threat mainly to bush roads; they believed that their utilisation of buffalo as a source of food kept numbers under control and constituted an effective land management strategy. I recommended that if an eradication program was needed in Arnhem Land, then the people living at outstations could be mobilised to participate more actively in culling, including as professional shooters on their own lands. Owing to the significance of buffalo as a source of meat in the contemporary economy, I was sceptical that an eradication program would be acceptable to land owners.

It eventuated that the BTEC did not extend into Arnhem Land for a variety of reasons, but mainly because some early culling and testing indicated that the herds there were almost entirely disease-free. Hence, there was no need to undertake the expensive and politically complex task of buffalo eradication throughout this region.

A decade later, in 1993, 'conservation' in a Western sense emerged with the formal establishment of a community-based conservation group called the Djelk Rangers. In the 1980s, a missionary in Maningrida had released some domesticated pigs into Barlparnarra swamp to the east of the township. At about the same time, a renowned Kuninjku man – the late Jerry Jirriminmin – released some pigs brought from the township of Gunbalanya to the west. A decade later, Aboriginal people living at outstations in the region were concerned at the very visible damage from rapidly growing populations of pig evident on flood plains like Bulkay and billabong and riparian margins. As such, the Djelk Rangers

started as a feral pig control program with funding assistance
from the Commonwealth government's Contract Employment
for Aboriginals in Natural and Cultural Resource Management
program with a Gurrgoni-speaking man Dean Yibarbuk as their
founding father.[7] Djelk is a Gurrgoni word for 'land' and 'caring
for land'. The Djelk Rangers were supported by the regional outstation resource agency, the Bawinanga Aboriginal Corporation,
and aimed to eradicate the pigs. This proved an impossible task.
Not long afterwards, in 1995, the rangers broadened their conservation efforts to deal with mimosa *(Mimosa pigra)*, a voracious
and wetlands-choking exotic plant. John Mawurndjul, the internationally renowned artist and senior manager for Bulkay, spotted
an outbreak on the Bulkay flood plains, and his deep Indigenous
environmental knowledge told him this was a foreign species.[8]

The Djelk Rangers worked closely with the Kuninjku from
the outset, in part because of the close kinship and geographic
relations between Dean Yibarbuk and themselves, but also because
Kuninjku were among the most committed group in the region to
live on their country at about ten outstations. During the 1990s,
the Djelk Rangers rapidly grew as a natural and cultural resource
management arm of Bawinanga, funded under the Community
Development Employment Projects (CDEP) scheme and the
Natural Heritage Trust.

Emergence of the Buffalo 'Problem'

The buffalo...tendency to increase is so great, that their
numbers may eventually prove a nuisance – G. W.
Earl, 1839, 'Enterprises, Discoveries and Adventures in
Australia'.[9]

During the 1990s the numbers of buffalo and pig in the region expanded exponentially, something that people living on country were well aware of, and also partially welcomed as a ready source of meat. Possibly because pigs and weeds were seen as higher ecological priorities, Kuninjku people paid less attention to buffalo. As in the boiled frog parable, no-one seemed to notice the buffalo's population growth owing to its creeping incrementalism and other priorities.

In the late 1990s Bawinanga and the Djelk Rangers were increasingly collaborating with Western scientists at the Australian Research Council Key Centre for Tropical Wildlife Management and the Tropical Savannas Management Cooperative Research Centre based at Charles Darwin University in Darwin. The goal of the Djelk Rangers was 'to develop herd management plans to minimise ecological impacts [of buffalo and pig] whilst maintaining food and trophy hunting benefits'.[10] As an element of these growing collaborations with Western scientists there were some aerial counts of buffalo, with a figure of between 4,000 and 6,000 estimated in the Maningrida region at the end of the twentieth century.[11]

Not long afterwards, in 2002 and 2003, I coordinated a field project as a part of these collaborations that saw a number of biologists camp with Kuninjku in various locations to monitor wildlife utilisation. This research was associated with a project to assess the sustainable use of wildlife with an eye to possible commercialisation of key species via wild harvest or capture. The project's main scientific finding, under-reported over a decade later, was that the range of flora and fauna utilised by Kuninjku had declined since 1979–80, but key bush resources remained readily available.[12]

With the benefit of hindsight, the alarm bells about buffalo and pig should have sounded more loudly, but even then people were camping on the flood plains and evidence of environmental degradation and species decline was limited. The greatest concern, expressed by all, was about the sudden arrival of the poisonous cane toad *(Bufo marinus)* or 'rubbish frog', as Kuninjku call them, in 2002. Almost overnight, goannas and monitors, important species both as food and totemically, were wiped out almost to extinction.[13] One important indicator that we missed was that people were sourcing their drinking water from a groundwater tap at Mumeka outstation, some 15 kilometres away, rather than from the Bulkay billabongs which they assessed as unsavoury.

Figure 3.2: Kuninjku people butchering buffalo at Bulkay, 2002. Photo: Tony Griffiths.

Formalising Conservation in the Djelk IPA

In 1997 the Howard government established the Indigenous Protected Areas (IPA) program as a vehicle to support Indigenous land management and to increase the size of the National Reserve

System, Australia's terrestrial network of protected areas and to improve its comprehensiveness, adequacy, and representativeness.[14] In the years that followed, the well-established Djelk Rangers carefully considered whether they wanted to participate in this program, as it required all local land owners to commit to managing their lands for the maintenance of biological diversity according to one of six internationally recognised land management categories, as defined by the International Union for the Conservation of Nature. In the Djelk case, this meant Category VI: 'protected area with sustainable use of natural resources'.[15]

There was a degree of regional ambivalence to this embrace of environmental management according to externally stipulated conservation criteria.[16] There was also the practical challenge of negotiating with 102 regional land-owning corporate groups (patri-clan members) to commit their lands to a conservation commons. The political complexity of this process saw a prolonged consultation phase, funded by the Commonwealth, extend over seven years before the requisite consensus was achieved among all land owners. The minister for the environment Peter Garrett officially declared the Djelk IPA on 25 September 2009, a day after the abutting and jurisdictionally overlapping 'sister' Warddeken IPA was declared.

Members of the Kuninjku clans were key players in the formation of the Djelk IPA because their estates extended from the Arnhem Land Plateau to the flood plains and tidal river margins, including key parts of the catchments of the Tomkinson, Mann and Liverpool rivers. These were among the most biodiversity-complex sub-regions in the IPA quite similar to the World Heritage listed Kakadu National Park in the Alligator Rivers region.

While Kuninjku might not see it quite this way, committing their ten estates covering well over 1,000 square kilometres to the

IPA fundamentally altered their relationship with the Australian state and the conservation movement. They were now variously required to deliver environmental 'outcomes', especially when employed as salaried rangers under the federally funded Working on Country program or engaged as 'custodial consultants' to assist rangers with advice about environmental management around sites of cultural significance and with traditional eco-logical knowledge. I, too, became more conservation-minded in my regional collaborations, working on two major projects with the Djelk Rangers between 2002 and 2012.[17] In 2009 I was nominated by Bawinanga as a foundation director and secretary of Karrkad-Kanjdji Limited, a company established to raise funds for environmental purposes and manage a charitable trust with goals to protect, restore and enhance the natural environment of the West Arnhem region including the Djelk and Warddeken IPAs.[18] It was this role that put me in the helicopter with 'Batman' and the potential donors.

Planning to Manage Wild Buffalo

Indigenous Protected Areas are required to develop 5-year plans with the first one for the Djelk IPA being completed in 2008. Throughout 2014, Bawinanga and the Djelk Rangers commissioned some external conservation consultants with well-established regional associations to assist them with their next plan, for the period 2015 to 2025, using an emerging conservation plan-ning instrument called 'Healthy Country Planning', sponsored by the conservation NGO Bush Heritage Australia.[19]

Also, in June 2014, the first aerial survey in 16 years was conducted to determine the distribution and abundance of buffalo (and other large 'feral' vertebrates) in Arnhem Land.[20] This survey estimated that there were now 97,823 buffalo in Arnhem Land (plus or minus 9,327), at a density of one per square kilometre overall. There were about 20,000 buffalo in the Djelk IPA, at a density of about two per square kilometre, with enormous variations across ecological zones. In some wetlands such as Bulkay, herds like those seen from the helicopter in May 2014 could push the seasonal density to more than forty buffalo per square kilometres. The Western science experts seem to be in agreement that the buffalo population has quadrupled since the last comprehensive regional survey in 1998 and that it could be currently growing at a rate of 15 to 20 per cent per annum.[21]

The Healthy Country Planning meetings provided an ideal forum for the planning team and traditional land owners to consider how this population explosion had come about and what should be done about it. In February 2015, the planning team invited Murray Garde and me to participate in and help facilitate two meetings with Kuninjku land owners, in part because of our long associations with these people and in part because Murray's exceptional linguistic skills were invaluable in ensuring clear communications.

Two meetings with land owners, opposite moiety land managers, rangers and members of the planning team were interspersed with a number of other discussions Murray and I conducted with our Kuninjku interlocutors exploring the meaning of 'the good life' for them in the precarious present.[22]

Kuninjku clearly and unequivocally recognised the environmental problems and biodiversity threats posed by the buffalo population explosion, alongside the pig population explosion that is less evident in aerial population counts, but more visible in terms of damage to billabongs. The problems caused by growing populations of estuarine crocodiles and cane toads were also universally acknowledged, with somewhat lesser concern about the impact of feral cats on small mammal populations.

Kuninjku were well aware that their country was being 'trashed', as Batman the chopper pilot put it. Buffalo have become highly visible in the landscape and they were identified as destructive not just of the wetlands environment, but also of freshwater supplies. As Mawurndjul noted:

> ...when buffalo go into our drinking water, it makes the water dangerous and we cannot drink it anymore. Buffalo have different toilet! They make the billabong yellow and they put sickness in the water.

Buffalo were also damaging rock art sites, riparian vegetation, a long list of edible plants and animals and sacred sites as Obed, a Kuninjku ranger and the Djelk's deadliest platform marksman, noted:

> When travelling in the chopper around Mankorlod I have seen a lot of buffalo track. At Kolbbe, which is a really sacred site, a lot of buffalo there in that swamp. We can't see the red lilies there anymore. Long time, pigs eat them, buffaloes wreck them.

Terrah Guymala, a senior ranger and renowned Nabarlek band lead singer, put it this way:

> Buffalo are a big problem, they are ruining our land, they are doing a lot of damage to rivers, creeks, billabongs and springs; they are causing erosion and changing

our waterholes so that we cannot fish and cannot get freshwater mussels anymore. I remember when I was young and we moved up from Table Hill to Manmoyi, we would walk everywhere, the country was lovely, there were wallabies and kangaroos everywhere and we drank as we walked from springs with good water. We only used to see the occasional buffalo or *bulukki* [wild cattle]. Today buffalo are everywhere, yesterday I drove to Maningrida to shop early in the morning and there were buffalo at every creek crossing. When you drive at night they are all over the road. Recently I went up in a helicopter near Manbulkardi [on the Liverpool River not far from Bulkay] and from the air we saw mobs of buffalo, it was like they were having a big meeting, a corroboree.[23]

At the same time Kuninjku have become increasingly dependent on buffalo, and to a lesser extent on pig, as a source of meat. Indeed over the past fifteen years buffalo meat has become a staple food; Kuninjku people like eating it and value it highly. This can be contrasted with the sentiments expressed by Commandant McArthur from Victoria Settlement on the Cobourg Peninsula, who wrote in 1843 that 'buffalo meat is not only inferior, but absolutely injurious to some...we have a few men who can never eat it'.[24] This is a sentiment that only some Kuninjku with no teeth would share.

In 1981, I estimated that 25 per cent of bush protein came from buffalo and that the community at Mumeka where I lived exploited about one buffalo a month.[25] Today, I estimate that this percentage might be as high as 75 per cent.[26] This growth is partly linked to abundance and, if one has access to a rifle, ease in killing. But there are other factors at work, foremost the related decline in the availability of other bush foods that buffalo and pig either destroy or eat or compete with for edible vegetation.[27] As buffalo come to out-compete other species the more significant they become in Kuninjku dietary intake.

Let me briefly crunch some more numbers. To put buffalo numbers in the Maningrida regional context, the Aboriginal population (inclusive of the township of Maningrida) to buffalo population ratio is about 1:7 whereas out in the bush the ratio is more like 1:40. In both cases, buffalo greatly outnumber people. Given that swamp buffalo weigh an estimated 300 to 550 kilograms each – with older males sometimes weighing as much as 1,200 kilograms and females 800 kilograms – the regional herd represents a likely minimum 8.5 million kilograms of buffalo. With an estimated dressing percentage (amount of useful meat) of just over 50 per cent per animal, this represents a massive 'protein capital' of 4.25 million kilograms of meat. Given the way that megafauna is generously shared when successfully hunted, buffalo also represent a massive stock of 'cultural capital' as it allows Kuninjku and others in the region to maintain key aspects of their customary kin-based relations of production.

Like the Western-trained non-Aboriginal scientists that I interviewed in September 2015, Kuninjku interlocutors are far from sure how this population explosion came about. One theory is that the relative absence of *Bininj* (Kuninjku people) in the landscape has allowed *nganabbarru* (or buffalo) to become the dominant species. As Namunjdja noted, 'we have been in Maningrida [township] and these things have arrived while we have been away'. When Mawurndjul stated that 'Before at Bulkay *Bininj* were camping all the time, but not now', his son-in-law Larry responded only half-jokingly: 'The buffaloes are now the land owners'.[28]

Others attributed the population explosion to growing difficulties in accessing guns owing to enhanced policing and stricter controls after the 1996 Port Arthur massacre, at the southern extremity of Australia, and in accessing both guns and vehicles after the 2007 Northern Territory Emergency Response (or 'Intervention'); the latter, in particular, has seen an escalated and increasingly vigilant police presence in remote Indigenous lives. What is clear is that the absence of *Bininj* living on country has been associated with rising numbers of *nganabbarru* and rising numbers of *nganabbarru* are correlated with less *Bininj* living in the landscape, but whether there is a direct causality between these two developments is unclear. The whole issue of why outstations today are less populated than in the past is a complex one which I cannot explore in detail here, except to note that the tension between living in the bush and living in the town is what my key interlocutor and close friend Mawurndjul refers to as a 'contradiction' as I will explain below.

When it comes to what to do about the *nganabbarru* boom Kuninjku land owners are far from certain, bearing in mind that our discussions were largely framed by the IPA management planning process. There is nonetheless a clear recognition by all that something needed to be done and done urgently as the population is estimated to be rapidly increasing by 4,000 per annum despite the site-specific culling by the rangers in recent years.[29] Mawurndjul was adamant: 'Pigs and buffalo, kill them. Well three, and crocodiles'. But he also noted affectionately that 'I like the buffalo', and indeed when I visited him in 2014 he had one called *Wamud* (the same subsection or kinship term as his father) living as a domesticated pet in his unfenced yard in Maningrida. He then instructed the rangers and planners sternly: 'Pigs start on them first before you do the buffalo', and 'Just promise me you'll kill all the pigs first. Pigs I want you to finish them up', revealing his own ranking of species.

Figure 3.3: A juvenile buffalo called Wamud *in John Mawurndjul's yard, Maningrida. Photo: Jon Altman.*

Namunjdja wanted to know from the *Balandas* at the planning meeting if Kuninjku would be paid compensation for culled buffalo, being aware that some payments had been made under the BTEC for the limited shooting for disease-testing in Arnhem Land. He was deeply concerned that a Kuninjku safari hunting joint venture nearby at Namokardabu would suffer, saying: 'I don't know what they are going to say if we tell them we are killing all the buffalo'. When confronted with the prospect of aerial shooting of buffalo to waste, which would take out large numbers in a single day, people were uncomfortable, despite assurances that meat would be shared with land owners and that some could be stored for local consumption in the chilling facility at the ranger shed. When Namirrki said to the rangers, 'If you shoot buffalo, then let us know so we can have some of the meat', everyone responded enthusiastically, '*yo yo!* [yes yes!]'.

The upshot of the meetings was that permission was granted by traditional owners of the land to cull 5,000 buffalo in the Djelk IPA, but in the wet season when the flood plains were inundated and the carcasses would rot away quickly so that *Bininj* would not be confronted by all the wasted meat and rotten stench. I, too, as someone who had both shared the thrill of hunting buffalo with Kuninjku in the past and had seen the carnage from aerial shooting, found myself deeply disturbed and saddened by the prospect of shooting to waste. I am reminded of anthropologist Basil Sansom writing about 'the Holocaust of the buffalo' he had seen at Wagait and his evocative reference to aerial militarised massacre of buffalo from 'helicopter gunships', when some of the professional platform shooters in that locality were Vietnam veterans.[30]

Intra-Cultural, Intercultural and Regional Contestations over Buffalo

I want to move now to further complicate this unfolding story of contradictions by exploring some of the 'unstable relations' that have emerged around what appears from a modernist resource management perspective as a fairly straightforward task: the radical cull of an out-of-control exotic population. In saying this I am aware that animal welfare and animal rights interest groups might argue that such culling is unnecessary or unethical or cruel,[31] the last two sentiments that I share in some measure.

The outcome of the planning consultations outlined above, the Djelk Healthy Country Plan, ranks buffalo as the fourth highest of twelve identified threats to healthy country – behind empty country, loss of knowledge, and pigs – and as a high threat to rivers and wetlands and cultural places.[32] Goals have been set: to ensure no increase in buffalo numbers from the 2014 estimate of 20,000 in year one; to reduce the population to 10,000 in five years; and, to reduce the population to 5,000 in ten years, back where it was in the late twentieth century.

In the context of the Healthy Country Planning exercise many of the tensions around the killing of large numbers of *nganabbarru* were bubbling away subliminally, below the surface in side conversations both during and after the formal meetings concluded. As Bowman and Robinson asked over a decade ago, noting conflicting views about controlling buffalo in cross-cultural settings, there is no simple answer to the question: 'What is the *nganabbarru*?'[33]

To begin, Kuninjku are unsure if *nganabbarru* is *Bininj* and endemic or *Balanda* and introduced. Western colonial history documents unequivocally that buffalo were imported to Fort Dundas (Melville Island) from Timor for food in 1826 and transferred to the mainland (Cobourg Peninsula) in 1828. More buffalo were then imported to Victoria settlement (Cobourg Peninsula) in 1838; and abandoned along with the settlement in 1849.[34]

Bininj see things more ambiguously or 'two-way'; buffalo might be *Bininj* or might be *Balanda* or might be both, depending on how the question is framed and the context.[35] This is similar to making a living where there is some tension between engaging with the market or the customary or both; or the tension between Kuninjku religion and ritual and *Yiwarrudj* (Christian fellowship) or both; or between outstation and township living or both; or between seeing buffalo like a ranger or as a Kuninjku hunter or both; or between the perceptions about buffalo of the old people and the 'new' generation or both. I won't explore all these potential contradictions and ambiguities here but merely note that, in the past, Kuninjku used to say that buffalo had moiety and skin (kin) name and the older generations still do. *Nganabbarru* also has associated myths and an ongoing role in secret male regional ceremonies.

When discussion is framed in the formal land management register these days, the English word 'feral' creeps into the lexicon, a term that is rarely used by Kuninjku in relation to buffalo, as my linguistic collaborator Murray Garde confirmed. He notes that:

> ...animals like buffalo have an Indigenous name whereas most others don't, e.g. pigs are 'bik', feral cats 'budjiket' etc. I always have this problem when I'm interpreting and we come to the feral topic. Things like 'weeds' are literally 'bad grasses/plants from *Balanda*' or '*Balanda* animals that wreck the country', but buffalo are easy because they have a name *nganabbarru*.[36]

This name is shared across all the *Bininj Gunwok* dialects and beyond, but its origin is unknown.

The endemic/introduced question has legal and biological implications. Even if the buffalo is not endemic, Kuninjku (and others) may have special native title property rights in this species that wandered into western Arnhem Land before *Balandas*. The important section 211 of the Commonwealth *Native Title Act 1993* guarantees the right of land owners to harvest species for domestic or non-commercial use, a right that overrides state wildlife regulatory powers. And if *nganabbarru* has links to myth and ceremony then the recent population explosion might have a non-biological explanation from a Kuninjku perspective, an issue I need to explore further. I personally find it increasingly difficult to think of *nganabbarru* as a feral or exotic presence. It is a mega–herbivore that has proven itself extraordinarily adaptable and resilient within a difficult environment. Borrowing a phrase attributed to Bruce Rose, Bowman and Robinson note that buffalo fit in so well that they 'belong to country'.[37] Certainly, in terms of physical visibility, this is increasingly the case, as is clear to anyone driving the bush roads around Arnhem Land. In my own mind I increasingly consider *nganabbarru* not as some long-ago undomesticated wild *Bubalus bubalis*, but as '*Bubalus arnhemica*'. *Bubalus arnhemica*: a buffalo species that has adapted over two centuries to the west Arnhem Land flood plains where it is of the *Dua* moiety, as well as to the perched wetlands of the Arnhem Land Plateau,[38] where it is of *Yirritja* moiety, as still classified by the old people today.

Intra-Kuninjku tensions are palpable for Kuninjku rangers like Obed and Dickson. As conservation rangers they are of the younger generation and have 'two tool-box knowledge'[39] about the ecological problems caused by buffalo but also respect the views of the old people about buffalo. They need to constantly mediate these two perspectives while being suitably deferential to more senior land owners, their parents and immediate family. At the same time, they have been bestowed with a great deal of power through the Working on Country program. Unlike most in their community, especially those living at outstations where there is no labour market, rangers are some of the lucky few on wages. And as rangers they enjoy access to high-quality work vehicles, high-powered rifles and training as marksmen, including in platform shooting. All this both empowers and lumbers them with more and more relational responsibility to deliver meat to their families in Maningrida and at outstations. But simultaneously those living at Maningrida and outstations without guns and vehicles are disempowered and can be disgruntled by the fortunes of the few. These tensions between being a ranger and being Kuninjku are poorly recognised, even by their employer the Bawinanga Aboriginal Corporation and can at times erupt in work absenteeism.

Intercultural and intergovernmental contradictions can also arise in regional and national contexts generating cross-cutting cleavages, tensions and unusual alliances. For example, the plan to cull 5,000 buffalo was thwarted in 2015 from an unexpected quarter, the Bawinanga Aboriginal Corporation itself, whose *Balanda* senior management were working on a business plan to turn 'pests into profit'.[40] Attracted by talk of an exciting new live export trade to Vietnam, promoted by the Northern Territory Chief Minister Adam Giles,[41] and by the experience of the Gulin Gulin Buffalo Company in nearby southern Arnhem Land, which has regularly caught and on-sold about 2,000 buffalo per annum, there was a view prevalent among key members of Bawinanga's senior management that the conservation threat of buffalo could be dealt with profitably via commercial contracting. In the aftermath of its recent financial difficulties, which saw the organisation in special administration between 2012 and 2014, income is a pressing priority for Bawinanga.

Consequently, there was a disjunct between the Djelk plan to shoot an agreed number of buffalo and the Bawinanga management's desire for live export. The outcome was that culling was administratively undermined by the latter and only 2,400 buffalo were killed in the late wet season of 2015, 400 to 500 on the Bulkay wetlands.[42] This level of culling will result in a buffalo population increase but, according to livestock experts I have talked to, live export from the Djelk IPA is neither commercially or politically viable. In any case, although some may be swayed by the promise of royalty payments, such an approach is counter to the wishes of most traditional owners. Meanwhile, the live export enterprise stalled, the main local proponents at Bawinanga were sacked; their inability to listen to traditional owners being one of their alleged indiscretions.

The cross–cutting contradictions around buffalo abound, with the Australian government keen to develop northern Australia, while simultaneously keen to support a growing number of IPAs to demonstrate environmental credentials domestically and inter-nationally. I am sure that the wild husbandry of environmentally damaging buffalo contravenes the IUCN definition of Category VI 'sustainable use' protected areas. Hence a live buffalo export trade might potentially harm international conservation standings. On the one hand, the Northern Land Council is committed to supporting traditional owners wishes and to simultaneously show openness to sustainable enterprise on Aboriginal-owned land and, thereby, the live export possibility.[43] On the other, environmental philanthropies and NGOs such as Bush Heritage Australia and The Nature Conservancy with influence in the environmental governance of western Arnhem Land have conservation as a priority.

At the same time those who are looking to manage buffalo numbers in IPAs, like the Djelk Rangers, are adamant that if they cull and others wild farm (which generally means focusing on the live export of young bulls leaving cows to breed) the required rapid decline in numbers will never occur. The ranger groups thus face a moral dilemma: why cull if this will merely result in the in-migration of buffalo from elsewhere? And the commercial operators, mainly *Balanda* contractors, also face profit-motivated moral hazard. Why cull females, the reproductive means to regen-erate stock and future profit? A major moral dilemma all face is when to cull buffalo and by how much given that there is ample evidence from the nearby Alligator Rivers region and local exclusion fencing experiments set up by rangers that wetlands recover once buffalo numbers are drastically reduced.[44]

Being Black and Green: Emerging Tensions

In this chapter I have used buffalo as one indicator of the difficult challenges of engaging with a conservation framework, such as the relatively new IPA framework, in Arnhem Land; the difficulties of trying to be, if you like, simultaneously black and green, Aboriginal and conservationist. I hope I have demonstrated unequivocally that living in an IUCN Category VI IPA is not as straightforward as some might think or idealise; it is a form of being that is riven with contradictions, tensions, political conflicts and difficult decisions.

In February 2015, responding to a discussion we were conducting about the trade-offs for Kuninjku in aspiring to live on their ancestral lands and the counter-pressures to reside in the township of Maningrida, John Mawurndjul captured this existential tension poetically. Murray Garde translates Mawurndjul's dilemma in the following terms:

> Balang [Mawurndjul] describes a situation that would be a 'contradiction' in English, but for which there is no word in Kuninjku. Effectively he is saying, 'We want to live out on our country but then we want to come back in to Maningrida and then we want to go back out again, but what can we do, we are tied up'. The English word 'contradiction' conveys the same meaning as this phrasal translation. To be 'tying up ourselves' can be translated as 'we are frustrated'.

A similar frustration is evident in relation to *Bining dja nganabbarru* (Aboriginal people and buffalo) in the Djelk IPA that I interpret as: 'We want the buffalo to eat, but we also want to look after our country, it's a contradiction that frustrates us'.

Buffalo are only one of many ecological threats. As noted above, the Djelk Healthy Country Plan lists twelve: empty country, loss of knowledge, pigs, buffalo, weeds, unhealthy fire, problem animals, visitors, mining, climate change, commercial and illegal fishing and coastal pollution.[45] Most of these threats are interlinked, as, for example, buffalo spread weeds and denude vegetation and therefore are associated with other threats such as unhealthy fires, emptied (unoccupied) country, and loss of knowledge owing to a decline in biodiversity. And as ungulates, great emitters of methane, a greenhouse gas, buffalo even contribute to climate change with negative biodiversity consequences.

In a 2012 Boyer Lecture 'The conceit of wilderness ideology' – later retitled 'The First Australians Gift to the World: 30 Million Hectares of Protected Areas to Conserve Environments and Biodiversity' – Langton notes that Aboriginal people like other humans have an economic life, are caught up in the transforming encounter with modernity and have economic rights.[46] This is indisputable. To concretise from this abstraction to the case material presented here, buffalo are a big part of Kuninjku people's economic life as hunted meat. Kuninjku are caught up with the transforming encounter with modernity as they face relentless pressure from state-normalising policies such as the Indigenous Advancement Strategy and Closing the Gap to change their norms and values to comply with those of mainstream Australians. One possibility currently available to comply with this state-promoted project of improvement is to gain 'real' employment as a ranger.

But Kuninjku also hold economic rights, supported by Australian law; in this case to hunt buffalo for livelihood and to live in a different way from mainstream Australians. This is what the hybrid economy framework that I have developed across my career seeks to convey: how Aboriginal people like the Kuninjku are reconfiguring their transforming economy to engage with the customary, the market and the state simultaneously and interdependently. In earlier research I argued, with reference to the Djelk IPA, that rangering work is evolving into an exemplar of intercultural production; rangers work simultaneously in the customary, state and market sectors, in an intersecting production space that I refer to as a 'bliss point'.[47]

Clearly, though, this is not an unproblematic 'bliss point'. This is because there is growing potential for conflict between Aboriginal land owners and members of environmental NGOs and philanthropists, who are political and financial supporters of IPAs. These 'greenies' might question whether the explosion of buffalo populations in areas of Aboriginal land vested in the National Reserve System constitute a conservation 'gift', as per Langton's phrase. They might instead ask if Aboriginal people like the Kuninjku are, to use Langton's evocative language, 'the enemies of nature'? In any case, can this vesting really be described as a gift in the sense of prestation, or is it an exchange, a strategic decision to manage lands in a particular ecologically sound manner in return for support from the Australian government, and a range of environmental interest groups?

There are certainly some who highlight the neoliberalisation of nature in Australia and the bureaucratic requirements imposed by the Australian state on Indigenous ranger groups.[48] As Nancy Peluso noted some time ago, conservation can be used by governments and others to control remote places and peoples.[49] Arguably, the decision to declare an IPA is less of a 'gift' and more of a Hobson's choice: if land owners want to retain the natural and cultural values of their estates, faced with diverse threatening processes while also looking to make a livelihood from both wages and hunting for meat, then they need financial support. Given the vastness of most IPA jurisdictions, the Australian state is clearly the most affluent and likely potential benefactor for a number of compounding and compelling reasons including opportunity cost, public good, national interest and social justice. But despite these compelling reasons the state has proven to be a perennial under-investor in conservation. To avoid both over-reliance on the state and to provide additional support other environmental interests have to be recruited to the cause of Indigenous conservation alongside sustainable use. It is for this reason that the environmental damage that we saw from the helicopter over Bulkay needs to be actively managed.

An important and more straightforward example of regional cooperation and sound governance is evident in the management of wild fires in Arnhem Land. While the management of fire is less contentious than the management of buffalo, the case of the West Arnhem Land Fire Abatement (WALFA) scheme could be instructive for the challenge of managing buffalo especially as the Djelk Rangers are partners in this project. A coalition of five Aboriginal ranger groups in western Arnhem Land (including the Warddeken Rangers) has established this highly innovative savanna burning carbon abatement scheme.[50] Since 2006, the WALFA project has been paid under a long-term contract between Darwin Liquefied Natural Gas and the Northern Territory government to abate a remotely-verified 100,000 tonnes of CO_2 equivalents per annum. As with the management of IPAs generally, WALFA has been a highly intercultural institutional arrangement dependent on close collaboration between Aboriginal traditional owners and their families, collaborating scientists, researchers and long-term advocates for Indigenous rights to live on their country.

Despite concern expressed by some that fire management regimes are dominated by Western scientific ideas and outsiders,[51] in my experience this is not the case in Arnhem Land. Here, land owners play a crucial role not only in lighting ground fires in accord with customary practice, but also in directing aerial burning from helicopters. Unlike contentious proposals to cull buffalo, there is a widespread view that early burning is beneficial for the environment and in reducing the intensity of late dry season hot fires that emit far greater quantities of greenhouse gases. Also, unlike with buffalo, there has been a high level of regional cooperation among the five partners in WALFA operating over a large area of 28,000 square kilometres.

The results from managing fire to abate greenhouse gas emissions in Arnhem Land are verified by Western science and settler government. In 2014, the short-lived Abbott government negotiated the passage of the *Carbon Farming Initiative Amendment Act*, making the management of fires in savanna grasslands eligible for payments from the $2.55 billion Emissions Reduction Fund under the Coalition government's Direct Action Plan. WALFA has expanded into central Arnhem Land and into south-east Arnhem Land and a new business entity, Arnhem Land Fire Abatement (NT) Ltd, has recently been formed to operate as an Eligible Offsets Project within this Plan. ALFA (NT) Ltd now covers 69,000 square kilometres of Arnhem Land and could potentially include virtually the entire region. It is early days, but this entity has contracted to deliver nearly 300,000 Australian Carbon Credit Units (equivalent to a tonne of CO_2 equivalent each) every year for ten years through abatement; it could potentially deliver three times this amount if new methodology to measure sequestered carbon is approved.[52]

Managing the landscape with fire and abating carbon is currently a more straightforward intercultural enterprise than the management of buffalo that remains tense, contested and contradictory: there is global concern about climate change and multinational corporations, such as ConocoPhillips, are keen to purchase the emissions reduction offsets which abatement projects such as WALFA and other projects on Aboriginal (and non-Aboriginal) savanna grasslands deliver to market.[53] Importantly, the collaborative governance model developed by ALFA (NT) Ltd might prove instructive for the management of wild buffalo and other environmental threats. And profits earned by ALFA might be earmarked for buffalo management, as has occurred already with the underwriting of the limited aerial culling undertaken by the Djelk Rangers in 2015.

Conclusion: Contradictions and Livelihoods

In this chapter I have explored one species, the wild buffalo, in one jurisdiction to highlight 'contradictions' that generate unstable and emerging conflict-ridden relations between diverse interest groups including Aboriginal land owners, the Australian state and conservation interests. I give priority to the interests of the Kuninjku land owners to show how making strategic decisions comparing the value of buffalo as food and the biodiversity and cultural values of land is difficult, especially when residing in a regional conservation commons. And yet difficult decisions are being negotiated and action, even if currently too limited, is being taken.

In truth any production, either for mere livelihood or for massive super profits, faces trade-offs and contradictions, and this is surely something that many now recognise in the Anthropocene as the sustainability of late capitalism is increasingly questioned. In much of my writings about livelihood alternatives for remote-living Indigenous people I have emphasised the need for both flexibility and diversity of production, deploying the notion of 'economic hybridity'.[54] In marked contrast, much of the focus in policy discourse on developing northern Australia emphasises resource extraction of one form or another. And yet recent history shows that major resource extraction projects such as the Ranger uranium mine at Jabiru and the Alcan bauxite and alumina processing plant at Gove have failed to deliver livelihood benefits to most of the 14,000 Aboriginal people of Arnhem Land. Both mines now appear to have no financially viable futures.

There will be elements of an alternate hybrid economy that are less contradictory and frustrating than others. One possibility that might assist to transform prospects in Arnhem Land is carbon farming, what Russell-Smith et al. refer to as 'rekindling the *Wurrk* [managed fire] tradition'.[55] Optimistically, managing the landscape with fire might prove less contradictory and frustrating for Kuninjku and other Aboriginal people in Arnhem Land than other options, be they engagement with market capitalism or dealing with a number of conservation threats like buffalo. Carbon farming might provide an important plank for the building of an alternate Arnhem Land economy for the rest of the twenty-first century. But, as with the buffalo, emerging and currently unimagined contradictions and contestations will likely arise. Fire may appear less contradictory, but the main site of contradiction is actually the intersecting and culture-specific attitudes to resource use more generally. Risky interdependencies occur in all forms of resource use; unstable relations are inevitable and are more manageable if recognised as such.

Managing and utilising buffalo for livelihood demonstrates the difficult decisions that people living on the ground face as they seek to balance competing obligations and viewpoints. I empathise for I, too, am frustrated in my academic and advocacy work by the tensions between retaining resources for their use and exchange values and supporting conservation that prioritises environmental values. Without doubt, Kuninjku decision-making is influenced by neoliberal governmentality, state dependence and conservation interests. But the particular internal dynamics of their agency as land owners with resource rights and a desire to retain the integrity of their ancestral lands intergenerationally should not be understated. Today, under Australian settler law they have final, even if compromised and highly contested, authority. This will result in relations whose instability and tensions need to be marshalled to ensure challenges, like the buffalo now deeply embedded in the local economy, can be managed in a manner that does not jeopardise the environmental and cultural values of lands of global environmental and cultural significance.

References

Altman, J., 'What Future for Remote Indigenous Australia? Economic Hybridity and the Neoliberal Turn', in J. Altman & M. Hinkson (eds), *Culture Crisis: Anthropology and Politics in Aboriginal Australia*, UNSW Press, Sydney, 2010, pp. 259–80.

Altman, J. & Kerins, S. (eds), *People on Country: Vital Landscapes, Indigenous Futures*, The Federation Press, Sydney, NSW, 2012.

Altman, J. C., *Submission to the Feral Animals Committee, Buffalo Working Party, Department of Primary Production*, typescript, AIATSIS, Canberra, 22 October 1981.

Altman, J. C., 'Hunting Buffalo in North-Central Arnhem Land: A Case of Rapid Adaptation among Aborigines', *Oceania*, vol. 52, no. 4, 1982, pp. 274–85.

Altman, J. C., *Hunter-Gatherers Today: an Aboriginal Economy in North Australia*, Australian Institute of Aboriginal and Torres Strait Island, Canberra, 1987.

Altman, J. C., *Living the Good Life in Precarious Times*, 2015, viewed 28 March 2016 <http://insidestory.org.au/living-the-good-life-in-precarious-times>.

Altman, J. C., Griffiths, A. D. & Whitehead, P. J., 'Invasion of the rubbish frogs', *Nature Australia*, vol. Spring, 2003, pp. 44–51.

ANAO, *Indigenous Protected Areas, ANAO Audit Report No. 14 2011–12*, Australian National Audit Office, Canberra, 2012.

Ansell, J., *Djelk Rangers Annual Report 2013–2014*, Djelk Rangers and Bawinanga Aboriginal Corporation, Maningrida, 2014.

Ansell, J., *Djelk Rangers Annual Report 2014–2015*, Djelk Rangers and Bawinanga Aboriginal Corporation, Maningrida, 2015.

Bowman, D. M. & Robinson, C. J., 'The getting of the *Nganabbarru*: Observations and reflections on Aboriginal buffalo hunting in northern Australia', *Australian Geographer*, vol. 33, no. 2, 2002, pp. 191–206.

Brann, M., 'Territory buffalo exported to Vietnam for first time', *ABC Rural*, 11 February 2014.

Cochrane, M., *The Djelk Ranger Program: An Outsider's Perspective*, CAEPR Working Paper 27/2005, Centre for Aboriginal Economic Policy Research, Canberra, 2005.

Collier, N., Austin, B. J., Bradshaw, C. J. & McMahon, C. R., 'Turning pests into profits: introduced buffalo provide multiple benefits to indigenous people of northern Australia', *Human Ecology*, vol. 39, no. 2, 2011, pp. 155–64.

Cooke, P., 'A long way home to the warddewarrde', in J. C. Altman & S. Kerins (eds), *People on Country, Vital Landscapes, Indigenous Futures*, Federation Press, Sydney, 2012, pp. 146–61.

Ens, E., 'Conducting two-way ecological research', in *People on Country, Vital landscapes, Indigenous futures*, Federation Press, Sydney, 2012, pp. 45–64.

Fache, E., 'Caring for Country, a Form of Bureaucratic Participation: Conservation, Development, and Neoliberalism in Indigenous Australia', *Anthropological Forum*, vol. 24, no. 3, 2014, pp. 267–86.

Fache, E. & Moizo, B., 'Do Burning Practices Contribute to Caring for Country? Contemporary Uses of Fire for Conservation Purposes in Indigenous Australia', *Journal of Ethnobiology*, vol. 35, no. 1, 2015, pp. 163–82.

Fitzgerald, D., 'Permits allowing muster of buffalo on Top End Indigenous land will not be available until at least mid-June', *NT Country Hour*, 21 May 2015.

Garde, M., *Culture, Interaction and Person Reference in an Australian Language: An Ethnography of Bininj Gunwok Communication*, John Benjamins, Amsterdam, 2013.

Goffman, E., *Frame Analysis: An Essay on the Organization of Experience*, Harvard University Press, 1974.

Hage, G., *Alter-politics: Critical Anthropology and the Radical Imagination*, Melbourne University Press, Melbourne, 2014.

Higgins, V., Dibden, J. & Cocklin, C., 'Market instruments and the neoliberalisation of land management in rural Australia', *Geoforum*, vol. 43, no. 3, 2012, pp. 377–86.

Hunter, F., Yibarbuk, D. & Cooke, P., *Buffalo and the Perched Wetlands of the Arnhem Land Plateau*, Department of Sustainability, Environment, Water, Population and Communities, Darwin, 3–4 December 2008.

IUCN, *IUCN: Protected Area Category IV*, International Union for Conservation of Nature, 2012, viewed 28 March 2016 <https://www.iucn.org/about/work/programmes/gpap_home/gpap_quality/gpap_pacategories/gpap_category6/>.

Jesser, P., Markula, A. & Csurhes, S., *Pest Animal Risk Assessment, Water Buffalo, Bubalus bubalis*, Department of Primary Industries and Fisheries, Brisbane, 2008.

Johnson, V., *Bawinanga Aboriginal Corporation Annual Report 1999–2000*, Bawinanga Aboriginal Corporation, Maningrida, 2000.

Karrkad Kanjdji, *Karrkad Kanjdji Trust*, 2016, viewed 28 March 2016 <http://www.karrkad-kandji.org.au>.

Koenig, J., Griffiths, A., Godjuwa, C. & Campion, O., 'Aerial survey of vertebrates in the Mann river district, central Arnhem Land', *Northern Territory Naturalist*, vol. 17, 2003, pp. 7-19.

Langton, M., *The Conceit of Wilderness Ideology*, ABC, 2012, viewed 26 March 2016, <http://www.abc.net.au/radionational/programs/boyerlectures/2012-boyer-lectures-234/4409022>.

Langton, M., *The Quiet Revolution: Indigenous People and the Resources Boom*, Boyer Lectures, ABC Books, Sydney, NSW, 2013.

Letts, G. A., Bassingthwaite, A. & De Ver, W. E. L., *Feral Animals in the Northern Territory: Report of the Board of Inquiry*, Northern Territory Government Printer, Darwin, 1979.

May, K., Ansell, S. & Koenig, J., *Djelk Annual Report 2009–2010*, Djelk Rangers and Bawinanga Aboriginal Corporation, Maningrida, 2010.

Peluso, N. L., 'Coercing conservation?: The politics of state resource control', *Global Environmental Change*, vol. 3, no. 2, 1993, pp. 199–217.

Robinson, C. J. & Whitehead, P., 'Cross-cultural management of pest animal damage: a case study of feral buffalo control in Australia's Kakadu National Park', *Environmental Management*, vol. 32, no. 4, 2003, pp. 445–58.

Rostron, V., Campion, W., Namarnyilk, I. & Fogarty, W., 'Countrymen standing together', in J. Altman & S. Kerins (eds), *People on Country, Vital Landscapes, Indigenous Futures*, The Federation Press, Sydney, 2012, pp. 162–73.

Russell-Smith, J., Whitehead, P. & Cooke, P., *Culture, Ecology and Economy of Fire Management in North Australian Savannas: Rekindling the Wurrk Tradition*, CSIRO Publishing, Collingwood, 2009.

Saalfeld, K., *Feral Buffalo (Bubalus bubalis) Distribution and Abundance in Arnhem Land, Northern Territory, June 2014*, Department of Land Resource Management, Darwin, 2014.

Sansom, B., 'Irruptions of the Dreamings in Post-Colonial Australia', *Oceania*, vol. 72, no. 1, 2001, pp. 1–32.

Territory NRM 2013, *Developing a New Djelk Management Plan*, Territory Natural Resource Management, 2013, viewed 28 March 2016, <http://www.territorynrm.org.au/wp-content/uploads/2013/06/1430-Djelk.pdf>.

Whitehead, P, *Indigenous Livelihoods – Background Paper*, Knowledge Series 11/2012, North Australian Indigenous Land and Sea Management Alliance, Darwin, 2012.

Notes

1   Kuninjku is one of six dialects of the pan-dialectical *Bininj Gunwok* language, see: M. Garde, *Culture, Interaction and Person Reference in an Australian Language: An Ethnography of Bininj Gunwok Communication*, John Benjamins, Amsterdam, 2013.

2   J. C. Altman, 'What Future for Remote Indigenous Australia? Economic Hybridity and the Neoliberal Turn', in J. C. Altman & M. Hinkson (eds), *Culture Crisis: Anthropology and Politics in Aboriginal Australia*, UNSW Press, Sydney, 2010, pp. 259–80.

3   G. Hage, *Alter-politics: Critical Anthropology and the Radical Imagination*, Melbourne University Press, Melbourne, 2014.

4   J. C. Altman, *Living the Good Life in Precarious Times*, 2015, viewed 28 March 2016 <http://insidestory.org.au/living-the-good-life-in-precarious-times>.

5   J. C. Altman, *Hunter-Gatherers Today: an Aboriginal Economy in North Australia*, Australian Institute of Aboriginal and Torres Strait Island, Canberra, 1987.

6   J. C. Altman, *Submission to the Feral Animals Committee, Buffalo Working Party, Department of Primary Production*, typescript, AIATSIS, Canberra, 22 October 1981.

7   V. Johnson, *Bawinanga Aboriginal Corporation Annual Report 1999–2000*, Bawinanga Aboriginal Corporation, Maningrida, 2000, p. 22.

8   M. Cochrane, *The Djelk Ranger Program: An Outsider's Perspective*, CAEPR
     Working Paper 27/2005, Centre for Aboriginal Economic Policy Research,
     Canberra, 2005; Johnson, *Bawinanga Annual Report 1999–2000*.
9   G. A. Letts, A. Bassingthwaite & W. E. L. De Ver, *Feral Animals in the
     Northern Territory: Report of the Board of Inquiry*, Northern Territory
     Government Printer, Darwin, 1979.
10   Johnson, *Bawinanga Annual Report 1999–2000*, p. 23.
11   Ian Munro, personal communication, 9 September 2015; J. Koenig,
     A. Griffiths, C. Godjuwa & O. Campion, 'Aerial survey of vertebrates in
     the Mann river district, central Arnhem Land', *Northern Territory Naturalist*,
     vol. 17, 2003, pp. 7–19. The original count in the late 1990s was linked to
     a feasibility study for a short-lived joint venture buffalo and pig hunting
     safari enterprise between Bawinanga and Wildlife North Australia (see:
     Johnson, *Bawinanga Annual Report 1999–2000*, pp. 25–6).
12   I should declare my professional entanglements in much of this work; I was
     a member of the Scientific Program Advisory Group of the Cooperative
     Research Centre from 1994–2008 and a member of the Board of the Key
     Centre 1999–2005 as well as an active research collaborator.
13   J. C. Altman, A. D. Griffiths & P. J. Whitehead, 'Invasion of the rubbish frogs',
     Nature Australia, vol. Spring, 2003, pp. 44–51.
14   ANAO, *Indigenous Protected Areas, ANAO Audit Report No. 14 2011–12*,
     Australian National Audit Office, Canberra, 2012.
15   More specifically: 'Protected areas that conserve ecosystems and habitats,
     together with associated cultural values and traditional natural resource
     management systems. They are generally large, with most of the area
     in a natural condition, where a proportion is under sustainable natural
     resource management and where low-level, non-industrial use of natural
     resources compatible with nature conservation is seen as one of the main
     aims of the area' (IUCN, *IUCN: Protected Area Category IV*, International
     Union for Conservation of Nature, 2012, viewed 28 March 2016 https://
     www.iucn.org/theme/protected-areas/about/protected-area-categories/
     category-iv-habitatspecies-management-area.
16   Ian Munro, personal communication, 9 September 2015.
17   J. C. Altman & S. Kerins (eds), *People on Country: Vital Landscapes, Indigenous
     Futures*, The Federation Press, Sydney, NSW, 2012.
18   Karrkad Kanjdji, *Karrkad Kanjdji Trust*, 2016, viewed 28 March 2016
     <http://www.karrkad-kandji.org.au>.
19   See: Territory NRM 2013, *Developing a New Djelk Management
     Plan*, Territory Natural Resource Management, 2013, viewed
     28 March 2016, <http://www.territorynrm.org.au/wp-content/

uploads/2013/06/1430-Djelk.pdf>.

20 K. Saalfeld, *Feral Buffalo (Bubalus bubalis) Distribution and Abundance in Arnhem Land, Northern Territory, June 2014*, Department of Land Resource Management, Darwin, 2014.

21 According to a number of experts consulted in September 2015 including Keith Saafield, Peter Whitehead, Shaun Ansell, Alys Stevens and Pat Carrick.

22 Altman, *Living the Good Life in Precarious Times*. All quotes are from interviews and meetings during the week 2–6 February 2015 recorded and transcribed from Kuninjku to English by Murray Garde.

23 Discussion with Terrah Guymala, senior ranger at Manmoyi on 4 September 2015 conducted in a mix of Kuninjku/Kunwinjku dialects and English, translated by me into English.

24 Letts et al., *Feral Animals in the Northern Territory*, p. 211.

25 J. C. Altman, 'Hunting Buffalo in North-Central Arnhem Land: A Case of Rapid Adaptation among Aborigines', *Oceania*, vol. 52, no. 4, 1982, pp. 280–3.

26 This estimate is based on random observations made during visits and discussions with Djelk rangers and not as in earlier work on rigorous quantification. And it is only for Kuninjku who exploit more buffalo than other groups in the region. That said people still hunt wallabies, magpie geese and ducks and fish for barramundi and catfish that are seasonally consumed at high rates. But the sheer size of buffalo accounts for its high dietary contributions, especially of protein.

27 At uplands Manmoyi, an outstation with fifty to sixty people, Guymala estimates that as many as two to three buffalo are exploited weekly: 'We feed everyone and the dogs too, we have healthy dogs' (Terrah Guymala, personal communication, 4 September 2015). Buffalo can consume 30 kilograms of vegetable matter a day (P. Jesser, A. Markula & S. Csurhes, *Pest Animal Risk Assessment, Water buffalo, Bubalus bubalis*, Department of Primary Industries and Fisheries, Brisbane, 2008).

28 Interview with author, 3 February 2015.

29 For example, 662 in 2009–10 and over 1,000 in 2013–14 (see: J. Ansell, *Djelk Rangers Annual Report 2013–2014*, Djelk Rangers and Bawinanga Aboriginal Corporation, Maningrida, 2014, p. 21; K. May, S. Ansell & J. Koenig, *Djelk Annual Report 2009–2010*, Djelk Rangers and Bawinanga Aboriginal Corporation, Maningrida, 2010, p. 14).

30 B. Sansom, 'Irruptions of the Dreamings in Post-Colonial Australia', *Oceania*, vol. 72, no. 1, 2001, pp. 26–7. Similar semi-automatic .308 calibre rifles are used by the military and buffalo shooters, in part because .308 ammunition is relatively cheap. But this calibre is far more effective in killing soft-skinned humans than tough-skinned buffalo resulting in

buffalo often being wounded and requiring several shots to kill.

31 P. Whitehead, *Indigenous Livelihoods – Background Paper*, Knowledge Series 11/2012, North Australian Indigenous Land and Sea Management Alliance, Darwin, 2012, pp. 59–60.

32 J. Ansell, *Djelk Rangers Annual Report 2014–2015*, Djelk Rangers and Bawinanga Aboriginal Corporation, Maningrida, 2015, p. 43.

33 D. M. Bowman & C. J. Robinson, 'The getting of the *Nganabbarru*: Observations and reflections on Aboriginal buffalo hunting in northern Australia', *Australian Geographer*, vol. 33, no. 2, 2002, pp. 191–206. There are some similarities and some differences in our analyses, but bear in mind their research was undertaken over a decade ago before the population explosion was quantified and before the declaration of the Djelk IPA and the escalation of conservation discourse and priorities in regional resource management.

34 Letts et al., *Feral Animals in the Northern Territory*, p. 211.

35 Goffman's notion of 'front stage' and 'back stage' and performativity is highly apposite to how such tensions are framed and discussed (E. Goffman, *Frame Analysis: An Essay on the Organization of Experience*, Harvard University Press, 1974).

36 Murray Garde, personal communication, 7 September 2015.

37 Bowman & Robinson, *Australian Geographer*, p. 202.

38 F. Hunter, D. Yibarbuk & P. Cooke, *Buffalo and the Perched Wetlands of the Arnhem Land Plateau*, Department of Sustainability, Environment, Water, Population and Communities, Darwin, 3–4 December 2008, p. 66.

39 E. Ens, 'Conducting two-way ecological research', in J. C. Altman and S. Kerins (eds), *People on Country, Vital Landscapes, Indigenous Futures*, Federation Press, Sydney, 2012, pp. 45–64; V. Rostron, W. Campion, I. Namarnyilk & W. Fogarty, 'Countrymen standing together', in J. Altman & S. Kerins (eds), *People on Country, Vital Landscapes, Indigenous Futures*, The Federation Press, Sydney, 2012, pp. 162–73.

40 N. Collier, B. J. Austin, C. J. Bradshaw & C. R. McMahon, 'Turning pests into profits: introduced buffalo provide multiple benefits to indigenous people of northern Australia', *Human Ecology*, vol. 39, no. 2, 2011, pp. 155–64.

41 M. Brann, 'Territory buffalo exported to Vietnam for first time', *ABC Rural*, 11 February 2014.

42 The cull was financed from a diversity of sources including windfall profits earned from the sale of excess carbon abatement generated under the West Arnhem Land Fire Abatement project.

43 D. Fitzgerald, 'Permits allowing muster of buffalo on Top End Indigenous

land will not be available until at least mid-June', *NT Country Hour*, 21 May 2015.

44 C. J. Robinson & P. Whitehead, 'Cross-cultural management of pest animal damage: a case study of feral buffalo control in Australia's Kakadu National Park', *Environmental Management*, vol. 32, no. 4, 2003, pp. 445–58.

45 J. Ansell, *Djelk Rangers Annual Report 2014–2015*.

46 M. Langton, *The Conceit of Wilderness Ideology*, ABC, 26 March 2016 <http://www.abc.net.au/radionational/programs/boyerlectures/2012-boyer-lectures-234/4409022>.

47 J. C. Altman, 'What Future for Remote Indigenous Australia? Economic Hybridity and the Neoliberal Turn', pp. 274–5.

48 E. Fache, 'Caring for Country, a Form of Bureaucratic Participation: Conservation, Development, and Neoliberalism in Indigenous Australia', *Anthropological Forum*, vol. 24, no. 3, 2014, pp. 267–86; V. Higgins, J. Dibden & C. Cocklin, 'Market instruments and the neoliberalisation of land management in rural Australia', *Geoforum*, vol. 43, no. 3, 2012, pp. 377–86.

49 N. L. Peluso, 'Coercing conservation?: The politics of state resource control', *Global Environmental Change*, vol. 3, no. 2, 1993, pp. 199–217.

50 M. Langton, *The Quiet Revolution: Indigenous People and the Resources Boom*, Boyer Lectures, ABC Books, Sydney, 2013, p. 122; P. Cooke, 'A long way home to the warddewarrde', in J. C. Altman & S. Kerins (eds), *People on Country, Vital Landscapes, Indigenous Futures*, Federation Press, Sydney, 2012, pp. 146–61.

51 E. Fache, & B. Moizo, 'Do Burning Practices Contribute to Caring for Country? Contemporary Uses of Fire for Conservation Purposes in Indigenous Australia', *Journal of Ethnobiology*, vol. 35, no. 1, 2015, pp. 163–82.

52 Thanks to Jennifer Ansell, CEO of ALFA (NT) Ltd, for providing much of this information for a collaborative research project on which we are embarking.

53 It is noteworthy that there is debate about whether carbon abatement projects are effective in tackling climate change. Here I am focusing on economic and political rather than environmental questions associated with WALFA, although the regional biodiversity benefits of the patchy and cooler burning of the seasonal savanna burning that generates offsets are not to my knowledge questioned by Western science.

54 Altman, 'What Future for Remote Indigenous Australia?'.

55 J. Russell-Smith, P. Whitehead & P. Cooke, *Culture, Ecology and Economy of Fire Management in North Australian Savannas: Rekindling the Wurrk Tradition*, CSIRO Publishing, Collingwood, 2009.

4

INTIMACIES WITH COUNTRY, ENVIRONMENTALISM AND INTERCULTURAL RELATIONS IN NORTHERN AUSTRALIA'S GULF COUNTRY

Richard J. Martin and David Trigger

In 1980, as a young man conducting research at Doomadgee in the Gulf Country, the anthropologist David Trigger noted much talk among older Aboriginal people about a place called Pungalina on the Calvert River near the border between the Northern Territory and Queensland – a pastoral lease, far from any town or settlement, which few had visited in recent decades. Trigger's work across the months and years before then, beginning in 1978, had involved visiting areas around Doomadgee with knowledgeable people; a process which had generated considerable enthusiasm about Aboriginal tradition amongst those with whom he worked. The prospect of a visit to remote Pungalina was eagerly anticipated by those who had lived there in their younger days, including one man – known affectionately as 'the oldest man in Doomadgee' – who linked himself passionately to a Dreaming in the area with the cryptic statement: 'me really emu!'

While 'the oldest man in Doomadgee' was unable to travel, others who similarly connected themselves to the Emu Dreaming near Pungalina accompanied Trigger on the trip. Upon reaching their destination, the old homestead location abandoned two years before, much information was recorded, including knowledge of sacred things as well as more mundane matters. As they entered Emu Dreaming country just to the west of Pungalina, an actual emu was shot and butchered. For some hours Trigger recorded the detailed knowledge of the bird's body parts as they were assembled for cooking and consumption, patiently explained by the older people in the group. The party's spiritual relationship to this animal as Dreaming was commensurate with their extraordinary knowledge of it as food and a material resource. Fourteen terms for the animal's body parts were recorded, including *lalaluya* (the thigh beef), *jamurrija* (the liver), *gargardija* (the 'milk guts' that can be eaten or used as fish bait), as well as *madarji* (the feathers used for decoration). Expert skills turned part of the large intestine, the *jalugi,* inside out, and cleaned it of contents (noting the fruits emus consume that include only one variety also edible by humans) to make a bag in which to insert and then cook some of the fat *(nganamira)*. Clara Bob (nee Charly), who was *mungguji* for, or connected patrifilially with, Emu Dreaming country and who described herself as *jibiya,* or belonging intimately to, that area, led her family in preparing the animal for consumption (see Figure 4.1). Her

Figure 4.1: Clara Bob plucking emu feathers (madarji) *for use as decoration for dancers. Photo: David Trigger, September 1980.*

personal Garawa name was *maningarri*, taken from the term for the emu's forearm. Like the oldest man in Doomadgee, this woman and her family were, in some respects, 'really emu': connected to this non-human through complex traditions and histories which are clearly 'intimate', with all the connotations of closeness, affect, expression, intensity, singularity, immanence and permeability that the term suggests.

Yet, as discussed in this chapter, such intimacies were complicated by the broader context of settler colonialism and the political economy of the contemporary Australian society: by pastoral settlement, abandonment, and land rights. By the time of a repeat visit undertaken by Trigger and Richard Martin with another group of Garawa people in 2012, some thirty-two years later, this context had shifted; the Pungalina lease had been purchased by an environmentalist organisation called the Australian Wildlife Conservancy, or AWC. This purchase resulted in the creation of a 3,060-square-kilometre nature reserve entitled the Pungalina-Seven Emu Sanctuary, encompassing the Pungalina lease as well as a sublease of 1,100 square kilometres of the neighbouring Seven Emu station for conservation purposes. Obliged by the conditions of its lease to continue to run cattle, the AWC's interest in the property actually encompasses a different range of values and interests to those of a conventional station, such as Pungalina historically had been. In short, it is now managed to promote biodiversity rather than maximise beef yield. This objective has impacted on Garawa Aboriginal people with continuing connections to the area, whose aspirations for employment and 'development', as well as the subsistence economic use of country, both overlap and conflict with the AWC's objectives. How the intimate Aboriginal ancestral connections to country described above have been affected by these changes form the subject of this chapter.

While a single property in a remote region, the shift in land and water use occurring on Pungalina with its purchase by the AWC reflects broader shifts across northern Australia. Over the past several decades, landscapes like the Gulf Country have transitioned from a focus on the production of commercial cattle herds towards more multifunctional understandings of value.[1] This chapter presents a natural and social history of this place across this transition, while posing questions about shifting Aboriginal connections to places like Pungalina as well as the connections of non-Aboriginal people, such as those associated with the AWC, who are locally known as 'whitefellas'. By adopting an analysis which focuses on comparison across historical conjunctures – between the first visit in 1980 and the repeat visit in 2012 – we discuss how Aboriginal intimacies with country intersect with the concept of 'environmentalism' as implemented by the AWC; a concept promoting other kinds of human intimacies with country. Here, we reject the idea that such non-Aboriginal relationships with land are completely distinct from Aboriginal ones, while noting a considerable separation of worldviews. Instead, we focus on the relationships that environmentalism, as a practice as well as an ideology, involves. Building on earlier work which has considered the negotiation of 'nativeness' and 'indigeneity' with respect to the environment,[2] we focus here on relations between Aboriginal people and others, considering the meanings that arise in and through their interactions with each other, as well as with different types of species at Pungalina, and ultimately with the land and waters of Pungalina itself. Analyses of comparable settings in Australia have tended to either depict the relationship between Aboriginal people and environmentalists such as those associated with the AWC as a fractious 'alliance', with environmentalists tending to emphasise shared values between 'green' (i.e. environmentalists) and 'black' (i.e. Aboriginal people), or to point instead towards significant differences in priorities and assessments of social realities and futures between these parties.[3] We begin with an analysis of these characterisations.

Blackfellas, Whitefellas and 'Greenies'

As Vincent and Neale explain, Marcia Langton's 2012 Boyer Lectures voiced a strong critique of environmentalists and environmentalism in Australia, focusing attention on relations between Aboriginal people and what Langton called 'the green left'.[4] In Langton's view, 'greenies' are poorly acquainted with the realities of Aboriginal people's lives, particularly the lives of those living in remote settings. As a result, 'greenies' – whom she characterised as predominantly non-Aboriginal, urban-based, and wealthy – tend to underestimate the challenges facing remote-living Aboriginal people seeking to reconceptualise their societies and economies in the wake of colonialism. Langton's view is that 'greenies' risk condemning Aboriginal people to penury by objecting to natural resource extraction projects, denying them the benefits of economic participation.[5] Relayed to a national radio audience and subsequently published in book form, Langton shattered the perception prevalent in parts of Australia that the interests of Aboriginal people and environmentalists necessarily coincide – a view which has tended to emphasise Indigenous culture as a 'cosmovision'[6] connecting people with nature – highlighting instead the politics of the 'green-black alliance' and the complexity of Aboriginal responses to the prospect of 'development'.

As Vincent and Neale also point out, Langton's lectures position 'greenie' and 'Aboriginal' as clearly distinct, with separate identities that exist prior to the interaction between them. It is inadequate, they suggest, to maintain such distinctions without analytical attention to the 'intercultural' relations which produced them, and continue to reproduce them, 'meaning the configuration and constitution of indigeneity and environmentalism in relation to one another is ongoing'.[7] In Australia, anthropological and other academic literature on such 'intercultural' relations is extensive and growing.[8] Such studies have generally sought to highlight the increasingly complex ways in which people with Indigenous, settler, and migrant ancestries and identities live together or alongside each other in contemporary Australia in ways that do not easily fit within ready dichotomies.[9] This has prompted investigation of ambiguities in the articulation of Aboriginal and non-Aboriginal identities, with Australianist scholars following Bhabha and other postcolonial theorists in emphasising the 'differential and strategic rather than originary, ambivalent rather than accumulative, doubl[ed] rather than dialectical' nature of these identities.[10]

The notion of 'greenies' itself goes some way towards complicating the dichotomy of Blackfellas and Whitefellas, and the 'moral and political binaries...[the] façade of unified positions... [and] left/right orthodoxies' upon which it thrives, which, as Gillian Cowlishaw memorably put it, 'caricature the complexity of racialized relationships being lived out across the nation'.[11] As David Ritter, the Chief Executive Officer of Greenpeace Australia Pacific argues, the category of 'greenie' not only distinguishes those described as distinct from other whitefellas – like pastoralists, fishers, and miners – but is further variegated to include all of those who participate in the 'environmental movement':

> ...not only the large national and international environmental non-government organisations (NGOs) but also the conservation councils and a plethora of other smaller entities; various think tanks and digital campaigning

organisations; numerous quasi-governmental and wholly private initiatives; and, of course, individual citizens who may become involved in a particular environmental issue.[12]

Such parties, Ritter notes, possess 'significant and legitimate differences in priorities, methods and underlying notions of the functioning of society...underpinned or influenced by the full ambit of ideological possibilities [within environmentalism]'.[13] While 'greenie' is often utilised in popular discourse to characterise – indeed caricature – those who express an interest in or concern for 'nature' or 'the environment', Ritter's emphasis on the diversity of the movement is salutary. As well as more sophisticated analyses of the identity categories of blackfellas and whitefellas, attention focused on 'greenies' reveals the great diversity contained in this category, which again arises only through interaction with others.

Like the plethora of entities that participate in the environmental movement, the proliferation of collectives representing the interests of blackfellas and whitefellas likewise complicates this analysis. Ethnographies of Australian society have historically approached governments, non-government organisations and the private sector as manifesting the will of the state and the broad settler society, being opposed to and even inimical with Aboriginal people's culture and identity.[14] However, as studies by Smith and others have shown, Aboriginal people are also closely involved in many such collectives and 'reshape and reform [them] via their involvement'.[15] Hence negotiations between blackfellas, whitefellas and 'greenies' must be understood not simply as relations between discrete social constructs and representations, but as relations between formally constituted collective actors with all the recursive and mimetic dimensions this introduces into the analysis.[16]

Hence, while we find significant differences between Aboriginal and non-Aboriginal people in their relations with place, our point is that analyses that remain confined to a rigid separation of identity categories, and the political struggles between them, tell only part of the story. While environmentalists had yet to enter the social field encountered by Trigger in the remote Gulf Country in the late 1970s and early 1980s, Aboriginal people were already intensely entwined with members of the broader society through more than 100 years of engagements with the same land and its species. Since then, these engagements have continued and intensified; in focusing our analysis on Pungalina and the changes that have taken place there since 1980, we raise questions of property, economy and ecology as these arise in, and affect, relations between blackfellas, whitefellas and greenies, while seeking to move beyond the basic questions of political ecology ('who owns what, who does what, who gets what, and what they do with it', to quote Li),[17] towards a consideration of effects, affordances and possibilities. The notion that a person might be 'intimate with country' invites these considerations. What does it mean to be intimate with land and water, the sea, and sky, with the 'vibratory cosmic forces' of life?[18] And to what extent are such intimacies shared between people across cultures?

The Gulf of Carpentaria

Pungalina is suitable for our analysis for a number of reasons. Firstly, Garawa Aboriginal people, like other Indigenous people in the Gulf Country and across the broader north of Australia, maintain a complex system of adapted traditional law and custom connecting them with country that derives from pre-colonial times. For Garawa people, country is richly imbued with spiritual significance, with different areas believed to represent, contain or be constituted by Dreamings such as the Emu Dreaming referred to above. Such Dreamings infuse the landscape with powers which may be dangerous if people behave inappropriately, or else accommodative to those with the appropriate knowledge and connections. Persons, Dreamings and country have a particular 'skin', an inner essential distinguishing quality known as *nginyi* in Garawa and glossed also as 'smell' in Aboriginal English. Individuals like Clara Bob (pictured earlier) generally inherit connections to country through their four grandparents, although other forms of connection are possible (such as through spiritual 'conception' at specific locations, or through the life events or deaths of close relatives in the area). In the ideal system, Garawa people maintain primary ties to their father's father's country, for which they occupy the role of *mingaringgi*, or 'owners', being supported by those with a secondary tie to their mother's and mother's father's country, known as *junggayi*, or managers, as termed in anthropological literature (with supportive *mingaringgi* and *junggayi* roles for relatives to whom the country stands as mother's mother and father's mother's country respectively).[19] At the time of writing, these connections have become understood flexibly across the relevant Garawa-identifying body politic, while knowledge about country and its appropriate 'skin-ship' continues to be a matter of intense politicking.

As well as such complex traditional connections and understandings of country, the Gulf was intensely affected by British colonisation with the arrival of Europeans and other settlers – including Chinese, Afghans and others of broadly Asian ancestry – from the mid-1860s. Colonisation began with a land rush of pastoralists driving cattle and sheep into the area, which precipitated intense conflict with Aboriginal people and eventually resulted in the gradual sedentarisation of Garawa people and others on pastoral stations, around small-scale mining developments, police station ration depots, in Borroloola and Burketown, and later at Doomadgee and Mornington Island missions.[20] While the violence introduced by the settlers dramatically and severely impacted on Garawa people and others around the Gulf Country with many murdered and dislocated from their traditional areas, colonisation also produced a complex history of intercultural relationships as initial violent contact gave way to an uneasy accommodation. Garawa people generally refer to this as the transition between 'Wild Time' (c. 1860s to early 1900s) and 'Station Time' (1900s to the early 1970s), as people settled into a semi-sedentary life and the country 'quietened down'.[21] On the stations and elsewhere, Garawa people came to form relationships with non-Aboriginal people, including connections between Aboriginal women and European, Chinese, Japanese, Malay and Afghani men.[22]

On Pungalina, these relationships began after the block was resumed from the larger neighbouring lease of Wollogorang and a Norwegian migrant named Andy Anderson (in partnership with Jim Nolan) built a hut on the property which he shared with an Aboriginal woman, likely from the mid-1920s. In 1943, Andy Anderson sold this block to George Anderson (no relation), who is said to have come to the Gulf Country from Victoria in southern Australia. George Anderson settled in the hut at Pungalina with two Aboriginal women, as well as with his children by them. When George Anderson died intestate in 1954, the lease reverted to the state, and George's Aboriginal partners and their children left. After George Anderson's death, the property was 'idle' until 1961 when the neighbouring pastoralist Willy Shadforth, a man of Aboriginal and non-Aboriginal descent, took it over. In 1978,

Shadforth sold Pungalina to a whitefella, who promptly went bankrupt, abandoning the lease and the dwelling located on the Calvert River. It was two years after this that Trigger and Garawa people traversed from the west through Emu Dreaming country to reach the old Pungalina homestead. This history complicates our presentation of Aboriginal 'intimacies with country' at Pungalina, suggesting attention to the broader context of colonial pastoral settlement and abandonment, including the recent land rights legislation (the *Aboriginal Land Rights Act 1976* (NT)) which shaped the 1980 field trip.

Pastoral Settlement, Abandonment and Land Rights

Colonial settlement in the Gulf Country was predicated on the profitability of the pastoral industry. In the early years, properties were run as open ranges similar to those found in other settler colonies like the United States. With few fences, country tended to be stocked according to the carrying capacity of the waterholes rather than the boundaries of any particular lease, resulting in intense pressure on Aboriginal people, who were excluded even from 'legally unoccupied' land. As the Northern Protector of Aborigines complained in 1901: 'where the cattle are – and where legally they have not th[e] slightest right to remain – the blacks have to be hunted away'.[23] Colonial archives attest to the severity of this process and its impact on Aboriginal people.[24] However, despite the violence and depredation that Aboriginal people suffered, settlement was never complete, particularly in remote areas where the 'promise' of the colonial frontier proved illusory, like at Pungalina. While numerous settlers sought profit there, by the late 1970s all such ventures had failed as agricultural overcapacity and associated shifts in the northern economy led to the loss of the commercial viability of the property.

This context shaped Trigger's first visit to the property in 1980, which was funded by the Australian Institute of Aboriginal Studies to help Garawa and other Aboriginal people record knowledge about sites and significant areas in the region. While connected to Trigger's academic studies, this research took place against the backdrop of recently instituted land rights legislation and other foreshadowed legislative reform to recognise Aboriginal rights. His field notes record the negotiations which took place as to the 'right people' to be involved on this trip; a matter subject to some politicking as to the appropriate persons with the strongest connections. This meant persons who related to estate areas on Pungalina as their patrifilial and matrifilial countries, relationships to the spiritual forces in the land based on descent and/or the system of 'skins', about which these persons were appropriately positioned to provide information. On this trip, the main *mingar-inggi* ('owner') who participated, a senior man who was last in the area as a young boy, played a lead role in providing knowledge about sites and significant areas which was duly documented by Trigger, including Garawa place names extending both upstream and downstream with groups of locations along the river jointly connected to particular 'skins' and Dreamings, including a site upstream that could only be looked at from a distance. Of interest, the name for the pastoral lease itself was said to come from the Garawa name for the junction of what are marked on maps as the Calvert River and Pungalina Creek: the junction of the water-courses being known as *banggilina*.

However, in addition to such traditional knowledge, as the group travelled to Pungalina, Trigger documented extensive Garawa knowledge of places connected to cattle station histories, such as 'Wanwansi creek', for example, which got its name because a horse with that brand died there. While, as the party travelled, older people gestured towards a few locations said to contain 'turnout all in a cave there', referring to stored artefacts and possibly human burials, just as significant was 'Black Charly's Mine' where a whitefella had dug for copper during earlier decades, living in a cave with two Aboriginal women. Garawa people associated the location with the family name, 'Charly', of the Aboriginal man believed to have 'found' the deposit – a location known to others as Redbank Mine – located some distance south of the destination of Pungalina on the neighbouring property Wollogorang. Further, at Pungalina, those participating recalled historical stories about the station, including an account about a remembered young Garawa man who once occupied the traditional estate area around the Banggilina site during 'wild time' when there was violence from both settlers and Aboriginal people. The recalled man is said to have killed a whitefella. He was subsequently caught and went to jail in Darwin, but returned to the Gulf after serving his sentence to father at least two children. The group also discussed the material environment around the station and the connections these indicated, with one woman commenting that she 'grew up', that is nurtured to maturity, a huge mango tree still living at the site of the abandoned homestead.

As well as such historical stories reflecting the incorporation of Aboriginal people within the pastoral economy, this field trip was also shaped by negotiations between Trigger (on behalf of the Garawa party) and pastoralists on neighbouring properties who controlled access roads to the abandoned Pungalina lease, reflecting more recent histories of exclusion of Aboriginal people from the stations. The most direct route was blocked, with the Euro-Australian owner of that lease stating: 'I would rather not have you down there'. While not hostile to the considerable number of Garawa people he had known over a lengthy period through employing them in cattle work, he was convinced that any traditional knowledge they had of the bush would be confined to the immediate homestead area where they 'grew up' when families lived on the stations. He reported how he had asked men about the surrounding country and concluded that they 'were pretty vague about it'; 'you can't turn the clock back' was his summary dismissal of the idea of land rights. His view was that, first, 'all the stations are touchy [about land claims]', and, second, 'why should there be two laws for White and Black?'[25]

The more circuitous route through Seven Emu Station was negotiated with Willy Shadforth, who was himself concerned that mapping the country of his mother's Garawa people could deprive him of the asset he had come to own in Australian law. This man's son, who was strongly opposed to tradition-based claims, put it as follows: 'some people think we got Seven Emus Station through the Aboriginal land rights, not true…[my father] won it in a lottery'. A young man, he boasted of having previously 'kicked' an anthropologist in a 'fancy Toyota' off his 'country', menacing that 'I've got a shotgun for every tourist'. Access to Pungalina through the neighbouring station was only secured when Trigger sat down to drink beer with the older Shadforth to discuss the trip. While unsympathetic, he did not prevent access, likely reluctant to disappoint his Garawa relations who were accompanying Trigger and exerting some social pressure. Indeed, this family's ambivalence about facilitating the visit to Pungalina prompted a later criticism from a senior Garawa woman for whom the Calvert River area was 'mother country': 'Yellafella where they got black mother and white father, they got all the station, they no more [do not] follow mother blood, they follow father blood'. At the time, over several beers, this man explained his own traditional connections, describing his relationship to the Aboriginal 'king Yilibara' of the neighbouring station Wollogorang.[26] Illustrating a strong grasp of Garawa history, this man explained how his mother's father, 'king Yilibara', had a fight with his younger brother in earlier days, this younger brother being the father's father of a senior Garawa person on the trip. From this fight the younger brother got the name *guyidalu*, he explained, *guyi* meaning head and *dalu* meaning rock, because 'no blood came out' of the latter's head from the fight with 'king Yilibara'. The repetition of this story reflected the long and close relations across the Garawa body politic despite the different life experiences of those, like Willy Shadforth, who had come to own stations.

In sum, this field trip involved the documentation of considerable Aboriginal intimacies with country as well as complications arising from the vexed history of colonisation; colonialism dislocating Garawa people from their traditional country, as pastoralists appropriated their land, but also coming to affect the ways in which people maintained knowledge and connection to parts of their country. In the case of Pungalina, this history is further complicated by the abandonment of the lease, as running cattle in this remote location proved unprofitable. Abandonment resulted in further dislocation, as people were removed from places like Pungalina towards towns like Borroloola and Burketown and Doomadgee and Mornington Island missions.

Tourism, Environmentalism and Indigenous Livelihoods

Since the 1980s, considerable changes have taken place at Pungalina, and more broadly across the Gulf Country and northern Australia. As the geographer John Holmes argues, agricultural redundancy in rangelands (such as at Pungalina) has been accompanied by the emergence of alternative market-driven amenity-oriented land and water uses. Holmes particularly discusses increasing tourism, as well as the impact of changing social values producing 'concerns tied to sustainable resource management, biodiversity preservation, landscape protection and Indigenous land rights', the latter of which have occurred at Pungalina.[27] After Trigger's visit with Garawa people, Pungalina remained abandoned for some time, its lands and waters effectively resumed by neighbouring properties and used (without legal rights) for the production of cattle. In the early 1990s, the lease was taken up by a non-Aboriginal man seeking to run an 'outback remote eco-wilderness' tourism venture particularly catering for amateur fishers and hunters, managing this tourism business in conjunction with the running of cattle (a requirement of the lease). However, by the time Richard Martin began fieldwork in the Gulf Country in 2007, this tourist business was defunct, and the Australian Wildlife Conservancy (AWC) was involved in negotiations to purchase the lease. In 2009, these negotiations were completed, and the old cattle property became part of the nature 'sanctuary' described above. This transition from pastoralism as a dominant land use towards more multifunctional understandings of country has significantly affected Aboriginal people with continuing connections to the area, as the following account of our 2012 field trip demonstrates.

As in 1980, access to Pungalina for Garawa people in 2012 remained a matter of negotiation with leaseholders, including the AWC. And, as in 1980, there were some sensitivities expressed during negotiations about tradition-based access and foreshadowed claims to land, with a native title claim over Pungalina (since determined) having succeeded the earlier regime of statutory land claims.

Further, like Trigger's first field trip to Pungalina, the 2012 visit was preceded by negotiations amongst Garawa people about who were 'the right people for country', with the role relationships of *mingaringgi* and *junggayi* still regarded as mean-ingful, being represented amongst the seven women, four men and one child who participated. However, contrary to the earlier visit, this field trip was interpreted by participants – including some of the children and grandchildren of those who participated in 1980 – as an opportunity to revitalise cultural knowledge by working with Trigger, himself now seen as someone who learnt from now-deceased 'old people'. The politics of such revitalisation were contested, with negotiations about who should come to the occasion for displays of tactical etiquette relating to the possession of knowledge and the pursuit of social honour. While not blocked, one participant's wish to be recognised as a traditional owner was particularly critiqued by others due to the alleged relevance of his non-Aboriginal ancestry (his father's father was a Euro-Australian), with another Garawa person of solely Aboriginal descent asserting: 'when they got a *mandagi* [i.e. whitefella] father they should sit down quiet'.[28]

Like the earlier visit, the 2012 field trip was eagerly anticipated as an opportunity to see country, and hunt and fish in a location not routinely visited. As one participant put it: '[Pungalina] is the land of plenty...'cause not too many people come'. Indeed, this man recalled a rare previous visit to the lease in which he successfully shot a wallaby and 'cut the tail to check the fat and the fat jumped out about that much [gesturing], it was like a bullock inside just too rich hey' – this view of fat functioning as a synecdoche for country, its abundance and fertility. Aboriginal interest in hunting and fishing at Pungalina was a significant cause of concern amongst the new leaseholders, the AWC. While Pungalina remains a pastoral lease as it was in 1980, it is now described as a 'refuge for many species that are in sharp decline elsewhere in northern Australia' rather than solely as a cattle business. On its website, the AWC uses descriptive and technical scientific language to accompany photographs of the landscape taken from the air interspersed with close-up images of animals to substantiate its representation of the lease as a biodiverse 'refuge':

> [T]he vast Pungalina-Seven Emu Wildlife Sanctuary protects an area of extraordinary conservation signifi-cance...The property captures a remarkable ecological gradient which extends from the ocean and its adjacent lowland plains to the top of the rugged sandstone plateau which dominates the Gulf region. Within this gradient lies a rich montage of habitats including coastal rainfor-est, mangroves, extensive riparian forest, vast eucalypt woodlands, perched wetlands and bubbling thermal springs.[29]

In an ABC report, a wildlife ecologist employed by the AWC expressed the view that this 'diversity of habitat types' is part of what makes the lease 'pretty special':

> Pungalina is pretty special 'cause it's been fairly well looked after in the past, I guess, in terms of um, it's been fairly low stocked, I think, it does have, it has in the past had a feral animal problem, but as far as, it's quite good condition as far as weeds go, so not many weeds, it's just an incredible landscape, it's a good example of the Gulf Country, that we can try and look after and keep it for the animals.[30]

In the same broadcast, the Chief Executive Officer of the AWC claims, 'We're like any other land manager really...we're trying to get the fire management right, we're trying to get across feral animals...and keep the weeds out'. However, the AWC's interest in 'keep[ing] it for the animals', as a biodiverse 'refuge', is in clear tension with Aboriginal people's interests in hunting and fishing. As we travelled into the property in 2012 this conflict produced some clear and strongly expressed concerns.

Upon arriving at the new homestead at Pungalina, in a different location to the old homestead area visited in 1980, the group split. Martin and Trigger interviewed the non-Aboriginal caretakers employed by the AWC, while Aboriginal participants fished for bream and turtle in the creek nearby. In the interview, the caretakers explained their role as maintaining a presence on the property, to cater for seasonal visits from scientists employed by the AWC and to protect the built infrastructure as well as the natural environment. Conscious of Aboriginal people fishing as we spoke, one of the caretakers stated:

> This is a sanctuary, we're looking after it...this is me speaking, nothing to do with AWC, but my feeling is that if we let these people come then our emus and things [i.e. species] would suffer...It would break my heart to have those people spear an emu.

Our inquiries established that these non-Aboriginal caretakers were advised by an ecologist not to take anything from the environment besides cattle. As a result, the caretakers expressed discomfort with Garawa people's exploitation of bush resources, seen as 'our emus and things'. For these caretakers, while coming from conventionally urban backgrounds in Holland and New Zealand, respectively, and having lived in the outback city of Alice Springs, as well as the Northern Territory's capital Darwin,

Pungalina was 'home', commenting: 'It's wonderful to be able to say, this is our home. When we were on leave it was so nice to be able to say: "Can't wait to get *home*"...I've always been a very rabid environmentalist...so when you talk about a sense of place, I think to me home is very much where I'm living at the time but it has to be someplace with an environmental sensitivity'. This 'sensitivity', this caretaker explained, involved 'beautiful' and 'wild' places, a point that was illustrated with reference to riparian vegetation around the homestead, but did not exclude an appreciation of Aboriginal traditional 'spirituality', for which both caretakers expressed respect.

But access to bush foods form an important material and symbolic part of many Garawa people's lives which connect with Aboriginal traditions in complex ways. The right to take them is jealously guarded, with people understanding such species as property tied into a system of thinking about the world glossed in English as 'law'. Our 2012 field trip to the sanctuary with Garawa people resulted in a catch of several dozen fish (known generically as *gagu* or *wajarrijba,* though many varieties have their own terms in Garawa) and turtles (*gulgul,* a short-necked variety valued as a delicacy) [31] as well as two *wundirri*, Australian bustards,[32] in two days. As in 1980, the rules associated with taking and preparing such species for eating were explained, with breaches believed to invite the censure of Aboriginal spirits: 'Country make you sick, somebody from this country come for you, spirit, all them old people for this country again, old *wanggala nganinyi*, old time people'. Yet, tactfully conscious of the attitude of the caretakers, such hunting and gathering mostly took place away from the homestead and the gaze of the environmentalists.

As well as hunting and fishing such native species, Garawa people participating on this field trip expressed some resistance to the AWC's aspiration to reduce the amount of cattle and other introduced species on the property. As one Garawa person explained on the field trip:

> They [i.e. introduced species] belong to here now, breed up in this large planet. Same as buffalo, pig, horse, [and] you see these little birds, brown ones, they [come] from Africa, every year they go fly everywhere where they want to go. Even the horse and cattle, their home [is] here, how you going to take them back? [There is] cruelty to animals these days, like the cattle, buffalo, killing to buffalo all the time but they're still here.

Cattle, as well as horses, were particularly associated with potential future 'development'. As we left the property, one of the senior men with whom we travelled expressed interest in returning in the future to work with cattle, assisting the organisation in the upcoming cattle muster. For this man, 'ringing' (stock work) was seen as part of Garawa traditions, recalling a time when people were productively employed on the stations in significant numbers. This man liaised with the caretakers to take a 'killer', a slaughtered beast, back to his home community at Robinson River at the end of our trip – such meat being valued much like the native species as food, but also as an indication of connection with the region's pastoral history.

In sum, this field trip, like the 1980 journey with Garawa people from Doomadgee, identified Aboriginal intimacies with country derived from pre-colonial traditions as well as adaptations arising from engagements with the broader society and introduced species. However, unlike the earlier visit, this trip involved some documentation of non-Aboriginal people's connections to the area, in the form of the AWC scientists' appreciation of it as a biodiverse 'refuge', which is 'pretty special', and further in the form of the caretakers' feelings of 'home' in this 'wild' and 'natural' place and connection to particular animals like emus. In the following section, we build on the contrast between these connections and the conflict between aspirations for 'development' and futures which they disclose.

Aboriginal Development, Intimacies with Country and Intercultural Relations

Around the same time as Langton's critique of the 'green-left' was broadcast in 2012, former Australian of the Year and prominent environment activist Tim Flannery published *After the Future: Australia's New Extinction Crisis*, in which he argued for a new way forward in natural resource management based on the involvement of not-for-profit private enterprises like the AWC. Emphasising the AWC's success in eliminating cats, foxes, rabbits and other 'ferals', and 'reintroducing endangered species' into fenced areas which 'effectively act as arks, keeping the survivors safe from extinction and genetically diverse', Flannery calls for further 'partnerships' between governments and the AWC (and other groups like it) to build on this success.[33] According to Flannery, humans are the 'keystone species in Australia's varied environments', both the largest and most significant threat, and the sole remaining hope. For Flannery, this role as keystone species is best filled by scientists such as those employed by the AWC: committed technical specialists who will seek to exclude human beings, and other introduced species, from places like Pungalina — a management plan which leaves little role for Aboriginal people and their continuing intimate connections to country. Research with Garawa people in the Gulf suggests a more complex approach is

advisable, reflecting the diversity – and instability – of contemporary Aboriginal-environmentalist relationships, which indeed is
already occurring at places like Pungalina as Aboriginal rights and
interests are negotiated.

In the first place, it is necessary to acknowledge the existence
of considerable Aboriginal knowledge of the environments like
Pungalina which might be seen to complement the expertise
produced by scientists and others such as those employed by the
AWC. Working with Aboriginal knowledge does not equate to
romanticism about the traditional wisdom of the pre-colonial
past. It necessarily also involves an awareness of change among
people such as the Garawa of the Gulf Country, not just as forms
of cultural loss (a perception of contemporary Aboriginal culture
common across the broader society), but also change as transformation, with many Aboriginal people expressing an attachment
to places on the basis of historical engagements with the cattle
industry and a desire to develop economic enterprises, as well
as maintain adapted practices of traditional hunting, fishing and
other subsistence use of bush resources. This approach to the
presence of introduced species presents a challenge to the kind of
radical nativism espoused by many environmentalists with respect
to what is seen to be valuable and authentic 'nature'.[34] This is
not to suggest that many Garawa and other Aboriginal people
throughout the Gulf do not perceive some of the negative impacts
of introduced species on the environment, or the damaging effects
of pastoralism and other development, and sometimes express the
desire to moderate such impacts and effects. However, Aboriginal
concerns for country include aspirations to develop viable jobs and
businesses based on the land and waters of their ancestral areas, with
tradition-based claims such as land rights and native title seen at
least in part as an opportunity to leverage legal rights and interests;

not simply to reinstate traditional lifestyles but rather to promote economic participation. Such change presents both challenges and opportunities for the relationship between the AWC and other environment groups and Aboriginal people – opportunities for organisations like the AWC to engage Aboriginal people in the conduct of surveys, the delivery of mustering and other services, and the implementation of fire-management (which is already occurring at Pungalina), as well as in other ways. At stake are questions of property and economy, as well as ecology. Who owns what, and what they wish to do with it, still needs to be 'settled' in this postcolonial society, as the issues of Aboriginal people's past and future place in Australia is negotiated, and renegotiated across the generations.

But as well as a neat illustration of the negotiation of questions of property, economy and ecology in a settler society, our analysis of Pungalina suggests that these things are entangled, and that such entanglements incorporate animals (such as emus) and other living things, as well as place itself. Rather than conflict or collaboration, our focus on historical conjunctions highlights intimacies here that a straightforward analysis of politics ignores. In 1980, there were Aboriginal stories of spiritual significance of the land together with oral histories of relationships with settler Australians and introduced species. Some mixed-descent individuals who had achieved legal leases over at least three pastoral properties (whether through inheritance from a settler forebear or some other means) were a complicating part of the entanglement between blackfellas and whitefellas. At the same time, whitefellas knew little if anything of Garawa spiritual beliefs such as stories of the Emu Dreaming near Pungalina: although they shared knowledge of the same locations as Garawa people, and had historically lived alongside Aboriginal people at Pungalina, the sense in which whitefellas shared the same place was questionable. A generation later, a new type of whitefella – environmentalists – likewise remain largely ignorant of Garawa beliefs; however, the interchange of meanings across cultures continues, as questions of property, economy, and ecology are renegotiated with the institution of the environmentalists' goals. Whether animals such as emus and other threatened species will continue to survive and thrive in the landscapes of the Gulf Country may depend on further exchange of meanings and values, as blackfellas, whitefellas and greenies manage their 'unstable relations' into the future.

References

Anderson, C., 'Aborigines and Conservationism: The Daintree-Bloomfield Road', *Australian Journal of Social Issues*, vol. 24, no. 3, 1989, pp. 214–27.

Anderson, C., 'Multiple views of paradise: perspectives on the Daintree rainforest', in J. Verstraete & D. Hafner (eds), *Land and Language in Cape York Peninsula and the Gulf Country*, John Benjamins, Amsterdam, 2016, pp. 263–84.

Australian Wildlife Conservancy, *Overview*, viewed 22 March 2016 <http://www.australianwildlife.org/sanctuaries/pungalina-seven-emu-sanctuary.aspx>.

Babidge, S., *Aboriginal Family and the State: the Conditions of History*, Ashgate, Farnham, 2010.

Bhabha, H. K., *The Location of Culture*, Routledge, London, 1994.

Cowlishaw, G., 'Cultures of complaint: an ethnography of rural racial rivalry', *Journal of Sociology*, vol. 42, no. 4, 2006, pp. 429–45.

Dalley, C. & Martin, R. J., 'Dichotomous identities? Indigenous and non-Indigenous people and the intercultural in Australia', *The Australian Journal of Anthropology*, vol. 26, no. 1, 2015, pp. 1-23.

Engle, K., *The Elusive Promise of Indigenous Development*, Duke University Press, Durham, 2010.

Fitzgerald, D., 'Wildlife surveys helping to understand native animals in remote Gulf of Carpentaria region,' *Northern Territory Country Hour*, ABC, 10 September 2015, viewed 1 March 2016 <http://www.abc.net.au/news/2015-08-07/pungalina-sanctuary-wildlife-survey-awc/6673356>.

Flannery, T., 'After the Future: Australia's new extinction crisis', *Quarterly Essay*, vol. 48, 2012, pp. 1–80.

Grosz, E. A., *Chaos, Territory, Art: Deleuze and the Framing of the Earth*, Columbia University Press, New York, 2008.

Head, L., 'Decentering 1788: beyond biotic nativeness', *Geographical Research*, vol. 50, 2012, pp.166–78.

Hinkson, M. & Smith, B., 'Introduction: Conceptual moves towards an intercultural analysis', *Oceania*, vol. 75, no. 3, 2005, pp. 157–66.

Holcombe, S., 'Luritja management of the state', *Oceania*, vol. 75, no. 3, 2005, pp. 222–33.

Holmes, J., 'Impulses Towards a Multifunctional Transition in Rural Australia: gaps in the research agenda', *Journal of Rural Studies*, vol. 22, no. 2, 2006, pp. 142-60.

Kapferer, B. & Morris, B., 'The Australian society of the state: egalitarian ideologies and new directions in exclusionary practice', *Social Analysis*, vol. 47, no. 3, 2003, pp. 80–107.

Kyle-Little, S. H. (Patrol Officer, Northern Territory Department of Native Affairs), 'Report relative to mines and cattle stations employing native labour in the Borroloola district, 16 December', *Australian Archives* (NT Branch) F315,49/393 A II, 1948.

Kyle-Little, S. H., 'Report of patrol of Borroloola district to Wollogorang Station by way of Seven Emus Station and return by way of Robinson River Station, 21 December', *Australian Archives* (NT Branch) F315,49/393 A II, 1948.

Langton, M., *The Quiet Revolution: Indigenous People and the Resources Boom*, Boyer Lectures, ABC Books, Sydney, 2013.

Li, T. M., *Land's End Capitalist Relations on an Indigenous Frontier*, Duke University Press, Durham, 2014.

Macdonald, G., 'Autonomous selves in a bureaucratised world: challenges for Mardu and Wiradjuri', *Anthropological Forum*, vol. 23, no. 4, 2013, pp. 399–413.

Martin, R. J., 'Reconfiguring indigeneity in the mainland Gulf country: Mimicry, mimesis, and the colonial exchange of difference', *The Australian Journal of Anthropology*, vol. 26, no. 1, 2015, pp. 55–73.

Martin, R. J. & Trigger, D. S., 'Negotiating belonging: plants, people, and indigeneity in northern Australia', *Journal of the Royal Anthropological Institute*, vol. 21, no. 2, 2015, pp. 276–95.

Merlan, F., *Caging the Rainbow: Places, Politics, and Aborigines in a North Australian town*, 1998, University of Hawaii Press, Honolulu.

Merlan, F., 'Theorizing Relationality: A Response to the Morphys', *American Anthropologist*, vol. 115, no. 4, 2013, pp. 637–8.

Reynolds, H., *The Other Side of the Frontier: Aboriginal Resistance to the European Invasion of Australia*, James Cook University, Townsville, Qld, 1981.

Ritter, D., 'Black and green revisited: Understanding the relationship between Indigenous and environmental political formations', *Land, Rights, Laws: Issues of Native Title*, vol. 6, no. 2, 2014.

Roberts, T., *Frontier Justice: A History of the Gulf country to 1900*, University of Queensland Press, St Lucia, 2005.

Roth, W. E., 'The Northern Territory–Queensland border, north of "Urandangie"', m.s., *Queensland State Archives* A/45400, 1901.

Smith, B. R., 'Still Under the Act? Subjectivity and the State in Aboriginal North Queensland', *Oceania*, vol. 78, 2008, pp. 199–216.

Trigger, D., Mulcock, J., Gaynor, A. & Toussaint, Y., 'Ecological restoration, cultural preferences and the negotiation of "nativeness" in Australia', *Geoforum*, vol. 39, no. 3, 2008, pp. 1273–83.

Trigger, D. S., *Whitefella Comin': Aboriginal Responses to Colonialism in Northern Australia*, Cambridge University Press, Cambridge, 1992.

Trigger, D. S., 'Indigeneity, Ferality, and What "Belongs" in the Australian Bush: Aboriginal responses to "introduced" animals and plants in a settler-descendant society', *Journal of the Royal Anthropological Institute*, vol. 14, no. 3, 2008, pp. 628–46.

Trigger, D. S., 'Anthropology and the resolution of native title claims', in T. Bauman & G. Macdonald (eds), *Unsettling Anthropology: the Demands of Native Title on Worn Concepts and Changing Lives*, AIATSIS, Canberra, 2011.

Trigger, D. S. & Martin R. J., 'Chinese History, Aboriginal Identity, and Mixed Ancestry in North Australia's Gulf Country', in F. Fozdar & K. McGavin (eds), *Mixed Signals: Perspectives on Mixed Race Identities in Australia, New Zealand and the Pacific Islands*, Routledge, London, In Press.

Trigger, D. S. & Martin, R. J., 'Place, Indigeneity, and Identity in Australia's Gulf Country', *American Anthropologist*, Forthcoming.

Vincent, E. & Neale, T., 'Unstable Relations: a critical appraisal of indigeneity and environmentalism in contemporary Australia', *The Australian Journal of Anthropology*, In Press, <http://onlinelibrary.wiley.com/doi/10.1111/taja.12186\ abstract>.

Notes

1   J. Holmes, 'Impulses Towards a Multifunctional Transition in Rural Australia: gaps in the research agenda', *Journal of Rural Studies*, vol. 22, no. 2, 2006, pp. 142–60.

2   R. J. Martin & D. S. Trigger, 'Negotiating belonging: plants, people, and indigeneity in northern Australia', *Journal of the Royal Anthropological Institute*, vol. 21, no. 2, 2015, pp. 276–95; D. S. Trigger, J. Mulcock, A. Gaynor &

Y. Toussaint, 'Ecological restoration, cultural preferences and the negotiation of "nativeness" in Australia', *Geoforum*, vol. 39, no. 3, 2008, pp. 1273–83; D. S. Trigger, 'Indigeneity, Ferality, and What "Belongs" in the Australian Bush: Aboriginal responses to "introduced" animals and plants in a settler-descendant society', *Journal of the Royal Anthropological Institute*, vol. 14, no. 3, 2008, pp. 628–46.

3   C. Anderson, 'Aborigines and Conservationism: The Daintree-Bloomfield Road', *Australian Journal of Social Issues*, vol. 24, no. 3, 1989, pp. 214–27; C. Anderson, 'Multiple views of paradise: perspectives on the Daintree rainforest', in J. Verstraete & D. Hafner (eds), *Land and Language in Cape York Peninsula and the Gulf Country*, John Benjamins, Amsterdam, 2016, pp. 263–84; M. Langton, *The Quiet Revolution: Indigenous People and the Resources Boom*, Boyer Lectures, ABC Books, Sydney, 2013; D. Ritter, 'Black and green revisited: Understanding the relationship between Indigenous and environmental political formations', *Land, Rights, Laws: Issues of Native Title*, vol. 6, no. 2, 2014.

4   E. Vincent & T. Neale, 'Unstable Relations: a critical appraisal of indigeneity and environmentalism in contemporary Australia', *The Australian Journal of Anthropology*, In Press, <http://onlinelibrary.wiley.com/doi/10.1111/taja.12186\ abstract>.

5   Langton, *The Quiet Revolution*.

6   K. Engle, *The Elusive Promise of Indigenous Development*, Duke University Press, Durham, 2010.

7   Vincent & Neale, *The Australian Journal of Anthropology*, p. 16.

8   C. Dalley & R. J. Martin, 'Dichotomous identities? Indigenous and non-Indigenous people and the intercultural in Australia', *The Australian Journal of Anthropology*, vol. 26, no. 1, 2015, pp. 1–23; M. Hinkson & B. R. Smith, 'Introduction: Conceptual moves towards an intercultural analysis', *Oceania*, vol. 75, no. 3, 2005, pp. 157–66; F. Merlan, *Caging the Rainbow: Places, Politics, and Aborigines in a North Australian town*, University of Hawaii Press, Honolulu, 1998.

9   D. Trigger & R. J. Martin, 'Place, Indigeneity, and Identity in Australia's Gulf Country', *American Anthropologist*, forthcoming.

10 H. K. Bhabha, *The Location of Culture*, Routledge, London, 1994.

11 G. Cowlishaw, 'Cultures of complaint: an ethnography of rural racial rivalry', *Journal of Sociology*, vol. 42, no. 4, 2006, p. 431.

12 Ritter, *Land, Rights, Laws*, p. 1.

13 ibid., p. 2.

14 G. Macdonald, 'Autonomous selves in a bureaucratised world: challenges for Mardu and Wiradjuri', *Anthropological Forum*, vol. 23, no. 4, 2013, p. 409;

B. Kapferer & B. Morris, 'The Australian society of the state: egalitarian ideologies and new directions in exclusionary practice', *Social Analysis*, vol. 47, no. 3, 2003, p. 86.

15 S. Babidge, *Aboriginal Family and the State: the Conditions of History*, Ashgate, Farnham, 2010; C. Dalley & R. J. Martin, 'Dichotomous identities?'; S. Holcombe, 'Luritja management of the state', *Oceania*, vol. 75, no. 3, 2005, pp. 222–33; F. Merlan, 'Theorizing Relationality: A Response to the Morphys', *American Anthropologist*, vol. 115, no. 4, 2013, pp. 637–8; B. R. Smith, 'Still Under the Act? Subjectivity and the State in Aboriginal North Queensland', *Oceania*, vol. 78, 2008, pp. 199–216.

16 R. J. Martin, 'Reconfiguring indigeneity in the mainland Gulf country: Mimicry, mimesis, and the colonial exchange of difference', *The Australian Journal of Anthropology*, vol. 26, no. 1, 2015, pp. 55–73.

17 T. M. Li, *Land's End Capitalist Relations on an Indigenous Frontier*, Duke University Press, Durham, 2014, p. 6.

18 E. A. Grosz, *Chaos, Territory, Art: Deleuze and the Framing of the Earth*, Columbia University Press, New York, 2008, p. 102.

19 D. S. Trigger, 'Anthropology and the resolution of native title claims', in T. Bauman & G. Macdonald (eds), *Unsettling Anthropology*, AIATSIS, Canberra, Australia, 2011, pp. 145–46; Figures 1 & 2.

20 H. Reynolds, *The Other Side of the Frontier: Aboriginal Resistance to the European Invasion of Australia*, James Cook University, Townsville, 1981; T. Roberts, *Frontier Justice: A History of the Gulf country to 1900*, University of Queensland Press, St Lucia, 2005; D. S. Trigger, *Whitefella Comin': Aboriginal Responses to Colonialism in Northern Australia*, Cambridge University Press, Cambridge, 1992.

21 In the late 1940s, the patrol officer Kyle-Little undertook a horseback tour of Gulf Country pastoral stations as part of his responsibilities as Protector of Aborigines with the Northern Territory Department of Native Affairs. On this trip, he reported on numbers of Aboriginal people living on stations adjoining Pungalina, with sixty people living at Manangoora, forty at Seven Emu, thirty at Robinson River, and forty at Wollogorang, meeting another small party on the Foelsche River whom he described as 'nomadic natives'. On that trip, Kyle-Little appears not to have visited Pungalina. See: S. H. Kyle-Little (Patrol Officer, Northern Territory Department of Native Affairs), 'Report relative to mines and cattle stations employing native labour in the Borroloola district, 16 December', *Australian Archives* (NT Branch) F315,49/393 A II, 1948; S. H. Kyle-Little, 'Report of patrol of Borroloola district to Wollogorang Station by way of Seven Emus Station and return by way of Robinson River Station, 21 December', *Australian Archives* (NT

Branch) F315,49/393 A II, 1948.

22 Throughout Garawa country, such relationships were common despite the existence of legal acts prohibiting 'consorting with', or having 'carnal knowledge' of, Aboriginal women (see, e.g. Queensland's *Aboriginal Preservation and Protection Acts* between 1939 and 1946, Section 29; the Northern Territory's *Aboriginals Ordinance of 1918*, Sections 28, 45, 51 and 53). Remote from the administrative centres of Darwin (in the Northern Territory) and Brisbane (in Queensland), non-Aboriginal men lived relatively openly with Aboriginal women across most of the stations having mixed-descent children with women at Manangoora, Spring Creek and Pungalina stations (as well as on Redbank mine and at diggings across the Lawn Hill mineral field). See: D. S. Trigger & R. J. Martin, 'Chinese History, Aboriginal Identity, and Mixed Ancestry in North Australia's Gulf Country', in F. Fozdar & K. McGavin (eds), *Mixed Signals: Perspectives on Mixed Race Identities in Australia, New Zealand and the Pacific Islands*, Routledge, London, In Press.

23 W. E. Roth, 'The Northern Territory–Queensland border, north of "Urandangie"', m.s., *Queensland State Archives* A/45400, 1901, p. 3.

24 Martin, *The Australian Journal of Anthropology*; Trigger, *Whitefella Comin'*.

25 D. S. Trigger, Field notes, September 1980. Subsequent quotations in this section are from the same field notes.

26 Martin, *The Australian Journal of Anthropology*.

27 Holmes, *Journal of Rural Studies*, pp. 143–4.

28 R. J. Martin, Field notes, October 2012. Subsequent quotations in this section are from the same field notes.

29 Australian Wildlife Conservancy, *Overview*, viewed 22 March 2016 <http://www.australianwildlife.org/sanctuaries/pungalina-seven-emu-sanctuary.aspx>.

30 D. Fitzgerald, 'Wildlife surveys helping to understand native animals in remote Gulf of Carpentaria region', 10 September 2015, *Northern Territory Country Hour*, ABC, viewed 1 March 2016 <http://www.abc.net.au/news/2015-08-07/pungalina-sanctuary-wildlife-survey-awc/6673356>.

31 This is most likely what is scientifically classified as *Elseya* spp. known by the English common name 'snapping turtle'.

32 Classified scientifically as *Ardeotis australis* with the common name of 'bush turkey'.

33 T. Flannery, 'After the Future: Australia's new extinction crisis', *Quarterly Essay*, vol. 48, 2012, pp. 64–5.

34 L. Head, 'Decentering 1788: beyond biotic nativeness', *Geographical Research*, vol. 50, 2012, pp. 166–78.

5

HOPE AND FARCE:
INDIGENOUS PEOPLES' WATER REFORMS DURING
THE MILLENNIUM DROUGHT

Jessica K. Weir

Introduction

The profoundly interconnected character of river systems and the centrality of water in facilitating life mean that large water engineering projects have a transformative capacity far beyond localised structures and distribution points, affecting all kinds of life forms and our relationships with them. Conflicts over the flow and distribution of water 'resources' have followed their industrialisation, moving the focus of such large river regulation projects from the technical to the political, from instrumental questions of water management to (often fraught) inquiries into whose water issues are prioritised within transformed river systems.[1] This is exemplified in Australia's Murray-Darling Basin, an over one million square kilometre catchment in the continent's south-east, where riverine ecologies have co-evolved with highly variable cycles of drought and deluge (see Figure 5.1). In this hot, dry place, the agency of the rivers to flood is celebrated by the Indigenous 'traditional owners' for sustaining all lives, including their own. Since the 1920s, large-scale schemes have sought to order this variability, and today the Murray River is both ancestral creator bringing life-giving waters and an extraordinary project of modernity. However, river regulation and changes to land use have had a negative effect on river integrity and water quality, and the Murray-Darling Basin is now also renowned for river dysfunction. Severe drought conditions from 2001 to 2009 – the 'Millennium Drought' – amplified what were already extensive and seemingly intractable 'environmental' problems. In 2010, the federal government initiated unprecedented water reforms which included the politically contentious step of buying water entitlements, previously allocated for consumptive uses, and reallocating them as 'environmental water' for river health.

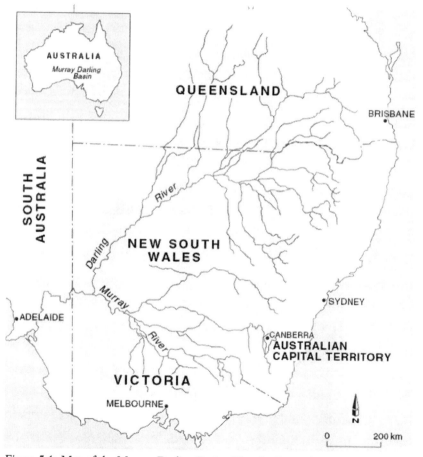

Figure 5.1: Map of the Murray-Darling Basin. Chandra Jayasuriya

Water scarcity highlights where water interests align and where they compete. As the Millennium Drought continued, the economic value of water increased, whilst water quality and the health of riverine ecologies continued to diminish. Clashes intensified between the dominant agricultural and environmental interest groups, despite both having a shared interest in the river integrity. These clashes highlighted the significance of the agriculture/environment dichotomy, and the role of hyper-separated dualisms. Hyper-separated dualisms are a knowledge tradition within which paired categories are placed in distinctly irreconcilable positions, such as nature/culture, tradition/change, subject/object, mind/body, male/female, and so on. The water debates about the Murray River were dominated by the flashpoint of production/conservation, with Indigenous peoples' water interests either absent or marginalised.[2] Their water interests fit neatly into neither agricultural nor environmental camps. Indeed, their water interests and their speaking position are split by agriculture/environment incommensurability assumptions that can be promulgated in each camp. Diverse Indigenous peoples thus have to strategise how to speak through and with the dominant dualistic knowledge traditions in order to gain purchase for their own priorities. It is an activity that is invested with a lot of hope, but one that can also be reduced to farce.

This chapter sets out some of the challenges of engagement that Indigenous people face within the very connected context of river degradation and water reform, living as a minority within Australia's colonial-settler state. In particular, this paper considers: how 'environmental' issues are framed by the nature/culture dualism; how Indigenous peoples' identities are positioned by the tradition/change dualism; how nature/culture and tradition/change interact to constrain what Indigenous people can say in response to river degradation, including their water rights agenda; and, critically, how the dualisms constrain what all people can say and hear. I will show how a particular kind of thinking has been normalised as culturally neutral universal knowledge, whilst simultaneously marginalising the contribution of other knowledge traditions. I will explore these issues by first establishing the socio-ecological context, and then considering the political-legal position of Indigenous people and their water issues. This is followed by a discussion of the water reform concept of 'cultural flows', including a critique of this concept and a response. The discussion concludes with an analysis of environmental and Indigenous or 'green-black' relations in this space. I reiterate the warnings of the traditional owners – we need to use a different kind of thinking to address river health, rather than continuing to rely on approaches that enabled over-allocation. Our capacity to effectively respond to the diminishment of our river ecosystems has become even more crucial with the expanding effects of climate change. Power of course is influential is this response, but so too is knowledge.

My analysis arises out of research I undertook during the Millennium Drought with the Murray Lower Darling Rivers Indigenous Nations (MLDRIN).[3] MLDRIN is an alliance of Indigenous people formed to strengthen the governance capacity of their traditional owner groups and to engage with water issues. At the time of my research agreement with them (particularly 2003–07), the groups represented by MLDRIN were: the Wiradjuri, Yorta Yorta, Taungurung, Wamba Wamba, Barapa Barapa, Mutthi Mutthi, Wadi Wadi, Latji Latji, Wergaia and Ngarrindjeri nations.[4] Their homelands or 'country' is in the southern part of the Murray-Darling Basin, where the Murray River begins in the snowy mountains, and travels west and south through semi-arid and arid lands until reaching the Southern Ocean. The concept of 'cultural flows' is just one of MLDRIN's strategies, but it has attracted a lot of attention, becoming federal policy in 2012, and also influencing the national Indigenous water agenda. In this chapter I review the positions that led up to, and are evident within, MLDRIN's 2007 Echuca Declaration on cultural flows, and what this tells us about knowledge diversity and new water questions.[5] I combine approaches from human geography and the environmental humanities to synthesise field-work findings with critical theory, connecting what I learnt from MLDRIN delegates with literature that critiques the abstraction of nature from its places, histories and cultures.[6]

River Regulation, Disorder and Response

Water variability and connectivity is central to understanding the rivers of the Murray-Darling Basin, their regulation, and the water management disputes. Very high rainfall and run-off variability is experienced across seasons, years, and decades. Drought followed by flood followed by drought is normal. Riverine plants and ani-mals have co-evolved with this variability. For example, river red gums drop leaves in times of drought and establish new genera-tions in times of flood. Fish, frogs, birds, snakes and many other species take advantage of flood waters to breed rapidly. However, it is precisely this variability which river regulation has sought to address; to protect towns from floods and ensure water during severe droughts when the 'mighty' Murray River can recede to a small stream. Large-scale interstate and intrastate river regulation became possible in 1915 when New South Wales, Victoria, and South Australia agreed on how to share the water.[7] Between 1934 and 1978, immense water storages were completed in mountain catchments and downstream as on-river and off-river storages. The stored water is distributed through a network of weirs, locks and canals. Flood plains have dried up as the regulated flow fails to break the river bank. Winter rains and snow melt are held back for the spring–summer 'irrigation season', and the Murray's flow on the riverine plains is now the *reverse* of seasonal patterns. Because it is constantly moving and connecting, river water once fresh enough to drink is now loaded with sediment, salt and other pollutants. As I write this, in 2016, a toxic outbreak of blue-green algae occurred for over 1,700 kilometres of the Murray River, lasting three months, killing animals and requiring farmers to find other water sources for their stock. Blue-green algal blooms have always been a feature of the riverine ecologies, but large-scale blooms are only a relatively recent phenomenon. In 1991 a state of emergency was declared when the first algal bloom over 1,000 kilometres occurred. The 2016 algal bloom is noteworthy here not just for the destruction of life but also because it was less remarked upon – as such effects of river degradation become accepted as the new normal.[8]

Land use transformations – such as the introduction of new crops, stock, and pest species and changes in farm practices to intensive industrial methods – also contribute to the diminishment of riverine ecologies. The acidification of ephemeral wetlands has been a striking loss of fertility. These wetlands had existed on the variable presence of water, but were permanently drowned as additional water storage facilities to support river regulation. During the Millennium Drought this stored water was released and, as a result, the long submerged acid-sulphate soils were oxygenated and became more toxic than battery acid. Wetlands, known as billabongs, have always been an important refuge for wildlife during drought times. Now, these poisoned wetlands no longer just fail to support life, their toxicity actually kills. This and other effects of land use change and river regulation are often recorded in the declining health and threatened status of the native plants and animals. River red gum forests are now largely dead or in decline. Native fish are estimated to be only 10 per cent of pre-European settlement levels.[9] Nesting birds are particularly affected by changes to the timing and duration of floodwaters; they will abandon their young if floodwaters start receding before the chicks can fly.

Environmental projects to improve river health are run by those seeking relief for local plants, animals, birds, fish, shellfish and other species. At the same time, improved water supply is sought by agriculturalists affected by the over-allocation of water licences and declines in water quality. Whilst the agriculture/environment split dominates water debates, there are irrigators who manage con-sumptive water to also achieve ecological objectives, and ecologists arguing for river health as part of also supporting river industries. The Millennium Drought intensified divisions over water use, but also brought people together as shared interests in river health were revealed. Water was so scarce that unprecedented emergency water measures were introduced to ensure, at the very least, water supply for towns. Under these measures some farmers received no water allocations at all and most others received only a fraction of pre-drought allocations. Images of farmers cutting down orchards and grapevines made metropolitan news at the same time as aerial photographs of river red gum forests standing dead on their former flood plains. Water management had become much more complex than originally envisioned.

Effective responses to these new water questions are ham-pered by the self-interest that arises in upstream/downstream river relationships between jurisdictions, companies, communities and individuals. For example, in the 1960s salinity had become a major concern and South Australia moved to limit surface water extraction (1968). Such a limit to 'progress' was not replicated by upstream states until 1995–96, when 'The Cap' was agreed upon for surface water extractions (but not ground water). To better address catchment complexity, in the 1980s institutional arrangements were expanded. The Murray-Darling Basin Initiative was formed with six interested jurisdictions: the federal government, the Australian Capital Territory, New South Wales, Queensland, South Australian and Victoria. However, by 2007 the situation was so dire that the federal government drew on its constitutional powers to intervene. With the federal government setting the water-sharing parameters, the states and territory governments became responsible for implementation.[10] In the Murray-Darling Basin Plan, the federal government proposed to return water to the rivers by buying consumptive water entitlements from willing sellers as well as improving water infrastructure. At a public meeting held to consult on the proposed reforms, upstream irrigation-dependent communities dramatically burnt copies of the water-planning documents. After much public controversy, and the breaking of the drought in 2010, the amount of water to be returned to the rivers was revised downwards. Again, agricultural and environmental interests clashed: environmentalists and ecologists said that too little water was being returned, while irrigators said that it was too much.[11]

Indigenous Peoples' Political-Legal Position

These entrenched contestations over scarce, degraded and valuable water provide a difficult context for Indigenous people to argue their own water interests, not least because of their historical and contemporary exclusion from political-legal arrangements. Commonwealth, state and territory ownership and management of water has long been premised on the *absence* of Indigenous peoples' property rights to land and water. As a result, Indigenous people are often seen as new entrants into water debates, and new competitors for scarce water allocations. This is deeply unjust. For tens of thousands of years Indigenous people were the only people who lived here, with sovereign titles across the entire continent. Before colonisation, the fertile Murray River was one of the most densely populated places in Australia.[12]

To say that the negotiation position facing Indigenous people today in the Murray-Darling Basin is fraught is an understatement. They are now 3.4 per cent of the population in the Basin, have small land and water holdings,[13] and, like many Indigenous people nationally, typically rate low on standardised social-economic indicators. They are thus thwarted by Westminster electoral systems based on majority votes and the pathways of influence that come with holding property or other material wealth. This situation of disadvantage arises out of the violence of colonisation and ongoing discriminatory treatment by Australia's successive settler colonial courts and governments. In the nineteenth and twentieth centuries their land was taken from them and given to other people, a recent history alive both in current memories and the day-to-day experience of living as neighbours to the beneficiaries of confiscations and their descendants. Despite the redress afforded by the historic 1992 High Court *Mabo* decision, which recognised 'native title' as surviving colonisation,[14] the scope of native title rights in the Murray-Darling Basin is heavily curtailed by the way even these laws are designed. Where recognised, native title rights to water are usually limited to small amounts for domestic and customary use.

For the Indigenous people whose country has been transformed by river regulation, theirs is an experience of violence that is so much more than the denial of their polities and property rights. Their experience is embedded in the diminishment of variable freshwater flows, and the destruction of their lands and waters that has followed. This destruction has been wrought not just on a particular place or species, or a particular traditional owner group, but on *peoples, species and places* over a vast river basin. Furthermore, the destruction has been rapid, much of it occurring over the lifetime of the current elders who grew up with healthy river ecologies. River regulation has shaped a contemporary wave of dispossession, compounding past losses and rupturing connections into the future.

In 2004 I conducted interviews with MLDRIN delegates and founders. The late Ngarrindjeri elder Agnes Rigney spoke to me about the immense changes she had witnessed over her lifetime. She grew up fishing on the clear waters of the Murray with bamboo spears her father made:

> It is not alive today; it is a dead river. Not only from just looking at it, but what it produces. Yes, I've seen the changes. I've seen the time when the river did produce for us well, when the river was clean, you could see the bottom of it. But to see it now it makes you wonder how anything could live in it actually, like the fish and the micro-organisms and all that.[15]

Yorta Yorta elder Henry Atkinson was able to live off the land with his family in the 1930s, catching fish, crayfish, mussels and turtles. In 2004, he found otherwise:

> The Murray River is being treated as a drain. The quality of the water is what you would find in a gutter. In fact, I would not go swimming in the river in Echuca as I used to anymore, there's no way.[16]

Yorta Yorta woman Monica Morgan spoke about the river as experienced in her childhood in the 1960s in Yorta Yorta country.[17] Her elders taught her the ecological cues that would tell her when swan eggs would be available up in the Barmah-Millewa lakes:

> There was life…You'd sit there and they'd say, 'Oh well the duckweed is coming down; that means the swan eggs are ready to go and be collected up in the lakes'. So there were seasons happening.

Now the water flows out of season, and both the swans and the duckweed are rarely sighted. Monica states:

> So if I am seeing in just a short time, twenty, thirty years, the disappearance of things that I took for granted, and were a real reflection of nature, and also governed my life cycles, then what is going to be left for our children?[18]

Along the length of the Murray, the MLDRIN delegates talked about how they are unable to pass on to their children and grandchildren the skills of living with country because the fish, birds, animals and plants are just no longer there, or only present in small and vulnerable populations. The MLDRIN delegates include the last generation of elders who grew up drinking from these rivers. Younger generations and others, who do not even know what they do not know, now accept muddy river water as normal. This is not just a loss of knowledge, but a loss of even the knowledge of the loss — a 'double-loss'.

Political-legal water rights are a core part of reparations for Indigenous people, but how meaningful are these rights when the creeks and wetlands are desiccated, drowned, or poisoned? In the Murray-Darling Basin, Indigenous peoples' water rights, their content and the capacity to exercise them, are dependent on healthy river ecosystems. Although it is true that degraded polluted water can be traded on the water market for money, and that money can then be used for ecological restoration projects, such work does not address the outstanding priority of variable freshwater flows. Because the magnitude and timing of water flows are so influential, and the river disorder problems are so connected, the Indigenous water rights agenda requires a bigger response than redistributing water allocations between humans; it requires a water policy that is supported to prioritise river health as the necessary prerequisite for all else, including our agricultural industries. This is evident in federal government law and policy which now accept that over-allocated rivers need to have their water returned.

Knowledge Interactions

The Indigenous water reform agenda is also difficult because it involves both the intersection and synthesis of Indigenous and (predominately) Western knowledge in an intercultural context, within which Indigenous knowledge has already undergone a profound syncretism with Western knowledge.[19] This is not to imply a unidirectional transfer, as Western knowledge has been influenced by Indigenous knowledge and indeed by the country itself – such as the new science of ecology.[20]

The British colony, established in 1788, was brutal, bringing violence and disease, with frontier wars and, later, assimilation policies that have led to the loss and transformation of Indigenous peoples' knowledge and language. However, many Indigenous people continue to speak a language steeped in their unique inheritance, including Indigenous people whose main language is English. In this, they draw on both dualistic and connected thinking, whether deliberately or less consciously as part of the integration of knowledge practices within settler colonial societies.

Many of the MLDRIN delegates speak of their country, being and knowledge as co-created, with origin stories detailing roles and responsibilities with the natural world, including kinship relationships with other species, places and things. These are intimate relationships, as Yorta Yorta Elder Henry Atkinson has described:

> As an Indigenous person, the environment, which includes the forests, the lands – the whole lot – is the core of our very being. It is our past and our future.[21]

This language of connection is not an undifferentiated holism, but an assembly of relationships variegated as strong, weak, important, distant – with fresh water explicitly recognised as the life-sustaining force it is. Speaking from 'country', a term used here to describe their homelands, the traditional owners speak of cultural and ethical domains of responsibility and reciprocity with the multiplicity of agencies that form sentient ecologies. Nature has the capacity to act and communicate, and the rivers are respected as the key connecting life force. As described by Yorta Yorta man Lee Joachim:

> The importance of the river is to ensure that it is seen as a continuing living being. That it is respected like any

other person should be respected. It has got the ability to cleanse itself. It has got the ability to nurture itself. And it has got the ability to ensure that the life that it touches upon also has an ongoing process.[22]

Yorta Yorta people speak of when *Baiame* sent a giant snake to follow his wife as she travelled from the mountains to the sea, thereby creating *Dhungala* (the Murray River). Much further downstream, Ngarrindjeri people speak of their ancestral creator *Ngurunderi*, who chased a giant *pondee* (Murray cod), widening the Murray River and eventually creating all the salt and freshwater fish. Such stories tie people to their distinctive part of the river in a potent spiritual way. These knowledges do not exclude instrumental approaches to water; rather, they are not dominated by instrumentalism.

In 1824, when European explorers first sighted the Murray River, Euro-American knowledge traditions were continuing to transform as part of the Enlightenment's quest for universal knowledge. Enlightenment intellectuals sought, and continue to seek, to establish science and reason as the foundation of knowledge, and thus free the world from superstition and religious beliefs. This has included the fundamental split of nature and culture.[23] The philosopher René Descartes argued that science and philosophy would empower men to be the masters of nature. He theorised a mechanistic view of nature, with the exception of the human mind, so that nature became simple matter without agency.[24] With the separation of nature and culture, believers are able to transform places without regard for the delicate web of relations that enmesh all kinds of natures and cultures.[25] Nature has become subordinate to humans, and it becomes possible to deny that human lives rely on nature for their very survival.[26] The split of nature and culture underscored the development of the natural sciences, but, whilst the natural sciences conduct their own critiques of this legacy (such as in the work of ecologists, anthrozoologists and others), the nature/culture dualism has become formalised across a range of disciplines and expert knowledges.[27] This dualism has been essential to the large-scale aggregation and organisation of nature as 'natural resources'. Diverse forests become lumber, and diverse waters become gigalitres.[28] Nature as resource can be claimed and managed by the state for the nation's benefit (for example, Figure 5.2).[29]

TREES WHICH HAVE BEEN "DROWNED IN THEIR COUNTRY'S SERVICE"   Photo: P. J. Hurley

47

Figure 5.2: Photo taken in 1946 of a drowned red gum forest with caption reading: 'Trees which have been "drowned in their country's service"'.[30]

In addition to negotiating with nature/culture, Indigenous people have to work with the influence of the tradition/modern dualism. In Australia, 'tradition' has become a defining marker of what it means to be Indigenous. For example, to apply for native title rights, applicants are required to establish not just occupation and polity, but also continuous 'traditional laws and customs'. This is the required performance to secure their collective rights. This emphasis on tradition presumes Indigenous people have a certain type of culture that does not grow.[31] Their culture will be lost on a path that goes from tradition to modern, or from custom to rationality; and as their culture is lost, so too do they lose their Indigenous rights. For example, Yorta Yorta people were judged as not Indigenous enough to be recognised as holding native title rights by Federal Court Justice Olney.[32] Justice Olney was looking for contemporary evidence of ceremonial and religious activities, and not the cultural heritage and environmental management work that was presented by Yorta Yorta.

Whilst the defining feature of tradition is connection with the past, traditions are always changing in every culture, as they constantly evolve for contemporary purposes.[33] However, in Western culture, the loss of culture – the shedding of romantic or superstitious beliefs which 'hold people back' – is often considered necessary for progress, and they can remain Western; but Indigenous people must shed their 'inferior' Indigenous culture if they wish to become modern. This thinking is known as the theory of hierarchical civilisation.[34] It is another example of a hyper-separated dualism which can become an unexamined societal norm. This is evident in Justice Olney words describing the (perceived) loss of Yorta Yorta traditions as being the result of 'the tide of history'.[35]

Philosophers Val Plumwood and Bruno Latour have each described how dualisms are created and then separated into oppositional corners with a tension that cannot be resolved.[36] Plumwood calls this hyper-incommensurability. What is natural cannot be cultural, what is traditional cannot be modern, what is rational cannot be emotional, and so on. Conceptual strategies are used to exaggerate differences and deny commonality. Nature is lacking human attributes: mind, rationality, spirit or the outward expression of these in language and communication.[37] Indigenous people are essentialised as traditional spiritual beings, distinctly different from other humans, otherwise they lose their indigeneity. To counter the weight of these conceptual frames, Plumwood says we need to make 'a double movement or gesture of affirming kinship and also affirming the Other's difference, as an independent presence to be engaged with on their own terms'.[38]

Universal Staging

The capacity of dualistic thinking to marginalise other knowledge traditions is underpinned by the staging of this knowledge as a universal knowledge. The Enlightenment's pursuit of 'universal knowledge' is expressed explicitly through documents such as the 1789 French Declaration of the Rights of Man and of the Citizen and later the United Nations 1948 Universal Declaration of Human Rights. Universal knowledge was also pursued in the natural sciences quest for an understanding of nature as universal, as known through a universal science.[39] Such universalisms form 'grand narratives' which involve an ordering of people, places, species, things and time. For example, the pathway of progressive reason, which purportedly begins in the West and unfolds across the globe, is part of rendering global events into a singular historical narrative. As political scientist Timothy Mitchell has written:

> The narrative is structured by the progression of principle, whether it be the principle of human reason or enlightenment, technical rationality or power over nature. Even when discovered acting precociously overseas, these powers of production, technology, or reason constitute a single story of unfolding potential.[40]

In the pursuit of establishing reason, science and rationality as the foundation of knowledge, Enlightenment scholars simultaneously establish Western knowledge as universal knowledge: omnipotent and culturally neutral. Yet, at each step of the way, the creation of universal approaches was hotly debated within Western societies. For example, political scientist James Tully has documented the gradual movement of governments away from practices that were responsive to cultural diversity, towards the establishment of a uniform citizenship (in theory at least).[41] Key 'universal' terms in modernity, such as 'nature', 'nation', and 'economy', have been repeated so often and so effectively that it seems that these conceptual objects 'exist prior to any such representation'.[42] However, identifying that universals are flawed does not require endorsing the post-modern critique of cultural relativism, within which all knowledges are local and cannot be translated across cultures.[43] Instead, we can retain the valuable knowledge generated by so-called universals, and not dismiss them for their subjectivity. Anthropologist Anna Tsing argues for a different kind of universalism, a 'sticky universal' that can travel and communicate across contexts, but which is recognised for its origins and partial objectivity.[44]

Meanwhile, hyper-separated dualistic knowledge traditions continue to do their work. As the grand narratives unfold from the West, Indigenous people across the world are found to be remote, isolated and primitive. The spiritual homelands of the Murray River peoples necessarily give way to the contemporary priorities of modern agricultural production. With the 'rule of experts', life-giving waters are disentangled from messy cultural and ethical connections, and measured instead as discrete, separate units that can be stored and allocated for human consumption.[45]

In this water management culture, Indigenous people face the choice of either co-option or marginalisation. They can speak the dualistic language and be involved, or they can continue to express their holistic connections of complexity and remain marginalised. But this is a *false choice*.[46] Instead, by re-setting the terms of the dialogue, other options become possible. For this to happen, there needs to be greater reflexivity about the presumed 'naturalness' of the concepts 'nature', 'natural resources', and 'natural resource management'. With greater reflexivity, water management conversations framed around so-called 'universal knowledges' become more open to hearing what Indigenous people are saying.

Table 5.1: Some false assumptions about modern and Indigenous water management.

Modern (i.e. 'non-Indigenous') water management	Indigenous water management
Modern	Traditional
Universal	Local
Technical	Spiritual
Rational	Emotional
Culturally neutral	Culturally specific

Intercultural life is much more complicated and enmeshed than what I have briefly scoped in this chapter. I have presented a simplification to navigate through complexity, rather than simplifying it, in line with cultural theorist Ien Ang's notion of 'cultural intelligence'.[47] My intention has been to focus on how Indigenous people and their interests are stereotyped and then used to discriminate in fields of differential power and loaded discourse. I have summarised this context in a table of some of the acknowledged and unacknowledged assumptions that Indigenous people repeatedly face within water management negotiations in the Murray-Darling Basin (see Table 5.1). It is not a problem that categories such as 'traditional', 'local' and 'spiritual' are identified as appropriate to Indigenous peoples' interests – because they are all these things. However, Indigenous people also have Indigenous interests that are 'modern', 'universal', and 'technical'.

Effecting Change

How, then, to effect change? The traditional owners decided to build their authority and capacity to speak, and set up processes and structures to secure a greater influence in water issues. Not the least complicating factor in this work is that Indigenous people, as with all peoples, hold diverse views within and between polities and individuals.

In 1998, the Yorta Yorta people called a meeting of traditional owners from along the Murray River, mobilising traditional authority partly in response to Justice Olney's native title judgement, as well as to collaborate on issues of river health. In 2001, MLDRIN met for the first time as a group of representative delegates from each nation group. In 2003, they negotiated funding for an executive officer and meeting costs from the Murray-Darling Basin Commission (MDBC). The MLDRIN delegates continued to build capacity on their own terms by establishing policies that ensured authority remained with the traditional owner groups and not the newly formed alliance. For example, MLDRIN worked with the nations to set up their own incorporated bodies, so that they could enter into contracts for any water reform outcomes that might be achieved. The design of MLDRIN itself as based in country rather than state/territory jurisdictions, also responded to the fragmentation of Indigenous peoples' representation in water issues.

In 2006, MLDRIN signed a Memorandum of Understanding (MoU) with the MDBC. The MoU was a mutual act of cultural

recognition on agreed terms. Significantly, the MoU's acknowledgement of the nations as the traditional owners of country was
in itself a highly valued outcome. Their experience of colonisation
and marginalisation means they are repeatedly challenged on not
just their legitimacy to be involved, but also their very identity
as traditional owners.[48] The content of the MoU also reflected
MLDRIN's priority to support the nations as the political-legal
structures for engagement. For example, clause 6.4 states:

> The parties will develop agreed general frameworks
> and processes to enable each of the Indigenous nations
> to reach understandings and agreements with the
> Commission on all issues of common concern in order
> to facilitate the resourcing of activities...

The activities listed within this clause include natural resource
management, cultural heritage, social and economic outcomes,
and other activities of mutual interest. These are processes of
nation-building that do not require the sanction of native title
courts.

The MLDRIN delegates' other key objective was to have a
greater say in water management. Long before the Millennium
Drought the river country had been suffering. The jurisdictions
began to acknowledge that The Cap was not sufficient for water
reform, and that 'environmental water' needed to be identified
for river health. In 2002, the Murray-Darling Basin Ministerial
Council (MDBMC), which oversees the MDBC, introduced
The Living Murray program. The aim of The Living Murray
was to achieve a 'healthy working river', defined as 'one that is
managed to provide a compromise, agreed to by the community,
between the condition of the river and the level of human use'.[49]

Environmental water was to be found through water recovery measures, such as improvements to infrastructure, rather than addressing the over-allocation of consumptive licences. After consultations on three possible amounts of water to return annually – whether 350 gigalitres, 750 gigalitres or 1,500 gigalitres – in 2003 the MDBMC announced that 500 gigalitres would be recovered over five years at a cost of $500 million.[50] As part of this, 'icon sites' or Significant Ecological Assets were identified to receive environmental water for ecological objectives.[51]

We now know that the original goals of The Living Murray were eclipsed by the federal government's intervention in response to the Millennium Drought. By 2010, the federal government was proposing to return 3,000 to 4,000 gigalitres of environmental water. This became law in 2012 as a reduced annual return of 2,750 gigalitres. The terms of the conversation had also moved, from the compromised working river described above, to a greater emphasis on ecosystem function. The scientific advice is that 6,983 gigalitres of environmental water is needed to return healthy ecosystem functions.[52] Whereas, at the start of The Living Murray program, the MDBMC had been provided scientific advice that to achieve 'a healthy working River Murray System' a return of: 750 gigalitres per year would have a low-moderate chance of success; 1,630 gigalitres per year a moderate chance; and, 3,350 gigalitres per year a high chance.[53]

The MDBMC's 2003 decision to allocate 500 gigalitres may have been a pragmatic policy within a tough socio-political context; however, it received a lot of criticism from environmental groups and MLDRIN. MLDRIN conducted their own consultative process about these environmental water reforms, reporting back that the nation groups were critical of the three reference points which were unsatisfactory, and falling far short of returning the rivers to health.[54] Political historian Daniel Connell aptly described how such 'business-as-usual' approaches to water management have 'indefinite decline' of the rivers as an 'unspoken premise'; and, the then goal of The Living Murray as 'a philosophy of despair'.[55] The MDBC literature identified the relationship between agricultural interests and river health, but vested interests in the status quo prevailed. MLDRIN pursued opportunities within The Living Murray environmental management program, including: Cultural Heritage Management Plans at each of the icon sites; employment specifically for Indigenous people in water management; and, funds for 'Indigenous use and occupancy' maps.[56] However, it remained that the core problem of over-allocated river water was not being addressed.

With the new idea of environmental water or environmental flows becoming part of mainstream water management, the MLDRIN delegates unsurprisingly responded with cultural flows. For many of the delegates, the purpose of this was very straight-forward – to get a little more water for country in this period of harsh policy constraints and harsh drought conditions.[57] Cultural flows attracted attention from water managers who could consider how this water might also be about river restoration, but with a focus on Indigenous peoples' values. But there was a lot of uncertainty around the concept, and the joint desire that it be better articulated was expressed by MLDRIN and the Community Advisory Council (CAC), which advised the MDBMC. In 2005, the two groups met in Wagga Wagga for a day's discussion. At this meeting, the late Ngarrindjeri Elder Matt Rigney, who grew up on the Coorong in South Australia, and was the then chair of MLDRIN, succinctly said: 'Cultural flows – it's about the regeneration of life'.[58]

From the Macquarie River in central New South Wales, Wiradjuri elder Tony Peachey described cultural flows as a flush of fresh water, because:

> ...unless you get that fresh water in to flush it out, the river itself just gets sick. That's as simple as it is; because the flows aren't there.[59]

The delegates are stating the obvious – but they needed to. They express a fundamental point about water and river health that they cannot see in the bleak goals of The Living Murray. They are exasperated by a water reform context that cannot respond with action to the seriousness of the situation and the central role of variable freshwater flows in restoring life. Without fresh water, everything dies. Yorta Yorta Elder Henry Atkinson brought it all together when he said:

> Cultural flows are a natural flow which allows everything to grow. Cultural flows include your history and your culture.[60]

Cultural Flows and the Echuca Declaration

With over-allocated agriculturally valuable river catchments, powerful vested interests and severe drought, effecting change was never going to be simple for MLDRIN. Interestingly, the concept of cultural flows has found some traction. The 2012 Murray-Darling Basin Plan requires that regional-based water resource plans 'must be prepared having regard to the views of Indigenous people regarding cultural flows'; and, a national cultural flows research project has been funded.[61] Yet the concept of cultural flows remains a difficult agenda,[62] and it has also attracted criticism for being a confusing diversion to the Indigenous water rights agenda. As a match with environmental flows, cultural flows also unfortunately matches with the nature/culture dualism: this is a cultural flow that is disconnected from nature, and also one that is likely to require the production of a 'traditional' culture. By using the word 'culture' to leverage off their indigeneity, the proponents of cultural flows have risked being limited by what culture means within mainstream water management.

In 2007 in the Murray River town of Echuca, the MLDRIN delegates met for two days to develop a statement on cultural flows: the 'Echuca Declaration'. It was an Indigenous-only meeting, with the delegates each allowed to bring a couple of support people from their nation. A draft was negotiated and this was then taken on the road to each delegate nation to seek their support, a process undertaken either by the MLDRIN coordinator or through the nation's own governance processes. The most cited part of the Echuca Declaration is the Part 1, Article 1 definition:

> 'Cultural Flows' are water entitlements that are legally and beneficially owned by the Nations of a sufficient and adequate quantity and quality to improve the spiritual, cultural, natural, environmental, social and economic conditions of those Nations.[63]

This definition combines the language of water entitlements with the 'rights language' used in international contexts, such as in the United Nations Permanent Forum on Indigenous Issues. It is a declaration of their legitimacy to have water rights recognised in law, in a context where, both in perception and actuality, they have very few rights as traditional owners. The evocative language of connection has been replaced by a list of conditions and references to water quality and quantity, ostensibly to better fit with the language norms of water law and management. The language of connection remains in other parts of the Declaration, which sets out MLDRIN's comprehensive cultural flows agenda. Article 2 defines the cultural flows outcomes for the survival of the rivers, with the full spectrum of priorities they have for cultural flows preceded by the qualification ... if our country is healthy enough'. Whilst I did not attend the meetings in which the Echuca Declaration was drafted and then agreed upon, at previous MLDRIN meetings I had observed discussions about cultural flows. Informing these conversations was the understanding that *any* quantifiable Indigenous/cultural water allocation would be insufficient to address the critical state of riverine ecologies throughout the river country. No less so than in 2007, when parts of the Murray–Darling Basin were suffering from 'ecosystem collapse'.[64]

The restitution of Indigenous peoples' water property rights has always been raised by traditional owners as part of their water agenda. For example, in the consultations MLDRIN conducted about The Living Murray, prior to the language of cultural flows, it was argued that a water allocation was necessary for each traditional owner group. This allocation was to be for their 'cultural economy', whether that water be used to increase environmental flows or for an economic base. This could be a distinct Indigenous water allocation itself, or an allocation of water out of both environmental and consumptive water 'pools'. Ideally, this water would be a legally defined right or, at the very least, a renewable tradable water entitlement, as realised through the different water management schemes of the states and territories.[65] In the dominant language of water management it is much easier, and thus arguably more strategic, to express 'cultural flow' as an 'Indigenous water allocation'; an amount of water allocated for Indigenous peoples' use. Indeed, ecologists have made strategic compromises when lobbying for 'environmental water allocations', despite it being obvious in their professional opinion that the river is the source of the water.

Sue Jackson and Marcia Langton, senior academics in the field of Indigenous peoples' water issues, have criticised cultural flows, or, their term, 'cultural water entitlements' (in which they exclude consumptive values), for being an 'overloaded and weak concept'.[66] They define their scope as 'an analysis of the legal model for recognizing indigenous interests in water that has emerged from neo-liberal reforms to water governance.'[67] They find that the Echuca Declaration definition 'should be avoided' for multiple reasons, including: because of 'the simple and misleading contrast of environmental flows to "cultural flows"'; because it 'confuses entitlements, allocations and flows'; and, because it is 'an unfortunate elision of Indigenous secular and religious concerns'.[68] They argue:

> Water regulation in Australia should not have to carry the cultural and political weight of capturing cultural identity, especially when marginalized indigenous groups require water allocations for basic community and environmental needs, and are delayed in their aspirations by the confusion caused by the term cultural flows...
>
> This is a problem of incommensurability between a cultural domain and a regulatory system.[69]

148

Technical-managerial analyses into the political economy of water rights are important work, particularly during water forum periods. In 2004, the water reforms went nationwide with the National Water Initiative providing the framework for separating water titles from land titles to facilitate water trading and increase the efficiency of consumptive water use. [70] In this, there was a clear opportunity for governments to, albeit belatedly and pro-visionally, recognise Indigenous peoples' water rights, including their consumptive water rights. Indigenous people require robust technical, legal and political advice to push their agenda in these forums. As Jackson and Langton note, a lack of understanding about Indigenous peoples' world views contributes to their mar-ginalisation in mainstream water management.

My main reply to this analysis is that it only discusses MLDRIN's cultural flows arguments in a regulatory context. There is no mention of the five pages of the Echuca Declaration that frames this cultural flows agenda or any specific insights from the MLDRIN delegates themselves on the choices they face. Instead, Jackson and Langton consider the definition on its own, so as to discuss what they see as being the problem with cultural flows as argued for in southern Australia.

When I had access to observe MLDRIN meetings during an intense period of water scarcity and reform, I found that what were saying about cultural flows was important precisely because it did not fit into mainstream water management. The delegates prioritise the restoration of variable fresh water flows, whilst also articulating a rights agenda that is dependent on that restorative activity. However, Jackson and Langton do not consider this perspective, and instead draw on their expertise from Northern Australia to recommend the Indigenous reserve strategy as the exemplar alternative to cultural water entitlements.[71] In the north, fresh water sources are largely unallocated, Indigenous people own some 30 per cent of the land, there are well-established Indigenous organisations with secure funding streams, and Indigenous people are less likely to be questioned over their authenticity. Jackson and Langton illustrate with a water plan that will potentially allocate 25 per cent of water to Indigenous land owners for their commercial use. These are indeed significant outcomes.

Unfortunately, in the Murray-Darling Basin the traditional owners cannot even presume the continuity of river health, and, for at least one moment in time, the federal government agreed. At the peak of the Millennium Drought, farmers started the irrigation season with allocations of just 2 per cent of their entitlements, thirty-three wetlands were drained of water, the Coorong became five times saltier than the sea, 20,000 hectares of acid-sulphate soils were exposed, and the flow of water across the South Australian border was just 960 gigalitres per year.[72] Research from Antarctic ice cores reveals that decadal-long 'megadroughts' have historically been a normal feature of the hydrological cycle, and their effects are anticipated to worsen as the Basin's climate becomes hotter.[73]

Indigenous peoples' cultures have always changed and adapted to new circumstances, including surviving an ice age; but in 2006 Yorta Yorta woman Monica Morgan described the ongoing failure of water institutions to return water to the rivers as a 'bureaucratic genocide' on her people. As Yorta Yorta man Lee Joachim also said:

We just don't all come from Adam and Eve. We come from the simple dirt that we walk upon. And our spirits, and our *Baiame*, our makers, it's all interconnected there. And people don't even show respect, you know, for that.

If our river and environment is dying, then I believe that we as a people are also dying.[74]

Here, there are no consumptive water licences, nor environmental flows, nor cultural flows, nor Indigenous water allocations, if there is no Murray River or if it is so degraded as to be a toxic polluted mess. The political-legal aspect is critical in arguing for Indigenous water rights, but it is not the only water work that needs to be done. The river must come first. However, to say this is to fall into abusive and dismissive categories reserved for environmentalists, Indigenous people and others who do not use the technical, rational language of land and water management.

Offside

Indigenous people and environmental groups share many common agendas; however, green-black relationships are often strained. For example, in the temperate rainforests of British Columbia, Canada, environmentalists first sought to *exclude* the existence of the Aboriginal Nuu-chah-nulth people by using external and universal concepts of a pristine nature, and then, when that was unsuccessful, to *collapse* the Nuu-chah-nulth into the same category as the forest – as primitives in harmony with a pre-modern nature.[75] This second exclusion relates to the depiction of Indigenous people as ecological saviours, with the remedy for the global ecological destruction of modernity.[76] In this iteration, they are required to have certain values that are antithetical to capitalist or market economy pursuits: described as a 'Green Orientalism' in the South East Asian context.[77] When making ecological alliances, Indigenous people have to consider whether to also remain free of commercial aspirations; realising some rights this way requires that they deny themselves the other rights.[78]

But there are also very successful collaborations between environmental groups and Indigenous people. In the Murray-Darling Basin, environmental groups have much greater political influence than Indigenous people, and MLDRIN has strategically made alliances to seek common ends. This is exemplified by the successful campaign to persuade state governments to revest river red gum forests from state forestry land to national parks.[79] River red gums live for up to a thousand years, but these wetland and flood plain forests are in such poor health that their economic value as lumber has become negligible. In 2010, Victoria and (later) New South Wales revested the forests as reserved lands; but the management change was contested and resulted in an inquiry. Bitter local disputes within rural communities were documented in this process, including tired and limiting exchanges relying on the nature/culture and tradition/change dualisms to discriminate and exclude, with one person even insisting that the forests were 'grown by the white man'.[80] Yarkuwa, a local Indigenous organisation, is building acceptance for a 'cultural and environmental management' that includes all people, prioritises traditional owner use, and selected timber harvesting is just one of many activities supported by healthy forest wetlands.[81] They are growing acceptance for these narratives of inclusion and connection.

Green-black alliances are inherently complex and so, in order to set a stronger basis for partnership, in 2007 MLDRIN negotiated a cooperative agreement with representatives from several environmental non-government organisations (NGOs), representing a diversity of interests from retiree bushwalkers to so-called radical greenies.[82] This agreement recognised the Indigenous nations as the traditional owners of country and their inherent right to speak for country. The agreement also recognised the role of environmental groups in representing the concerns of their membership, and the role they play in the creation of an equitable, healthy and sustainable country. A real sticking point in negotiating the 2007 agreement was the insistence by MLDRIN that Indigenous people have scientific knowledge too. This was recognised in the final text in the following points:

- that Indigenous science and Western science each have their own value and role in caring for country;
- that knowledge and management work together – caring for country creates new knowledge and knowledge helps us better care for country.

According to MLDRIN's executive officer at the time, Wamba Wamba man Steven Ross, some of the environmental NGOs were initially concerned that calling traditional knowledge 'Indigenous science' would undermine the presumed universal authority of Western science.[83] To counter, the delegates revealed how their understandings of the rivers, including direct observation and experimentation, form the basis of their science. Since colonisation, this science has been informed and influenced by Euro-American science. The environmental NGOs more experienced in engaging with Indigenous people were quicker to accept MLDRIN's position on Indigenous science.

Support for cultural flows was another agenda item requiring negotiation, including how they differed from environmental flows. Cultural flows were initially raised by MLDRIN as an addition to environmental flows during drought times, for example, so the water could reach further out onto a flood plain. The question then arises, if environmental flows restore river health, why are cultural flows needed? Environmental flows are based on ecological criteria, and are blind to Indigenous law, language, culture and country. The traditional owners cannot rely on these flows to water places important to them. Further, environmental flows are limited amounts of water, and judgements about which places get this water are based on ecological criteria, as evident in The Living Murray's 'icon sites'. The option of involving Indigenous people in the governance of environmental flows requires the ecological criteria to be broadened out. Otherwise, if decisions remain based on ecological science, then Indigenous people do not need to be consulted about their values.[84] In these negotiations, MLDRIN used empirical evidence from their use and occupancy mapping work to lend weight to their arguments. Critically, environmental flows do not address the broader agenda that Indigenous people bring to water reform, including reparations.

Differences between MLDRIN's agenda and the environmental NGOs were also evident during the river red gum campaign. Steven Ross found himself emphasising to environmental partners that the campaign is not just about trees; that it also has to include water and capacity building for the nations.[85] Presumably, the isolation of the river red gums as a campaign issue by the environmental groups reflects a pragmatic decision about what makes an effect with metropolitan audiences: in this case, a charismatic species. From Steven Ross's perspective, the capacity of the nation's to speak for country is central to how best to care for country, but this is a more political and complex issue. 'Speaking for country' was another sticking point in the environmental agreement. Many people have visions of what is best for country, including scientists and environmental groups who sometimes contend that they 'speak for' nature.[86] However, scientists should not expect to have special standing to decide value questions for society.[87] That MLDRIN and the environmental groups reached agreement reveals how strategic compromises are part of partnerships towards shared goals and the transformative effect of the dialogue.

Unfortunately, an alarmed defensiveness arises from parts of the academy when Indigenous people express concern for environmental issues. Environmental humanities scholar Deborah Rose has analysed how scholars use knowledge policing strategies to marginalise or outlaw a class of positive statements in this respect.[88] Dualisms are used to create a double-bind position, based on two stereotypes: the Noble (Indigenous) Ecologist living in harmony with nature; and, the Dismal (Indigenous) Ecologist, who is pragmatic and ruthless, and only their limited toolkit constrained them from being just as destructive as the colonialists. Rose writes:

> Noble savage or dismal savage, it hardly seems to matter. Both images are dead ends. And yet, they are often wielded as weapons: if a settler-descended person says something positive about Indigenous people's ecological knowledge and/or ethics, one is accused of romanticism or primitivism; if one says something negative, one may be accused of racism. Indigenous people themselves are by no means exempt; they too are accused of romanticism or, alternatively, of cynicism. [89]

By casting Indigenous people who make positive environmental statements as primitives living in harmony with nature, the noble savage can be easily critiqued as false, and the noble dismal becomes the default position for Indigenous people, without addressing the dualisms that constructed the noble savage stereotype in the first place. This work makes it possible to constrain debates on environmental crises to the monologue of Western universals, rather than engaging with Indigenous people on their own terms.[90]

The first step to engendering change is to be able to acknowledge something is wrong, but the proponents of instrumental modernism are particularly ill-placed to respond to ecological devastation because this devastation challenges their hyper-separated beliefs. They have to deny these problems if they wish to continue their work.[91] But in the Murray-Darling Basin, the very connectedness of the problems offers the challenges required for mainstream water management to think its way out of the 'slow violence' of grinding ecological damage that creates 'broken' country.[92]

Scholars in the environmental humanities bring two conceptual tasks to this work: to resituate humans within their environments; and, to resituate non-humans or more-than-humans within cultural and ethical domains.[93] Hopefully, mainstream water management will eventually make and formalise these conceptual steps. Instrumental approaches to nature that already recognise the dependency of human lives on fresh water, fresh air, and so on, are not enough. We also need to engage with the experiences of rivers, plants, animals and other creatures as beings with cultural and ethical values. Otherwise, our connections are still impoverished, and we risk treating the interests and ethics of the more-than-human as sharply discontinuous from the human.[94] Indigenous knowledges are not interesting stories that illustrate another aspect of the river country, to be displayed alongside scientific or expert knowledges, but provide the tools to rethink our relationships with nature.

Hope and Farce

There are many ways to support Indigenous peoples' water issues in water reform. In this chapter, my intention has been to reveal how conceptual tools are used to constrain and shape water debates, and how greater insight into the culture of mainstream water management is a necessary precursor to facilitate the knowledge diversity needed to address the new water questions of over-allocated river systems.

What do you do when your country is dying? Do you ask for a slice of the water pie? Do you concede to grand narratives of singular historical time in which your culture and traditions must give way to modern Australia? Or do you insist that what you are losing is worth saving, explain how it is irreducible from your very understanding of water, and offer up these insights as ways forward for all. But even to say that your country is dying is to appear overly dramatic in the discourse of water managerialism. What else is happening when the soil is destroyed, water is poisoned, and species have become locally or forever extinct? Deborah Bird Rose writes about the obliteration of ecological violence:

> This violence produces vast expanses where life founders. It amplifies death not only by killing pieces of living systems, but by diminishing the capacity of living systems to repair themselves. What can a living system do if huge parts of it are exterminated? Where are the thresholds beyond which death takes over from life? Surely we exceed those thresholds violently and massively in the conjoined processes of conquest and development?[95]

Water variability – the droughts and deluges – is not an anomaly that requires regulation, but a complex thriving eco-system supporting relationships between people, species, places and other things over vast distances. In their identification of the diverse values connected by water, the traditional owners have the capacity to evocatively and powerfully build and deepen conversations that have long been constrained by dualisms. Consider the potential of engaging with what the elders from along the rivers have been saying. They are responding to the brutal destruction of their country on a scale and at a pace of loss that is hard to conceive. Of course, water is a resource for human consumption, but it is also so much more than that.

Acknowledgements

I would like to thank all the people who have collaborated with me in this research, particularly the traditional owners involved with MLDRIN when I did my doctoral scholarship with them, and my supervisory panel. I also thank Tim Neale, Eve Fesl and the anonymous reviewer for their assistance in preparing the paper for publication. All errors remain my own.

References

Arnold, A., 'Turning back the tide of history', *The Sunday Age*, 8 January 2006, p. 18.

Arthur, W. S., *The Murray–Darling Basin Regional and Basin Plans: Indigenous Water and Land Data*, Murray-Darling Basin Authority, 2010.

Atkinson, H., 'Yorta Yorta Co-operative Land Management Agreement: Impact on the Yorta Yorta Nation', *Indigenous Law Bulletin*, vol. 6, no. 5, 2004, pp. 23–5.

Baldwin, D., 'Are toxic algal blooms the new normal for Australia's major rivers?', *The Conversation*, 18 May 2016.

Braun, B., *The Intemperate Rainforest: Nature, Culture, and Power on Canada's West Coast*, University of Minnesota Press, Minneapolis, 2002.

Brennan, S., Davis, M., Edgeworth, B. & Terrill, L. (eds), *Native Title from Mabo to Akiba: a Vehicle for Change and Empowerment?*, Federation Press, Sydney, 2015.

Chong, J. & Ladson, A. R., 'Analysis and management of unseasonal flooding in the Barmah–Millewa Forest, Australia', *River Research and Applications*, vol. 19, no. 2, 2003, pp. 161–80.

Connell, D., 'The Chariot Wheels of the Commonwealth: The past present and future of inter-jurisdictional water management in the Murray-Darling Basin', *Australian National University*, 2005.

Connell, D., *Water Politics in the Murray-Darling Basin*, Federation Press, Sydney, 2007.

Connell, D., 'Catchment management across borders in the Murray–Darling Basin', *International Journal of River Basin Management*, vol. 11, no. 2, 2013, pp. 167–73.

Council of Australian Governments, 'Intergovernmental agreement on a National Water Initiative', *COAG*, 2004.

Cullen, P., 'Science and politics: speaking truth to power', paper presented to North American Benthological Society Annual Conference, Anchorage, 2006.

Escobar, A., 'Culture Sits in Places: reflections on globalism and subaltern strategies of localization', *Political Geography*, vol. 20, no. 2, 2001, pp. 139–74.

Gibbs, L. M., 'Valuing water: variability and the Lake Eyre Basin, central Australia', *Australian Geographer*, vol. 37, no. 1, 2006, pp. 73–85.

Godden, L. & Gunther, M., 'Realising capacity: Indigenous involvement in water law and policy reform in south-eastern Australia', *Journal of Water Law*, vol. 20, pp. 243–53, 2012.

Grafton, R. Q. & Connell, D., *Basin Futures: Water Reform in the Murray-Darling Basin*, ANU EPress, 2011.

Hall, K., Baldwin, D. S., Rees, G. & Richardson, A., 'Distribution of inland wetlands with sulfidic sediments in the Murray–Darling Basin, Australia', *Science of the Total Environment*, vol. 370, no. 1, 2006, pp. 235–44.

Hurley, PJ, *From Kosciusko to the Sea: A Journey Along the River Murray*, Dymock's Book Arcade, Sydney, 1946.

Ingold, T., *The Perception of the Environment: essays on livelihood, dwelling and skill*, Routledge, New York, 2000.

Jackson, S. & Langton, M., 'Trends in the recognition of indigenous water needs in Australian water reform: limitations of "cultural" entitlements in achieving water equity', *Journal of Water Law*, vol. 22, no. 2/3, 2012, pp. 109–23

Jones, G., Hillman, T. J., Kingsford, R., McMahon, T., Walker, K., Arthington,

A., Whittington, J. & Cartwright, S., 'Independent report of the expert reference panel on environmental flows and water quality requirements for the River Murray System', *Report to the Murray–Darling Basin Ministerial Council*, Cooperative Research Centre for Freshwater Ecology, 2002.

Kalland, A., 'Anthropology and the concept of "sustainability": Some reflections', in A. Roepstorff, N. Bubandt & K. Kull (eds), *Imagining Nature*, Aarhus University Press, Aarhus, 2003.

Kingsford, R. T., 'Will the Murray-Darling plan do enough for the environment? The truth is, we don't know,' *The Conversation*, 28 November 2011 <https://theconversation.com/will-the-murray-darling-plan-do-enough-for-the-environment-the-truth-is-we-dont-know-4485>.

Kinnane, S., 'Recurring visions of Australindia', in A. Gaynor, M. Trinca & A. Haebich (eds), *Country: Visions of Land and People in Western Australia*, Western Australian Museum, Perth, 2002, pp. 21–31.

Latour, B., *We Have Never Been Modern*, Harvard University Press, Cambridge, 1993.

Lintermans, M., *Fishes of the Murray-Darling Basin: an Introductory Guide*, Murray-Darling Commission, Canberra, ACT, 2007.

Lohmann, L., *Green Orientalism*, The Corner House, Dorset, 1993.

Matthews, F., *The Ecological Self*, Routledge, New York, 2006.

MDBMC, *The Living Murray*, Murray-Darling Basin Ministerial Council, Canberra, 2002.

Merlan, F., 'Explorations Towards Intercultural Accounts of Socio-Cultural Reproduction and Change', *Oceania*, vol. 75, no. 3, 2005, pp. 167–82.

Mitchell, T., 'The stage of modernity', in T. Mitchell (ed.), *Questions of modernity*, University of Minnesota Press, 2000, pp. 1–34.

Mitchell, T., *Rule of experts : Egypt, techno-politics, modernity*, University of California Press, Berkeley, 2002.

MLDRIN (Murray Lower Darling Rivers Indigenous Nations), Echuca Declaration, 14 November 2007, Echuca.

Muir, C., 'Broken: Living Lexicon for the Environmental Humanities', *Environmental Humanities*, vol. 5, 2014, pp. 287–90.

Nixon, R., *Slow Violence and the Environmentalism of the Poor*, Harvard University Press, Cambridge, 2011.

Otto, T. & Pedersen, P., 'Disentangling traditions: Culture, agency and power', in T. Otto & P. Pedersen (eds), *Tradition and Agency: Tracing Cultural Continuity and Invention*, Aarhus University Press, Aarhus, 2005, pp. 11–49.

Plumwood, V., *Feminism and the Mastery of Nature*, Routledge, New York, 2002.

Plumwood, V., 'Decolonising relationships with nature', *PAN: Philosophy Activism Nature*, no. 2, 2002.

Robin, L., *How a Continent Created a Nation*, UNSW Press, Sydney, 2007.

Robin, L., 'Resilience in the Anthropocene: a biography', in J. Frawley & I McCalman (eds), *Rethinking Invasion Ecologies from the Environmental Humanities*, Routledge, Abingdon, 2014, pp. 45–63.

Rose, D. B., *Nourishing Terrains: Australian Aboriginal Views of Landscape and Wilderness*, Australian Heritage Commission, Canberra, 1996.

Rose, D. B., 'The Rain Keeps Falling', *Cultural Studies Review*, vol. 11, no. 1, 2005, pp. 122–7.

Rose, D. B, 'Decolonising the Discourse of Environmental Knowledge in Settler Societies', in T. Neale, C. McKinnon & E. Vincent (eds), *History, Power, Text: Cultural Studies and Indigenous Studies*, UTS ePress, Sydney, NSW, 2014.

Rose, D. B., van Dooren, T., Chrulew, M., Cooke, S., Kearnes, M. & O'Gorman, E., 'Thinking through the environment, unsettling the humanities', *Environmental Humanities*, vol. 1, 2012, pp. 1–5.

Sahlins, M., 'What is anthropological enlightenment? Some lessons of the twentieth century', *Annual Review of Anthropology*, vol. 28, no. 1, 1999, pp. 1–23.

Scott, J. C., *Seeing Like a State: How Certain Schemes to Improve the Human Condition Have Failed*, Yale University Press, New Haven, 1998.

Sillitoe, P., 'Local science vs. global science: An overview', in P. Sillitoe (ed.), *Local Science vs. Global Science: Approaches to Indigenous Knowledge in International Development*, Berghan Books, New York, 2007, pp. 1–22.

Smith, B. R., '"Indigenous" and "scientific" knowledge in Central Cape York Peninsula', in P. Sillitoe (ed.), *Local Science vs. Global Science: Approaches to Indigenous Knowledge in International Development*, Berghahn Books, New York, pp. 75–90.

Smith, D. I., *Water in Australia: Resources and Management*, Oxford University Press, Melbourne, 1998.

Taylor, J. & Biddle, N. G., 'Indigenous people in the Murray-Darling Basin: a statistical profile', CAEPR Discussion Paper 264, 2004.

Tran, T., 'Water is country, country is culture: the translation of Indigenous relationships to water into law', PhD Thesis, University of Dundee, 2013.

Tsing, A. L., *Friction: an Ethnography of Global Connection*, Princeton University Press, Princeton, 2005.

Tully, J., *Strange Multiplicity: Constitutionalism in an Age of Diversity*, Cambridge University Press, 1995.

Vance, T. R., Roberts, J. L., Plummer, C. T., Kiem, A. S. & van Ommen, T. D., 'Interdecadal Pacific variability and eastern Australian mega-droughts over the last millennium', *Geophysical Research Letters*, 42, 2015, pp. 129–37.

Ward, N., 'Good methodology travels: Australian case study', *Living Proof: The Essential Data-collection Guide for Indigenous Use-and-occupancy Map Surveys, Ecotrust Canada and Union of British Columbia Indian Chiefs, Vancouver, 2009, pp. 339-64.

Webb, S., 'Intensification, population and social change in southeastern Australia: the skeletal evidence', *Aboriginal History*, 1984 pp. 154–72.

Weir, J. K., *Murray River Country: an Ecological Dialogue with Traditional Owners*, Aboriginal Studies Press, Canberra, 2009.

Weir, J. K., 'How to keep the river flowing', in S. Pincock (ed.), *Best Australian Science Writing*, NewSouth, Sydney, 2011.

Weir, J. K., Crew, D. & Crew, J., 'Wetland forest culture: Indigenous activity for management change in the Southern Riverina, New South Wales', *Australasian Journal of Environmental Management*, vol. 20, no. 3, 2013, pp. 193–207.

Weir, J. K. & Ross, S., 'Beyond Native Title: the Murray Lower Darling Rivers Indigenous nations', in B. R. Smith & F. Morphy (eds), *The Social Effects of Native Title*, ANU EPress, Canberra, 2007, pp. 185–202.

Weir, J. K., Ross, S. L., Crew, D. R. J. & Crew, J. L., *Cultural Water and the Edward/Kolety and Wakool River System*, research report, AIATSIS Centre for Land and Water Research, Australian Institute of Aboriginal and Torres Strait Islander Studies, Canberra, 2013.

Zwarteveen, M., 'A masculine water world: the politics of gender and identity in irrigation expert thinking', in R. Boelens, D. Getches & A. Guevara (eds), *Out of the Mainstream: Water Rights, Politics and Identity*, Earthscan, London, 2010, pp. 75-98.

Notes

1   M. Zwarteveen, 'A masculine water world: the politics of gender and identity in irrigation expert thinking', in R. Boelens, D. Getches & A. Guevara (eds), *Out of the Mainstream: Water Rights, Politics and Identity*, Earthscan, London, 2010, pp. 75–98.

2   R. Q. Grafton & D. Connell, *Basin Futures: Water Reform in the Murray-Darling Basin*, ANU EPress, 2011.

3   J. W. Weir, *Murray River Country: an Ecological Dialogue with Traditional Owners*, Aboriginal Studies Press, Canberra, 2009; J. W. Weir & S. Ross, 'Beyond Native Title: the Murray Lower Darling Rivers Indigenous nations', in B. R. Smith & F. Morphy (eds), *The Social Effects of Native Title*, ANU EPress, Canberra, 2007, pp. 185–202.

4   MLDRIN is much larger today, see: <www.mldrin.org.au>.

5   This paper focuses on the early days of the concept of cultural flows,

and unfortunately it is beyond the scope to engage with the subsequent iterations of cultural flows and the research that has accompanied this.

6 B. Latour, *We Have Never Been Modern*, Harvard University Press, Cambridge, 1993; F. Matthews, *The Ecological Self*, Routledge, 2006; T. Mitchell, *Rule of Experts: Egypt, Techno-politics, Modernity*, University of California Press, Berkeley, 2002; V. Plumwood, *Feminism and the Mastery of Nature*, Routledge, 2002; D. B. Rose, T. van Dooren, M. Chrulew, S. Cooke, M. Kearnes & E. O'Gorman, 'Thinking through the environment, unsettling the humanities', *Environmental Humanities*, vol. 1, 2012, pp. 1–5.

7 D. Connell, *Water Politics in the Murray-Darling Basin*, Federation Press, Sydney, 2007, p. 95.

8 D. Baldwin, 'Are toxic algal blooms the new normal for Australia's major rivers?', *The Conversation*, 18 May 2016.

9 M. Lintermans, *Fishes of the Murray-Darling Basin: an Introductory Guide*, Murray-Darling Commission, Canberra, 2007.

10 D. Connell, 'Catchment management across borders in the Murray–Darling Basin', *International Journal of River Basin Management*, vol. 11, no. 2, 2013, pp. 167–73.

11 R. T. Kingsford, 'Will the Murray-Darling plan do enough for the environment? The truth is, we don't know', 2011 <https://theconversation.com/will-the-murray-darling-plan-do-enough-for-the-environment-the-truth-is-we-dont-know-4485>.

12 S. Webb, 'Intensification, population and social change in southeastern Australia: the skeletal evidence', *Aboriginal History*, 1984, pp. 154–72.

13 W. S. Arthur, *The Murray–Darling Basin Regional and Basin Plans: Indigenous Water and Land Data*, Murray-Darling Basin Authority, 2010; J. Taylor & N. G. Biddle, 'Indigenous people in the Murray-Darling Basin: a statistical profile', CAEPR Discussion Paper 264, 2004.

14 S. Brennan, M. Davis, B. Edgeworth, & L. Terrill (eds), *Native Title from Mabo to Akiba: a Vehicle for Change and Empowerment?*, Federation Press, Sydney, 2015.

15 Interview with author, 21 July 2004.

16 Interview with author, 7 August 2004.

17 See also M. Morgan in this volume.

18 Interview with author, 1 July 2004.

19 B. R. Smith, '"Indigenous" and "scientific" knowledge in Central Cape York peninsula', in P. Sillitoe (ed), *Local Science vs. Global Science: Approaches to Indigenous Knowledge in International Development*, Berghahn Books, New York, 2007, pp. 75–90; F. Merlan, 'Explorations Towards Intercultural Accounts of Socio-Cultural Reproduction and Change', *Oceania*, vol. 75,

no. 3, 2005, pp. 167–82.

20   L. Robin 'Resilience in the Anthropocene: a biography', in J. Frawley &
     I. McCalman (eds), *Rethinking Invasion Ecologies from the Environmental
     Humanities*, Routledge, Abingdon, 2014, pp. 45–63.

21   Interview with author, 7 August 2004.

22   Interview with author, 25 June 2004.

23   Plumwood, *Feminism and the Mastery of Nature*.

24   Matthews, *The Ecological Self*, pp. 17, 31.

25   Latour, *We Have Never Been Modern*, pp. 32, 39.

26   Plumwood, *Feminism and the Mastery of Nature*; V. Plumwood, 'Decolonising
     relationships with nature', *PAN: Philosophy Activism Nature*, no. 2, 2002, p. 11.

27   Mitchell, *Rule of Experts*.

28   For example, see: B. Braun, *The Intemperate Rainforest: Nature, Culture, and
     Power on Canada's West Coast*, University of Minnesota Press, Minneapolis,
     2002; L. M. Gibbs, 'Valuing Water: variability and the Lake Eyre Basin,
     Central Australia', *Australian Geographer*, vol. 37, no. 1, 2006, pp. 73–85;

29   J. C. Scott, *Seeing Like a State: How Certain Schemes to Improve the Human
     Condition Have Failed*, Yale University Press, New Haven, 1998.

30   P. J. Hurley, *From Kosciusko to the Sea: A Journey Along the River Murray*,
     Dymock's Book Arcade Ltd, Sydney, 1946, p. 47.

31   Tsing, *Friction*, p. 9.

32   A. Arnold, 'Turning back the tide of history', *The Sunday Age*, 8 January
     2006, p. 18; H. Atkinson, 'Yorta Yorta Co-operative Land Management
     Agreement: Impact on the Yorta Yorta Nation', *Indigenous Law Bulletin*,
     vol. 6, no. 5, 2004, pp. 23–5; Weir, *Murray River Country*, 74–5.

33   T. Otto & P. Pedersen, 'Disentangling traditions: Culture, agency and
     power', in T. Otto & P. Pedersen (eds), *Tradition and Agency: Tracing Cultural
     Continuity and Invention*, Aarhus University Press, Aarhus, 2005, pp. 11–49.

34   M. Sahlins, 'What is anthropological enlightenment? Some lessons of the
     twentieth century', *Annual Review of Anthropology*, vol. 28, no. 1, 1999,
     pp. 1–23.

35   *Yorta Yorta Aboriginal Community v the State of Victoria and Ors* (1998
     unreported), para 19; this phrase was used repeatedly in the determination,
     see paras 3, 126, 129.

36   Latour, *We Have Never Been Modern*; Plumwood, *Feminism and the Mastery
     of Nature*.

37   Plumwood, *Feminism and the Mastery of Nature*.

38   ibid., p. 15.

39   Latour, *We Have Never Been Modern*; Smith, *Local science vs. Global Science*;
     P. Sillitoe, 'Local science vs. global science: An overview', in P. Sillitoe

(ed.), *Local Science vs. Global Science: Approaches to Indigenous Knowledge in International Development*, Berghan Books, New York, 2007, pp. 1–22.

40 T. Mitchell, 'The stage of modernity', in T. Mitchell (ed), *Questions of Modernity*, University of Minnesota Press, Minnesota, 2000, pp. 8–9.

41 J. Tully, *Strange Multiplicity: Constitutionalism in an Age of Diversity*, Cambridge University Press, 1995.

42 Mitchell, *Questions of Modernity*, p. 19.

43 A. Escobar, 'Culture Sits in Places: reflections on globalism and subaltern strategies of localization', *Political Geography*, vol. 20, no. 2, 2001, pp. 139–74.

44 A. L. Tsing, *Friction: An Ethnography of Global Connection*, Princeton University Press, Princeton, 2005.

45 Taken from the title of Mitchell, *Rule of Experts*; Gibbs, *Australian Geographer*.

46 Tully, *Strange Multiplicity*, pp. 56–8.

47 I. Ang, 'Navigating Complexity: from cultural critique to cultural intelligence', *Continuum*, 25, pp. 779–94.

48 See, for example: J. K. Weir, D. Crew & J. Crew, 'Wetland forest culture: Indigenous activity for management change in the Southern Riverina, New South Wales', *Australasian Journal of Environmental Management*, vol. 20, no. 3, 2013, pp. 193–207.

49 MDBMC, *The Living Murray*, MDBMC, Canberra, 2002, p. 47.

50 MDBMC, 'Murray-Darling Basin Ministerial Council Communiqué', 14 November 2003.

51 The icon sites are the Barmah-Millewa forest; Gunbower and Koondrook-Perricoota forests; Hattah Lakes; Chowilla Floodplain (including Lindsay-Wallpolla); the Murray Mouth, Coorong and Lower Lakes; and the River Murray channel.

52 Grafton & Connell, *Basin Futures*.

53 G. Jones, T. J. Hillman, R. Kingsford, T. McMahon, K. Walker, A. Arthington, J. Whittington & S. Cartwright, 'Independent report of the expert reference panel on environmental flows and water quality requirements for the River Murray System', *Report to the Murray–Darling Basin Ministerial Council*, Cooperative Research Centre for Freshwater Ecology, 2002.

54 The MLDRIN report and responses are contained within: Farley Consulting Group, *Indigenous Response to The Living Murray Initiative*, Murray Darling Basin Commission, Canberra, 2003.

55 D. Connell, 'The Chariot Wheels of the Commonwealth: The past present and future of inter-jurisdictional water management in the Murray-Darling Basin', *Australian National University*, 2005, pp. 206, 285.

56 N. Ward, 'Good methodology travels: Australian case study', in T. N. Tobias

Living Proof: The Essential Data-collection Guide for Indigenous Use-and-occupancy Map Surveys, Ecotrust Canada and Union of British Columbia Indian Chiefs, Vancouver, 2009, pp. 339–64.

57   Monica Morgan, personal communication, June 2016.

58   Wagga Wagga, MLDRIN joint-meeting with Murray-Darling Basin Commission's Community Advisory Council, 13 July 2005, cited in Weir, *Murray River Country*, p. 121.

59   ibid., p. 120

60   ibid.

61   The National Cultural Flows Research Project at <www.culturalflows.com.au>.

62   For example, Weir, J.K., Ross, S. L., Crew, D. R. J. and Crew, J. L., *Cultural Water and the Edward/Kolety and Wakool River System*, research report, AIATSIS Centre for Land and Water Research, Australian Institute of Aboriginal and Torres Strait Islander Studies, Canberra, 2013.

63   MLDRIN (Murray Lower Darling Rivers Indigenous Nations) 2007, Echuca Declaration, 14 November, Echuca.

64   Vance, T. R., Roberts, J. L., Plummer, C. T., Kiem, A. S. & van Ommen, T. D., 'Interdecadal Pacific variability and eastern Australian mega-droughts over the last millennium', *Geophysical Research Letters*, 42, 2015, 129–37.

65   Godden, L. & Gunther, M., 'Realising capacity: Indigenous involvement in water law and policy reform in south-eastern Australia', *Journal of Water Law*, vol. 20, 2012, pp. 243–53.

66   Jackson, S. & Langton, M., 'Trends in the recognition of indigenous water needs in Australian water reform: limitations of "cultural" entitlements in achieving water equity', *Journal of Water Law*, vol. 22, no. 2/3, 2012, pp. 109–23, 116.

67   ibid., p. 110.

68   ibid., p. 116.

69   ibid., pp. 116–7.

70   Council of Australian Governments 2004, 'Intergovernmental agreement on a National Water Initiative'.

71   Jackson and Langton, Journal of Water Law, p. 117.

72   Government of South Australia, 'Millennium Drought', Department of Environment, Water and Natural Resources, viewed 1 July 2016 http://www.environment.sa.gov.au/managing-natural-resources/river-murray/about-the-river/millennium-drought.

73   T. Vance et al., *Geophysical Research Letters*.

74   Interview with author, 25 June 2004.

75   Braun, *The Intemperate Rainforest*, pp. 71, 83, 86.

76 ibid., pp. 92–3.

77 L. Lohmann, *Green Orientialism*, The Corner House, Dorset, 1993.

78 A. Kalland, 'Anthropology and the concept of "sustainability": Some reflections', in A. Roepstorff, N. Bubandt & K. Kull (eds), *Imagining Nature*, Aarhus University Press, Aarhus, 2003, p. 170.

79 Weir et al., *Australasian Journal of Environmental Management*.

80 NSW Legislative Council, *Inquiry into Public Land Management*, General Purpose Standing Committee No. 5, 1 & 2 August 2012, Deniliquin, Australia; see further Weir et al., *Australasian Journal of Environmental Management*.

81 Weir et al., *Australasian Journal of Environmental Management*.

82 The National Parks Association of NSW, Friends of the Earth, The Wilderness Society, the Victorian National Parks Association, the Australian Conservation Foundation, Environment Victoria, and the Nature Conservation Council of NSW.

83 Steven Ross, personal communication, October 2007.

84 T. Tran, 'Water is country, country is culture: the translation of Indigenous relationships to water into law', PhD Thesis, University of Dundee, 2013.

85 Steven Ross, personal communication, September 2007.

86 L. Robin, *How a Continent Created a Nation*, UNSW Press, Sydney, 2007, p. 9.

87 P. Cullen, 'Science and politics: speaking truth to power', paper presented to North American Benthological Society Annual Conference, Anchorage, 2006.

88 D. B. Rose, 'Decolonising the Discourse of Environmental Knowledge in Settler Societies', in T. Neale, C. McKinnon & E. Vincent (eds), *History, Power, Text: Cultural Studies and Indigenous Studies*, UTS ePress, Sydney, NSW, 2014, p. 208.

89 ibid.

90 ibid., p. 209.

91 Latour, *We Have Never Been Modern*.

92 Muir, *Environmental Humanities*; Plumwood, *Australian Humanities Review*; R. Nixon, *Slow Violence and the Environmentalism of the Poor*, Harvard University Press, Cambridge, 2011.

93 Plumwood, unpublished, cited in Rose et al. *Environmental Humanities*.

94 Plumwood, *PAN*, pp. 3–4.

95 D. B. Rose, 'The Rain Keeps Falling', *Cultural Studies Review*, vol. 11, no. 1, 2005, p. 125.

6

ABORIGINAL PEOPLE AND WILDERNESS: DAVE LINDNER, INTERIORITY AND THE SELF-WILLED LAND

Robert Levitus

Introduction: The Debate over Aboriginal People and Wilderness

The word 'wilderness' has accumulated a range of literal and metaphorical meanings.[1] It is not a term of art in the environmental sciences and so does not have any agreed technical meaning for ecologists. In defining the word where it is intended to refer to a kind of environmental zone, dictionaries commonly use the terms 'wild', 'uncultivated' and 'uninhabited', sometimes adding an absence of roads and towns. More useful in that it reduces these various descriptors to a single criterion is 'a large tract of land that has not been significantly affected by human activities'.[2]

This concept of wilderness, though widely accepted, has been criticised from many directions.[3] One prominent issue in the debate over its use to describe the uncultivated environments of Australia has been whether it allows for the presence and environmental agency of Aboriginal people. Significantly, the early English form 'wildēornes' meant 'land inhabited only by wild animals', and was derived from the words for 'wild deer'.[4] The dictionary conception of wilderness thus reveals its historical origins in northern European agricultural societies in which human residence, sociality and production were concentrated in towns, villages and fields. The remaining landscape was not lived in, but travelled through or visited as a source of game, herbs, medicines and perhaps supernatural power.

The later application of such a concept in European settler societies, and then on a global scale, encountered the anomaly of peoples that persisted with shifting or nomadic lifeways, for whom such remaining landscape was conceived as the centre of their worlds, rather than as periphery or residuum.[5] While colonial attitudes, and subsequently the policies of national governments and international conservation organisations, often demanded the removal and resettlement of such peoples,[6] recent attempts to preserve the wilderness concept for its special conservation value have had to try to accommodate this anomaly.

In the revised categories of protected areas adopted by the International Union for the Conservation of Nature (IUCN) in 2008, 'wilderness area' is given a separate sub-category 1b, and defined as 'usually large unmodified or slightly modified areas, retaining their natural character and influence, without permanent or significant human habitation, which are protected and managed so as to preserve their natural condition'.[7] In setting out the primary objective for management of such areas, the IUCN further defines them as 'natural areas that are undisturbed by significant human activity, free of modern infrastructure and where natural forces and processes predominate'.[8] But then included among the IUCN's other management objectives is provision 'to enable indigenous communities to maintain their traditional wilderness-based lifestyle and customs, living at low density and using the available resources in ways compatible with the conservation objectives'.[9] The indigenous anomaly is thus accommodated by conceiving of traditional adaptation as a mode of living that treads lightly upon the earth. The priority of wilderness preservation is thereby able to make allowance for indigenous peoples.

In Australia, campaigning experience from the 1970s to the 1990s, especially around major issues of mining in the Kakadu area of the Northern Territory and broad questions of land use on Cape York Peninsula, forged difficult but successful tactical alliances between Aboriginal and conservationist groups.[10] However, on the conservationist side, these moves toward concord evoked differences between those who, like the IUCN later on, hoped that Aboriginal land-use aspirations would be environmentally sustainable, and those who feared they would not.[11] In 1998, the Australian Heritage Commission (AHC) convened a meeting between government agencies, Aboriginal representatives and environmental NGOs which produced the Malimup Communique.[12] What the AHC described as the underlying commitment of this document illustrates this conservationist anxiety about Aboriginal land use:

Indigenous use of [areas reserved as] 'wilderness' should be undertaken in ways that ensure that all natural and cultural values are protected in the long term. The protection of 'wilderness' values requires that, where possible, technology used should be low impact to minimise detrimental effects. The effects of the use of 'wilderness' by rightful indigenous communities should be monitored by all stakeholders.[13]

Keith Muir, Director of the Colong Foundation for Wilderness, worried that even this was going too far.[14] Hunting with firearms, use of four-wheel-drive vehicles and erection of permanent accommodation signalled the distance between what he called the 'two wilderness dreamings': the ancient and spiritually meaningful indigenous wilderness that now allowed for such things, and the purist non-indigenous wilderness:

> Where the last remnants of the natural world are safe from the spoiling forces of modern technology…Motor vehicles form a barrier between wilderness and the human soul. You must 'walk the land' to fully relate and belong to the land. Surely the most sacred, most biodiverse places should be visited on their own terms?[15]

He urged Indigenous leaders to allow 'a place for wilderness in the Indigenous landscape',[16] free of roads and permanent settlements.

It was clear, however, that Aboriginal criticism took issue not only with conservationists' reservations about possible land uses, but also, more fundamentally, with the presumption implicit in their attachment to the concept of wilderness. The Ecopolitics Association of Australia held sixteen conferences between 1986 and 2005.[17] In 1995 it handed over organisation of the ninth con-ference to the Northern Land Council in Darwin for the purpose of addressing 'the fundamental question of post-colonialism – who controls indigenous lands and under what conditions'[18] with respect to the Australian conservation estate. That conference resolved:

> Noting the changes which have occurred in statements from some conservation agencies, that Ecopolitics IX reiterates the unacceptability of the term 'wilderness' and related concepts such as wild resources, food, etc. as it is popularised. The term has the connotations of *terra nullius* theory and as such all concerned people and organisa-tions should look for alternative terminology which does not exclude indigenous history and meaning.[19]

This challenge to the conservationists' preferred order of things was set out at length by Marcia Langton.[20] Langton's attack was directed in the first instance at those environmentalists who had, in her view, enshrined in the public imaginary a fanciful conception of wilderness as a zone of pure nature untouched by humanity, the preservation of which demands the exclusion of all human activity. This, she argued, is a new dimension of *terra nullius*, the doctrine under which Australia was colonised by Europeans and which denied that Aboriginal peoples had any pre-existing and legally recognisable relationships to land. The white imagining of parts of Australia as wilderness was only possible once its original inhabitants had been destroyed or pushed aside. The notion is therefore 'fundamentally colonialist', 'a mystification of genocide'.[21]

In the years since this issue emerged, the Australian Conservation Foundation has shifted policy to accord with that argument.

> Knowing that language is an important tool that can empower or oppress, the ACF has communications protocols that dictate, for example, that when describing landscapes that have been occupied by indigenous people, 'the word "wilderness" should not be used as it incorrectly denotes a place that is uncultivated and uninhabited and reinforces the fallacy of *Terra nullius*'.[22]

The Australian Wildlife Conservancy, Bush Heritage Australia and the National Parks Association of NSW use such expressions as 'land for conservation',[23] 'ecologically important land'[24] and 'core natural places'[25] on their respective websites, without necessarily eschewing 'wilderness'. However, two organisations that defend the continued use of the term, as their names insist, are The Wilderness Society (TWS) and the Colong Foundation for Wilderness.

On its website and in other publications,[26] TWS addresses the claimed exclusive connotations by taking an explicitly inclusive position, listing 'indigenous conservation'[27] as one of the four pillars on which its work to protect and restore wilderness is based. The explanatory paragraph under that heading fulsomely acknowledges Australian Indigenous land and sea rights and the past and present record of Indigenous environmental management, and supports sustainable usage of homelands. The Society's efforts to engage with Aboriginal concerns extended to the publication of an article by Langton in its news magazine in which she summarised her arguments denying the existence of wilderness in Australia and condemning the continued declaration of national parks as a further stage of colonial conquest.[28]

The Colong Foundation published a Wilderness Resurgence Statement in 2004, locating wilderness at the wild end of a spectrum of possible land uses, and asserting its intrinsic value and right to exist. But while the statement viewed the existence of wilderness as a tribute to the long history of Aboriginal custodianship, it gave a particular characterisation of that traditional Aboriginal impact. Aboriginal people, it said, 'may have influenced these areas, but did so without destroying their ecological integrity':[29]

Compared to the wholesale destruction and fragmentation of native vegetation in the last 215 years (under European 'management') – traditional Aboriginal land practices have only 'slightly modified' (in reference to

IUCN definition of wilderness) such areas. It is thus appropriate to refer to large, natural areas of the bush in Australia as 'wilderness'.[30]

In conceiving of the Aboriginal influence upon natural areas as comparatively minimal and not sufficiently altering as to corrupt their wilderness status, the Foundation implicitly regards Europeans and traditional Aboriginal people as change-agents of different degree, but not of different kind. In this passage, wilderness is seen as a thing apart from humans, who exert varying, but always external, impacts upon it. In similar vein, and despite its more open and embracing attitude to Aboriginal traditional attachment, TWS says that the 'crucial issue in the identification of wilderness is not whether an area has been modified by humans, but the extent and nature of the modification'.[31]

The vantage point that locates Aboriginal people as external to wilderness is necessarily also open, in principle, to the view that their impact upon it is negative. This position can also be found in the Colong Foundation's literature, where writers such as Muir and Colley have argued that traditional Aboriginal burning severely damaged the Australian environment by causing erosion and nutrient depletion of soils.[32] Such negative evaluations further reveal the necessary baseline of wilderness management for this school of conservationist thought: 'to create conditions in which natural forces and processes can operate to the maximum extent and visitors can enjoy these conditions without damaging them'.[33] Logically then, human usage must be vetted for its impact upon pre-human nature. This view of wilderness preservation implicitly puts nature before humans, in both senses of the word 'before'.

Langton will have none of this. For her, in the 1996 paper cited earlier, Aboriginal action made Australian nature into what it was at the time of colonisation, having 'shaped even the reproductive mechanisms of forests'.[34] The fashioning work of Aboriginal people turned all those parts of the continent that they occupied into cultural landscapes. She has reiterated her position, most recently, in the 2012 Boyer Lectures:

> These vast areas owned by Aboriginal people are the repository of Australia's megadiversity of fauna, flora and ecosystems because of the ancient Aboriginal system of management, and because, Aboriginal people fought to protect their territories from white incursion. They are not wilderness areas. They are Aboriginal homelands, shaped over millennia by Aboriginal people.[35]

My account of this issue to this point is not intended to be historically complete, neither is it to assess the current balance of contending positions. Indeed, for many on both sides, the issue is no longer of much interest, despite such occasional flare-ups as the *Wild Rivers Act* issue in Cape York.[36] What I have tried to do instead in this section is record the principal positions that have been adopted in a way that points out their assumptions about the nature of nature in Australia and the past relationship of Aboriginal people to it. It is worth noting further, however, that not only do contending views still exist, but also that debate about wilderness internationally is less accommodating to indigenous claims. As Dowie noted in 2009, Australia is the only country that had come close to accepting the idea of transferring management powers over high-conservation-value areas to indigenous custodians.[37]

Aboriginal People in Wilderness: Dave Lindner and the Management of Kakadu National Park

In this section I introduce the views of a practical conservationist who has never been a member of any organisation, but who has worked on the wetlands of the South Alligator River in Kakadu National Park in the Northern Territory since 1972, and lived near or next to them since 1979, shortly after they were included in the newly declared first stage of Kakadu. I have known Dave Lindner since 1981 when I arrived in Kakadu to begin social history research. I have recorded his ideas and observations since then, and in recent years have had access to his private archive of notebooks and other resources.

Lindner is broadly knowledgeable of natural history and has been a close and consistent observer of the Kakadu environment. He is also a dedicated hunter with a deep knowledge of firearms. For decades, firstly as an employee of a local Aboriginal association and then on his own account, he has maintained a fresh meat supply to the Aboriginal camps of the Park. He has had a series of local Aboriginal wives, but no interest in learning anything of their language or formal culture. He has an uncompromising dedication to a vision of Kakadu as a publicly accessible and properly conserved Park, and has been an unrelenting critic of national park management.

Lindner unreservedly regards the environment in which he has worked as a wilderness, one which was heavily populated by Aboriginal people until the mid-nineteenth century. His interpretations of environmental issues in Kakadu are based on his understandings of how Aboriginal people lived in that environment, and they inform a particular view of the pre-European relationship between Aboriginal people and wilderness. I discuss here how Lindner's understanding of the prehistoric Aboriginal presence has affected his interpretation of four areas of environmental management in Kakadu. These four discussions reproduce both the style and content, in places verbatim, of his explanations to me.

Figure 6.1: Dave Lindner, 6 November 2009. Photo by Robert Levitus.

Living Areas and Landscape Repair

Like wetlands and flood plains across a large portion of the Top End of the Northern Territory, especially between Darwin and Gunbalanya, the South Alligator River plains were seriously impacted by a drastic overpopulation of water buffalo in the 1960s and 1970s. Through most of the 1970s, Lindner was the senior Northern Territory conservation officer in the Alligator Rivers region and across the buffalo country generally.[38] From the beginning of 1972, he led the effort to reduce buffalo populations across all of the impacted Top End rivers, but especially the South Alligator. Lindner himself shot thousands of animals. The mandatory program later funded under the Brucellosis and Tuberculosis Eradication Campaign finally achieved complete, though not permanent, removal of feral buffalo from Kakadu.

Lindner's commitment extended to understanding the mechanisms by which buffalo had impacted the wetlands and beginning the work of landscape repair. Based on his experience of other Northern Territory wetlands, his own ground observations and changes observable on the decadal sequence of aerial photographs, he developed a holistic interpretation of the buffalo impact that amounted to systemic degrading of the entire hydrology of the wetlands, the net long-term effect of which was to reduce a complex of saline, semi-saline and freshwater zones into a uniform saltwater flood plain.

The principal process of wetland degradation set in train by the buffalo was the destruction of natural levees followed by dry-season penetration of saltwater from the tidal sections of the river upstream into what had been naturally semi-saline or freshwater domains. The inflowing tidal waters carried muds that silted upstream billabongs and freshwater swamps. Some swamp beds were raised to the level of the surrounding flood plain so they drained more completely in the dry season; some billabongs were made shallower or disappeared altogether.

Trees of various kinds – *Cathormion, Barringtonia, Pandanus,* paperbark – that fringed billabongs or grew on the flood plains, were killed by saltwater or by the buffalo themselves. The lush grasses remembered by the pre-war buffalo shooter Tom Cole,[39] on which his horses had grazed, had been eaten out by buffalo, and replaced by sedges. *Hymenachne,* an aquatic grass which develops into thick floating mats that affect wetland hydrology by channelling the wet season outflow, and *Phragmites,* a segmented reed that was used traditionally to make goose spears, had almost disappeared from the South Alligator. The *Eleocharis* rush, which geese eat and use to make nests, had also been eaten out.

As buffalo numbers reduced, Lindner turned his efforts to landscape restoration. But now the extent and rapidity of the buffalo impact created a problem of interpreting on the ground what the pre-buffalo South Alligator landscape might have looked like. At this point, evidence of traditional Aboriginal occupation and usage, available from archaeological deposits, the diary of the explorer Ludwig Leichhardt, and the memories of senior Aboriginal people, provided guidance. These sources showed that the processes set in train by buffalo destroyed a very rich wetland environment that had traditionally supported large numbers of people.

The camping areas around the South Alligator wetlands had been almost completely abandoned long before the major buffalo impact occurred, as people succumbed to epidemic disease and the remnants adopted new modes of life and residential options. The places and their surrounds had themselves changed. The extensive occupation sites were heavily impacted by buffalo. Groves of trees that people had camped under near the flood plain edge had often disappeared, so Lindner found that people returning to these places after years away found them very different in appearance.

But the signs of previous occupation were still abundant. Where there were large scatters of stone artefacts indicating Aboriginal camping locations, people who were old enough and who had passed through or lived in that country remembered those places as having been adjacent to freshwater swamps with their abundance of foods. Restoration work could thus be guided directly by surviving Aboriginal memories of what places used to look like before the explosion of buffalo numbers, and by inference from the archaeology. The presence of old cooking hearths and an enormous number of axes and worked stones at the edge of the plain indicated that the adjacent area had been a freshwater swamp.

Lindner adopted a method pioneered by other rangers in the area, of building new levees to block off the influx of saltwater and allow wet season flushing to restore the freshwater domains further upstream. At one location on the western side of the river, the memories of a local woman, Minnie Alderson, were critical to Lindner's decision to place a levy and restore at least something of what had been lost. Projects like this expanded the available habitat for geese and other freshwater species, further reversed the decline of the South Alligator wetlands and enhanced their value as a traditional food source.

Lindner took further steps to begin restoring the surrounding flood plain by reintroducing *Hymenachne* and *Phragmites* from wetlands to the west. Here again, Lindner's restoration efforts were guided by local Aboriginal memory, this time from one of the Park's senior traditional owners, Toby Gangele, or by inference from Minnie Alderson's statements. These two Aboriginal people had experience of camping around and using the traditional

resources of the South Alligator wetlands alongside their engagement with the introduced economy. Alderson and Gangele
remembered particularities of what the country used to look like
and thus supplied some geographical specificity to the environmental values that Lindner sought to restore.

*Figure 6.2: Minnie Alderson, west side of South Alligator River plains, 1980.
Photo by Dave Lindner.*

During that first phase of Lindner's work on the South
Alligator River, evidence of the distribution of the Aboriginal
presence provided a critical but passive indicator of the shape and
structure of the pre-buffalo wetland wilderness. As post-buffalo
landscape processes have revealed themselves in the years since,
Lindner has identified other management issues which he inter-
prets as signs of the contemporary condition of wilderness without
people. He argues that proper management of these problems
requires an effort to replicate pre-colonial Aboriginal behaviour
on a scale comparable to that of the large population that once
lived there.[40] His interpretation of the traditional Aboriginal presence has thus moved beyond the passivity of demographic patterns

and now incorporates Aboriginal action as a constitutive impact in the production and maintenance of wilderness.

Burning to Control Vegetation: the Wetlands

As the years passed with the buffalo gone and saltwater controlled, a new and contrary environmental problem of too much vegetation has emerged on the wetlands. For Lindner, *Hymenachne* grass mats spreading over the swamps, paperbark saplings colonising flood plain fringes, and *Cathormion* and *Barringtonia* expanding across the plains, are all signs of not just a post-buffalo wetland, but also of a post-Aboriginal wetland. But whereas the remains of large-scale pre-colonial occupation had provided a passive indicator of the Aboriginal environment for the purpose of post-buffalo landscape restoration, these new problems of excessive native plant colonisation pointed to the absence of specific features of Aboriginal environmental agency. This is evident in two respects.

That native plants are growing widely where they did not grow in pre-contact times is evident in that they now obscure areas that were once identifiable as open Aboriginal occupation sites. Lindner comments that places such as these would have been kept denuded of vegetation by the simple and incidental trampling impact of many human feet. The level of traditional occupation around the edges of freshwater swamp areas would have been so heavy that they would have been worn down to gravel very early every year.[41]

Of wider significance, however, is the cessation of Aboriginal burning. Lindner emphasises the presence of Aboriginal people traditionally living year-round on the flood plain, and burning continually, as essential to pre-contact ecology. Aboriginal people occupied the area that is now freshwater wetlands since before the wetlands were deposited, which occurred after post-glacial sea levels rose. That late prehistoric transition from salt-flat mangrove to freshwater wetland was directed towards grassland in many areas by the practice of Aboriginal burning. There is now almost no-one there. While in my view it is impossible to be certain as to the cause of the depopulation of the wetlands, Lindner argues from the absence of European artefacts for a quick and almost total collapse in the mid-nineteenth century, brought about by a smallpox epidemic. This brought to an end an intensive and almost uninterrupted burning effort by a permanently resident and seasonally very large Aboriginal population.

Lindner identifies the characteristic sign of Aboriginal occupation on Top End river systems as 'smoke in the trees'. People burn as a matter of course. But for many years the only smoke to be seen across this entire section of the South Alligator catchment was Minnie Alderson's campfire at Spring Peak. When the British wildlife documentarian David Attenborough visited in the early 1960s he commented that the South Alligator country was empty of people, except for the few people at the safari camp where he stayed.[42] In 1981, the archaeologist Rhys Jones told Lindner that, compared to his earlier experience of being with the Anbarra on the central north coast of Arnhem Land, 'the South Alligator was lonely'.[43]

Under traditional circumstances, the extent of *Hymenachne* grass was controlled by saltwater and fire. Both would have been necessary to restrict *Hymenachne* and keep open space for the *Eleocharis* rush, which has some salt tolerance and is what makes the South Alligator so important for geese. The numbers of geese are limited by food supply rather than by breeding habitat. In the naturally freshwater domains, *Hymenachne* will dominate in the absence of regular burning and reduce the geese feeding areas.

Lindner says Aboriginal people similarly limited the growth of paperbarks, *Cathormion* and other woodland trees by burning, and so created the open wetlands. Increased contemporary abundance of these plant species does not indicate a healthy wetland, rather it indicates a choked-up wetland changing from grassland to scrubland. A high-wind fire is necessary to kill *Cathormion* and paperbark. *Cathormion* needs to be burnt when it is small because beyond a certain height it is unaffected by fire. Fire also limits the distribution of paperbarks, because late in the year their root systems become flammable when the supporting substrate of the sloping wetland margins dries out.

To illustrate the Aboriginal attitude to fire, Lindner cites the response of Galurrwuy Yunupingu, a prominent north-east Arnhem Aboriginal leader, to the biologist Mike Ridpath, who expressed regret over a late dry-season fire that destroyed some paperbarks at the former CSIRO research station in Kakadu. Yunupingu advised that it was good for encouraging yams. Lindner further hypothesises that, were the program to reintroduce *Phragmites* into the wetlands resumed, its limits would be reached at the point when Aboriginal people would have seen a need to burn it. He conjectures that without Aboriginal interference there would probably have been thickets of *Phragmites* across the prehistoric flood plain.

So for Lindner, the wetlands of the pre-contact Aboriginal, which were later degraded by buffalo, 'were never like the wetlands we have now'. Their post-buffalo recovery has taken place in the absence of Aboriginal people whose burning restricted these wetland flora to a lesser ecological niche than that which they are able to fill naturally. This is shown by the fact that areas which the archaeological record shows to have been heavily used by Aborigines, are being invaded by shrub growth. Lindner

184

considers Aboriginal burning to have been ubiquitous. Contrary to contemporary Park managers' qualms about restricting burning programs to the early dry season, Aboriginal people burnt at any time they were able. The explorer Leichhardt observed people burning flood plain grasses in late November, something which would be regarded as unacceptable by many today.[44]

Burning to Protect Vegetation: the Uplands

The cessation of Aboriginal burning has had similarly critical implications, but for opposite reasons, on the Arnhem Land Plateau, which extends into Kakadu from the east. In this case Lindner agrees with what is now a well-researched and widely accepted historical scenario.[45] Those Aboriginal groups that survived into the last century increasingly left their homelands to go to places of contact with non-Aboriginal people and so their traditional, low-intensity, patchwork burning ceased over large areas, with disastrous consequences for some widespread woodland species. In the absence of Aboriginal people, huge fires came from fringing areas almost annually and swept across flammable sections of the plateau. Lightning strikes also became important. Lindner argues that even if only a very small percentage of strikes result in dry fires, that is fires that are able to burn because they are not quickly extinguished by rainfall accompanying the lightning, then that is a major impact.

Biologists refer to *Callitris intratropica*, or cypress pine, and *Allosyncarpia ternata*, as 'key charismatic plant species' for diagnosing recent change in fire regimes.[46] Because *Callitris* is resistant to termites the dead tree remains on the ground for many years. Lindner recognised the extent of the loss when, as he recalls, he looked around the Snowdrop area of the upper Katherine River in south-west Arnhem Land in the late 1980s and early 1990s 'and found the *Callitris* were all dead. *Callitris* is the one species that registers the massive change that has occurred in the plateau landscape as a result of the cessation of traditional Aboriginal burning. *Callitris* is the barometer of what has happened since the removal of Aborigines'. *Allosyncarpia*, a tree which defines a particular form of closed rainforest assemblage on the plateau,[47] is also losing ground to fire. The destruction of these species also signalled the larger impact of uncontrolled fires because of the impact on the biological communities associated with them.

Lindner therefore welcomed the publication of historian Bill Gammage's celebrated recent book, *The Biggest Estate On Earth: How Aborigines Made Australia*, containing images of park-like country in southern Australia attributable not to nineteenth-century artistic misrepresentations, but to Aboriginal burning.[48] Those park-like conditions, Lindner says, could be lost within a few years when Aboriginal burning stopped; that is the level of burning that sustained the pre-contact Arnhem Plateau wilderness.

Hunting Saltwater Crocodiles

The saltwater, or estuarine, crocodile is a species that has always held a particular fascination for Lindner. Like the ecological elements already discussed, its recent history has been one of dramatic change, and Lindner's view of its current status flows in part from his interpretation of its longer-term history in the presence of Aboriginal people.

Lindner considers that the environmental conditions for saltwater crocodiles are now probably unique in history in that all external controls on population have been removed. Under the conditions existing prior to any non-Aboriginal environmental impact, the sandy upper reaches of the major rivers and creeks, below the Arnhem Land escarpment, were poor environments for saltwater crocodiles. Their only food in those areas was freshwater crocodiles and other prey such as the occasional turtle. A saltwater crocodile in such a location, such as a plunge-pool waterhole at the base of the escarpment, would wipe out the freshwater crocodiles present there and then starve. The survival of freshwater crocodiles depends on the existence of that zone in which saltwater crocodiles could not establish themselves. In their new authoritative compendium, Grigg and Kirshner conclude that, for the north Australian saltwater crocodile, 'the carrying capacity of an area will not be determined by proximity to nesting habitat, but, more likely, by food availability'.[49]

Lindner observes that, in addition to those natural limits, Aboriginal people were moving up and down the rivers constantly and preying on crocodiles. He speculates that the availability of a crocodile during lean times of the year would have been welcome news for a resident band. That incessant hunting impact would have countered the movement of saltwater crocodiles upstream into the lowland forest zone of ephemeral streams.

Lindner suggests those limits probably always applied in prehistoric times to crocodile numbers in the current river systems. Aboriginal hunters have lived along the rivers and creeks of this area for 50,000 years. Until 12,000 years ago, when the last ice age ended, what we now know as the sub-coastal and lowland areas were much further inland, and the saltwater crocodile population was further north. It is likely that saltwater crocodiles only entered the present-day river systems in the last 12,000 years, and that their numbers expanded to a level somewhere below current numbers on the lower flood plains during the most recent freshwater phase. Aboriginal hunters were present throughout.

Now we have a completely opposite set of conditions. Since the nineteenth-century population collapse, the presence of hunters in the bush has been reduced almost to nothing, removing that significant predatory pressure on saltwater crocodiles. In addition, the hostile, sub-subsistence quality of upper catchment streams for saltwater crocodiles has changed. Pigs, thriving on waterholes retrieved and revegetated since the removal of buffalo, now provide crocodiles with a major food source in the upstream areas. In many areas, crocodiles have more food available than they need, and they are living in places they would never have previously inhabited.

Lindner argues this is a dramatic reversal of recent history. When saltwater crocodiles were reduced almost to extinction by commercial hunting after World War II, freshwater crocodiles invaded saltwater crocodile habitat.[50] From the moment saltwater crocodiles were afforded effective protection in the Northern Territory in 1971,[51] they reinvaded their former range, then they extended their range beyond what it had formerly been, into what was previously exclusively freshwater crocodile habitat. Human predators have gone, and pigs now provide a food source over the crocodiles' present expanded range.

Today saltwater crocodiles are at maximum populations, and male crocodiles of less than 5 metres are forced out of the larger dominant crocodiles' territories into every accessible refuge waterhole. This situation is probably unique in the long-run history of the region. Saltwater crocodiles are now heavily impacting the freshwater crocodile populations below the plateau, an impact that Lindner considers more serious than that of cane toads.

Wilderness and Interiority

Immediately apparent from Lindner's approach to these four environmental management issues is his adherence to a restorative approach to conservation. This has entailed not only the removal of deleterious external impact factors, principal among them being buffalo, but also an assertive interventionist attitude to the containment and then reversal of processes of environmental decline set in train by such recent historical factors. The restorative strategies that Lindner has advocated or implemented arise from his diagnosis of the dynamic processes of the systems he observed. This actively restorative attitude brought Lindner into almost immediate conflict with the hands-off, steady-state approach initially favoured by some of the more cautious Park managers in Kakadu.

A restorative attitude needs an interior perspective, a dedication to understanding the workings of wilderness, and to what is required to repair and reinstate those workings. Aboriginal people are central to Lindner's interpretations of the interior workings of wilderness. Those who have seen in the concept of wilderness a resurrection of *terra nullius*, have argued that the concept is cancelled by acknowledgement of the human presence and its humanising impact on the land. Lindner goes in the opposite direction. He takes as given that the north Australian wilderness has included people for tens of thousands of years and argues for the internal impacts, most importantly fire, through which those people were constitutive of that place.

To refer again to the discussion in the introductory section, Lindner's view is thus distinguished from those wilderness conservation organisations that see all human action as an external impact, but is rather in accord with Langton's view that Aboriginal action has been creative of the Australian environment. But while Lindner recognises what they have created in wilderness, Langton sees homelands. This is clearly a difference that goes beyond terminology. Lindner embeds Aboriginal people within wilderness, and emphasises the essentialising force of tens of thousands of years of hunter-gatherer adaptation for understanding what Aboriginal people were in that context. In other words, wilderness is the antithesis of modernity, and the Aboriginal person in wilderness was not a modern person in the cultural sense, but modern in the evolutionary sense.

The point at which this critical historical breach began is recognised by the environmental philosopher Max Oelschlaeger: 'Viewed retrospectively, the idea of wilderness represents a heightened awareness by the agrarian or Neolithic mind, as farming and herding supplanted hunting and gathering, of distinctions between humankind and nature'.[52] The issue is one of ontology, of the nature of our being as humans in relation to other beings in the world. The Neolithic revolution allowed humans to create secure, separate, cultivated domains. Lindner insists that humans must be understood firstly as another species. He conceives of pre-colonial Aboriginal hunter-gatherers, and those few who more recently maintained a voluntary bush orientation, as 'wild people' or 'natural people', distinct from modern people, because they lived within and with respect to the natural environment, rather than attempting to seal themselves off from that environment in the manner of modern humanity (an attempt that Lindner sees as a conceit and a delusion).

This is a troubling idea for contemporary political sensibilities, because it locates 'real' Aboriginality within that natural setting; it evokes the spectre of the assimilation of Aboriginal people to fauna in Australian colonial law, and suggests a dissonant echo of nineteenth- and early twentieth-century debates about the evolutionary status of Aboriginal people, in which 'it was an open question whether Aborigines were closer to the animal world or to modern man'.[53]

But while Lindner insists on the essential difference of the hunter-gatherer, he will have nothing of social Darwinist hierarchies.[54] For Lindner, 'the modern world is shit'; a fraudulent, excessive, self-indulgent, hypocritical catastrophe-in-the-making. His psychology tends towards the anticipation of doom. He falls readily within that type that Oelschlaeger labels the 'Paleolithic counterrevolutionary', who:

> ...actually sees the deep past. From such a perspective the relation between the human species and the 'other' – that is, the wilderness itself – is not simply one of exploitation and domination. Instead, wild nature and culture are understood as organically related. So viewed, the destruction of things wild and free will entail the collapse of any civilization that rests upon them. Insofar as this thesis is correct, then the modern project, which has long promised the total humanization of the earth's surface, is paradoxically destined to fail through its own success.[55]

Lindner further diverges from others who have recognised and celebrated the environmentally transformative impact of Aboriginal adaptation. Rhys Jones famously characterised Aboriginal people as 'fire-stick farmers'.[56] In a similar vein, environmental manager Peter Cooke has written of the creation of a 'modern wilderness' in western Arnhem Land, caused by the abandonment of the landscape by its Aboriginal 'gardeners'.[57] We can recognise in these representations not only a broad understanding of the Australian continent as a cultural landscape, that is an assimilation of nature to culture as symbolised in the Aboriginal concept of 'country', but an inclination also to regard the figure of the passively opportunistic hunter-gatherer as inadequate to the magnitude of Aboriginal environmental agency. They must, it is implied, have been something more than that. While Lindner certainly sees them as more than that, he resists the corresponding desire to bring the traditional Aboriginal person closer to modernity.

The urge to not only represent traditional Aboriginal practice as something more than hunter-gatherer, more than simple extraction, but to also rename it as 'farming' or 'gardening' – that is, to advance that practice up an implicitly evolutionary ladder and thereby to separate Aboriginal people from a state of pre-modernity in prehistory and to approximate them more closely to ourselves – begs that question of ontology from across the watershed of the Neolithic revolution. While it is central to his Park management agenda to emphasise that Aboriginal practice was much more than passive opportunistic hunter-gatherer extraction, Lindner regards their characterisation as 'farmers' or 'gardeners' as an elision of the specificity of hunter-gatherers and their radical difference from modern people.[58]

The Anthropology of Aboriginal People and Landscape

In an important respect, the idea of Aboriginal people being located within and constitutive of wilderness should be entirely unremarkable to anthropologists, except that this has been known to them within a different domain of discourse conducted with a different terminology. The ideas of Dreaming beings embedding language in land and quickening the first ancestors of the social groups who arose from that land and owned those languages, of totemic classifications cutting across the domains of the natural and social, and of increase ceremonies performed to guarantee the reproduction of species, are all basic fare in Australianist anthropology and provide the groundwork for approaching that different ontology of relationships between Aboriginal people and environment signalled in the previous section.

In recent decades ethnographers have given us more insight into the interactive character of these relationships, making familiar the notion of the sentient landscape and documenting the intentionality of places and the things that country does to people. In one of the earlier statements, Nancy Williams gave us this scenario from north-east Arnhem Land:

> When, for example, a person enters an area of land owned by another group for the first time, he anticipates a certain guardedness that verges on hostility to emanate from the land and all that animates that land and is in it. For his part, he should be cautious and reserved, because he is not known and has not been appropriately recognized by that land. A spirit of that land may show itself explicitly suspicious or hostile. Should he attempt to utilize any of the resources of that land during his first visit, he expects that his efforts may be unsuccessful: the land will not yield up its creatures or its plants to strangers.[59]

I do not have space here to review what is now a significant literature.[60] It is pertinent, however, to focus for a moment on Elizabeth Povinelli's account of the Belyuen people of the Cox Peninsula, west of Darwin, because she explicitly recognises the reciprocal movement of communication and influence between people and country, entitling one of her chapter sub-headings 'The action of the mythic countryside on the human hunter', and the next 'The action of the human hunter on the mythic countryside'.[61] For the former, her examples go beyond the passive rejection of the foreign hunter depicted in the Williams passage above. Povinelli recorded occasions when a plague of freshwater crocodiles, a spread of invasive weed, or entanglement in vines, were predicted or interpreted as responses of various sites to the presence of people unknown to the spirits of these places.

A long history of everyday encounters in the bush with the actions of Dreamings has laid down sediments of relatedness between Belyuen people and places that has eventually made the Cox Peninsula into country that was right for them even though they do not claim traditional ownership of it. Most important of these encounters are with conception Dreamings that make women pregnant, leave identifying marks on the bodies of children, and even make people feel obliged to hunt in particular places. Descent-based Dreamings can also emerge from the ground to reward or punish people. Conversely, features of country can take on the likeness of people who go there, and people's spirits can reside after death at places that were familiar to them, and later appear to the living. People's talk and sweat penetrate the countryside, allowing it to recognise and respond to individuals and languages.

What country responds to is the shared substance of Dreamings. A person is the embodiment of various totems, such that the relatedness between people and Dreamings is one of consubstantiality. Again, the specifics of this are reciprocal. On the Cox Peninsula, Dreamings have age, sex and language. According to Povinelli, Dreamings are 'critically present, touching and commenting on the actions of the living and acting as ancestors, successors, consociates, and contemporaries to Aboriginal families'.[62] This ontological reality means that their respective wills are of the same kind. Dreaming intentionality and action are knowable to humans, just as human intentionality and action are knowable to Dreamings.

These communicative connections apply also to fire and hunting in western Arnhem Land. On the Liverpool River, the linguist Murray Garde recorded an increase ritual at a native honey site which in part was intended to subdue any fires that came through that area so that the hives were undamaged.[63] On another occasion he translated an explanation from the senior traditional owner, Lofty Nadjamerrek, as to why, in the camps of groups that have gathered before a kangaroo fire drive, spears must be laid flat on the ground.

> If we were to put the spears upright in the camp, then the mind of the kangaroo would be alerted because *yirridjdja* moiety kangaroos are like humans. Those kangaroos know everything about our intentions and can think, 'Oh, I can feel energy welling up in my body, there must be humans coming'...Those *yirridjdja* moiety kangaroos are associated with the Ubarr and the Lorrkkon ceremonies and have supernatural power. *Yirridjdja* moiety kangaroos are like 'clever men', like human witch doctors.[64]

What this, and other ethnography in this vein, gives us is the substance of that hunter-gatherer difference that Lindner intuits. It shows, in the detail of belief and practice, some of the specificity of Aboriginal relatedness with environments that they know as country.

Self-willed Land

I turn now to consider a growing school of ecological and environmentalist thought for the bearing it might have on matters considered so far. The rewilding movement is a major recent

development within global conservation, which advocates the restoration of a sustainable ecological balance in large protected areas
by the reintroduction of apex predators.[65] Rewilding movement
activists, especially in Europe and North America, have adopted
the concept of 'self-willed land' as a central ideological tenet.
The concept arises from the etymology of the term 'wilderness'.
Proponents of this concept draw on two sources in the literature
that go behind the early English 'wildēornes', or land of wild
animals, mentioned in the first section.

The first source is the seminal *Wilderness and the American
Mind*, which historian Roderick Nash begins with the suggestion
that in early Teutonic and Norse languages, the root of the first
syllable was 'will', meaning 'self-willed, willful, or uncontrollable',
such that 'wild' was a contraction of 'willed'.[66] The second is a
paper presented at the third World Wilderness Conference in
1983, in which Native American scholar Jay H. C. Vest takes up
the origin of the suffix '-ness'. He cites a late nineteenth-century
etymological dictionary which derives it from the Anglo-Saxon
'naes' or 'nes', 'defined first as "the ground"; secondly as "a prom-
ontory, headland, as in *Beowulf*", that is, a prominence of land or
a prominent mass of land'.

> Wilderness then means 'self-willed-land' or 'self-willed-
> place' with an emphasis upon its own intrinsic volition.
> The middle syllable *der* of wilderness possibly represents
> the preposition-article combination 'of the'. Hence, in
> wil-der-ness, there is a 'will-of-the-land'; and in wildeor,
> there is 'will of the animal'. A wild animal is a 'self-
> willed animal' – an undomesticated animal – similarly,
> wildland is 'self-willed land'.[67]

Vest finds the cultural context for this etymology in ancient Celtic and other nature-oriented European belief systems centred on sites of divination or worship, often trees or groves located in deep forest, that were charged with the presence of spirits. The details of this cultural setting are little to the point. There is no analogy to be drawn here with the ethnography above. These European cultures were post-Neolithic, there is no suggestion of an individualised commonality of substance between human and spiritual entities, and communication with spiritual sites was the preserve of a priestly class. Their practice shows the emergence of 'religion' as a discrete institution, and the receding of sites of power away from the traffic of everyday life. So communication between people and the spiritual entities of the land was more institutionally specialised and less socially diffuse than in the Aboriginal cultures discussed above.

Moreover, rewilding emphasises the creation of conditions in which natural processes can be left to restore environmental health. Its more purist advocates insist that self-willed land is land that is independent of humans. Indeed, one of the websites dedicated to the application of this concept in Europe begins with the statement that 'true wilderness is a land that has supreme naturalness and is free of any human control'.[68] But the philosophical appeal of self-willed land within wilderness discourse arises from the one point that it has in common both with its Celtic cultural origins and with Aboriginal perceptions of landscape: the attribution of agency to nature.

Three Discourses

To this point I have drawn upon three fields of discourse. The first is that of recent views of the relationship between Aboriginal people and wilderness, within which I have highlighted the environmental interpretations of Dave Lindner. The second is that of ethnographic investigation and anthropological interpretation of the relationship between Aboriginal people and environment. The third is the rewilding movement's concept of the self-willed land. I now seek to show how these latter two can be connected to the first, to form a revised conception of that relationship between Aboriginal people and wilderness that is the focus of this chapter. To show concisely what is to be gained from this proposed complementarity, it may first be useful to set out what each of these perspectives offers, and what it lacks.

Lindner locates traditional Aboriginal people within wilderness. For him, they are part of the wild. But he recognises only one-half of the relationship, that of the constitutive impacts of Aboriginal action upon wilderness, because that is all that is necessary for his management-oriented purposes. This leaves his characterisation of Aboriginal people as wild people with no basis outside his own intuitions, motivated by a defiantly anti-modernist impulse. Anthropology shows that the interactions between traditional Aboriginal people and country are intimately reciprocal, and that within Aboriginal ontology, the intentionalities of people, and those of the diverse agents within country, are of the same kind. But this literature has accumulated around a different intellectual object, that of interpreting the cultural other, and is oblivious to the question of whether the environments at hand should be called wilderness. The rewilding movement promotes a conception of wilderness as self-willed land that has an important underlying philosophical commonality with the Aboriginal conception of the environment. But its advocates maintain a doctrinaire rejection of any human presence, much less a reciprocally and constitutively active one, within those places.

What I propose is that the rewilding movement's conception of wilderness as self-willed land, by reason of a congruence
with Aboriginal conceptions of environment and in spite of its
implied exclusion of Aboriginal people themselves, offers an analytical connection. It provides a conceptual and terminological
bridge across which anthropological interpretations of reciprocal
Aboriginal-environmental relationships can be imported into the
discursive domain of the relation between Aboriginal people and
wilderness. The idea of wilderness as self-willed land offers a
connection between those two discursive fields.

In turn, Lindner's conception of that relation between
Aboriginal people and wilderness, by reason of its positive and
interior perspective, can be located within the context of that more
complete conception of Aboriginal-environmental relations supplied by anthropology. The anthropology provides ethnographic
substance to Lindner's conception of Aboriginal people as a part
of the wild. But the meetings and meldings between people and
countryside that it documents extend his remark into dimensions
beyond his reckoning. It also supplies a richer matrix within which
to locate his interpretations of the diversely constitutive impacts of
Aboriginal action upon wilderness. Those interpretations now
appear as a suite of impacts selected for their management implications and extracted from that matrix of interactions.

From a starting point of utter contempt for modernity and
its environmental destructiveness, and nil interest in formal
Aboriginal cultural systems, Lindner locates the traditional culture
of Aboriginal people in their intimate and continuous engagement with nature. This is echoed by Povinelli in her emphasis on
everyday hunting activities for informing Belyuen people's sense
of relations to place, each other, and other groups. Anthropology
shows the fuller dimensions of that intimacy, in the multiple

symbolic and communicative connections with a self-willed land that is thereby seen to partake of the same world of signs and powers, or culture, as do people.

Conclusion: The Question of Management

I earlier noted Lindner's insistence on hunter-gatherer difference, and that terms such as farming and gardening misrepresented the character of their environmental action and consciousness, a view shared, at least implicitly, by Nash and Oelschlaeger. Another term that has appeared in this chapter is management. Lindner takes as first principle that Aboriginal people were part of the ecosystem and that we should be managing for an Aboriginal Australian ecosystem, not an ecosystem without Aboriginal traditional practices.

Aboriginal hunter-gatherers, with all the evolutionarily unique capacities of *homo sapiens*, were the agents of pervasive and regularised internal environmental impacts. They were an integral and necessary part of the workings of wilderness. With respect to the management issues discussed earlier, the actions required to address and redirect current environmental processes are deducible from an interpretation of the Aboriginal presence and their everyday behaviours of camping, walking around, hunting and burning. For contemporary environmental managers, such as the Parks Service and new Aboriginal ranger groups, that means that attention to what traditional Aboriginal people did, and how to replicate their impacts under current conditions, is the essential task. It is therefore tempting, indeed conventional, to characterise traditional Aboriginal environmental action itself as management.

Space requires that a full discussion be left for another time, but for Lindner, the term 'management' is misplaced. To emphasise the interiority of their position, he prefers to say that

'Aboriginal people *lived* in the environment; they did not manage it'. This is reminiscent of anthropologist Tim Ingold's 'ontology of dwelling...not of making a view *of* the world but of taking up a view *in* it'.[69] From an etic perspective, the term 'adaptation' seems the closest. From an emic perspective, for example, John Bradley describes the relationship of the Yanyuwa people to their environment in the Northern Territory Gulf Country as one of 'negotiation'.[70] The integration of the three discourses above makes the idea of management – unidirectional and controlling – seem an incongruous imposition into a wilderness world of relatedness, interdependencies, communication, and mutually constitutive influences and impacts.

Acknowledgements

My first and most obvious debt is to Dave Lindner, who has spent many hours over many years patiently explaining things to a sometimes dense student. My thanks to Eve Vincent for inviting me to contribute to this collection and for her encouragement during a discouraging phase of the work. Thanks also to David Trigger for directing my attention to the rewilding phenomenon, to Andrew Picone of the Australian Conservation Foundation for discussing his organisation's view, and to an anonymous referee.

References

APSA Environmental Politics and Policy Standing Research Group, 'The Ecopolitics Association', n.d., viewed 23 February 2016 <http://www.ecopolitics.org.au/ecopolitics-association/>.

Attenborough, D., *Quest Under Capricorn*, Lutterworth Press, London, 1963.

Australian Conservation Foundation, 'Policy statement No. 64 – Wilderness and Indigenous cultural landscapes in Australia', 1999, viewed 10 March 2016 <https://www.acfonline.org.au/sites/default/files/resources/64%20-%20Wilderness%20&%20Indigenous%20Cultural%20Landscape%20in%20Australia.pdf>.

Australian Heritage Commission, 'Wilderness: We call it home', n.d., viewed 8 March 2016 <http://olr.npi.gov.au/heritage/publications/anlr/callithome.html>.

Australian Wildlife Conservancy, 'About AWC', n.d., viewed 24 February 2016 <http://www.australianwildlife.org/about/about.aspx>.

Bowman, D. M. J. S., Garde, M. & Saulwick, A., '*Kunj-ken Makka Man-wurrk* – Fire is for kangaroos: Interpreting Aboriginal accounts of landscape burning in central Arnhem Land', in A. Anderson, I. Lilley & S. O'Connor (eds), *Histories of Old Ages: Essays in Honour of Rhys Jones*, Pandanus Books, Australian National University, Canberra, 2001, p. 75.

Bradley, J. M., 'Landscapes of the mind, landscapes of the spirit', in R. Baker, J. Davies and E. Young (eds), *Working On Country: Contemporary Indigenous Management of Australia's Lands and Coastal Regions*, Oxford University Press, South Melbourne, 2001.

Brockwell, S., Clarke, A. & Levitus, R., 'Seasonal movement in the prehistoric human ecology of the Alligator Rivers region, north Australia' in A. Anderson, I. Lilley & S. O'Connor (eds), *Histories of Old Ages: Essays in Honour of Rhys Jones*, Pandanus Books, Australian National University, Canberra, 2001, pp. 361–80.

Bush Heritage Australia, 'What we do', 2015, viewed 24 February 2016 <http://www.bushheritage.org.au/what_we_do>.

Chaloupka, G., *Journey In Time*, Reed, Chatswood, 1993.

Colley, A., 'Fires burning', *Colong Bulletin*, no. 183, 2000.

Colong Foundation for Wilderness, 'Resources: the wilderness resurgence statement', 2004, viewed 8 March 2016 <https://www.colongwilderness.org.au/resources/wilderness-advocacy/the-wilderness-resurgence-statement>.

Cooke, P., 'Buffalo and tin, baki and Jesus: the creation of a modern wilderness', in J. Russell-Smith, P. Whitehead & P. Cooke (eds), *Culture, Ecology and Economy of Fire Management in North Australian Savannas: Rekindling the Wurrk Tradition*, CSIRO Publishing, Collingwood, 2009.

Dowie, M., *Conservation Refugees: The Hundred-Year Conflict Between Global Conservation and Native Peoples*, MIT Press, Cambridge, 2009.

Dudley, N. (ed.), *Guidelines for Applying Protected Area Management Categories*, IUCN, Gland, Switzerland, 2008, viewed 17 February 2016 <https://portals.iucn.org/library/efiles/documents/PAPS-016.pdf>.

Fisher, M., 'Self willed land: Advocacy for wild land and nature', 2016, viewed 9 May 2016 <http://www.self-willed-land.org.uk/>.

Gammage, B., *The Biggest Estate on Earth: How Aborigines Made Australia*, Allen & Unwin, Crows Nest, 2011.

Garde, M., with Nadjamerrek, B. L., Kolkkiwarra, M., Kalayirra, J.,

Djandjomerr, J., Birriyabirriya, B., Bilindja, R., Kubarkku, M. & Biless, P., 'The language of fire: seasonality, resources and landscape burning on the Arnhem Land plateau', in J. Russell-Smith, P. Whitehead & P. Cooke (eds.), *Culture, Ecology and Economy of Fire Management in North Australian Savannas: Rekindling the Wurrk Tradition*, CSIRO Publishing, Collingwood, 2009, p. 161.

Gerritsen, R., *Australians and the Origins of Agriculture*, BAR International Series 1874, Archaeopress, Oxford, 2008.

Grigg, G. & Kirshner, D., *Biology and Evolution of Crocodylians*, CSIRO Publishing, Clayton, 2015.

Hutton, D. & Connors, L., *A History of the Australian Environment Movement*, Cambridge University Press, Cambridge, 1999.

Ingold, T., *The Perception of the Environment: Essays on Livelihood, Dwelling and Skill*, Routledge, London and New York, 2000.

Jones, R., 'Fire-stick farming', *Australian Natural History*, vol. 16, 1969, pp. 224–8.

Langton, M., 'The European construction of wilderness', *Wilderness News*, no. 143, Summer, 1995/96, pp. 16–17.

Langton, M., 'Art, wilderness and *terra nullius*', in R. Sultan, P. Josif, C. Mackinolty and J. Mackinolty (eds), *Ecopolitics IX: Perspectives on Indigenous Peoples Management of Environment Resources*, Northern Land Council, Casuarina, 1996, pp. 16–24.

Langton, M., An Aboriginal Ontology of Being and Place: The Performance of Aboriginal Property Relations in the Princess Charlotte Bay Area of Eastern Cape York Peninsula, Australia, unpublished Ph.D. thesis, Macquarie University, 2005.

Langton, M., 'Lecture 4: The conceit of wilderness ideology', *2012 Boyer Lectures: The Quiet Revolution: Indigenous People and the Resources Boom*, ABC RN, 2012, viewed 8 March 2016 <http://www.abc.net.au/radionational/programs/boyerlectures/2012-boyer-lectures-234/4409022#transcript>.

Leichhardt, L., *Journal of an Overland Expedition in Australia*, T. and W. Boone, London, 1847.

Lucas, D., Gapindi, M. & Russell-Smith, J., 'Cultural perspectives of the South Alligator River floodplain', in D. B. Rose & A. Clarke (eds), *Tracking Knowledge in North Australian Landscapes*, North Australia Research Unit, The Australian National University, Canberra and Darwin, 1997.

Markus, A., *Governing Savages*, Allen and Unwin, Sydney, 1990.

McGregor, R., *Imagined Destinies: Aboriginal Australians and the Doomed Race Theory, 1880–1939*, Melbourne University Press, Carlton South, 1997.

Meehan, B., Brockwell, S., Allen, J. & Jones, R., 'The wetlands sites', in

R. Jones (ed.), *Archaeological Research in Kakadu National Park*, Special Publication 13, Australian National Parks and Wildlife Service and Australian National University, Canberra, 1985.

Monbiot, G., 'The British Thermopylae and the case for reintroducing big cats: a weird and wonderful tale', 2014, viewed 9 June 2016 <http://www.monbiot.com/2014/08/28/the-british-thermopylae/>.

Mosley, G., 'Major threat to south east Australian wilderness landscape looms', *Colong Bulletin*, no. 170, 1998, p. 3.

Muir, K., 'Aboriginal reconciliation and wilderness', *Colong Bulletin*, no. 162, 1997, pp. 2, 4–5.

Muir, K., 'Indigenous wilderness: Malimup Communique', *Colong Bulletin*, no. 169, 1998, p. 12.

Muir, K., 'The pure state of nature: book review', *Colong Bulletin*, no. 181, 2000, p. 8.

Muir, K., 'Action toward wilderness protection in Australia', n.d. [2006], viewed 8 March 2016 <https://www.colongwilderness.org.au/files/pages/kmuir.pdf>.

Nash, R. F., *Wilderness and the American Mind*, 5th edn, Yale University Press, New Haven, 2014.

National Parks Association of NSW, 'About NPA', 2015, viewed 24 February 2016 <http://www.npansw.org.au/index.php/home/what-we-do>.

Oelschlaeger, M., *The Idea of Wilderness: From Prehistory to the Age of Ecology*, Yale University Press, New Haven, 1991.

Pascoe, B., *Dark Emu: Black Seeds, Agriculture or Accident?*, Magabala Books, Broome, 2014.

Peterson, N., 'Is the Aboriginal landscape sentient?: Animism, the new animism, and the Warlpiri', *Oceania*, vol. 81, no. 2, July 2011, pp. 167–79.

Poirier, S., *A World of Relationships: Itineraries, Dreams, and Events in the Australian Western Desert*, University of Toronto Press, Toronto, 2005.

Povinelli, E. A., *Labor's Lot: The Power, History, and Culture of Aboriginal Action*, University of Chicago Press, Chicago, 1993.

Queensland Environment Groups, 'Native Title and Protected Areas Project support document: Malimup Communique', n.d., viewed 8 March 2016 <http://www.indig-enviro.asn.au/Support21.htm>.

The Rewilding Institute, 'Around the campfire with Uncle Dave: Wilderness – self-willed land', 2013, viewed 12 June 2016 <http://rewilding.org/rewildit/around-the-campfire-with-uncle-dave-wilderness-self-willed-land/>.

Rose, D. B., *Nourishing Terrains: Australian Aboriginal Views of Landscape and Wilderness*, Australian Heritage Commission, Canberra, 1996.

Sultan, R., 'Foreword', in R. Sultan, P. Josif, C. Mackinolty and J. Mackinolty (eds), *Ecopolitics IX: Perspectives on Indigenous Peoples Management of Environment Resources*, Northern Land Council, Casuarina, 1996.

Sweeney, O., 'Who's afraid of the big bad wolf?: The influence of predators and their role in rewilding', *Nature New South Wales: Journal of National Parks Association of NSW*, vol. 60, no. 1, Autumn, 2016, pp. 14–15.

Talbot L. & Sweeney, D., 'Green movement is here to help, not hinder, Aboriginal people', *Sydney Morning Herald*, 21 December 2012 <http://www.smh.com.au/federal-politics/political-opinion/green-movement-is-here-to-help-not-hinder-Aboriginal people-20121220-2bpim.html>.

'Updating wilderness in Australia', *Wilderness News: Special Report*, no. 154, 1999.

Vest, J. H. C., 'Will-of-the-land: Wilderness among primal Indo-Europeans', *Environmental Review*, vol. 9, no. 4, Special Issue: Roots of Ecological Thought, Winter, 1985, pp. 323–9.

Vincent, E. & Neale, T., 'Unstable Relations: a critical appraisal of indigeneity and environmentalism in contemporary Australia', *The Australian Journal of Anthropology*, In Press <http://onlinelibrary.wiley.com/doi/10.1111/taja.12186\ abstract>.

Washington, H., 'Wilderness truths: Debunking wilderness myths', 2016, viewed 19 February 2016 <http://www.wildernesstruths.com/>.

Washington H. G., 'The "wilderness knot"', in Watson, A., J. Sproull & L. Dean (eds), *Science and Stewardship to Protect and Sustain Wilderness Values*, Eighth World Wilderness Congress Symposium, September 30 – October 6, 2005, Anchorage Alaska, Proceedings RMRS-P-49. U.S. Department of Agriculture, Forest Service, Rocky Mountain Research Station, Fort Collins, Colorado, 2007 <http://www.fs.fed.us/rm/pubs/rmrs_p049.pdf>.

'What is wilderness?', in *Wilderness No Compromise: a Profile of The Wilderness Society*, n.d. [1999].

The Wilderness Society, 'Our purpose', n.d., viewed 26 February 2016 <https://www.wilderness.org.au/our-purpose>.

Williams, N. M., 'A boundary is to cross: observations on Yolngu boundaries and permission', in N. M. Williams & E. S. Hunn (eds), *Resource Managers: North American and Australian Hunter-Gatherers*, AAAS Selected Symposium 67, Westview Press, Boulder, 1982.

Woinarski, J. C. Z., Russell-Smith, J., Andersen, A. N. & Brennan, K., 'Fire management and biodiversity of the western Arnhem Land Plateau', in J. Russell-Smith, P. Whitehead & P. Cooke (eds.), *Culture, Ecology and Economy of Fire Management in North Australian Savannas: Rekindling the Wurrk Tradition*, CSIRO Publishing, Collingwood, 2009, p. 246.

Notes

1   For example, see: M. Oelschlaeger, *The Idea of Wilderness: From Prehistory to the Age of Ecology*, Yale University Press, New Haven, 1991, pp. 356–7.

2   *The Free Dictionary by Farlex*, viewed 12 February 2016 <http://www.thefreedictionary.com/wildernesshttp://www.thefreedictionary.com/wilderness>.

3   H. Washington, 'Wilderness truths: Debunking wilderness myths', 2016, viewed 19 February 2016 <http://www.wildernesstruths.com/>; H. G. Washington, 'The "wilderness knot"', in A. Watson, J. Sproull and L. Dean (eds), *Science and Stewardship to Protect and Sustain Wilderness Values*, Eighth World Wilderness Congress Symposium, September 30 – October 6, 2005, Anchorage, Alaska, Proceedings RMRS-P-49. U.S. Department of Agriculture, Fort Collins, Colorado, 2007, pp. 441–6, <http://www.fs.fed.us/rm/pubs/rmrs_p049.pdf>.

4   'Oxford dictionaries: Language matters', 2016, viewed 16 February 2016 <http://www.oxforddictionaries.com/definition/english/wilderness>.

5   R. F. Nash, *Wilderness and the American Mind*, 5th edn, Yale University Press, New Haven and London, 2014, pp. 277–8; M. Dowie, *Conservation Refugees: The Hundred-Year Conflict Between Global Conservation and Native Peoples*, MIT Press, Cambridge, 2009, pp. 19–20; J. M. Bradley, 'Landscapes of the mind, landscapes of the spirit', in R. Baker, J. Davies and E. Young (eds), *Working On Country: Contemporary Indigenous Management of Australia's Lands and Coastal Regions*, Oxford University Press, South Melbourne, 2001, p. 305.

6   M. Dowie, *Conservation Refugees*, 2009; and see the references cited by C. Miller, 'Foreword', in R. F. Nash, *Wilderness and the American Mind*, 2014, p. xiii.

7   N. Dudley (ed.), *Guidelines for Applying Protected Area Management Categories*, IUCN, Gland, Switzerland, 2008, viewed 17 February 2016, p. 14 <https://portals.iucn.org/library/efiles/documents/PAPS-016.pdf>.

8   ibid.

9   ibid.

10 D. Hutton and L. Connors, *A History of the Australian Environment Movement*, Cambridge University Press, Cambridge, 1999, pp. 138, 178–9, 251–2; E. Vincent and T. Neale, 'Unstable Relations: a critical appraisal of indigeneity and environmentalism in contemporary Australia', *The Australian Journal of Anthropology*, In Press <http://onlinelibrary.wiley.com/doi/10.1111/taja.12186\ abstract>.

11 ibid., p. 252; G. Mosley, 'Major threat to south east Australian wilderness landscape looms', *Colong Bulletin*, 170, September 1998, p. 3.

12 Australian Heritage Commission, 'Wilderness: We call it home', viewed 8 March 2016 <http://olr.npi.gov.au/heritage/publications/anlr/callithome. html>.

13 Queensland Environment Groups, 'Native Title and Protected Areas Project support document: Malimup Communique', viewed 8 March 2016 <http://www.indig-enviro.asn.au/Support21.htm>. See also Australian Conservation Foundation, 'Policy Statement No. 64 – Wilderness and Indigenous cultural landscapes in Australia', 1 August 1999, viewed 10 March 2016 <https://www.acfonline.org.au/sites/default/files/ resources/64%20-%20Wilderness%20&%20Indigenous%20Cultural%20 Landscape%20in%20Australia.pdf>.

14 K. Muir, 'Indigenous wilderness: Malimup Communique', *Colong Bulletin*, no. 169, July 1998, p. 12.

15 K. Muir, 'Action toward wilderness protection in Australia', 2006, pp. 8, 10–11, viewed 8 March 2016 <https://www.colongwilderness.org.au/ files/pages/kmuir.pdf>.

16 ibid., p. 4.

17 APSA Environmental Politics and Policy Standing Research Group, 'The Ecopolitics Association', viewed 23 February 2016 <http://www. ecopolitics.org.au/ecopolitics-association/>.

18 R. Sultan, 'Foreword', in R. Sultan, P. Josif, C. Mackinolty and J. Mackinolty (eds.), *Ecopolitics IX: Perspectives on Indigenous Peoples Management of Environment Resources*, Northern Land Council, Casuarina, 1996, p. 3.

19 'Conference resolutions', in R. Sultan, P. Josif, C. Mackinolty and J. Mackinolty (eds.), *Ecopolitics IX*, p. 166.

20 M. Langton, 'Art, wilderness and *terra nullius*', in R. Sultan, P. Josif, C. Mackinolty and J. Mackinolty (eds), *Ecopolitics IX*, pp. 16–24; M. Langton, 'The European construction of wilderness', *Wilderness News*, no. 143, Summer 1995/96, pp. 16–17.

21 M. Langton, 'Art, wilderness and *terra nullius*', pp. 24, 17; see also D. B. Rose, *Nourishing Terrains: Australian Aboriginal Views of Landscape and Wilderness*, Australian Heritage Commission, Canberra, 1996, pp. 17–18.

22 L. Talbot and D. Sweeney, 'Green movement is here to help, not hinder, Aboriginal people', *Sydney Morning Herald*, 21 December 2012 <http:// www.smh.com.au/federal-politics/political-opinion/green-movement-is- here-to-help-not-hinder-Aboriginal people-20121220-2bpim.html>.

23 Australian Wildlife Conservancy, 'About AWC', viewed 24 February 2016 <http://www.australianwildlife.org/about/about.aspx>.

24 Bush Heritage Australia, 'What we do', 2015, viewed 24 February 2016 <http://www.bushheritage.org.au/what_we_do>.

25 National Parks Association of NSW, 'About NPA', 2015, viewed 24 February 2016 <http://www.npansw.org.au/index.php/home/what-we-do>.

26 See also 'What is wilderness?', in *Wilderness No Compromise: a Profile of The Wilderness Society*, n.d. [1999], n.p.; 'Updating wilderness in Australia', *Wilderness News: Special Report*, no. 154, March 1999, p. 2.

27 The Wilderness Society, 'Our purpose', viewed 26 February 2016 <https://www.wilderness.org.au/our-purpose>.

28 Langton, 'The European construction of wilderness'.

29 Colong Foundation for Wilderness, 'Resources: the wilderness resurgence statement', 2004, viewed 8 March 2016 <https://www.colongwilderness.org.au/resources/wilderness-advocacy/the-wilderness-resurgence-statement>.

30 Colong Foundation, 'Resources'.

31 'Updating wilderness in Australia', *Wilderness News*.

32 K. Muir, 'The pure state of nature: book review', *Colong Bulletin*, no. 181, July 2000, p. 8; A. Colley, 'Fires burning', *Colong Bulletin*, no. 183, November 2000, p. 6.

33 G. Mosley, 'Major threat to south east Australian wilderness landscape looms'.

34 Langton, 'Art, wilderness and *terra nullius*', p. 24.

35 M. Langton, 'The conceit of wilderness ideology', *2012 Boyer Lectures: The Quiet Revolution: Indigenous People and the Resources Boom*, ABC, 2012, viewed 8 March 2016 <http://www.abc.net.au/radionational/programs/boyerlectures/2012-boyer-lectures-234/4409022#transcript>.

36 T. Neale, 'Re-reading the *Wild Rivers Act* Controversy', this volume.

37 M. Dowie, *Conservation Refugees*, p. 114.

38 The agency employing him had a series of names during these years. Some of these were Wildlife and National Parks section within the Animal Industries Branch, the Forestry, Fisheries, Wildlife and National Parks Branch, the NT Conservation Commission.

39 Personal communication, n.d.

40 See, for example, D. Lucas, M. Gapindi and J. Russell-Smith, 'Cultural perspectives of the South Alligator River floodplain', in D. B. Rose and A. Clarke (eds.), *Tracking Knowledge in North Australian Landscapes*, North Australia Research Unit, The Australian National University, Canberra and Darwin, 1997, p. 134.

41 For an estimate based on archaeological evidence and comparative observations, see B. Meehan, S. Brockwell, J. Allen & R. Jones, 'The wetlands sites', in R. Jones (ed), *Archaeological Research in Kakadu National*

Park, Australian National Parks and Wildlife Service and Australian National University, Canberra, 1985, pp. 135–6.

42 D. Attenborough, *Quest Under Capricorn*, Lutterworth Press, London, 1963, pp. 43–4.

43 D. Lindner, personal communication; B. Meehan et al., 'The wetlands sites', p. 135.

44 L. Leichhardt, *Journal of an Overland Expedition in Australia*, T. and W. Boone, London, 1847, p. 493.

45 P. Cooke, 'Buffalo and tin, baki and Jesus: the creation of a modern wilderness', in J. Russell-Smith, P. Whitehead & P. Cooke (eds.), *Culture, Ecology and Economy of Fire Management in North Australian Savannas: Rekindling the Wurrk Tradition*, CSIRO Publishing, Collingwood, 2009, pp. 92–7.

46 J. C. Z. Woinarski, J. Russell-Smith, A. N. Andersen & K. Brennan, 'Fire management and biodiversity of the western Arnhem Land Plateau', in J. Russell-Smith et. al., 2009, p. 246; see also: Cooke, 'Buffalo and tin, baki and Jesus', p. 89.

47 Woinarski et. al., 'Fire management', pp. 241–2.

48 B. Gammage, *The Biggest Estate on Earth: How Aborigines Made Australia*, Allen & Unwin, Crows Nest, 2011.

49 G. Grigg and D. Kirshner, *Biology and Evolution of Crocodylians*, CSIRO Publishing, Clayton, 2015, p. 561.

50 ibid., p. 527.

51 ibid., pp. 557–8.

52 Oelschlaeger, *The Idea of Wilderness*, 1991, p. 3; and see Nash, *Wilderness and the American Mind*, 2014, p. xx.

53 A. Markus, *Governing Savages*, Allen and Unwin, Sydney, 1990, p. 37.

54 ibid., pp. 38–47; R. McGregor, *Imagined Destinies: Aboriginal Australians and the Doomed Race Theory, 1880–1939*, Melbourne University Press, Carlton South, 1997.

55 Oelschlaeger, *The Idea of Wilderness*, 1991, p. 8.

56 R. Jones, 'Fire-stick farming', *Australian Natural History*, vol. 16, 1969, pp. 224–8. For the reservations that have been expressed about the use of this term, see: D. M. J. S. Bowman, M. Garde & A. Saulwick, '*Kunj-ken Makka Man-wurrk* – Fire is for kangaroos: Interpreting Aboriginal accounts of landscape burning in central Arnhem Land', in A. Anderson, I. Lilley & S. O'Connor (eds), *Histories of Old Ages: Essays in Honour of Rhys Jones*, Pandanus Books, Australian National University, Canberra, 2001, p. 75.

57 Cooke, 'Buffalo and tin, baki and Jesus', pp. 85–7.

58 Rupert Gerritsen (*Australians and the Origins of Agriculture*, BAR

International Series 1874, Archaeopress, Oxford, 2008) argues for an early Neolithic stage of development in a few parts of the continent. Recently, Bruce Pascoe (*Dark Emu: Black Seeds, Agriculture or Accident?*, Magabala Books, Broome, 2014) has collated more widespread evidence for intensification of Aboriginal productive systems and argued that most Aboriginal societies were in the early stages of agriculture. For Arnhem Land, George Chaloupka (*Journey In Time*, Reed, Chatswood, 1993, p. 139) refers to 'yam gardens' at many places on the Arnhem Land Plateau, enhanced both by the replanting of the heads from harvested yams, and by the introduction of yam heads collected during travels across other areas. This does not require a significant revision of the existing model of a human ecology of mobile seasonal resource exploitation driven by the phases of the monsoonal climate (see: S. Brockwell, A. Clarke & R. Levitus, 'Seasonal movement in the prehistoric human ecology of the Alligator Rivers region, north Australia' in A. Anderson, I. Lilley & S. O'Connor (eds), *Histories of Old Ages*, pp. 361–80). The same adaptive principle applies to all the regions discussed in this chapter.

59 N. M. Williams, 'A boundary is to cross: observations on Yolngu boundaries and permission', in N. M. Williams & E. S. Hunn (eds), *Resource Managers: North American and Australian Hunter-Gatherers*, AAAS Selected Symposium 67, Westview Press, Boulder, 1982, p. 147.

60 See, for example: S. Poirier, *A World of Relationships: Itineraries, Dreams, and Events in the Australian Western Desert*, University of Toronto Press, Toronto, 2005 (especially regarding the importance of dreams); Bradley, 'Landscapes of the mind, landscapes of the spirit' (on the Yanyuwa of the Northern Territory Gulf country); M. Langton, An Aboriginal Ontology of Being and Place: The Performance of Aboriginal Property Relations in the Princess Charlotte Bay Area of Eastern Cape York Peninsula, Australia, unpublished Ph.D. thesis, Macquarie University, 2005. For a sceptical commentary on the idea of sentience in the landscape, see: N. Peterson, 'Is the Aboriginal landscape sentient?: Animism, the new animism, and the Warlpiri', *Oceania*, vol. 81, no. 2, July 2011, pp. 167–79.

61 E. A. Povinelli, *Labor's Lot: The Power, History, and Culture of Aboriginal Action*, University of Chicago Press, Chicago, 1993, pp. 137–67.

62 ibid., p. 138.

63 M. Garde with B. L. Nadjamerrek, M. Kolkkiwarra, J. Kalayirra, J. Djandjomerr, B. Birriyabirriya, R. Bilindja, M. Kubarkku & P. Biless, 'The language of fire: seasonality, resources and landscape burning on the Arnhem Land plateau', in J. Russell-Smith et al., 2009, p. 161.

64 ibid., p. 150. 'Yirridjdja' is the name of one of the two patrimoieties, the

other being Duwa, into which the world is divided in west Arnhem Land Aboriginal thought.

65 O. Sweeney, 'Who's afraid of the big bad wolf?: The influence of predators and their role in rewilding', *Nature New South Wales: Journal of National Parks Association of NSW*, vol. 60, no. 1, 2016, pp. 14–15; G. Monbiot, 'The British Thermopylae and the case for reintroducing big cats: a weird and wonderful tale', 2014, viewed 9 June 2016 <http://www.monbiot. com/2014/08/28/the-british-thermopylae/>.

66 Nash, *Wilderness and the American Mind*, pp. xx, 1.

67 J. H. C. Vest, 'Will-of-the-land: Wilderness among primal Indo-Europeans', *Environmental Review*, vol. 9, no. 4, 1985, p. 324.

68 M. Fisher, 'Self willed land: Advocacy for wild land and nature', 2016, viewed 9 May 2016 <http://www.self-willed-land.org.uk/>. And see: The Rewilding Institute, 'Around the campfire with Uncle Dave: Wilderness – self-willed land', 2013, viewed 12 June 2016 <http://rewilding.org/rewildit/around-the-campfire-with-uncle-dave-wilderness-self-willed-land/>.

69 T. Ingold, 'Hunting and gathering as ways of perceiving the environment', in *The Perception of the Environment: Essays on Livelihood, Dwelling and Skill*, Routledge, London, 2000, p. 42.

70 Bradley, 'Landscapes of the mind, landscapes of the spirit', p. 297.

7

KANGAROO TAILS FOR DINNER? ENVIRONMENTAL CULTURALISTS ENCOUNTER ABORIGINAL GREENIES

Eve Vincent

A captured echidna is liberated in secret, as conservationists and Aboriginal campers sleep. Why the subterfuge? An environmentalist leads a tourist over to a sacred site, respectfully relaying a story they have come to know well. Does this amount to transgression? Vegetarians sit quietly by the fire, while around them fellow 'greenies' and Aboriginal people relish wild meats. Why would their principled abstinence from meat eating become, in this moment, a source of shame?

In this chapter I offer an analysis of a set of face-to-face exchanges between environmental activists and Aboriginal conservationists. I deal here with marginal figures: on the periphery of Australian economic and cultural life, in an only-just-arable wheat-growing region, an Aboriginal group holds out against the promise that mining will deliver their economic salvation. While environmentalist imaginaries are taken by international scholars to be everywhere ascendant,[1] and concern with the environment is certainly pervasive,[2] industrial visions loom large in contemporary Australia. The state facilitates, even expedites, large-scale exploitation of resources by transnational ventures. Protest-based opposition groups are as much demonised as they are celebrated in public discourse. This is not to equate Aboriginal people's structural subordination with predominately middle-class greenies' perception of their own ideological embattlement, but rather to foreground that a shared sense of being both marginalised and right is fostered within these conditions.

The marginalised, as anthropologist Anna Tsing argues, make something of their marginality, 'protesting, reinterpreting and embellishing their exclusion' from political processes.[3] I seek to understand a series of fraught encounters that unfold in a particular political space forged out of the experience of exclusion, rather than the determinate political and cultural forces that produced that space. For all their particularity, these exchanges illuminate broader problems of race relations within a settler colonial society. Non-Indigenous desires for contact with Aboriginal people, reification of cultural otherness, and postcolonial guilt combine to shape, constrain and sometimes wreck these relations. Aboriginal objectives here are not nearly so transcendental. These Aboriginal greenies nurture a political support base, enabling them to harness resources to their attempt to amplify, and make efficacious, their locally unpopular anti-mining position.[4] To pre-empt some familiar criticisms: I do not regard the environmentalists I analyse here as muddle-headed individuals and I am not trying to point out the error of their ways. The task is to understand how broader problems are lived out at the level of the everyday. I begin by explaining how this green-Aboriginal collaboration came about, before detailing the background to this research.

'I Got Up and Asked for Help'

In 2003, at a bush camp called Kulini Kulini, over 300 anti-nuclear environmental activists met at the invitation of the Kupa Piti Kungka Tjuta – a council of senior Aboriginal women based in Coober Pedy. The gathering was part of a successful campaign against the siting of a nuclear waste dump in northern South Australia.[5] In attendance was a Kokatha woman I will call Aunty

Joan, from the coastal town of Ceduna in far west South Australia.[6] Ceduna lies approximately 600 kilometres south-west of Coober Pedy, via a stretch of highway and a long gravel road. Aunty Joan is related to a prominent Kungka, a Kokatha woman from Port Augusta (now deceased). At that gathering, Joan recalls, 'I got up and asked for help'. This request marks the beginning of the long-term collaboration between Joan's family group (or 'Aunty Joan Mob') and urban grassroots environmental activists, which now has national and international dimensions. Aunty Joan Mob are opposed to the extensive exploration for minerals such as uranium underway in their country. They have enjoined 'greenies', as they are affectionately tagged, to their marginal anti-mining struggle, capturing non-local resources as they continue to articulate, to local and broader publics, a refusal to embrace participation in the extractive resource industry.

In the following sections I critically examine the terms of the Aunty Joan Mob–greenie relationship as I observed it. Prominent Indigenous public intellectual Marcia Langton has recently sug-gested that greenies take up Aboriginal dissidents for their own ends, fomenting intra-Aboriginal conflict and potentially obstructing development.[7] By contrast, Aunty Joan had an active role in initi-ating and establishing the relationship I describe. Whereas Langton and others cast Aboriginal people in a passive role, here, as will become clearer, it is Aboriginal people who make use of greenies to realise manifold aims. In both the original argument and my brief counter-point this relationship is seen in overly instrumentalised terms: in reality much messier, contradictory interactions ensue.

Greenies value the opportunity for contact with 'real' Aboriginal people, more or less conscious that they are better acquainted with images and representations of indigeneity – a kind of 'hyperreal' Indigene[8] – than actual Aboriginal people. But some greenies welcome not just the opportunity to 'have some kind of meaningful engagement with Aboriginal people', as one greenie named Clare expressed it, and start to themselves enact a kind of Aboriginalisation of their everyday beings. While a subtle Aboriginalisation of the self is consciously undertaken by certain greenies, others are influenced by the politics of non-Indigenous 'solidarity', as developed in Australian cities since the 1970s. These greenies are well versed in 'postcolonial' questions of appropriation, representation and speaking positions, and constantly mark, rather than blur, the boundary between their own race 'privilege' and Aboriginal 'oppression'. Yet these greenies also seek personal transformation as they strive to become better (white) people. Ethnographic detail helps highlight the tensions and possibilities negotiated as part of this heady mix of demands and desires.

'Rockhole Recovery' Trips

Aunty Joan 'got up and asked for help' after observing that the Kungka Tjuta had formed productive working relationships with Melbourne-based green NGOs, as well as attracting the more specific support, between 2000 and 2004, of a small collective of activists called the 'Melbourne Kungkas'.[9] I was a member of the Melbourne Kungkas for the five years of its existence but did not make it to Kulini Kulini for various reasons. A flyer promoting this bush camp stated, 'We are going to stand up and fight strong. And you fellas have got to help us'.[10] At Kulini Kulini, Aunty Joan observed greenies in this helping role: facilitating meetings, seeing to camp logistics, collecting firewood, making cups of tea for elders and much more. Joan was explicit in her hope, now realised, of building her own 'greenie network'.

Aunty Joan's request 'for help' was met with a response, and in March 2006 she organised a week-long peripatetic camping trip into the scrub just north of Ceduna affected by mineral exploration leases, in close collaboration with a dynamic greenie she had met at Kulini Kulini. On this first trip Aunty Joan travelled with ten greenies, all of them women, under – in effect – her guardianship.

These trips later became known as 'Rockhole Recovery' or simply 'rockhole trips'. Itineraries centre around visiting granite outcrops, or 'rockholes', which are permanent water sources scattered across semi-arid country, and significant cultural sites connected to the Seven Sisters Dreaming complex.[11] The trips are ongoing, and take place each September, as the Seven Sisters or Pleiades constellation makes its appearance in the spring skies, and in March, before the Sisters slip beyond view. Travelling in convoy, between ten and twenty non-local, non-Indigenous participants traverse two contiguous conservation zones, Yumbarra Conservation Park and the Yellabinna Regional Reserve. This Park and reserve have been legally designated 'multi-use', their purpose apparently encompassing the protection of intact mallee habitat, recreational four-wheel driving, mining exploration and large-scale mining. Iluka Resources operates a mineral sands mine, Jacinth-Ambrosia, on the western edge of Yellabinna, and is one of the largest tenement holders across this area.

On the trips, rockholes are tended to, being drained of dirty water and decomposing animal remains, and left empty for rain to replenish. In pre-colonial times these would have been a vital source of drinking water for mobile hunter-gatherers. Their ongoing importance for species such as emus, wedge-tailed eagles, kangaroos and dingoes has been revealed through Aunty Joan Mob's use of sensor cameras at one particular rockhole site. I have partaken of five of these trips between March 2008 and September 2013.

Greenies contribute, minimally, their labour and resources to the task of monitoring and cleaning rockhole sites. They 'chuck in' money to cover fuel and food, and if they possess suitable four-wheel drives these are filled with trip participants, both Aboriginal and greenie. The idea is to stimulate in them, over the course of the trip, an awareness of the presence of this non-iconic, pristine mallee scrubland, and the threats facing it, which are dramatised as imminent but start to seem amorphous on further investigation. Aunty Joan hopes greenies go beyond being better 'informed'; the trips are experiential and are designed to awaken in greenies an affective response to being on country. If a viable deposit was discovered and developed in the future, especially one proximate to a rockhole site, Joan hopes greenies could be called upon to act. She sums up this strategy by saying she was taught by others, including the Kungkas, that if you bring 'white people with you' then 'in years to come they're gonna help you fight for the land'.

Indeed, in March 2007, members of a rockhole trip stumbled across local contractors engaged in exploration work for Iluka. This was before Iluka had finalised the Indigenous Land Use Agreement for Jacinth-Ambrosia with native title claimants, which was signed in December 2007, and the company was sensitive to conflict with local Aboriginal figures.[12] The greenies travelling with Aunty Joan on this particular rockhole trip established a spontaneous 'blockade', although the opacity of this simple phrase gives me pause. Joan's social identity is not simply that of a politicised troublemaker. She married into a white wheat-farming family in the 1960s, and has lived a life entwined with known black and white locals. In March 2007, two white contractors in a ute 'personified' Iluka, in anthropologist Alex Golub's terms.[13] In film footage of this particular mining company – Aboriginal protestor confrontation, Aunty Joan chats casually with the confused men. These are 'local boys' who call Joan by her first name. There is a familiarity in evidence despite greenies' construction of this event in terms of an ideological opposition. Exploration was temporarily halted after the contractors made radio contact with their supervisor. This moment confirmed Aunty Joan's faith in greenies' capacity to respond effectively when called upon.

Analysing Greenies

As suggested above, I am part of the world I analyse here. I was introduced to Aunty Joan by a fellow former Melbourne Kungka in late 2006. I moved to Ceduna in March 2008, my arrival timed to take part in a rockhole trip at the start of twelve months of fieldwork. At this stage I resolved to study the workings of a familiar scene. After a decade of being involved in Aboriginal–led environmental campaigns, I sought to understand the desire to be involved. I was at the time a kind of 'hybrid scholar–activist'[14] – both greenie and neophyte ethnographer. The focus on greenies was soon eclipsed by other concerns, environmental actors coming to play a more minor role in my work than I originally envisaged. But the conversations and interviews I draw on here were entered in to on the basis of this shared history and commitments, as much as I alerted interviewees, particularly through the blunt instrument of the academic consent form, that I was in the process of becoming something different. I retain an acute sense of my implication in all I describe, as well as Aunty Joan's loyalty to her ('my') greenies, whom she rarely criticises. However, they, or rather we, should not be spared scrutiny.

My plan to study greenies reflects growing anthropological attention to Anglo-Australians or 'whitefellas' involved in Aboriginal scenes in Australia.[15] This body of work clarifies the state of Indigenous–non-Indigenous interdependencies, long obscured by the treatment of Aboriginal people in isolation, as pure subjects of cultural difference, or as mendicant and a problem. Non-Indigenous greenie, bureaucratic and organisational workers' identities are all dependent, in some sense, on Aboriginal people for their sense of purpose and, in some cases, livelihoods.

My original research focus was further animated by broader political developments. By the mid-2000s a paradigm shift had taken place within Australian public debate of Indigenous issues. A realignment of the terms of political engagement saw prominent Indigenous leaders question the role of the Australian New Left in supporting Aboriginal campaigns for rights and recognition since the mid-1960s. Progressives were accused of being unable to face the effects of decades of 'welfare dependency', especially in remote areas, where impoverishment was depicted as a consequence of the self-determination policy era,[16] drawing impassioned responses and more detailed analysis of this shift.[17] Leftist sympathisers with Indigenous causes were accused of being overly oriented to past injustices and symbolic questions. While I gloss here more specific debates it now seems clear that a new paradigm has emerged, current Indigenous affairs policies revolving around disciplinary measures aimed at transforming Aboriginal sociality, as anthropologists Barry Morris and Andrew Lattas argue.[18] As I observed it, a dominant response to this situation within the Australian left was bewilderment, but this period of rapid realignments was also a stimulant to analysis. Tess Lea et al. argued, 'With Noel Pearson and others challenging left-wing or progressive orthodoxies the least we can do is respond with a willingness to examine the conditions which are seen as so corrupting, and to analyse the conceptual basis of our own progressivism'.[19]

In my case, undertaking this task involves analysis of the conceptual basis of a distinct branch of environmentalism, which

I term 'environmental culturalism'. Environmental culturalism involves lending *support* to Aboriginal-led campaigns for greater environmental protections for their traditional countries, where Aboriginal people are assumed to seek those protections because of their land-based cultural traditions. Aboriginal people are not encountered as secondary to the environmental issue, and are understood to be the rightful directors of the course of action to be embarked upon.

By 2012, Langton's more general attack on progressivism[20] had crystallised into a scathing assessment of green groups' role in allegedly retarding Aboriginal economic opportunities. Langton's critique of environmentalism is summarised elsewhere: environmentalists would deny Aboriginal groups the benefits that flow from native title–related agreements; environmentalists live at luxurious distance from the realities of remote and rural Aboriginal poverty and social problems; environmentalists exalt 'noble savages', preferring 'cultural' rather than 'economic Aborigines'.[21] As previously indicated, the accusation of ecological racism warrants serious attention, but needs to be tested through empirically grounded analysis.

Finally, it is worth noting that my interest in greenies puzzled greenies and Aunty Joan Mob alike. 'I'm wondering just what kind of field notes you write up?' Samantha, a middle-aged conservationist from Melbourne, challenged me out bush one night. She mimicked me writing, 'Tonight we all ate kangaroo tails for dinner'. How could I bear to sustain an interest in white people, Samantha seemed to be saying, while surrounded by the seemingly paradigmatic object of anthropological curiosity – Indigenous people involved in the regeneration of cultural traditions centred on mythological sites? While some greenies might be amused by the idea of being of analytical interest, others were actively hostile to it, as they invested in a morally charged opposition between action and reflection. Still other greenies welcomed the chance to be interviewed, in part because critical self-reflection was central to their activist practice.[22] These greenies believe white supporters of Indigenous political groups should be both self-inquiring and self-effacing, deferring to Aboriginal people to speak and taking care, in press releases for example, to always present Aboriginal people as the authors of significant actions, muting the sometimes crucial role greenies played in designing, organising or executing these actions (and in writing the press release).[23]

Interlopers?

'Australians do not know and relate to Aboriginal people', Langton argued in 1993. Instead, she continued, 'The most dense relationship is not between Aboriginal people, but between white Australians and the symbols created by their predecessors'.[24] Undoubtedly, the environment movement creates some of the most positive images of indigeneity in circulation in Australia today. These are images of custodianship, in which Indigenous traditional owners act as an 'inspirational symbol' of environmental ethics.[25] Familiar with these images, greenies may become aware they lack intersubjective relations across the racialised Australian boundary between Indigenous and non-Indigenous people. This realisation prompts them to seek out contact with actual Aboriginal people, whom they wish to come to 'know and relate to'.

Clare, quoted earlier, was typical of this scenario. Clare was in her late twenties when I interviewed her in 2009. She described herself as from a 'total whitey middle-class background'. Clare grew up in an inner suburb of a major Australian city and attended a private high school. As a child she had a 'pretty stereotypical idea of traditional Aboriginal culture', remembering an Aboriginal visitor coming to her school and playing the didgeridoo. However, Clare's mum had Aboriginal colleagues, working for a time in an organisation that facilitated anti-racism workshops. Conversations with her mum directed her towards issues of injustice as a teenager yet, while she remembered one of her mum's colleagues occasionally popping into their home to 'say hello', the engagement remained largely intellectual. When Clare went on her first rockhole trip in 2006 she did so with a strong awareness that 'up until that point I'd never had any meaningful relationships with any Aboriginal people'. Another greenie's story is similar – Rhiannon, also aged in her late twenties when I interviewed her, was attuned to issues of social justice in her adolescence but had no memory of 'ever meeting anyone...that talked about or was obviously from an Aboriginal background'. What she did remember were pivotal educational moments: as a teenager she was being driven to school by a friend's dad, and 'From Little Things, Big Things Grow', a song about the Gurindji people's equal wages and land rights struggle, came on the radio. The 'guy driving...turned it up really loud...He loved it and was singing along'. Stimulated by the Gurindji story and others, as a university student Rhiannon travelled to Coober Pedy to meet the Kungka Tjuta. This was not the case with all greenies, some of who grew up in and went to school in country towns with sizeable Aboriginal populations, but was true of most.

Many greenies, then, carry with them a discomforting sense of the distance between their lives and those of Aboriginal people, whom they *know about* through becoming politically interested and/or involved in a broad range of social justice issues, but whom they don't really *know*. They desire to bridge a social distance which is itself rendered literal by the geographical expanse they travel in order to access relationships with Aunty Joan Mob members.

And yet, of course, while greenies talk of wanting to make contact with 'Aboriginal people', they desire to make contact with particular kinds of Aboriginal people – that is, Aboriginal conservationists who wish to protect their country from commoditisation. Why is it that this more particular criteria that applies to the Aboriginal people greenies want to get to know is not made more explicit in greenies' accounts of the beginnings of these relationships? An implicit naturalising of the environmentalism of these Aboriginal people is effected; the particularity of the intellectual and political commitments of the Aboriginal people sought out is subsumed into an essentialised cultural identity. This observation is nothing new: it accords both with Langton's critique and Vassos Argyrou's analysis of the relatively recent transnational construction of 'native populations as repositories of ecological wisdom'.[26]

While the greenness of these Aboriginal actors goes unmarked – naturalised as an innate quality of Aboriginality, rather than a requisite attribute of particular kinds of Aboriginal people – greenies take care to mark pro-development Aboriginal people as aberrant. An explanation is needed for their particularity, which is regarded as a deviation from a cultural norm. These people are either explained away or not properly countenanced. They are explained away: as simply uninformed ('they are given the wrong information'); as 'brain-washed' and manipulated by 'mining company propaganda'; in more sympathetic terms, as worn down by structurally inequitable processes; or, as self-interested or representing a corrupted version of Aboriginality because they seek material gain at a personal or community level. When I say they are not countenanced, I mean that there is a disturbing lack of curiosity about these other Aboriginal people, despite greenies' putative interest in 'Aboriginal issues'.[27]

Greenies then are largely outsiders. This should not stand as a criticism but as a matter of fact: they do not pretend to be otherwise and often wrestle with feelings of being out-of-place in a small country town, withstanding anxiety and awkwardness in order to forge interpersonal relations with Aboriginal people and, in time, friendships. They have gratefully accepted an invitation to be here. 'Here's a group of people who are under-resourced and in a situation where they don't have as much power [as pro-mining Aboriginal groups, who are resourced by mining companies], asking for help', Judith told me. Aunty Joan Mob do not live in a hermetically sealed world, and have sought to draw closer resourceful, politically driven volunteers. Before meeting greenies in 2006, Aunty Joan's whitefella husband Gary, told me: 'I'd never even heard of greenies! But I found them to be beautiful people, absolutely beautiful'.

Does their outsider status make them interlopers, as Langton argues? The logic and consequences of large-scale commodity extraction are not just local questions, and greenies see themselves as active participants in a global movement faced with wide-spread environmental devastation. At the time of my fieldwork, Chinese demand drove the market for the mineral sands now trucked through Ceduna from Jacinth-Ambrosia, which are used in ceramics and other products. Local and global scales articulate[28] and greenies concern themselves with their interlocking: global capitalism, consumption, and anthropogenic climate change, habitat destruction and species loss, are all issues of concern. For greenies the modernist paradigm that establishes mastery over nature threatens all life on earth; new ways of relating to the complex, interdependent ecological whole are sought. In one sense, they are as legitimate actors as any on these issues. Yet the significance of *this* particular struggle is best understood in terms more resolutely local than many greenies grasp. Greenies have in fact been enjoined to an intra-Aboriginal dispute, throwing into relief the inadequacy of them purporting to stand 'in support of Aboriginal people'.

Interlocutors?

In a letter to the local paper, an Aboriginal resident of Ceduna complained bitterly about the activities of people who they argued lacked local cultural authority and recognition, mocking Aunty Joan Mob's following among the 'greenies you all seem to have latched on to'.[29] Whether greenies realise it or not, Aunty Joan Mob have coupled them to another kind of conflict, one that is intensely felt and which involves a broader network of Aboriginal people in Ceduna. While I cannot do a complex situation justice here, some background is necessary. In the mid-1990s, Aboriginal residents of Ceduna became involved in the preparation of native title claims, a series of which were eventually amalgamated in 2006 and finally resolved in late 2013.[30] The whole process proved highly divisive. Aunty Joan Mob became disillusioned with the very concept of native title, in part because the *Native Title Act 1993* (Cth) compels claimants and native title holders to negotiate with mining companies, whereas Aunty Joan, especially, sought to repel them.[31]

The other reason for Aunty Joan Mob's disillusionment with native title arises from the impact the claims process has had on local Aboriginal identities. Historical and anthropological research conducted for the claim stimulated the resurgence of 'Wirangu' as a local category of identification, and recognition of the newly (re)emerged Wirangu as the area's traditional owners. Aunty Joan Mob proudly identify as Kokatha people; they perceived that via the claims process they were being asked to learn and accept that

Kokatha country, *ipso facto*, lies north of Ceduna, and north of the birthplace of Joan's generation, the Koonibba Lutheran Mission. Aunty Joan Mob rejected this revision of the terms of their self-understanding, insisting that they are Kokatha people, living out their lives on Kokatha country, possessing cultural knowledge for sites that lie on Kokatha country, and speaking the Kokatha language.

I understand rockhole trips as a kind of narrative device, by which Aunty Joan Mob stabilise the terms of their self-understanding destabilised by the claims process. The Aunty Joan Mob–greenie encounter creates an intersubjective 'forcefield' like any other – 'charged with energy and driven by need'.[32] If Aunty Joan Mob are going to tell this story of self then they need the involvement of others. Greenies are involved then in an existential-political struggle, becoming vital interlocutors who take up, reproduce and circulate Aunty Joan Mob's claim: greenies understand themselves to be travelling through Kokatha country, learning about Kokatha culture, with Kokatha guides. Their visits are fleeting, and even those who make return visits have only a limited access to the bigger picture. Most greenies are not in a position to realise that another truth claim has overridden Aunty Joan Mob's self-understanding over recent years. It is left to the local letter writer to point to, however implicitly, a conflict intimately known to Aboriginal readers.

There is nothing duplicitous about Aunty Joan Mob's invitation to greenies. They reject native title wholesale, and talk freely of their experience of the claims process, revelations which can prove shocking to their supporters. I have disentangled the question of mining and local identities but for Aunty Joan Mob these remain enmeshed: they offer a critique of the state's limited terms of 'recognition' for Indigenous rights in land, and the state's terms for reckoning their identity, which gives rise to these rights.

Yet when environmental culturalists state that they stand in 'support of Aboriginal people', they unwittingly elide a much more conflicted reality. In fact, they act in support of *particular* Aboriginal people, on the condition that they share their political goals, even if they oppose mining for different reasons. This pits greenies into a contest not just with mining companies and the state but also with other Aboriginal people who welcome mining. This fact is as inescapable as it is unsettling, and I emphasise that some greenies are willing to grapple with it. My argument is that environmentalists need to reimagine Aboriginal people as agentive and politicised. Currently, a cultural determinism underpins imaginings of and investments in a homogenised Aboriginal self-state, the truth of which remains either accessible to contemporary Aboriginal people who are 'naturally' environmentalist in their outlook, or inaccessible to them, which might corrupt or confuse their position on environmental questions.

The Missing Echidna

These problems of distance, the seeking out of interpersonal relations and friendships, and the naturalisation of certain attributes as 'properly' Aboriginal can be further explored through the following case study. In the case of the missing echidna greenies make a familiar move. Particular Aboriginal subjects are incorporated into the Aboriginal as object, whom, having travelled many kilometres in order to get to know, greenies assume that they already know.

These events took place in September 2008. Two carloads of hunters left camp, piling most of the young men and boys as well as a couple of greenies into the back of the four-wheel

227

drives. They departed at dusk and returned after 10pm. It was a hot night and as the hunters 'cruised' slowly back into camp the women in the group were baking damper to have with honey, talking by the fire and keeping an eye out for scorpions scuttling along the dry ground. The hunting party told us they brought back two wombats, a rabbit and an echidna. A vegetarian greenie returned from the hunting trip ashen-faced and silent. 'You shot an echidna?' I asked him, one horrified vegetarian to another.

Then an Aboriginal teenager, Bryn, whose mother's mother is Aunty Joan's mother's sister, climbed out of the vehicle last, holding a blanket with the echidna curled up in it. He handed it to me gently, telling me that he wanted to show it to Joan's grandchildren and his other cousins in the morning, before letting it go. In my lap, it slowly uncurled.

A greenie named Gretta had not overheard my conversation with Bryn, and later put the echidna to bed in a box with a blanket. She sat quietly by the fire, but was clearly agitated, staying up after most of us had gone to bed. Later that night she convinced the few greenies who remained by the fire to help her stage an escape. Gretta tipped the box over so that it looked like the echidna had fought its way out, releasing it into the night. The next morning Aunty Joan and Bryn went looking for it, wanting to show it to the kids in camp before letting it go. They were disappointed and Gretta's hand in its disappearance was kept quiet.

For Gretta the echidna had became the focus of commonly shared anxieties. Greenies have a putative interest in Aboriginal cultural practices, which includes hunting, but this interest can prove arduous to sustain in the face of one's own ideological commitments. The echidna's staged escape involved self-negation on Gretta's part, and she effected an effacement of her own intimately

228

held beliefs – not approaching nor asking Bryn or Aunty Joan what they planned to do with the echidna, despite her distress. Instead she took care to act in secret. However, her beliefs were sublimated only to a degree, and she was intent on saving the echidna's life, having projected on to Aunty Joan Mob what she assumed they would do: eat this echidna.

Yet what Gretta seeks out, thinks she's found, and then recoils from, is not actually what she's come into contact with. These are not generic culturally different Aboriginal hunters and gatherers. Their cultural practices, in this particular case, are very much influenced by this family group's own interest in conservation issues. Their efforts at conservation might, of course, also be interpreted as reflecting a traditional principle. However, Aunty Joan Mob are enthusiastic about reconceptualising species in scientific as well as cultural terms. A shift is in evidence here. Aunty Joan has explained to me that echidnas are very rarely eaten now. 'They're way too hard too find, we're worried that they're getting extinct', she says. Indeed, she wanted to show the young people the echidna and talk about the past and the future with them, an opportunity that was lost.

I am arguing that Aunty Joan Mob need to be allowed to be Aboriginal greenies, whose greenness is not *predetermined* by their Aboriginality but whose environmentalism is culturally specific. I am not saying that Aunty Joan Mob and greenies are against mining or for conservation in this region for the *same* reasons. At stake for Aunty Joan Mob is a multilayered sense of the cultural, historical and (to a growing extent) ecological significance of *their* country, for which reasons it needs protection; for these environmentalist culturalists at stake is a more general sense of needing to protect country or habitats *of this kind*, which are of both cultural and ecological significance.

Interdependencies Obscured: the Greenie–Aunty Joan Mob Ratio

On three of the five trips I undertook greenies outnumbered Aunty Joan Mob members. But on one trip, in September 2008, around twenty-five greenies travelled with over sixty Aunty Joan Mob members (including children). This unusually large trip generated a genre of commentary from greenies that drew my attention to the value greenies place on an 'otherness which is not too readily available'.[33] I use here Ghassan Hage's work on white cosmo-multiculturalism, a mode of multicultural appreciation of ethnic others whereby the other should appear as 'existing for itself', while also, of course, needing to exist for and be made available to the cosmopolitan subject for their consumption.[34]

Greenies were enthusiastic about being numerically over-whelmed by Aboriginal people. Luce, a middle-aged woman, nicely summed up why:

> But I love that that's exactly what's really important... people who've got stories for country taking kids out, younger people and kids all doing that stuff together, several generations. It felt like the whitefellas were almost a tag along – welcomed but not essential to the process at all. That was fabulous, I liked that about it. It wasn't about us.

There is in this statement first an assumption about what it is that Aboriginal people should ideally be up to: intergenerational trips out on to country, dedicated to the transmission of cultural knowledge ('stories'). Where this involves greenies becoming a part of this process they should not be 'essential' to its facilitation.

In fact, in March 2008, an Aunty Joan Mob member vehemently complained to me that he sensed greenies *were* becoming essential to the facilitation of cultural maintenance and transmission. He resented what he saw as his dependence on the resources of middle-class greenies, whose access to well-maintained four-wheel drives and funds for fuel made it possible for impoverished Aboriginal people to visit relatively remote and inaccessible sacred sites. Both greenies and this Aunty Joan Mob member believed greenies should be irrelevant to these trips, obfuscating the trip's very origins in the relationship.

The frisson of excitement at the outset of the September 2008 trip soon gave way to ambivalence. The effort of running a large camp, namely cooking in huge cast-iron pots and washing piles of greasy dishes, burdened a few increasingly frazzled greenies. More significantly, the Aboriginal numerical dominance of this trip meant that the greenie and Aboriginal camps were each large enough that they were in effect separate, whereas usually no spatial distinction was evident. The hope of getting to know Aboriginal people had to be carefully balanced against appreciation of the heightened value accorded to Aboriginal people oriented to Aboriginal others, preferring to camp near and spend their evenings talking to their relations. These were exactly the sorts of Aboriginal people greenies wanted to get to know: Aboriginal people who were not especially keen to get to know greenies, as polite as they were to them. The fulfilment of the first hope ensured the ultimate failure of the larger hope.

The Walking/Driving Cultural Distinction

Other unforeseen consequences arose on the large trip described above: the more travellers, the more time spent travelling – in cars. The convoy bumped along, and numerous stops were made for cigarette breaks; to retrieve snacks; to *gumbu* (wee); to look around at animal tracks; to dive after *gulda* (sleepy lizards), which were knocked swiftly against the side of cars to be roasted later; to closely inspect a mallee fowl nest; to dig up water-storing plants to show to greenies; and, importantly, to interpret and mull over the tracks of mining exploration parties. Many greenies found the travelling excruciatingly slow and complained about the amount of time spent in cars. The driving involved lurching over a series of sand dunes, sending passengers and stuff flying as vehicles cleared soft tops before bumping down the other side. Particularly steep dunes were approached and cleared in turn, the engines in the queued convoy idling as one vehicle approached in low gear, picked up speed and disappeared from view. On larger trips, cars frequently became bogged, having to be dug out. Driving between sites could come to take up most of the day, a trip of around 100 kilometres consuming over six hours, for example.

Judith, Luce's partner, was characteristically restrained in commenting carefully, 'I don't *love* driving'. In general, Aunty Joan Mob members happily moved through country in vehicles. Greenies preferred to walk.[35] The walking/driving distinction is one example of unanticipated cultural differences that created tensions out bush. These Aboriginal people, descended from desert-dwelling mobile hunter-gatherers, like to drive through country (and to camp on it); greenies, born of a motorised modernity they repudiate (and of course share with Aunty Joan Mob members), seek to deepen their appreciation for this country by walking through it.

Greenies' love of walking caused Joan much stress. In September, greenies set out on a morning walk between two sites. While the Aboriginal teenage boys in camp walked with us, the remainder of Aunty Joan Mob stayed behind. Aunty Joan warned of 'killer heat', snakes and wild dogs, sending out vehicles in search of us before we had walked the full distance. Clare had stayed behind in camp, and reported the great unease generated by the thought of a pack of whitefellas moving through this country without Kokatha guides. Greenies were unaware that the bush was filled with ancestral spirits, to whom our presence and purpose might need to be explained.

Figure 7.1: Guldas *(sleepy lizards) were knocked swiftly against the side of cars to be roasted later. Photo by Eve Vincent.*

Further, the greenie/Aboriginal cultural distinction is as much an everyday class-based one as a reified cultural one. Our bodies bear the unequal conditions of our existence.[36] Greenies and Aunty Joan Mob members inhabited different kinds of classed and raced bodies – health-conscious greenies' self-disciplined bodies could generally handle walking distances that our adult Aboriginal companions, the majority of whom smoked, could not.

Mimicry or Yielding? Greenies' Use of 'Cuz' and 'Bruz'

Cameo Dalley and Richard Martin recently outlined a 'basic premise' that they argue needs further exploration, 'If it can be accepted that Indigenous people are changed through their inter-action with non-Indigenous people, then it stands to reason that non-Indigenous people might also be transformed and come to incorporate aspects of Indigenous ways of being into their own lives'.[37] Indeed, some greenies come to pepper their everyday idiom with Aboriginal English vernacular, saying terms such as 'fullah', the generic kin terms 'cuz' (cousin) and 'bruz' (brother), and using 'Country' as a proper noun. In this case an incorpora-tion of Indigenous ways of speaking – which points to Indigenous 'ways of being' sensed by greenies – happens even after greenies spend a short amount of time around Aunty Joan Mob. I am reluctant to overemphasise the prevalence of this phenomena as it surfaced occasionally and involved minimal experimentations with speech. It might sound very crude – a transparent, even desperate, attempted Aboriginalisation of stigmatised whiteness.[38] It can be more productively understood in light of Taussig's work on the weaving of mimesis, contact, primitivism and alterity within colonial relations.

Taussig, much like literary theorist Homi Bhabha, is drawn towards examining the capacious capacity of the colonised's mimetic faculties.[39] In one example, the power of the colonisers is captured through the wooden figurines used in Cuna healing rituals observed in the 1920s: the figurines are European in type.[40] In another, Taussig considers the outlawed Hauka movement of French colonial Africa; begun by Songhay people in 1925 this involved colonial subjects dancing until they became possessed by the spirits of colonial administrators.[41] In Taussig's examples the mimicking of white Others involves the acquisition, and/ or taming of 'strange powers',[42] whereas for Bhabha mimicry menaces, simultaneously revealing the ambivalence of colonial discourse and disrupting its authority.[43]

In the postcolonial present, it is the primordial power of Aboriginality that greenies can be seen to capture, becoming, if only partially, possessed by it – or perhaps of it. Greenies strongly share in the sentiments which, Lattas argues, defined the nation in the 1980s to 1990s: alienation and a lack of connection to the Australian landscape, Lattas states, became constitutive of an experience of an Australian self 'lacking in subjectivity'.[44] I am tempted to critique these superficial attempts to fill this lack; one cannot, as Michael Jackson concludes, enter the world of another mimetically.[45] A more sympathetic reading foregrounds the desire to be transformed through contact with another in evidence here, and might allow for a playful exploration of difference. Perhaps, in Taussig's terms, greenies are taking the opportunity to 'yield into and become Other'?[46]

Taussig returns to the Cuna figurines to reveal that while the outer form wore European clothes, the inner substance, 'the personified spirit of the wood itself', is in fact the powerful part of the object, which 'acts out the healer's song'.[47] What kind of interplay of exterior and interior forms exists in the case of the subtly Aboriginalised greenie? For certain greenies, these slight alterations in speech, I contend, give expression to the deeply problematic assumption that latent within all of humanity is a non-modern, ecologically attuned self: this lies buried within a universalised interior, from which emanates voice. As the historian William Cronon has shown, conservationists imagine 'wilderness' as a 'place of freedom in which we can recover the true selves we have lost to the corrupting influences of our artificial lives'.[48] Aboriginal people retain access to this uncorrupted self-state, assumes primitivist humanist logic, so that when greenies make contact with Aboriginal people they simultaneously make contact with this part of their true selves. That which looks like a disjunctive interior/exterior – a middle-class white person who 'even talks like a Nunga [Aboriginal person]', as Aunty Joan's teenage granddaughter exclaimed in amazement one evening – for greenies represents a coming into *alignment* of a way of being corrupted by modernity but re-sutured here.

Mimicry sometimes becomes a problem for the Aunty Joan Mob–greenie alliance. In July 2015 I spoke to Aunty Joan about this, reviewing an issue that arose in 2012–13, after which a greenie was asked not to come back on future trips. Two specific incidents brought an increasingly conflictual set of interactions, which unfolded over the course of two years, and which were more complex than I have space to discuss, to a head. First, this greenie used ochre collected at an old ceremonial site to 'do themselves up like a skeleton and put it all over Facebook', as Aunty Joan summarised. In general, Aunty Joan reckons, and I have experienced, 'We're pretty easy-going with the greenies'. But this use of cultural materials made Joan deeply uneasy; the latent power this material might potentially release was not for playing with, and it was treated carefully by Aunty Joan Mob members who had an attenuated relationship with the past of their antecedents, whose lives involved land-based rituals and ceremonies. On Facebook this greenie had played with and circulated an inappropriate representation of self. This self had been too opportunistically Aboriginalised, after pursing what was retrospectively assessed as an excessive amount of contact with Aunty Joan Mob. It is important to note that this greenie's Facebook self bore no resemblance whatsoever to the kind of everyday cultural selves they had actually come into contact with: Aunty Joan Mob members say 'cuz' and 'bruz' but they do not paint themselves up with ochre.

A second incident placed further stress on the relationship. This greenie came to act as a guide to other non-Indigenous people at a rockhole site. They were overheard repeating a story to a tourist; Aunty Joan relishes educating tourists but retains the authority to control the dissemination of cultural knowledge that has been entrusted to her, and which will be passed to her daughters. This greenie had forgotten that they were 'still just a visitor'. This was a very serious transgression.

'Last Night We All Ate Kangaroo Tails for Dinner'

Except that we didn't. Prior to rockhole trips, Joan and the two or three key greenies centrally involved in organising each particular trip collected a list of vegetarians present. Vegetarianism and other variants of ethically informed dietary restrictions were commonly practised among groups of greenies. Dylan Clark's excellent analysis of vegan punks in Seattle in the 1990s remains pertinent.[49] Clark understands punks as inverting Lévi-Strauss' culinary triangle, valuing the raw and the rotten over the cooked.[50] For these vegan punks, who didn't eat any animal products, too much culture had come to transfigure the natural state of food, whereas for Lévi-Strauss humanity's capacity to transform raw foods to cooked, through the discovery of fire, was central to the successful

237

mediation of what he understood as a nature/culture 'opposition'.[51] For Clark's punks, as well as many greenies, the highly processed foods of industrialised globalised food systems were the fare of interrelated systems of domination: humans over the environment, men over women, humans over animals. Greenies, in fact, embody inversions of these hierarchies: hirsute women and bare-footed men embrace their animality;[52] greenies strive for a non-gendered division of labour in the camp kitchen; vegan and vegetarian greenies desist in meat eating.

And yet it was not discourses about or practices of vegetarianism that made its way into my field notes when I travelled with greenies. Among environmental culturalists the eating of bush foods, indeed the savouring of the dripping, fatty *malu wipu* (kangaroo tails) and appreciative comments about the tender meat of *wardu* (wombat) cooked for five hours in a ground oven assumed predominance. Why was discussion and enactment of vegetarianism muted here?

Numerous scholars note that Australians are reluctant to eat kangaroo and native wild meats more generally.[53] The greenie embrace of wild meat eating is consistent with these analyses: their enthusiasm represents a conscious rejection of the disgust and discomfort apparent in the 'mainstream' aversion to eating kangaroo and wild meats. For Waitt and Appleby, kangaroo marks the boundary between domesticated and wild foods, their interviewees believing that humans should domesticate their food sources. Many greenies believe otherwise: hunting wild species allows for a restoration of 'natural' over industrial methods of food procurement.

Anthony Redmond describes the ways in which Kimberley Aboriginal people 'partially construct themselves (and each other) through the type of meat they effectively "own" and identify most strongly with'.[54] Redmond notes a 'local broad-brush distinction made between *ngarla*, fresh meat, and *mayi*, vegetable foods', the latter category encompassing sandwiches.[55] Meat, especially bush meat and beef, is valued over *mayi* by blackfellas, but also intriguingly by some whitefellas. In the case I describe, expressing an appreciation of and identification with bush meats involves greenies constructing, again, a subtly Aboriginalised self. These greenies have their mouths literally opened to alterity. Through this process they become other to the vegetarian white greenie. Since anthropology also presupposes an openness to others, being closed to meat eating became doubly troubling to me, and I forced myself to pathetically nibble once on *gibbera* (bush turkey) and another time on *wardu*.[56] My response was visceral disgust, and despite my shame I had to accept I was too sealed into my greenie cultural self for my long-term vegetarianism to yield.

Marking Racialised Boundaries

My attention so far has been directed towards a particular mode of interacting with Aboriginal otherness, and I have emphasised some greenies' desire to be transformed by others. Yet another mode is just as actively practiced in this space, and its precepts run counter to the assumptions that animate the exchanges already analysed.

Certain greenies conceive of themselves as enjoying 'white privilege', that is as possessing often-invisible benefits accrued by virtue of 'occupying the dominant position within an oppressive social hierarchy'.[57] These greenies strive to be 'privilege-cognisant'.[58] This involves bringing awareness to dimensions of their experience of white subjecthood, which might ordinarily have gone unnoticed, rendered invisible because of the hegemony of whiteness within Australian multicultural, settler colonial society.[59] Clare Land's analysis of the meeting of Aboriginal grass-roots activists and their non-Indigenous 'allies' has greatly aided my understanding of the political logics at work here. I summarise these before turning to a final ethnographic moment.

'To understand white privilege should also be to consider ways to undo it', advises Land.[60] This then is also a political project centred on transformation, of society but also of the self, activists seeking to unlearn certain internalised unconscious habits in order to 'reconstruct whiteness'.[61] As Michael Monahan argues, the concept of privilege involves a 'boundary condition': a way of clearly demarcating those who are privileged and those who are not.[62] Land acknowledges that the bounded identity categories employed in this model are themselves the product of colonial thought.[63] In effect the colonial order's binary terms – Indigenous/non-Indigenous, coloniser/colonised, black/white – are paradoxically reproduced through a project aimed at 'decolonising' the practices of solidarity activists. And yet, Land argues, these categories remain indispensible as historical, constructed social categories are determining of life experiences (explaining one's 'social locatedness'), and their critical invocation as structural and inherited, but not natural, categories is necessary. Any attempt to *blur* these categorical distinctions, via the notion of hybridity, is deemed impossible, indeed dangerous, given that key political gains, such as rights in land, are based on the assertion and reproduction of Indigenous difference. Land advocates instead a 'departure' from these categories, whereby new categories generated by Indigenous philosophical systems are deployed, before quickly cautioning that indigeneity should not be appropriated as part of this process. In sum, Land asserts that activists 'use' and also 'refuse' these categories, although the extended discussion highlights ongoing reliance on their use and the near impossibility of their refusal: at the very moment they are departed from, caveats such as 'no appropriation' serve to reinstate the distinction. I cannot solve the problem Land lucidly identifies. What I am interested in is: what happens when this categorical fixity is challenged by an Aboriginal political figure, of the kind that a good white 'ally' might be expected to listen to and learn from? This question presented itself most clearly in the following exchange.

'Tell me something: do you feel guilty?' Aunty Joan asked a group of greenies who were sitting by the fire after dinner one night. There was a pause and then a rush of talking, 'not guilty… but responsible', 'guilt's not the right word…' Then, a middle-aged woman spoke, clearly and firmly, 'I don't feel guilty. But I am aware that my privilege, as a white person, comes about as a result of your disempowerment'. Aunty Joan was seated right next to this speaker and looked at her vaguely alarmed and uncomfortable. She then cut us all off, saying, 'You know I wouldn't be here if my great-great-grandfather hadn't jumped ship at Eucla. He was a white man, he was Irish'.

At the risk of generalising, progressive greenies often understand colonial history as productive of both contemporary Indigenous people (and their unequal 'disempowered' circumstances) and contemporary non-Indigenous people (and their 'privileged' circumstances and *habitus*). They want to do something about this situation and change it. As part of this process they are committed to learning about Indigenous issues and from Indigenous people. And yet, here Aunty Joan was inviting greenies to pause and think slightly differently about the colonial past, unsettling an investment in the binary categories that structure the aforementioned historical narrative. Joan herself could not neatly be placed within a categorical distinction between coloniser and colonised. The colonial *relation*, she seemed to stress in this moment, was fundamental to her biography and being. Her Aboriginality could not be understood without taking into account the conditions of its creation: she is, in part, one of us.

However, greenies quickly restored their already existing understanding of the past, at a juncture inviting an enriched understanding. 'Well the Irish have a long history of fighting oppression!' said a greenie happily, and indeed Aunty Joan agreed, 'What were they thinking? Crossing Irish with Kokatha!' In effect, the invitation was declined, and the conversation moved on.

Earlier I noted that particular Aboriginal subjects might be integrated into the Aboriginal as object, whom, having travelled many kilometres in order to get to know, greenies assume that they already know. In the case of the missing echidna greenies could not see the Aboriginal greenie, seeing only the Aboriginal hunter-gatherer as a fixed cultural figure. In this case, greenies, whose political commitments involve casting Aboriginal people in the role of educators, could not countenance racial instability, moving to reinstate a fixed identity, such that the Aboriginal political figure was expected to embody. Greenies quickly and seamlessly reabsorbed Joan's comment, which I own is somewhat enigmatic, into a pre-existing teleology that located her firmly on one side of the oppressed/oppressor binary (contra-Ignatiev, the Irish were recast in this moment as not quite white).[64]

In the rural town of Ceduna racial binaries are certainly reconstituted in everyday social life, but the possibility of their dissolution is also everywhere apparent. White people and Aboriginal people share bedrooms, surnames, histories, workplaces, the schoolyard, and football fields. Many white residents and Aboriginal residents here trace their descent from either Aboriginal-white relations on the sexualised colonial frontier, or are born of and live immersed in the 'mixed up' state of the present, as Joan puts it. I do not have the space to elaborate these claims, nor to explain how a racialised social hierarchy and the hegemony of whiteness are maintained within these conditions. Of course greenies have no way of being already attuned to these local particularities. I am highlighting, first, that greenies as 'allies' import an 'anti-racist racial absolutism', as anthropologist Chris Vasantkumar might term it,[65] which is sometimes at odds with local specificities. Second, this racial absolutism is revealed as so central to their political logics that effort was expended in ensuring its maintenance, for its own sake, even where it proved inadequate to the particular scenario that presented itself.

Conclusion

One of the problems of attending to lived, everyday encounters is that broader processes and structures have escaped my attention. The state, for example, has disappeared from view. Yet the native title claims process, and the impossibility of maintaining an anti-mining position within it, has produced the condition of marginalisation I outline here. Aunty Joan Mob have created something out of this space, reinvigorating a cultural practice centred on relations with rockhole sites. With limited resources at their disposal, Aboriginal greenies realise largely although by no means exclusively practical goals through their relations with environmental activists, inviting greenies to join in this venture as the first step to building a political alliance. For greenies, Aboriginal people can become conduits for different kinds of projects of self-realisation and transformation. I have identified two greenie modalities in particular: the access to an ecologically attuned, non-modern self that contact with Aunty Joan Mob offers sees some greenies embrace of a subtle Aboriginalisation of the self. The determined maintenance of 'anti-racist racial absolutism' in a setting characterised by racial instability guides other greenies' inclination to mark their absolute difference from Aunty Joan Mob members, emphasising their 'privilege' as against Aboriginal subordination. In naming and probing these problems, I do not mean to reduce these complicated, affective, and often mutually rewarding relations to them: the substance of these encounters always produces an excess.

The second problem I face in writing about these questions through detailing lived intersubjective encounters is that individuals might feel betrayed and criticised *as individuals*. This is not my intention. I seek here to shed light on some of the unstable relational dynamics at work as environmentalists engage with Indigenous political agendas within a settler colonial setting. Nevertheless I worry that I have been mean about greenies, and further worry that Aunty Joan Mob won't appreciate my critical perspective on their loyal supporters. Throughout this process I have tried to also hold the habit of worrying at a critical distance, seeing that as a non-Indigenous person working with Indigenous people in a politicised space such as this I have long been enculturated into worrying about saying the wrong thing. My worries are of the same order as Gretta's and born of my familiarity with the world of environmentalist culturalists, which I have endeavoured to see in analytical terms here. These risks, however, are worth taking, lest the difficult dynamics germane to these real contexts continue to remain secreted.

Acknowledgements

Thanks to Juan Francisco Salazar, Tim Neale, Clare Land, Shane Reside and Breony Carbines for providing feedback on early drafts of this chapter. Many thanks to the Aunty Joan Mob members and greenies involved in this research, particularly those greenies interviewed throughout 2008–09.

References:

Argyrou, V., *The Logic of Environmentalism: Anthropology, Ecology and Postcoloniality*, Berghahn Books, Oxford & New York, 2005.

Batty, P., 'Private Politics, Public Strategies: White Advisers and their Aboriginal Subjects', *Oceania*, vol. 75, 2005, pp. 209–21.

Berlant, L., 'Slow Death (Sovereignty, Obesity, Lateral Agency)', *Critical Inquiry*, vol. 33, 2007, pp. 754–80.

Bhabha, H., 'The Other Question' in *The Location of Culture*, Routledge, London & New York, 2004, pp. 94–131.

Brown, N. & Brown, C. (eds), *Talking Straight Out: Stories from the Irati Wanti Campaigne*, Alapalatja Press, Coober Pedy, SA, 2005.

Clark, D. 'The Raw and the Rotten: Punk Cuisine', *Ethnology*, vol. 43, no. 1, 2004, pp. 19–31.

Clarke, P., 'The Aboriginal Cosmic Landscape of Southern South Australia', *Records of the South Australian Museum*, vol. 29, no. 2, 1997, pp. 125–45.

Cowlishaw, G., 'Euphemism, Banality, Propaganda: Anthropology, Public Debate and Indigenous Communities', *Australian Aboriginal Studies*, no. 1, 2003, pp. 2–18.

Cronon, W., 'The Trouble with Wilderness; or, Getting Back to the Wrong Nature', in W. Cronon (ed.), *Uncommon Ground: Rethinking the Human Place in Nature*, W. W. Norton & Company, New York & London, 1996.

Dalley, C. 'Love and the stranger: Intimate relationships between Aboriginal and non-Aboriginal people in a very remote Aboriginal town, northern Australia', *The Australian Journal of Anthropology*, vol. 26, no. 1, 2015, pp. 38–54.

Dalley, C. & Martin, R., 'Dichotomous Identities? Indigenous and non-Indigenous People and the Intercultural in Australia', *The Australian Journal of Anthropology*, 2015, vol. 26, no. 1, 2015, pp. 1–23.

Golub, A., *Leviathans at the Gold Mine: Creating Indigenous and Corporate Actors in Papua New Guinea*, Duke University Press, Durham & London, 2014.

Greer, G., *The Female Eunuch*, Paladin, London, 1971.

Gressier, C., 'Going Feral: Wild Meat Consumption and the Uncanny in Melbourne, Australia', *The Australian Journal of Anthropology*, vol. 27, no. 1, 2016, pp. 49–65.

Hage, G., 'At Home in the Entrails of the West: Multiculturalism, Ethnic Food and Migrant Home-Building ', in H. Grace, G. Hage, L. Johnson, J. Langsworth & M.Symonds (eds), *Home/world: Space, Community and Marginality in Sydney's West*, Annandale, Pluto Press, 1997, pp. 99–153.

Henry, R., *Performing Place, Practising Memories: Aboriginal Australians, Hippies and the State*, Berghahn Books, Oxford & New York, 2012.

Ignatiev, N., *How the Irish Became White*, Routledge, New York, 2009.

Jackson, M., *Minima Ethnographica: Intersubjectivity and the Anthropological Project*, University of Chicago Press, Chicago, 1998.

Kirsch, S., *Reverse Anthropology: Indigenous Analysis of Social and Environmental Relations in New Guinea*, Stanford University Press, Stanford, CA, 2006.

Kowal, E., 'The stigma of White privilege', *Cultural Studies*, vol. 25, no. 3, 2011, pp. 313–33.

Kowal, E., *Trapped in the Gap: Doing Good in Indigenous Australia*, Berghahn Books, New York & Oxford, 2015.

Land, C., *Decolonizing Solidarity: Dilemmas and Directions for Supporters of Indigenous Struggles*, Zed Books, London, 2015.

Langton, M., *"Well, I Heard It on the Radio and I Saw It on the Television": An Essay for the Australian Film Commission on the Politics and Aesthetics of Filmmaking By and About Aboriginal People and Things*, North Sydney, NSW, Australian Film Commission, 1993.

Langton, M., 'Trapped in the Aboriginal Reality Show', *Griffith Review*, vol. 19, 2008, pp. 143–59.

Langton, M., *The Quiet Revolution: Indigenous People and the Resources Boom*, ABC Books, Sydney, 2013.

Lattas, A., 'Aborigines and Contemporary Australian Nationalism: Primordiality and the Cultural Politics of Otherness', *Social Analysis*, vol. 27, 1990, pp. 50–69.

Lea, T., *Bureaucrats and Bleeding Hearts: Indigenous Health in Northern Australia*, UNSW Press, Sydney, 2008.

Lea, T., Kowal, E. & Cowlishaw, G., 'Double Binds', in T. Lea, E. Kowal & G. Cowlishaw (eds), *Moving Anthropology: Critical Indigenous Studies*, Charles Darwin University Press, Darwin, NT, 2006, pp. 1–15.

Lévi-Strauss, C., *The Raw and the Cooked: Mythologiques, Volume One*, The University of Chicago Press, Chicago, 1983 [1969].

Lévi-Strauss, C., 'The Culinary Triangle', in C. Counihan & P. Van Esterik (eds), *Food and Culture: A Reader (Second Edition)*, Routledge, New York & London, 1997, pp. 36–43.

Michaels, E., *Unbecoming*, Duke University Press, Durham, 1997.

Monahan, M., 'The Concept of Privilege: A Critical Appraisal', *South African Journal of Philosophy*, vol. 33, no. 1, 2014, pp. 73–83.

Moreton-Robinson, A., *The White Possessive: Property, Power, and Indigenous Sovereignty*, University of Minnesota Press, Minneapolis, MN, 2015.

Morris, B. & Lattas, A., 'Embedded Anthropology and the Intervention', *Arena Magazine*, no. 107, 2010, pp. 15–20.

Neale, T., 'Regarding Self-Governmentality: Transactional Accidents and

Indigeneity in Cape York Peninsula, Australia', in M. Griffiths (ed.), *Biopolitics and Memory in Postcolonial Literature and Culture*, Ashgate, Farnham, UK, 2016, pp. 29–46.

Peace, A., 'Kill Skippy? Red Meat versus Kangaroo Meat in the Australian Diet', *Australian Humanities Review*, vol. 51, 2011.

Peace, A., Connor, L. & Trigger, D., 'Environmentalism, Culture, Ethnography', *Oceania*, vol. 82, no. 3, 2012, pp. 217–27.

Pearson, N., 'Our Right To Take Responsibility', in *Up From The Mission: Selected Writings*, Black Inc., Melbourne, 2009, pp. 143–71.

Probyn, E., 'Eating Roo: Of Things That Become Food', *New Formations: A journal of culture, theory & politics*, vol. 74, no. 1, 2011, pp. 33–45.

Ramos, A., 'The Hyperreal Indian', *Critique of Anthropology*, vol. 14, no. 2, 1994, pp. 154–71.

Redmond, A., 'Meetings with and without meat: How images of consubstantiality shape intercultural relationships in the northern Kimberley region of Western Australia', *The Australian Journal of Anthropology*, vol. 26, no. 1, 2015, pp. 24–37.

Ritter, D., *The Native Title Market*, UWA Publishing, Crawley, WA, 2009.

Rothwell, N., 'Indigenous Insiders Chart an End to Victimhood', *The Australian Literary Review*, vol. 3, no. 8, 2008, pp. 14–17.

Strakosch, E., *Neoliberal Indigenous Policy: Settler Colonialism and the 'Post-Welfare' State*, Palgrave Macmillan, London, 2015.

Sutton, P., *The Politics of Suffering*, Melbourne University Press, Carlton, Vic, 2009.

Taussig, M., *Mimesis and Alterity: A Particular History of the Senses*, Routledge, New York, 1993.

Tsing, A., *Friction. An Ethnography of Global Connection*, Princeton University Press, Princeton, NJ, 2005.

Tsing, A., *In the Realm of the Diamond Queen: Marginality in an Out-of-the-way Place*, Princeton University Press, Princeton, NJ, 1993.

Vincent, E., 'Hosts and Guests: Interpreting Rockhole Recovery Trips', *Australian Humanities Review*, vol. 53, 2012.

Vincent, E. & Neale, T., 'Unstable Relations: a critical appraisal of indigeneity and environmentalism in contemporary Australia', *The Australian Journal of Anthropology*, In Press <http://onlinelibrary.wiley.com/doi/10.1111/taja.12186\ abstract>.

Waitt, G. & Appleby, B., '"It smells disgusting": plating up kangaroo for a changing climate', *Continuum: Journal of Media & Cultural Studies*, vol. 28, no. 1, 2014, pp. 88–100.

Notes

1   V. Argyrou, *The Logic of Environmentalism: Anthropology, Ecology and Postcoloniality*, Berghahn Books, Oxford & New York, 2005.

2   A. Peace, L. Connor & D. Trigger, 'Environmentalism, Culture, Ethnography', *Oceania*, vol. 82, no. 3, 2013, pp. 217–27.

3   A. Tsing, *In the Realm of the Diamond Queen: Marginality in an Out-of-the-way Place*, Princeton University Press, Princeton, NJ, 1993, p. 1.

4   See: C. Land, *Decolonizing Solidarity: Dilemmas and Directions for Supporters of Indigenous Struggles*, Zed Books, London, 2015, p. 82.

5   N. Brown & C. Brown (eds), *Talking Straight Out: Stories from the Irati Wanti Campaign* dnvols, Alapalatja Press, Coober Pedy, SA, 2005, p. 78.

6   Pseudonyms are used throughout this chapter.

7   M. Langton, *The Quiet Revolution: Indigenous People and the Resources Boom*, ABC Books, Sydney, 2013, pp. 62–64, 78.

8   A. Ramos, 'The Hyperreal Indian', *Critique of Anthropology*, vol. 14, no. 2, 1994, pp. 154–71.

9   *Kungka* is a common word for 'woman' across Central Australian desert languages. The title 'Melbourne Kungkas' was suggested to the activist women involved by one of the Coober Pedy *kungkas*, but for another the very idea of cosmopolitan white university students in the city referring to themselves as '*kungkas*' was a source of hilarity: wheezing, irrepressible laughter broke out whenever she heard the term.

10 Brown and Brown, *Talking Straight Out*, p. 75.

11 P. Clarke, 'The Aboriginal Cosmic Landscape of Southern South Australia', *Records of the South Australian Museum*, vol. 29, no. 2, 1997, p. 136.

12 For details of this agreement, see the entry in the Agreements, Treaties and Negotiated Settlements Project website: ATNS, viewed 10 August 2015 <http://www.atns.net.au/ agreement.asp?EntityID=4485>.

13 A. Golub, *Leviathans at the Gold Mine: Creating Indigenous and Corporate Actors in Papua New Guinea*, Duke University Press, Durham, 2014.

14 S. Kirsch, *Reverse Anthropology: Indigenous Analysis of Social and Environmental Relations in New Guinea*, Stanford University Press, Stanford, 2006, p. xi.

15 P. Batty, 'Private Politics, Public Strategies: White Advisers and their Aboriginal Subjects', *Oceania*, vol. 75, 2005, pp. 209–21; T. Lea, *Bureaucrats and Bleeding Hearts: Indigenous Health in Northern Australia*, UNSW Press, Sydney, 2008; R. Henry, *Performing Place, Practising Memories: Aboriginal Australians, Hippies and the State*, Berghahn Books, Oxford & New York, 2012; C. Dalley, 'Love and the stranger: Intimate relationships between Aboriginal and non-Aboriginal people in a very remote Aboriginal town, northern Australia', *The Australian Journal of Anthropology*, vol. 26, no. 1, 2015,

pp. 38–54; E. Kowal, *Trapped in the Gap: Doing Good in Indigenous Australia*, Berghahn Books, New York, 2015.

16 N. Rothwell, 'Indigenous Insiders Chart an End to Victimhood', *The Australian Literary Review*, vol. 3, no. 8, 2008, pp. 14–17; N. Pearson, 'Our Right To Take Responsibility', in *Up From The Mission: Selected Writings*, Black Inc., Melbourne, 2009, pp. 143–71; P. Sutton, *The Politics of Suffering*, Melbourne University Press, Carlton, Vic, 2009.

17 G. Cowlishaw, 'Euphemism, Banality, Propaganda: Anthropology, Public Debate and Indigenous Communities', *Australian Aboriginal Studies*, no. 1, 2003, pp. 2–18; T. Neale, 'Regarding Self-Governmentality: Transactional Accidents and Indigeneity in Cape York Peninsula, Australia', in M. Griffiths (ed.), *Biopolitics and Memory in Postcolonial Literature and Culture*, Ashgate, Farnham, UK, 2016, pp. 29–46; E. Strakosch, *Neoliberal Indigenous Policy: Settler Colonialism and the 'Post-Welfare' State*, Palgrave Macmillan, London, 2015.

18 B. Morris & A. Lattas, 'Embedded Anthropology and the Intervention', *Arena Magazine*, no. 107, 2010, pp. 15–20.

19 T. Lea, E. Kowal & G. Cowlishaw, 'Double Binds', in T. Lea, E. Kowal & G. Cowlishaw (eds), *Moving Anthropology: Critical Indigenous Studies*, Charles Darwin University Press, Darwin, NT, 2006, p. 2.

20 M. Langton, 'Trapped in the Aboriginal Reality Show', *Griffith Review*, vol. 19, 2008, pp. 143–59.

21 E. Vincent & T. Neale, 'Unstable Relations: a critical appraisal of indigeneity and environmentalism in contemporary Australia', *The Australian Journal of Anthropology*, In Press <http://onlinelibrary.wiley.com/doi/10.1111/taja.12186\ abstract>.

22 Land, *Decolonizing Solidarity*, p. 164.

23 E. Michaels, *Unbecoming*, Duke University Press, Durham, 1997, pp. 44–8.

24 M. Langton, *"Well, I Heard It on the Radio and I Saw It on the Television": An Essay for the Australian Film Commission on the Politics and Aesthetics of Filmmaking By and About Aboriginal People and Things*, Australian Film Commission, North Sydney, NSW, 1993, p. 33.

25 Argyrou, *The Logic of Environmentalism*, p. 71.

26 ibid., p. 72.

27 E. Vincent, 'Hosts and Guests: Interpreting Rockhole Recovery Trips', *Australian Humanities Review*, vol. 53, 2012.

28 A. Tsing, *Friction: An Ethnography of Global Connection*, Princeton University Press, Princeton, NJ, 2005.

29 'Shame job' (letter to the editor), *West Coast Sentinel*, November 13, 2008, p. 4.

30 Information on the Far West Coast native title determination is available from the website of South Australia Native Title Services (SANTS). See <http://www.nativetitlesa.org/our-news/sants-welcomes-far-west-coast-native-title-determination>. Last accessed 15 February 2016.

31 D. Ritter, *The Native Title Market*, UWA Press, Crawley, WA, 2009.

32 M. Jackson, *Minima Ethnographica: Intersubjectivity and the Anthropological Project*, University of Chicago Press, Chicago, 1998, p. 16.

33 G. Hage, 'At Home in the Entrails of the West: Multiculturalism, Ethnic Food and Migrant Home-Building', in H. Grace, et al. (eds), *Home/world: Space, Community and Marginality in Sydney's West*, Pluto Press, Annandale, 1997, p. 141.

34 ibid., p. 141.

35 A handful of heavily involved greenies had come to find this kind of driving thrilling and prided themselves on their learned competence on the sand, becoming competitive with each other about their acquisition of skills held by Aunty Joan Mob members. I'll admit I was filled with excessive pride when I was once praised as a 'deadly driver', even if the compliment came from a 10-year-old.

36 L. Berlant, 'Slow Death (Sovereignty, Obesity, Lateral Agency)', *Critical Inquiry*, vol. 33, 2007, pp. 754–80.

37 C. Dalley & R. Martin, 'Dichotomous identities? Indigenous and non-Indigenous people and the intercultural in Australia', *The Australian Journal of Anthropology*, vol. 26, no. 1, 2015, p. 8.

38 E. Kowal, 'The stigma of White privilege', *Cultural Studies*, vol. 25, no. 3, 2011, pp. 1–21.

39 M. Taussig, *Mimesis and Alterity: A Particular History of the Senses*, Routledge, New York, 1993; H. K. Bhabha, 'The Other Question', in *The Location of Culture*, Routledge, London & New York, 2004 [1994].

40 Taussig, *Mimesis and Alterity*, p. 7.

41 ibid., p. 240.

42 ibid.

43 Bhabha, *The Location of Culture*, p. 126.

44 A. Lattas, 'Aborigines and Contemporary Australian Nationalism: Primordiality and the Cultural Politics of Otherness', *Social Analysis*, vol. 27, 1990, p. 55.

45 Jackson, *Minima Ethnographica*, p. 97.

46 Taussig, *Mimesis and Alterity*, p. 1.

47 ibid., p. 186.

48 W. Cronon, 'The Trouble with Wilderness; or, Getting Back to the Wrong Nature', in W. Cronon (ed.), *Uncommon Ground: Rethinking the Human Place*

in Nature, W.W. Norton & Company, New York & London, 1996, p. 80.

49 D. Clark, 'The Raw and the Rotten: Punk Cuisine', *Ethnology*, vol. 43, no. 1, 2004, pp. 19–31.

50 C. Lévi-Strauss, 'The Culinary Triangle', in C. Counihan & P. Van Esterik (eds), *Food and Culture: A Reader (Second Edition)*, Routledge, New York & London, 1997, pp. 36–43.

51 C. Lévi-Strauss, *The Raw and the Cooked: Mythologiques, Volume One*, The University of Chicago Press, Chicago, 1983 [1969].

52 G. Greer, *The Female Eunuch*, Paladin, London, 1971, p. 38.

53 G. Waitt & B. Appleby, '"It smells disgusting": plating up kangaroo for a changing climate', *Continuum: Journal of Media & Cultural Studies*, vol. 28, no. 1, 2014, pp. 88–100; C. Gressier, 'Going Feral: Wild Meat Consumption and the Uncanny in Melbourne, Australia', *The Australian Journal of Anthropology*, vol. 27, no. 1, 2016, pp. 49-65; E. Probyn, 'Eating Roo: Of Things That Become Food', *New Formations: A Journal of Culture, Theory & Politics*, vol. 74, no. 1, 2011, pp. 33–45; A. Peace, 'Kill Skippy? Red Meat versus Kangaroo Meat in the Australian Diet', *Australian Humanities Review*, vol. 51, 2011.

54 T. Redmond, 'Meetings with and without meat: How images of consubstantiality shape intercultural relationships in the northern Kimberley region of Western Australia', *The Australian Journal of Anthropology*, vol. 26, no. 1, 2015, p. 27.

55 ibid., p. 27.

56 The Australian bustard is here called 'bush turkey'. The Southern hairy-nosed wombat is endemic to this region.

57 M. Monahan, 'The Concept of Privilege: A Critical Appraisal', *South African Journal of Philosophy*, vol. 33, no. 1, 2014, p. 75.

58 Land, *Decolonizing Solidarity*, p. 28.

59 See: A. Moreton-Robinson, *The White Possessive: Property, Power, and Indigenous Sovereignty*, University of Minnesota Press, 2015.

60 Land, *Decolonizing Solidarity*, p. 31.

61 ibid., pp. 31-3.

62 Monahan, *South African Journal of Philosophy*, p. 75.

63 Land, *Decolonizing Solidarity*, pp. 84–111.

64 N. Ignatiev, *How the Irish Became White*, Routledge, New York, 2009.

65 Personal communication, 2015.

8

INDIGENOUS-GREEN KNOWLEDGE COLLABORATIONS AND THE JAMES PRICE POINT DISPUTE

Stephen Muecke

A Major Indigenous-Green Alliance

Joseph Roe battled for four years to protect Walmadany (James Price Point, near Broome, Western Australia) in the name of the *Bugarrigarra* and ultimately died of heart failure in 2012. Two years later, the former federal Greens leader, Bob Brown, awarded him the honour of Environmentalist of the Year. During the long campaign to stop the Woodside oil and gas consortium from constructing a major gas plant and port, Roe had said, 'I don't have to be an environmental activist. If I do my job and look after country, protection for the environment will flow from our law and culture'.[1] This is exactly the kind of confidence that a senior *maja*, law man, can and should put in the power of *Bugarrigarra* (traditional law and culture), the law for which his grandfather Paddy Roe urged us to 'dig little bit more deep' to access under the surface appearance of things.[2] *Bugarrigarra* is manifest in 'living country' at sites designated as having 'something there', a power. It cannot operate by itself; it needs humans to cherish, sustain and actively look after it with activities on country. So while Joseph Roe asserted his responsibilities towards the *Bugarrigarra*, and did not need to claim any 'greenie' status, the campaign he was a leader of was strongly supported by a multiplicity of green organisations. I would claim it to be the most significant, and successful, Indigenous–green alliance in Australia's history;

significant because of the large numbers of organisations involved, and the financial and environmental stakes; successful because of the positive outcome for both the Indigenous anti-gas group and the greens with whom they enjoyed an intimate collaboration for a long period.

The Case for Institution-based Analysis

I want to think of the *Bugarrigarra* as an *institution*, rather than, say, the spiritual branch of a *culture*. Culture is the more amorphous concept, and, in the context of colonisation, weaker, because cultures tend to be dismissed as 'merely relative' compared to the solid factual grasp that science, or some other institutionally based knowledge, is supposed to have on the world. Mining companies come to Goolarabooloo country armed with this realist apparatus, strategically plugged in to *their* arrays of institutions that precisely articulate *financial* investment with the *objectivity* of the hard sciences (geology, chemistry, etc.) with the *technological* capacities of engineering, the *rights* afforded by the law and the *executive* powers of politics. This way of seeing the modern institutional complex – the financial-industrial-law enforcement complex – more usefully replaces catch-all concepts like 'society' and 'culture' because we can follow their courses of actions more precisely as they come prepared to industrialise, rolling out the universalist modernisation script of progress.

This is an approach championed by philosopher of anthropology Bruno Latour as a way of accounting for how 'the various ways in which the central institutions of our cultures produce truth'.[3] In *An Inquiry into Modes of Existence*, he focuses a philosophical anthropological gaze on the 'Moderns', that is, on Western European institutions. In that book, he wants to turn around a long history of mistrust of institutions, claiming the very act of 'pointing one's finger at institutions might work as a weapon to criticise them, but surely not as a tool for re-establishing confidence in established truths'.[4] It's a moderate position, because this kind of anti-institutional attitude is found more at Left and Right political extremes. The former, imagining themselves at the revolutionary barricades, have a long-cultivated mistrust of Ideological State Apparatuses. The latter, inheritors of Reaganesque attacks on 'big government', tolerate institutions only to the extent that they do the bidding of corporations.

To the Goolarabooloo mob and their allies, the industrial push into their country looks like colonisation as usual, in that it involves appropriating ancestral lands they have battled to protect on earlier occasions. But in other respects it is a new kind of game. Local Nyikina leader, Anne Poelina, is well aware of the historical exploitation of her own people in the earlier pearling and pastoral industries, but today she analyses the new 'neo-liberal context, with…the ever-increasing threat of massive industrialisation…by multi-national mining corporations – the new colonisers'. She pointedly adds: 'we are all being colonized: it is not a black or white question any longer'.[5] What differs with this new *extraction* economy, despite its promises of jobs for locals and financial compensation packages, is that it is even more disengaged from the region than pearling and pastoralism were, as classic instances of *settler* colonialism. FIFO (fly-in fly-out) workers are but one symptom of how a global corporation aspires to extract value efficiently by avoiding local infrastructure investment.

How did a core group of about a hundred Goolarabooloo successfully oppose the juggernaut lead by Woodside and its joint venture partners, which included Royal Dutch Shell, Japan Australia LNG and BHP Billiton? What part did the *Bugarrigarra* play in this? If I can provide an answer to these two questions, I think that it will furnish a glimpse of how an institutional analysis works by giving full weight to the ontological underpinnings of institutional knowledges. But first, I have to define 'Goolarabooloo' as a social and geographic entity. The word does not refer to a language or a 'tribe', even though Daisy Bates, the first European recorder of the word, saw it as a tribal name in 1901.[6] It is more interesting than that. It cannot be reduced to language groups like Bardi, Yawuru, Karajeri or Ngumbal, or to their territories, because it is underpinned by, and organised for the maintenance of, the *Bugarrigarra* songlines that traverse the Dampier Peninsula and beyond. These become manifest in the annual initiation ceremonies that put boys through the law; that *make* Aboriginal men. These are run by the *maja* who have the sole authority to open the law grounds and reanimate the *Bugarrigarra*.

During the anti-gas campaign, from 2009 to 2013, activists occupied camps along the coast. These camps are regular stops on the Lurujarri Heritage Trail run annually by the Goolarabooloo mob. Senior members of the Roe family were living permanently at Walmadany, an operations centre for the campaign, not far from where Woodside had built its compound. Some of the activists had been on the Trail at an earlier time, and were attracted back to Broome to lend a hand during the campaign. These people were known to the Goolarabooloo; others had to get elders' approval to camp at Walmadany, where there were up to 100 people at any given time. They did various kinds of jobs: some had scientific expertise, others legal, and others did media liaison work. Different kinds of knowledge were thus put into action, always under the direction of Goolarabooloo elders who chaired meetings and vetted proposals for 'actions' like lock-ons or blockades.

The activists, most untutored in anthropology, nevertheless came to understand the primacy of the *Bugarrigarra* and of the connection to 'living country'. These underpinned what I would call the concept of Goolarabooloo *world*. This world, in the sense of 'cosmos', is not clearly circumscribed. It is a network of numerous kinds of beings and entities: human beings, animals, plants, the ocean and freshwater sources, the stars, spirits (good and bad), ancestors from the *Bugarrigarra*, law and culture (including songs, stories and ceremonies, with all their concepts and feelings). While people are *maja* (bosses) for this world, in the sense of being responsible for its management, it is much more vast than their brief lives and it is out of their control. It is a network where everything is linked up, like the World Wide Web,[7] and it traditionally has strong links to other worlds, like the world of the Bardi up the road. Some beings have stronger links than others. Spiritual beings like *ngajayi*, for example, are simultaneously manifest in a story, in traces in the landscape, and in certain star formations. Today, aspects of the whitefella world can be incorporated in the Goolarabooloo world, but they tend to be peripheral rather than central.

For the Goolarabooloo mob, it is their whole world that is under threat because of industrialisation, not just a part of it; not for instance, the 'natural' part, an assumption that greenie sympathisers still make the mistake of assuming. Just as for Achuar people in Brazil, described by Phillipe Descola,[8] the Goolarabooloo (or any other Australian Indigenous community) do not have a singular concept of nature. Between the world of the Moderns and the world of the Goolarabooloo there is no clear common ground that is in dispute, and, importantly, their differences are not 'merely cultural'. Common ground would have to be found through negotiation. Of central value in the 'world of Woodside' is the 'natural' resource, methane gas, and they are passionate about it for strange financial reasons, while in the world of the Goolarabooloo the *Bugarrigarra* is of central value, and they are passionate about it for strange spiritual reasons.

Unlike the many anthropologists and philosophers who have endorsed an 'ontological turn' in their fields, I am not interested in the 'nature' or the essence of given entities. Following Latour (following Gabriele Tarde), I am more interested in their *attachments*, or how they *belong* (which is the word used in Indigenous Australia, where the verb 'to be' is not used):

> The verb 'to be' cannot capture the grid. In his last book, *Psychologie économique* (1902), Gabriel Tarde...set us on the right path: everything changes if we agree to choose the verb 'to have'. From the verb 'to be', Tarde says, we cannot draw anything interesting that would involve interests, except identity with the self, the 'easy way out' of substance; but from the verb 'to have', we could get a whole alternative philosophy, for the good reason that *avidity* (unlike *identity*) defines in reversible fashion the being that *possesses* and the being that *is possessed*. There is no better definition of any existent whatsoever beyond this list of *the other beings* through which it must, it can, it seeks to pass...[9]

So, despite the appearance that mining companies like Woodside hold their resources at an objective distance – out there in 'nature' – it is actually the case that they go to enormous trouble to secure their attachments (the rights to explore and exploit, the geological surveys, the commitment of capital, the engineering deployments, the political facilitation, the police protection, and so on). The pathways to secure these attachments are what an institutionally based analysis needs to follow, just as the Goolarabooloo attachment to the *Bugarrigarra* is networked and complex in a quite different way.

As appointed *maja* for law and culture, the Goolarabooloo elders make a point of their strong connection to country. The matriarchs of the family were two of Paddy Roe's daughters, one of whom, Teresa, is still alive. They locate their conception Dreamings (via spirits called *rayi*) in the same mid-Dampier country north of Broome. These connections are being tested in a native title case at the moment; a case contested by two other claimant groups, the Jabirr Jabirr and Bindunbur.[10] The Jabirr Jabirr, in particular, assert connection to country through genealogical descent, while the Goolarabooloo assert custodianship through genealogical ascent, from the *rayi* to the children.[11] The Jabirr Jabirr and Bindunbur claimants are backed by the Kimberley Land Council (KLC), which also played a key role in negotiating with Woodside and the Western Australian government. When Wayne Bergman was chair of the KLC he was working towards getting the gas plant built, and had the support of certain Jabirr Jabirr families, while cutting the Goolarabooloo out of the negotiations.[12] Pre-existing fractures in the Broome Indigenous community (traditional family rivalries for the most part) were turned into a major rift by the 'gas business' and this rivalry continues with the three-way contested native title claim over the same country today.

Cissy Djiagween, a Jabirr Jabirr leader, was crying when she was interviewed in mid-April 2013 after Woodside pulled out of the gas project. The Goolarabooloo supporters were down at the 'Roey' hotel celebrating the decision. 'I feel betrayed by my people', she said. 'Woodside had got our spirit up. It was our country and this was a way we could work the country to benefit us, our children and generations to come with health, education and jobs'.[13] She was referring to the $1.5 billion compensation package that was promised if the project had gone ahead. The way she put it, she wanted the country to be put to 'work' for the basic services she mentions, while her opponent, Teresa Roe, had a different attitude: 'we bin there from day one, from *Bugarrigarra*, and we don't want the country to get destroyed'.[14] While he was alive, Paddy Roe had the endorsement of Jabirr Jabirr elders, and his custodianship claim was not disputed. That all changed with the fight over the gas plant, and Jabirr Jabirr descendants, most of whom took little part in law and culture, began reasserting themselves.

As part of the pro-gas campaign, the Jabirr Jabirr were aligned with a huge array of institutions: Woodside (with its several partners), the KLC, the state government, the Murdoch press, and the marketing agents for the gas industry. But in order to reassert themselves as Aboriginal people and traditional owners, they had to demonstrate participation in ceremony and knowledge of country. These are the factors that relate to the *Bugarrigarra*. It is the central institution, tying together all aspects of the Indigenous 'cosmos', as defined above, that the Goolarabooloo seek to protect and maintain through knowledge and ritual performance. And as the Indigenous group at the heart of the anti-gas campaign, orchestrating its efforts, it is aligned with another set of institutions: local conservation groups such as Environs Kimberley, the No Gas Community and Save the Kimberley; national conservation groups such as the Australian Conservation Foundation and The Wilderness Society; various artists such as the Pigram family of musicians, Missy Higgins and John Butler; and, the organisation of fundraising protest concerts in major cities. This green alliance – with former-businessman and president of the Australian Conservation Foundation, Geoffrey Cousins, making that argument for them – was unconvinced by the business case put by Woodside and others. All of these green organisations acknowledge the power of the *Bugarrigarra*, and it is of interest that the Jabirr Jabirr claimants had to revive their interests. The KLC, for its part, has to acknowledge 'traditional law and culture' as core business, even if their day-to-day organisation does not directly engage with it.

The *Bugarrigarra* is an institution with its own truths and what Latour calls 'felicity conditions' that have stood the test of time, persisting through millennia. Traditional owners are inalienably *attached* to it, and white people, even if their knowledge is scant, can also become attached to it as a kind of icon of the sacred. They see glimpses of ritual (as a law ground is pointed out to them with some reverence); they hear mysterious stories of spiritual belonging that only locals can tell. For anthropologists, the truths of the *Bugarrigarra* are brought out more strongly: sacred objects are shown and songs given their meanings; the name of the most sacred ancestor uttered *sotto voce*, and, out of respect for the secret, glossed in the ethnographies as 'that man'. All this knowledge is intimately tied up, *attached*, to the *Bugarrigarra*. It can only persist in performances that tie humans to places and to other 'totemic' beings in cosmic networks. It does not *belong* in museums.

The point of institutional analysis is to investigate how organisations that sustain kinds of knowledges appear to other institutions that test or extend that knowledge. In that optic, the *Bugarrigarra* can't be seen as sequestered somewhere in remote corners of traditional culture and destined eventually to disappear because of the advance of secular, objective forms of truth. Those have not yet even managed to eliminate Catholicism! It can take root and flower in the romantic imaginations of somewhat naive greenies. After interrogation by ethnographers, traditional owners find their knowledge tested in traumatic native title hearings. As an institution, the *Bugarrigarra has things going for it* (i.e. attachments) among a necessary plurality of institutions with their different modes of existence and felicity conditions. It has been able to persist post-colonisation. It is ontologically distinct, but I want another philosophical term, since I have argued that its distinctiveness is not due to what it *is*, but because of what it *has*. I'll call it a *mode of belonging.*

Turtles, Whales, Bilbies, Scientists and Other Critters

If the *Bugarrigarra* is a mode of belonging that can continue to attract others to it, and can have its concerns translated into other knowledges (like Western law or social sciences), then in some respects it behaves like other institutions that strive to persist. What I want to investigate in this section is the crossover between the biological sciences and Goolarabooloo knowledge of the environment, what is sometimes dubbed traditional ecological knowledge (TEK). The problem here can be simply stated: what makes both TEK and Western science reliable forms of knowledge when their methods are so different? The definition of reliability, or repeatability, is that knowledge can persist though time, and across great distances, without losing validity. But while science might achieve this with *observing*, measuring, counting and recording (calendars, tables of statistics, maps and graphs), the Goolarabooloo might do it by *paying attention* to 'cosmic alignments' (as when Indigenous ecological knowledges were shared with Nia Emmanouil 'in the context of the six seasons': 'When the black kites are flying over the dunes, the salmon are running'[15]). In this section, encounters between these ways of knowing are foregrounded by the gas

261

plant dispute.

Woodside's 'hold' on the gas, before the pipeline was even built, was weakened at its point of overlap with institutions with environmental concerns. Woodside would, of course, like its passage to the gas to be unfettered by any other beings, like plants or animals, but it is obliged to get the usual environmental clearances from the settler government.[16] These come in the form of plausible and reliable knowledge about what is 'in' the immediate environment, and how it might be affected by gas mining activities.

Malcolm Lindsay was a doctoral student in marine biology when I first met him. He'd been on the Lurujarri Trail, worked as an activist and 'citizen scientist' during the campaign, and now works for Environs Kimberley. He has also had jobs as an environmental consultant. He was a good person to talk to about the encounter between public science (a university tradition), private science (contracted and not public domain) and citizen science (non-professional). We spoke in 2013 about the importance of scientists having a good reputation, deriving from their university training or ongoing connection. But once consultants are contracted privately, their work is limited by the scope of the contract. The area covered can be narrow, or it is a 'clock-ticking exercise', and this scope might be contained to increase the chances of getting environmental approvals. He gave me the example of turtles at James Price Point (JPP):

> The turtle nesting survey at JPP was done by the eco-
> logical consultants for the proponents. They said, 'Okay,
> we're going to walk the beaches and look for turtle tracks
> when they've nested. We are not just going to focus on
> the project area, we're also going to have a buffer zone,
> we're going to walk 10–30 km of coastline. [But] that's

too far to walk, so we're obviously going to restrict where we walk, because if there's a rocky headland, obviously turtles are not going to nest there'. So they started defining what they *thought* was turtle-nesting habitat. They walked it and didn't find any turtle nests.

And of course the Goolarabooloo have gone, 'Well we know there's turtles there. We eat eggs, and we have in the past'. And they were looking in the wrong spot.

So then we did a survey, and we examined the full extent of the 30 km. And Phillip [Roe] and Richard [Hunter] said, 'Oh don't worry about walking all that, all you need to walk is between JPP and the Gully', that's to the north, where the black sands are, 'that's the only place they nest'.

And of course, that's where we found them, in the only place they nested. And it looks like ridiculous and inappropriate turtle-nesting habitat. It's more like a scrabbly, pebbly beach. You've got Minariny up the road with beautiful white beaches, but the turtles don't like that. For some reason they like that spot. So by having the TOs [traditional owners] telling us, 'No, look here', instead of *us* defining what was turtle nesting habitat, we let the turtles define it.[17]

Madeline Goddard, who also worked on the turtle survey as a citizen scientist, was a Bachelor of Science graduate from Melbourne. She corroborates this account:

The turtle project is actually really interesting because the ecological consultancy that did the environmental assessment on the place, RPS, concluded that no turtles nest on the beaches. They found one old nest site they weren't even sure they could conclude on. But they did a desktop study, which is quite common for ecological consultancies; they'll look on Google Earth or work out what could potentially be there and then go, 'Oh, that's too rocky for nesting'. So they disregarded all these beaches where a lot of turtles do nest on.

Whereas we went, 'Hey, Phil, where are the turtles?'

And he went, 'Oh, they're from here, to here.'

And so we designed our methodology encompassing that traditional knowledge of where the turtles were. [18]

This point about the incorporation of TEK is crucial. One of the factors that makes the sciences reliable is peer review, the collective input from colleagues. The fact that the citizen scientists included Phillip Roe as a colleague made their knowledge *more* reliable. This suggests to me that universalist modernist science (attached to quick 'Google Earth' and 'desktop' surveys) is not *paying attention* in the way that the Goolarabooloo offer. A 'rebooted' environmental science will thus be redesigned with TEK extensions, and this is the way that scientists like Malcolm Lindsay now proceed at Environs Kimberley with Indigenous colleagues and ranger programs.

Madeline Goddard was able to follow up by taking the citizen scientists' turtle survey to a conference that exposed the limitations of the privatised science:

[DW] was the lead scientist on the turtle report that we were presenting on. With citizen/community science it is really important to incorporate that traditional knowledge, local knowledge. If you come in as a scientist, assuming that the textbook is right, that turtles won't nest near rocky areas, you are disregarding a wealth of knowledge that the people who have lived on that land have had for a very long time. And so, we were incorporating that into the story of James Price Point and the struggle for development and how we'd found all these turtle nests on these beaches where the ecological consultancy had deemed there to be none. And as we were doing this...there was Tegan [Mossop] and Kevin Smith who were presenting with me. They'd worked a lot on the turtle research.

And (laugh) [DW] was sitting in the first row *glowering* at us, this person who'd just presented about all this amazing research that Woodside was doing, spending thousands of dollars...a strange thing that happened, throughout this whole turtle conference, people were talking about scientific research being the equivalent of turtle conservation[...]They'd highlight that industry and development was the number one threat to the sea turtles globally and that there was this huge sea turtle decline. All of them are either vulnerable or endangered. Critically endangered in the case of the hawksbill turtle, which we actually found nesting on the beach at JPP. You know, an internationally, critically endangered species was nesting on the beach. And the structure of the nesting beaches, due to oil and gas developments, is actually the number one thing that is causing the decline.

SM: They'd acknowledge that?

MG: Yes, they'd acknowledge that (...) but their offset was to not interfere with the Lacipede Islands, where a far greater number of turtles do nest, but, they are saying, we'll protect that, but their dredge plumes would exceed the Lacipede Islands, and destroy all these turtle nests…so it's a kind of crazy duality of saying one thing, but knowing they are doing this opposite thing.

So, we're at this conference, and presented our story of how we utilised traditional knowledge and how we had gone about really scientifically, involving the community, involving TOs, to produce a report that was really, rigorous, independent and peer-reviewed by top turtle experts and (laugh) [DW], the guy who wrote the report informing the environmental assessment of JPP development, was sitting there looking increasingly awkward and kind of angry and I ended up later (…) bumping into him (laugh), 'Oh, hey, oh it's you', and he just looked so awkward and started gushing apologies, 'I didn't even think to look on those beaches. I just thought, um, this is what we do…but…'

And so I said 'Yeah, look, you know, the virtues of traditional knowledge, and bit more time in the field', and you know trying to understand him on the point of view that you are limited by the amount of time you get in the field because he is in Perth and all his research is in Perth. Probably got, to be fair to him, half a day in the field to work this out, that's how these things go, there's a huge…

SM: So Woodside put these constraints on him?

MG: Ah, yeah, Woodside *do* put these sort of constraints on. When we had a bit more of a conversation, we both realised that, pretty much exactly the same time that I was leading the whale research at Murdudun and he was leading the whale research that had concluded that there were 1,000 whales within 8 kilometres of the coast, and because I'd been using social media, such as Facebook, to get our results out there, he'd heard of us and known that we'd already gone ahead of that mark, we'd already counted over 1,000 whales, just within six weeks of counting. So he said to us, 'Oh, you're the girls that have found far more whales than I have'. And we both got a bit cagey from this point…and I was being quite nice to him. I asked him what sort of considerations he took in the flight times because they'd done it all by aerial flights and whether they took into consideration the tides, which up here at 10 metres are very big, and he said to me, 'Oh, you think that tides have an influence? I didn't even think of that, I just go when Woodside gives me the plane'.

Malcolm Lindsay and his team also intervened on behalf of the bilbies of Dampier Peninsula and gave these previously invisible beings a presence through the report and public discussion. As with some of the other critters, such as the new species of spinner dolphin that was confirmed, there was a risk of the private scientists not finding them. Lindsay stressed the importance of 'having people on the ground for a long time, because endangered animals are by nature very rare and hard to find'. The other consultants had come from Perth, were staying in Broome and only taking day trips to look for the animals. Lindsay had a core team of three and they spent six to eight months looking. While he was a qualified scientist, the others had different skills:

...there was Damo, who'd lived with the Goolarabooloo for a while. Non-Indigenous, but he'd spent a lot of time out in the bush and had incredible tracking and bush skills. And there's Craig who's a Koori man from southern NSW. Same thing, he'd done a lot of tracking with his mum when he was younger.[19]

Malcolm, as the ecologist, ended up doing 'all the *gardiya* [whitefella] stuff, drawing the maps, entering the GPS points, taking the photos, cataloguing and writing the report'.[20] They were able to confirm five bilbies and the possibility of ten. The bilbies they found were active and using their burrows, but there were confusing things, like an absence of scat. A bilby expert Malcolm spoke to considered the usual way to survey:

...is flying over in a helicopter, and see their burrows, 'cos they have a large spoil mound. And you can imagine lush vegetation with a big, fresh pindan pile. It is quite visible – in the Tanami Desert. And I said to him, 'Oh you won't see it here, there's too much foliage, undergrowth of acacias, etc. He said to me, 'Oh well if you can't see it from the air, they won't be there'.

And that was his expert opinion. The danger with that, according to Lindsay, is that when such an expert opinion is delivered, the ecologist will *not* assume that 'an absence of evidence is evidence of absence', but the corporate boss will make that leap for the executive summary. These are the kinds of shortcuts that can be made in the writing up, to enhance the chances of environmental clearance. Another example Lindsay gave was of a fish count:

They did a comparison with other studies and found JPP had a much higher abundance of these predatory fish, apex predators, ones that typically get lost when you have ecosystem damage. There is a similar high abundance at other places in the Kimberley, the Pilbara and the Great Barrier Reef. So you've got a really abundant, healthy ecosystem up here. When that then went into the main document, they removed the Great Barrier Reef comparison, because in terms of PR that would be really bad.[21]

Conclusion

The JPP dispute was the occasion for a major green–Indigenous collaboration. I have argued that there were two interconnected 'worlds' in the dispute, composed of different institutional configurations. The modern industrial complex deploys a realist scientific philosophy to drive towards the valuable commodity it wants to extract, but can be interrupted when legal requirements for environmental probity can activate the agency of non-human species whose survival is threatened. As it happens, most of these non-humans are linked to the central institution of the Goolarabooloo world, the *Bugarrigarra*, whose dreaming tracks traverse the country.

It was on behalf of the *Bugarrigarra*, and the maintenance of traditional law and culture, that the Goolarabooloo were prepared to fight to the bitter end, while other Indigenous groups in Broome battled for the compensatory benefits that the gas plant deal, brokered by the KLC, had on offer. Rather than being comprehensively dismissed or overridden historically, the *Bugarrigarra* has persisted as the central institution that offered a number of concepts and modes of belonging that served to animate the alliances that the Goolarabooloo was able to forge with the constellation of largely green organisations that campaigned against the gas plant.

With that conceptual apparatus in place, I looked at evidence for the failure of what I have called 'privatised science' in the dispute. Examples of alternative modes of generating knowledge, citizen sciences that included traditional owners as colleagues, demonstrated a scientific rigour that *extended* rather than limited the scope of their inquiries. Through more extended immersion in country, and the learning of Indigenous ways of paying attention, environmental scientists have embarked on rebooting their disciplines with the inclusion of TEK and traditional owner colleagues.[22]

Bibliography

Bates, D., *The Native Tribes of Western Australia*, National Library of Australia, Canberra, 1985.

Benterrak, K., Muecke S. & Roe P., *Reading the Country: Introduction to Nomadology*, 3rd edn, re.Press, Carlton, Vic, 2014.

Botsman, P. 'Law Below the Top Soil', 2012 <http://www.savethekimberley.com/site/wp-content/uploads/2012/10/Botsman-report-October-2012.pdf>.

Burton, A. (dir.), *Sunset Ethnography*, 2014 <https://vimeo.com/113130961>.

Cordingley, G., 'Hopes die with gas hub decision,' *The West Australian*, 15 April 2013.

Descola, P., *Beyond Nature and Culture*, University of Chicago Press, Chicago, 2013.

Emmanouil, N., 'You've got to drown in it', *PAN: Philosophy Activism Nature*, no. 11, 2014, pp. 41–7.

Environs Kimberley, 'Valuable and Endangered Working Together to Understand and Manage Threats to Monsoon Vine Thickets of the Dampier Peninsula, A Summary of Key Findings Environs Kimberley West Kimberley Nature Project 2011–2013', 2013 <http://www.environskimberley.org.au/wp-content/uploads/2012/02/

MVT_Valuable-and-endangered-Final.pdf>.

Glowczewski, B., *Totemic Becomings. The Cosmopolitics of the Dreaming/Devires Totemicos*, n-1 publications, Sao Paulo, 2015.

Goddard, M., Buckton, C., Leahy, L. & Lindsay, M. 'A community survey of humpback whales, *Megaptera novaeangliae*, near the site of the proposed James Price Point Browse Liquefied Natural Gas precinct', Report prepared for the Goolarabooloo and Broome Community No Gas Campaign, March 2013 <https://kimberleycommunitywhaleresearch.files. wordpress.com/2013/03/a-community-survey-of-humpback-whales-near-james-price-point-march-2013.pdf>.

Latour, B., *The Making of Law: An Ethnography of the Conseil d'Etat*, Polity Press, Cambridge, UK, 2010.

Latour, B., *An Inquiry Into Modes of Existence: An Athropology of the Moderns*, Harvard University Press, Cambridge, Mass, 2013.

Lindsay, M., 'Evidence of the Greater Bilby, Macrotis lagotis, at the site of the proposed James Price Point Browse LNG Precinct', report prepared for the Goolarabooloo and Broome No Gas Community, October 2011.

Poelina, A. (dir.), *Three Sisters: Women of High Degree*, Madjulla Inc., 2015.

Notes

1   G. Negus, paraphrasing Roe, personal communication with author, March 2012.

2   K. Benterrak, S. Muecke, & P. Roe, *Reading the Country: Introduction to Nomadology*, 3rd edn, re.Press, Carlton, Vic, 2014.

3   B. Latour, *The Making of Law: An Ethnography of the Conseil d'Etat*, Polity Press, Cambridge, 2010, p. ix.

4   B. Latour, *An Inquiry Into Modes of Existence: An Athropology of the Moderns*, Harvard University Press, Cambridge, 2013, p. 4.

5   See Anne Poelina's film, *Three Sisters: Women of High Degree*, 2015, <http://majala.com.au>.

6   'Kularrabulu (kularra = west, or seacoast; bulu = people)'. See: D. Bates, *The Native Tribes of Western Australia*, National Library of Australia, Canberra, 1985, pp. 89–90.

7   Barbara Glowczewski writes of the 'cognitive similarity between the reticular network of Dreaming songlines and the...hyperlink mapping of the internet', (*Totemic Becomings. The Cosmopolitics of the Dreaming/Devires Totemicos*, n-1 publications, Sao Paulo, 2015, p. 31).

8   P. Descola, *Beyond Nature and Culture*, University of Chicago Press, Chicago, 2013.

9   Latour, *An Inquiry Into Modes of Existence*, pp. 424–5.

10 The current native title claims for these groups are Goolarabooloo People (WC2013/008), Jabirr Jabirr (WC2013/007) and Bindunbur (Area B) (WC2014/003).

11 Thanks to Jennifer Biddle for suggesting *ascent*. The author's book, *The Children's Country: The Struggles of the Goolarabooloo in North-West Australia*, is in progress.

12 See Peter Botsman's report for Save the Kimberley organisation, 'Law Below the Top Soil', 2012 <http://www.savethekimberley.com/site/wp-content/uploads/2012/10/Botsman-report-October-2012.pdf>, p. 21.

13 G. Cordingley, 'Hopes die with gas hub decision', *The West Australian*, 15 April 2013.

14 A. Burton (dir.), *Sunset Ethnography*, 2014 <https://vimeo.com/113130961>.

15 N. Emmanouil, 2014, 'You've got to drown in it', *PAN: Philosophy Activism Nature*, no. 11, pp. 41–7.

16 For a detailed account of the political history of the strategic assessment process, see: Botsman, 'Law Below the Top Soil'.

17 M. Lindsay, interview with author in Broome, 10 May 2013.

18 M. Goddard, interview with author in Broome, 4 May 2013. See also the full report of their work: M. Goddard, C. Buckton, L. Leahy & M. Lindsay, 'A community survey of humpback whales, *Megaptera novaeangliae*, near the site of the proposed James Price Point Browse Liquefied Natural Gas precinct', Report prepared for the Goolarabooloo and Broome Community No Gas Campaign, March 2013 <https://kimberleycommunitywhaleresearch.files.wordpress.com/2013/03/a-community-survey-of-humpback-whales-near-james-price-point-march-2013.pdf>.

19 M. Lindsay, interview with author.

20 M. Lindsay, 'Evidence of the Greater Bilby, *Macrotis lagotis*, at the site of the proposed James Price Point Browse LNG Precinct', report prepared for the Goolarabooloo and Broome No Gas Community, October 2011.

21 M. Lindsay, interview with author.

22 For an account of a recent project, see: Environs Kimberley, 'Valuable and Endangered Working Together to Understand and Manage Threats to Monsoon Vine Thickets of the Dampier Peninsula, A Summary of Key Findings Environs Kimberley West Kimberley Nature Project 2011–2013', 2013 <http://www.environskimberley.org.au/wp-content/uploads/2012/02/MVT_Valuable-and-endangered-Final.pdf>.

9

EMPLACING AND ECONOMISING: NEOLIBERALISING AUSTRALIAN LANDSCAPES OF DEMOCRACY

Michaela Spencer

Introduction

Writing about the 2005 introduction of Shared Responsibility Agreements (SRA) by the Howard Coalition government, Elisabeth Strakosch described these SRAs as new technologies for allocating discretionary funding to Indigenous communities in a 'mutually responsible' way. However, beyond this, her suggestion was that the significant governance-building dimensions of these technologies, and their associated policy, went without comment. Her claim was that:

> Through the deployment of the conceptual tools of contract and governance, SRAs established new and depoliticised relationships between government and indigenous peoples, replacing the centralized political structure of [an alternative governance approach as exemplified by] the Aboriginal and Torres Strait Islander Commission.[1]

Pointing to an evaluation report completed several years after the SRA launch, Strakosch also foregrounded an interesting discrepancy between the responses to these agreements articulated by government and Indigenous community members. Many Indigenous people had described feeling disappointed and let down, because the SRA process had not had the effect of addressing major priorities or issues in their communities. However, from a government perspective the trials were a great success because they had achieved significant 'progress outcomes' in the form of new relationships, structures and leanings (that is new Indigenous governance structures) over the course of the trials.[2]

I begin with this brief description of responses to recent Australian government policy initiatives because it highlights particular tensions arising around the new technologies of governance emerging in the practice of Indigenous affairs and environmental management. In this chapter, I explore if and how 'depoliticisation' of relations between the Australian state and groups of its citizens is occurring in the wake of recent government policy initiatives in Australia, and detail what amount to wide discrepancies in understanding between those party to these policy initiatives. I consider the claim that technologies of neoliberal governance, such as SRAs, produce *depoliticised relationships* between governments and those that they seek to govern. I also pursue the distinction, made by Strakosch, between *local on-ground effects* and change in more *general and removed orders of governance*, occurring as part of a widespread economisation of collective life.

This distinction points to a tension within means for neo-liberalising Australian political landscapes. This tension embeds the potential for a politics that operates through dual moments of 'emplacing' and 'economising' and it is this politics which I suggest is currently at play within current practices of neoliberal governance enacted within regional and remote communities, in particular in relation to policies for Indigenous affairs and environmental management.

In telling this story, I speak from and to sites of fieldwork in Northern Australia and Tasmania, describing my research as a participant in work being undertaken by Yolŋu and environmentalists in these places. Throughout this research, I wrestled with a concern that the work we were doing – building people and places on the ground – was in some ways configured or betrayed by shifts towards economisation of government services for environment and Indigenous communities. Such a reading is encouraged by much of the literature on neoliberalism as it has been produced in Australia since the 1980s. This literature focuses on the depoliticisation that accompanies shifts towards market-based approaches towards governance and economy.

It is in taking these concerns seriously, at the same time as seeking to honour my commitment and involvement to the work that Yolŋu and environmentalists were carrying out, that, in the second half of this paper, I reach towards another way of reading our work and the role that it plays in partially subverting the neoliberalisation of Australian political landscapes.

1. Working with Yolŋu and Environmentalists in Arnhem Land and Tasmania

The ongoing project of neoliberalisation in Australia is not new, having been pursued by successive state and federal governments since the 1980s[3] as there has been an overall movement away from direct government intervention in attending to social and environmental problems in remote areas. With the emergence of this vacuum in government services, an ethic of self-sufficiency in management oriented around distributed arrangements for the delivery and coordination of social and environmental services has grown up.[4]

Concern over my own involvement in the ongoing emergence of neoliberal governance amongst people and within places in the course of my research fieldwork has set me on a path of looking towards more generative interpretations; responses that go beyond the normative story of economisation and depoliticisation as singularly destructive.

1.1 Nyälka Milingimbi Aboriginal Women's Corporation

In early 2015, I travelled to the remote community of Milingimbi in East Arnhem Land as part of an Indigenous Governance and Leadership Project. The project was funded by the Northern Territory government and was carried out in five project sites. I was one of two researchers from Charles Darwin University employed to work on the project at Milingimbi, with the aim of facilitating learning around Western and Yolŋu practices of governance and leadership, in particular through working on projects which may enhance governance and leadership capacities within these communities.[5]

Predictably, the learning of this project very quickly became a 'two-way' process, as we began to work with a group of Yolŋu women who were interested in bringing to life a new Yolŋu Women's Aboriginal Corporation. The corporation was to be called Nyälka,[6] and the women involved were clear that this organisation would be run by, and focused around, Yolŋu women, and it would support the practice and upkeep of Yolŋu law. It would assist young women and young mothers to learn from their elders out on country, and it would help to sustain the connections through which Yolŋu people and places remain strong.

Those involved also wanted to work towards the delivery of services in their community. The majority of these services, as envisaged within the planning stages of the corporation, were to involve going out on country, and helping to teach young women about ways of caring for themselves and others. This might be achieved through collecting bush medicines, pandanus and dyes, and it might also include activities such as mediation, language training, cultural competency courses and providing employment programs.

Of course, there has been a significant history of the development of corporations in remote Indigenous communities. There were already a number of other Indigenous corporations in Milingimbi. Some of these were active, and involved in work such as running the accommodation business, the Arts Centre and the Milingimbi music festival, while others seemed to remain inactive, with a nominal corporate structure in place. As a legacy of emerging forms of local management within remote communities taking place over several decades, the Arnhem Land Progress Association (ALPA) corporation also maintains a continually strong presence in community life, keeping the one local store open and providing funding and support for a number of community employment programs and initiatives.

As facilitators on this project, my colleague and I had many concerns about what it meant to be intervening to promote the creation of yet another Indigenous corporation, and the financial and bureaucratic responsibilities that this structure would entail for its members. However, there was a strong interest on the part of our government funders to be able to engage with active and identifiable organisational bodies in the community, as well as for governance training to be broadly offered within Milingimbi and other Indigenous communities across the Top End. At the same time, the women we were working with were very clear that this was the way they wanted to go. While there were other women's groups in Milingimbi there was not yet a Yolŋu women's corporation.

They were interested in the new kind of organisational structure that was offered by a corporation, and the way in which such a structure might enable them to continue the ongoing practice of Yolŋu law and women's work on country, whilst also being visible to government and future business opportunities. Instead of proposing yet another training module to be visited upon remote communities we moved ahead with the development of Nyälka. Rather than dealing with a distant and abstract version of corporate governance to be absorbed and learnt, we would be confronting the particular reality of these practices while setting up this new corporation. Nonetheless, the niggling concerns around the value of what we were doing, and whether we were somehow facilitating and presiding over new forms of neocolonial governance practices never really went away. It was the women themselves who continually assured us that they wanted to keep going with this project, and with the necessary financial and administrative responsibilities that running a corporation would entail.

This experience in Milingimbi was not the first time that I had worried over being caught up in new forms of collaboration that seemed, at times, to subvert the aims and outcomes that we were otherwise trying to achieve. While doing my doctoral research in north-east Tasmania I spent a considerable amount of time working with a group of conservationists and environmental activists who were committed to the protection of native bushland habitats in their local region and were prepared to work in new ways with the state and capital in order to promote their aims.

1.2 North East Bioregional Network
The North East Bioregional Network (NEBN) was made up of a number of local residents, conservationists and environmental activists who were keen to work towards the protection of native habitats in their region of north-east Tasmania. These members

were involved largely as volunteers who variously contributed to a number of large bush regeneration projects run by the group, and who frequently contested prospective land clearing, mining, logging or development projects by public or private organisations which might be fought in the courts.

The everyday work of NEBN was two-fold, involving protecting the integrity of native landscapes, contesting new proposals for development that would significantly damage pristine forests and other bushland habitats, as well as also working to repair and restore degraded areas of bushland by removing weeds, reactivating the seed bank and supporting the rejuvenation of the species native to the area.

Several of those in the group described this work as 'giving back' and a way of behaving responsibly in a place that has been radically changed since European settlement. It was by doing this work that they paid careful attention to the place where they lived, respecting landscapes which had evolved to be here in this place, and which have lately been so drastically disrupted by a push to develop, dominate and transform nature in new ways.

Over the years, much of the work of NEBN had involved keeping an eye on council and local private landowners, working through scientific assessments and the courts to successfully object to development applications, and enforce the remediation of legal and illegal land clearing activities. However, more recently they had begun to change as other groups, who had never before been actively interested in the protection of nature, began to investigate and explore the provision of environmental services.

It was in carrying out this work that NEBN became a collaborator with several mining and forestry companies. Working together with these organisations, they were collaboratively managing and restoring areas of degraded native bush and sought to deliver services in the management of biodiversity value for these areas of land. And, in working with these other organisations, the focus of NEBN's work seemed to shift from environmental protection to the delivery of environmental services. These emerging new forms of environmental governance were transforming the group. Members of NEBN insisted that the work of negotiating and delivering environmental services was an important political activity; yet, this was an insistence that seemed 'politically strange'. I remained concerned that working in this way involved giving up too many of the commitments and principles that featured so strongly in the history of this group's environmental protection work.

2. Critical Engagements with Australian Neoliberalisation

It is in looking for ways to understand these feelings of worry and concern about assisting these two groups pursue their rather disparate interests – which they insisted were generative but which felt politically strange and unfamiliar to me – that I have turned to literature addressing the advent of neoliberal governance in Australia. In particular, I am concerned here with literature articulating the effects of neoliberal governance practices in the arenas of Indigenous affairs and environmental management.

Much of this analytic work focuses on the means by which practices broadly characterised as neoliberal have the effect of reinvolving Indigenous communities and environmentalists in forms of exploitative and neocolonial relations. Writing on the development of Indigenous ranger programs, anthropologist Elodie Fache argues that community-based natural resource management programs entangle rationales of empowerment and neoliberalism in producing new forms of 'bureaucratic participation' for Indigenous people and the bureaucratisation of the Indigenous Australian world.[7] She proposes that via an Aboriginal corporation that is autonomous, and distinct from the local government structure, so-called 'community-based' rangers involved in natural resource management programs attempt to negotiate a degree of collective independence from the bureaucratic interventions and demands of the state, but also from their own community. Through close ethnographic analysis of the complex relationships between local practices and the bureaucratic requirements at the core of the Indigenous rangers' daily work and life, Fache discerns the pervasive neocolonialism of such activity.[8]

The ranger system therefore, though commonly presented as a means towards greater socioeconomic and political autonomy for Indigenous Australians, 'may actually be serving to extend state power into the very communities that it is supposedly empowering'.[9] In this context, the relationships between Indigenous Australians and their land and sea country come to reflect principles and practices of management that are enforced by the state at all governmental levels. These principles and practices are modelled on the corporate world and, in particular, their principles of accountability and performance.

Similarly, transitions from discourses and practices of environmental protection and sustainability towards the organisation and delivery of ecosystem services (or 'payment for ecosystem services') have been described as promoting technocratic and economic approaches to biodiversity. Managing environments through 'services' can be read as framing biodiversity in specific reductionist terms; that is, as something that can be represented with a single measure. It is such measures that in turn enable the commodification of these services by incorporating them into systems of exchange, rendering environments as the bearer of economic value. It is in this sense that the ecosystem services discourse contributes to the commodification of biodiversity.[10]

Environmental programs based on the production and trade of ecosystem services in this way enable authorities to bring together previously competing and contradictory imperatives under the rubric of singular political problems. Through discrete measures, issues of social order and governance are put into the same 'language' as practices of environmental management and regional economic development in the creation of new hybrid forms of governing. It is precisely this approach which often contributes to the continuing failure of these natural resource management programs to achieve their desired effects. As a consequence, neoliberal forms of governing tend to be characterised by experimentation with a range of governmental technologies in order to make programs workable in practice.[11]

As such, market-based instruments for environmental protection do not emanate from a single uniform neoliberal manifesto or toolkit, but from a contested, spatially uneven and flexible process of experimentation in economic and social reform.[12] Nonetheless, the forms of environmental regulation and decision-making which have emerged – technocratically imposed and administered by centralised state and quasi-state agencies – themselves work to reduce opportunities for political debate and contestation, producing a general depoliticisation alongside environmental service provision.[13]

The accounts that I have canvassed above focus on environments as what Bruno Latour calls an 'object of concern', and find that, in relation to the new practices of management that these objects now entail, there has been a novel and radical encroachment of governance practices into the public performance of what the problems *are*. A focus of these and many other contemporary analyses of neoliberalisation is the hollowing out of the democratic institutions of liberal democracy and the nation state. In the gradual movement towards market mechanisms, particularly in managing complex social and environmental problems, the familiar practices of political deliberation and decision-making which previously accompanied liberal democracy are no longer relevant; previously available means for contesting dominant social orders and their agents becoming subsumed and integrated and collaborative work dedicated to localised self-management in market contexts. However, what such accounts do not seem able to address is the fact that managing the encroachment of governance practices has long been part of the everyday practice of Indigenous affairs and environmental management. It's just that now it is done differently. While the onset of neoliberal governance may have changed the rules, the interrelatedness of on-ground work and governance practices is certainly not new.

It is this apparent oversight in articulating what is at issue that has me turning to the work of political scientist Wendy Brown, an author who has extensively examined the ontological transformations affected within neoliberal governance practices. Over more than a decade, Brown has presented a broad-ranging account of neoliberal rationalities and the transposing of constituent elements of democracy into an economic register. Drawing on experiences within the North American academy and other arenas, she places front and centre the concern that neoliberalism is bringing about an evacuation of the many democratic freedoms associated with liberal democracy, its knowledge practices and institutions.

For Brown, the changes brought about by neoliberal policy agendas amount to much more than a process of rearranging existing political furniture, she suggests that 'neoliberalism transmogrifies every human domain and endeavour, along with humans themselves, according to a specific image of the economic'.[14] It is in this metamorphosis that the practices and principles of liberal democracy, which have until now been seen to guarantee human freedoms, begin to become obscured; law, education, popular sovereignty and public goods all become transformed as means for producing capital value. In this process, personal and other freedoms begin to diminish, and there are no longer means to be able to voice individuality external to the maintenance of general modes of economisation.

It is within this transition that the individual democratic participant – the citizen – becomes reconfigured in the model of *homo oeconomicus* (or 'economic human'), and '*rule* transmutes into governance in the order that neoliberal rationality is bringing about'.[15] Within liberal democratic institutional practices, 'rule' was constituted through means such as governmental scientific review, and the mobilisation of apparatuses for the production and assessment of scientific facts or other knowledge claims. However, Brown suggests, neoliberalism abandons these apparatuses altogether, and instead operates through personal codes of conduct and schemes for valuation.

3. Neoliberalising Landscapes

In telling my fieldwork stories, I follow Brown but do not agree with her depoliticisation thesis. Instead, I suggest that attuning to practices of both emplacing and economising allows a politics of neoliberalising in Australian landscapes of democracy to appear. To this end, I shift to an ontological mode, one that implies that analysis evokes an active and emergent register in which worlds are in the making. Such an approach is proposed and mobilised by a number of American pragmatist philosophers such as James

Dewey and Kathryn Pyne Addelson, as they have sought to engage with public problems as emergent outcomes of collective action, as well as the science studies scholar Helen Verran, who has similarly detailed numbers as emergent outcomes of collective work which may be done in one way, or another.[16]

Rather than considering neoliberalism to be an agenda which governments roll out and apply in a careful and cognisant manner, engaging with *neoliberalising* as an active and emergent outcome of heterogeneous practices opens up new possibilities for analysis and critique. In this mode of formulating collective action, places emerge as outcomes of collective action which may be variously engaged in by diverse and heterogeneous participants. The work – which might be engaged by those involved in shifts towards new forms of service provision – may be recognised as means of shaping and reshaping the character of places which are themselves outcomes of such work.

Recognising places as constituted within various forms of heterogeneous practices opens up new sorts of questions about the manner in which these places may be reconstituted. It is not only those in the field who are involved in such work. Those in the academy, narrating such actions and activities, take part in these practices which themselves also contribute to the shaping and arranging of places. Writing in a manner which does not erase the possibility of contest, and which does not seek to simply comment on the loss of autonomy, culture and political agency by community groups, I have begun to reach towards this alternative analytic and narrative approach. One means looks towards the mobilisation of differing ways of enacting places by naming a politics implicit within these practices. The outcome of this sort of account is not a description of neoliberal governance that denies the possibility of political action on the part of those whom this politics concerns. Rather, the outcome is one which looks to the practice of this politics as it is already being enacted, to see how it might be more explicitly detailed and inhabited in the future.

Having refigured the analytic gaze through which I tell (or re-tell) my fieldwork stories, let me again return to the two sites of research where I initially became so worried. Perhaps by looking more closely, it is possible to learn from the insistence that such work is important for the people involved, and take seriously their implicit claim that it does not amount either to promoting a neoliberal form of intimate colonising as Australian analysts propose, nor to the radical depoliticisation Brown proposes.

4. Telling Fieldwork Stories as Episodes of 'Emplacing' and 'Economising'

Story 1: Developing a program for the reduction of violence against women
Engaging various processes across nearly two years, CDU researchers and a small group of Yolŋu women in Milingimbi worked towards the point where a meeting to elect members and directors of a corporation could be held, and the paperwork to register the organisation with the Office of the Registrar of Indigenous Corporations (ORIC) could be completed. Prior to these definitive stages there were many other provisional steps which had been taken as the group decided on a vision, and articulated objectives for the corporation, completed a Rule Book which would be the legal basis for its operation, and negotiated ways in which the aim to strengthen collective Yolŋu life 'on-country', and work with young women and young mothers, might be able to be realised within and through a new corporate structure.

Having become officially registered as a corporation, Nyälka were able to begin applying for grants. One of those that became available around this time was linked to Australian government funding for the provision of community services in remote Indigenous communities. Announced under the program 'Building Safer Communities for Women' were a number of sizable government grants that were directed towards organisations able to deliver projects as programs for the reduction of violence against women in remote and regional communities.[17]

During these very early days of the corporation, it was this Commonwealth program that the Nyälka directors focused their attention towards as they began to design a project to promote a reduction of violence against women and children within Milingimbi and nearby communities. The name of the project – *Gurrkurrkurru Manapanmirr* – loosely translates as coming together through our connections in place. Its focus was to remember and strengthen the connections through which Yolŋu family relates, and through which conflict and misunderstanding might both arise and be resolved, and to do so 'in-place'. Significantly, these connections were envisaged as extending out through the kinship relations of Yolŋu family and clan groups and their lands, as well as through *Balanda* (settler or white) organisations and outside service providers in the community.

The project was to be rolled out as an ongoing series of journeys on-country together that would involve women going out collecting and gathering food and other goods. The first of these trips would be close to home for the women, and involve heading out at the right times of year to collect bush medicines from a site out beyond the Milingimbi airstrip. Then other journeys would connect with women in Ramininging and travel further afield to the Dhipirri homeland for hunting, collecting pandanus and dyes for weaving. Through these movements in and through country, young Yolŋu women could learn from their elders about the

connections between each other and the places they come from
and should affiliate with. At the same time, *Balanda* women from
other organisations and services providers could also come to learn
about these connections and their significance in community life,
consolidating involvements of their work within these networks.

As proposed by the women in Milingimbi, these activities,
which they might carry out as part of a process of supporting and
educating young women on-country, could viably connect up to
the administrative practices of contemporary modern governance.
The work of sustaining Yolŋu connections to country would be
carried out in the process of also extending knowledge of these
connections beyond Yolŋu to also include *Balanda* women within
a skilled support network.

A key aspect of the corporation involved establishing the means
by which their proposed project could demonstrably reduce the
incidence of violence against women, and/or the effects of family
and domestic violence in the areas where the program was carried
out. There was much discussion around this question amongst the
Nyälka directors, both regarding how such an outcome would be
achieved and how it would be described in the grant application.
The work of *Gurrkurrkurru Manapanmirr* would be to re-enact
and strengthen the connections of people and places through
which Yolŋu could remember who they are, and the means by
which they relate to each other. This was described by Gwen
Warmbirrirr, one of the Nyälka directors, in the following way:

> *Gurrkurr* is strength, it is also called a muscle and in
> another way is also like rope connecting through one
> clan to another. My *nathi's* (grandfather's) connections
> come through to this country through the song cycle.
> He came to this country when he was young, and had

male and female children here. Then they also had their children, which was us, and we have had our children here. The connection goes back a long way, but the connection still goes through the *gurrkurr*. The connection to the other clan that we are connected to through our *yapa-pulu* (sister clan) or our *mari-pulu* (grandmother clan) through the song cycle.

Going out together to collect bush medicines and dyes is a way of making connections between one clan group and another. You can recognise who you are and where you are from, and recognise where other people are from. You can talk about this so that people understand. When there are fights or jealousy, people can come to agreement because you can dig back to the root and follow the connections.[18]

The work of delivering these services does not only concentrate on recovering and strengthening these connections, but also on expanding the networks so as to also include *Balanda* women and organisations (who may not participate or understand in networks of kin relations through which violence might both manifest and be healed). As Gwen Warmbirrirr stated:

The Nyälka women can help to connect between families and tribes if there is trouble or jealousy. They are people who are strong and who can talk to people and make connections to help deal with problems. If two women are fighting, sometimes they don't understand why because they aren't looking at the root of the problem and making the right connections. Nyälka women can help with this. Part of this is training Yolŋu people about awareness of the laws which are to be abided in the community, both *Balanda* and Yolŋu.

The point of connection that these activities made to the 'Building Safer Communities' grant application, and the emerging new forms of governance promoted by the Australian state, was through its focus on the 'the social good' of reduction of violence against women. The purpose of these grants – as the government saw it – was the provision of funding to organisations interested in providing local services in managing violence and supporting women through activities and programs which were administered locally. The tender process was open to all organisations interested in applying, including charities, service providers, private organisations and Indigenous community organisations. It was necessary that the programs being offered did not duplicate services already being offered in the community, and should not operate exclusively out of a silo such as the clinic or school but should work to connect different groups in the community.

The rules devised by government officials also required that the application specify the particular need for such a program in the community or region where it would be offered, and the precise manner in which improvements or reductions in incidences of violence might be remarked and recorded. These might take the form of statistical data on incidences of family and domestic violence within certain populations or areas, or be detailed in other ways, even including use of story. Similarly, the research necessarily associated with the rolling out and attesting the success of these programs, might be carried out as grounded research or draw on other research methods that might evidence outcomes.

Story 2: Negotiating the provision of biodiversity services

For a number of years prior to my arrival in Tasmania as an ethnographer, NEBN had tried to develop a working relationship with the private timber company Gunns Ltd. They had sought to engage the company around their use of chemicals on their nearby hardwood plantation, and around the management of remnant areas of native bushland remaining on this site. However, it was not until the announcement of a Tasmanian round of an Australian government funded biodiversity fund that this relationship began to flourish.

Previously Gunns had been required to adhere to legislative requirements for the management of native ecologies and natural values. Conservationists had policed these lines carefully, holding Gunns accountable to various established criteria, such as the legislated distance from a watercourse where logging was able to take place, the particular species which were protected and so could not be logged or cleared, which herbicides and pesticides might be legally used, and those that could not be applied. This form of engagement involved each party arguing for limitations on the other's work, but ignored the particular skills and expertise that each side developed and expressed while engaging in these forms of mutual opposition. However, as Gunns began to struggle financially when confronted with tightening economic markets, and a new federal Clean Energy Policy emerged in 2011 to fund the provision of biodiversity services (amongst other things), the demeanour of mutual opposition began to change.[19]

As NEBN and Gunns tentatively began to work together, a new environmental management plan for Gunns' Seaview plantation was developed. This plan was specifically focused around the large areas of remnant native bushland which NEBN wanted to see protected, and included protocols around the management of weeds and water quality, as well as identification of key protected species. Joining together GPS surveys of the plantation and its vegetation profile, as well as detailed evaluative explanation and illustration of bushland health – poor, good, excellent – a guide was developed to help support and direct Gunns' management of native bush on the property.

NEBN was keen for these areas to be managed 'properly', as areas of remnant bushland which were sustaining of local species and habitats and which offered important connecting corridors for wildlife. These areas needed to be managed so as to ensure there was no significant encroachment of feral species, and so that areas of the plantation that were no longer being used for forestry could be restored to their former state. In developing this plan together, the Gunns corporation would learn about and adopt appropriate practices and procedures for careful management of the biodiversity values of their property.

The funding available though the federal biodiversity fund was for those seeking to offer services in biodiversity management to the Australian government. Gunns was eager to put up its hand. It submitted the plan as the basis of an application to a special Tasmanian funding round, and was successful in receiving a generous grant for the ongoing provision of biodiversity management services at its site. This included ongoing weeding and restoration of streamside reserves and other remnant areas of bushland within the plantation property. The practices for carrying out this restoration work were, by its own admission, anathema to Gunns, who was skilled at the management of plantation monocultures and industrial techniques for timber harvesting and processing. It was through this collaboration that NEBN were able to ensure that more areas of native forest were protected and better managed than they otherwise would be, and

Gunns was able to earn financial and political capital as a company not only simply engaged in harvesting timber as a resource, but also in the maintenance of regional biodiversity values.

In delivering these services, the negotiation of the ongoing collaboration between NEBN and Gunns did not always run smoothly. At times, as part of a process of continuing to work together, heated contestations over the doing-of-place bubbled to the surface and needed to be discussed and dealt with by the parties involved. One of these occasions arose as Gunns discussed with NEBN its plan to restore the native ecology of some stream-side reserves running through the plantation property. When proposing to reseed areas of degraded areas along a newly logged section of plantation forest, the Gunns representatives pointed out that they would use Ironbark seeds on the riverbank. These were a common Eucalypt species in the area, and as a canopy species they would also support the regeneration of the sedges and shrubs in the lower vegetation stories. The company could easily source these seeds from their storehouse and bring them to the site to be scattered along the streamsides.

It was after some careful questioning around the origin of these seeds that NEBN became oppositional. This proposed way of working, they argued, would not achieve what was needed. Gunns collected and stored seeds of many different varieties. These were shipped to its storehouse from many different sites, where storage was organised and consolidated according to species. Any number of seeds from quite different corners of the country could, in this way, be gathered together and stored in an undifferentiated way in the one place. When then drawing on this stock to assist revegetation of streamside reserves in north-east Tasmania, it may be seeds from southern Tasmania, Victoria or Western Australia which ended up being scattered and putting down roots into the soil.

When Gunns proposed these reseeding activities it had fore-seen no trouble at all. The process of reseeding, it assumed, would go ahead without a problem. However, it was pulled up short as NEBN refused to allow the work to go ahead, insisting that any reseeding or replanting use only seed stock drawn from the replanting location itself. NEBN preferred to halt the restoration work, and instead develop a plan by which Gunns could integrate seed collection into its ordinary plantation management activities, creating locally collected stock to draw on for any future reseeding work.

It was important that the management of biodiversity values be carried out so as to remake a native habitat which had evolved in this place; a habitat which had been physically altered and rearranged, yet was genetically identical to the forest that had once thrived there. Using locally sourced seeds, the integrity of the biodiversity that Gunns and NEBN were working to manage would be guaranteed.

5. A Politics in Neoliberalising Australian Landscapes

Both of the stories I have told here detail a politics emerging in the practices through which particular entities – as places and natures – emerge. Shifting to an ontological mode, we recog-nise that this is a politics concerned with the manner in which these entities come to be and become governable. This work, as undertaken by these community groups, involves participating in government-endorsed practices of governance, at the same time as continuing to support and maintain practices of place-making that live outside and beyond those implicitly and collectively imagined in current government policy agendas.

Significantly, this is work that does not require those involved to acquiescence in any single set of political commitments as a precursor to collaboration. In neither of the two situations that I have discussed here was there any settled agreement between parties regarding how places and natures might be enacted. But in both cases, Nyälka and NEBN sought active collaboration with others in beginning to participate in newly invented markets for services provision. The outcomes of such collaborations were not imagined as significant quantitative gains to be achieved through the delivery of these services – for example, as increased numbers of women engaged, or increased area of native forest protected. Rather, what was proposed were qualitatively new ways for constituting Australian places, new means for place-making.

Read in this way, by engaging the problem of violence against women as an issue in remote communities, Nyälka showed themselves as willing to work with CDU researchers to develop services that were fundable by the Australian government. They were sanguine about accepting the administrative and financial responsibilities entailed in such work, and were keen about the potential financial benefits that might flow from such activities. At the same time, they were insistent about the means by which such services should be delivered. Any efforts by Nyälka to work within the community, and to engage problems such as domestic and family violence, must necessarily involve practices of constituting the relations of people to each other and to their places in Yolŋu ways. Seeking to mend a perceived breakdown in means for resolving conflicts and rifts in place, they provided means by proposing this work as an appropriate, locally endorsed and delivered, engagement with a government-identified problem of violence against women.

Similarly open to collaboration, NEBN were willing and interested to work with Gunns in the development of biodiversity services. Together NEBN and Gunns carried out preliminary work around the management of native areas of bushland on the plantation, and the prospect of collaborating around the delivery of biodiversity services funded through the government scheme was an attractive option for both parties. For the NEBN, the economisation of environmental services offered means by which they could ride on the coat-tails of government effort to access private land for the development of strong regional environments and economies. However, NEBN were also very clear about the means by which these services were to be delivered. The nature to be constituted within the production of biodiversity was to be a specifically native nature, one which was genetically identical to that which had existed on the site before and which would continue to be sustained there.

It has been in following these episodes, and attending to the political work being carried out within them, that I have named and emphasised these dual moments of 'emplacing' and 'economising'; moments in which the poles of differing political tensions within the practice of neoliberal governance are engaged and experienced by community groups and activists. While accepting governmentality analyses that propose that neoliberalising is accompanied by a radical economising of political landscapes, my interpretation of these stories suggests that there *is* an active politics of 'emplacing' which runs alongside that of 'economising'. It is by attending to this politics that possibilities for engaging and contesting practices of 'economisation' become visible.

It has been by naming and so differentiating this paradox as dual moments of 'emplacing' and 'economising' that I have tried to provide a way to read fieldwork episodes in which these moments might be discerned, and through which they have been briefly detailed. Instead of seeking to represent particular political (or de-politicising) practices associated with neoliberalism in the everyday life of community groups and regional communities, I have attempted to retain recognition of 'economisation' as a real effect of some government policy approaches, while at the same time as also permitting a reading that shows the presence of an embodied politics of place-making within the work of these same groups. It has been in attending empirically to the work of these groups that I have sought to reveal a particular paradox that they currently inhabit and work. This is a dual commitment to joining mainstream movements towards service delivery and an insistence that they are continuing to carry out political work.

By naming these dual political moments, it is perhaps also possible to discern ways in which they may be more or less carefully inhabited and worked as elements of an explicit politics of neoliberal governance. While I have proposed 'emplacing' and 'economising' as a set of dual relations which catch some of the relevant aspects of the work appearing in these two fieldwork situations, there are no doubt other tensions and working paradoxes which could likewise be named and explored.

Conclusion

As an ethnographer joining in the work of both Yolŋu and environmentalists, I have been inducted into very different means for knowing and enacting places; one in working to bring to life a new Aboriginal corporation and another in carrying out conservation and restoration work. However, attending to a sense of discomfort and discontinuity between the ways in which those I worked with understood their participation in the ongoing life of the places where they live, and some of the accounts of this participation available in the literature of neoliberalism, I have tried to steer a course which works with this tension. Looking for ways to account for radical shifts in the manner in which natures and places are configured within dominant governance practices, at the same time as recognising possibilities for contest and strategic collaboration that are already being enacted by those involved. It is in grappling with ways to carefully work with changing neoliberalising landscapes that Yolŋu and environmentalists share particular experiences of *doing politics*; participating in means for shaping and sustaining the places where they live, as well as the particular means by which these places and natures might be enduringly sustained.

References

Addelson, K. P., *Moral Passages: Toward a Collectivist Moral Theory*, Routledge, New York, 1994.

Australian Government, *Clean Energy Futures*, Department of Environment, 2011 <https://www.environment.gov.au/cleanenergyfuture/index.html>.

Australian Government, *Building Safer Communities for Women*, Department of Social Services, 2015 <https://www.dss.gov.au/grants/building-safe-communities-for-women>.

Brown, W., 'Neo-liberalism and the end of liberal democracy', *Theory & Event*, vol. 7, no. 1, 2003.

Brown, W., 'American Nightmare: Neoliberalism, Neoconservatism, and De-Democratization', *Political Theory*, vol. 34, no. 6, 2006, pp. 690–714.

Brown, W., *Undoing the Demos: Neoliberalism's Stealth Revolution*, MIT Press, Cambridge, MA, 2015.

Dewey, J., *The Public and its Problems: An Essay in Political Inquiry*, Ohio University Press, Athens, OH, 1991.

Fache, E., 'Caring for Country, a Form of Bureaucratic Participation: Conservation, Development, and Neoliberalism in Indigenous Australia', *Anthropological Forum*, vol. 24, no. 3, 2014, pp. 267–86.

Indigenous Governance Leadership Development, 2016, Charles Darwin University, <https://www.cdu.edu.au/centres/groundup/igld/>.

Lockie, S., 'Neoliberal Regimes of Environmental Governance: climate change, biodiversity and agriculture in Australia', in M. R. Redclift & G. Woodgate (eds), *The International Handbook of Environmental Sociology*, Edward Elgar, Cheltenham, UK, 2010, pp. 364–77.

Lockie, S. & Higgins, V., 'Roll-out neoliberalism and hybrid practices of regulation in Australian agri-environmental governance', *Journal of Rural Studies*, vol. 23, no. 1, 2007, pp. 1–11.

Stephens, A., Oppermann, E., Turnour, J., Brewer, T. & O'Brien, C., 'Identifying tensions in the development of northern Australia: Implications for governance', *Journal of Economic & Social Policy*, vol. 17, no. 1, 2015, pp. 96–118.

Strakosch, E., 'A Reconsideration of the Political Significance of Shared Responsibility Agreements', *Australian Journal of Politics and History*, vol. 55, no. 1, 2009, pp. 80–96.

Strakosch, E., *Neoliberal Indigenous Policy: Settler Colonialism and the 'Post-welfare' State*, Palgrave Macmillan, New York, 2015.

Tonts, M. & Haslam-McKenzie, F., 'Neoliberalism and changing regional policy in Australia', *International Planning Studies*, vol. 10, no. 3–4, 2005, pp. 183–200.

Turnhout, E., Waterton, C., Neves, K. & Buizer, M., 'Rethinking Biodiversity: from goods and services to "living with"', *Conservation Letters*, vol. 6, no. 3, 2013, pp. 154–61.

Verran, H., *Science and an African Logic*, University of Chicago Press, Chicago, 2001.

Notes

1 E. Strakosch, 'A Reconsideration of the Political Significance of Shared Responsibility Agreements', *Australian Journal of Politics and History*, vol. 55, no. 1, 2009, p. 80. See also: E. Strakosch, *Neoliberal Indigenous Policy: Settler Colonialism and the 'Post-welfare' State*, Palgrave Macmillan, New York, 2015.

2 ibid., p. 89.

3 M. Tonts, & F. Haslam-McKenzie, 'Neoliberalism and changing regional policy in Australia', *International Planning Studies*, vol. 10, no. 3–4, 2005, pp. 183–200.

4 A. Stephens, E. Oppermann, J. Turnour, T. Brewer & C. O'Brien, 'Identifying tensions in the development of northern Australia: Implications for governance', *Journal of Economic & Social Policy*, vol. 17, no. 1, 2015, pp. 96–118.

5 These project sites were Ramininging, Gapuwiak, Milingimbi, Wurrumiyanga and Ntaria. See: Indigenous Governance Leadership Development, Charles Darwin University, 2016 <https://www.cdu.edu.au/centres/groundup/igld/>.

6 The name Nyälka refers to the basket which Yolŋu women carry their children in. It was suggested that the name of the corporation might

support this metaphor – of a basket to carry children in – as well as evoking the notion of a basket into which all Milingimbi women could put their ideas and actions.

7   E. Fache, 'Caring for Country, a Form of Bureaucratic Participation: Conservation, Development, and Neoliberalism in Indigenous Australia', *Anthropological Forum*, vol. 24, no. 3, 2014, pp. 267–86.

8   ibid., pp. 269–75.

9   ibid., p. 283.

10   E. Turnhout, C. Waterton, K. Neves, & M. Buizer, 'Rethinking Biodiversity: from goods and services to "living with"', *Conservation Letters*, vol. 6, no. 3, 2013, p. 156.

11   S. Lockie & V. Higgins, 'Roll-out neoliberalism and hybrid practices of regulation in Australian agri-environmental governance', *Journal of Rural Studies*, vol. 23, no. 1, 2007, pp. 1–11.

12   S. Lockie, 'Neoliberal Regimes of Environmental Governance: climate change, biodiversity and agriculture in Australia', in M. R. Redclift & G. Woodgate (eds), *The International Handbook of Environmental Sociology*, Edward Elgar, Cheltenham, UK, 2010, pp. 364–77.

13   ibid.

14   W. Brown, 'Neo-liberalism and the end of liberal democracy', *Theory & Event*, vol. 7, no. 1, 2003; W. Brown, 'American Nightmare: Neoliberalism, Neoconservatism, and De-Democratization', *Political Theory*, vol. 34, no. 6, 2006, pp. 690–714; W. Brown, *Undoing the Demos: Neoliberalism's Stealth Revolution*, MIT Press, Cambridge, MA, 2015, p. 10.

15   Brown, *Undoing the Demos*, p. 20.

16   K. P. Addelson, *Moral Passages: Toward a collectivist Moral Theory*, Routledge, New York, 1994; J. Dewey, *The Public and its Problems: An Essay in Political Inquiry*, Ohio University Press, Athens, OH, 1991; H. Verran, *Science and an African Logic*, University of Chicago Press, Chicago, 2001.

17   Australian Government, *Building Safer Communities for Women*, Department of Social Services, 2015 <https://www.dss.gov.au/grants/building-safe-communities-for-women>.

18   Gwen Warmbirrirr, interview with author, 2015.

19   Australian Government, *Clean Energy Futures*, Department of Environment, 2011 <https://www.environment.gov.au/cleanenergyfuture/index.html>.

10

WE'RE ALWAYS PUSHING THE BOUNDARIES FOR FIRST NATIONS' RIGHTS

Monica Morgan (with Eve Vincent)

Monica Morgan is a well-known Yorta Yorta activist. She was involved in the Yorta Yorta native title claim, which was unsuccessful in 1998, and unsuccessfully appealed to the High Court in 2002. In 1998, Justice Olney found that the 'tide of history' had 'washed away' Yorta Yorta native title rights. Monica was central to the campaign to have national parks declared in the Barmah and Millewa river red gum forests on the Victorian–New South Wales border. These parks were declared in 2010. Monica helped found the Murray Lower Darling Rivers Indigenous Nations, and has also been involved in the Australian government–funded Living Murray initiative. When I spoke to her, Monica told me she had moved back to her country, and found herself fulfilled by living in her mother's house at Cummeragunja, 'right on her river', Dhungula.

The story starts with, of course, the British invasion, and the situation that all traditional sovereign First Nation Peoples of Australia find ourselves in. Our first experiences of the white invasion were around the 1850s with Edward Curr coming through to seize our Moira lands for his sheep run, which carved out the heartlands of our Yorta Yorta territory. Native title was just a reflection of our continuing struggle for recognition and land justice in our own country. That was what the experience was: we were able to tell our story of our connection to our country, in our own terms, continuing that long fight and struggle by our ancestors.

What is that story?

The story was about people who survived, our struggle. Our people would say, 'this is who are, who we have left', which was only a little over a dozen original ancestors that we could clearly [identify] as being left after disease and war and the killings of our people. We tried to start with that story and convey that to the respondents to the federal courts, which included the New South Wales and Victorian governments who were represented there.

We gave personal accounts as handed down by our ancestors and held in government records of the murders, the massacres, the waterholes being poisoned, the special places around country, the rapes of our women, the stealing of our children – it was very much weaved into our story. Also part of our story was our resilience, our connections, our ability to stay in country under all adversity. To proudly keep declaring, over and over, 'this is our land'. The opening statement was 'Yanika, yanika', or 'Go away, go away, leave our country', which was said as Curr was paddling down the Murray River. And the story of a young girl Undyarning and her Kaiya, an old man who said to Curr, 'Get out. You're not welcome here. This is our country'. His response was to raise his gun over them and fire a shot.

During the court case we went through the series of petitions and lots of things that our people put into place early on – particularly with water. In 1861, a deputation was made to a representative of the Victorian government requesting a fishing tax of £10, in lieu of the loss of our fish, on each steamboat going up and down the Murray River. Our demands have always been based on survival of our people, survival of our country and the ability for us to acknowledge that, 'Yes, it's a changed situation, but we still have our rights to our country'.

All of my Yorta Yorta Elders, we went all around our country, talking about sacred sites, talking about our cultural practices and places that we'd travel to around our country. We took court around with the expectation that what our people's words were about, were going to be believed. But of course the outcome wasn't to be that.

In 1881 our people spoke and put a petition saying, 'We need our own area of land'. During the native title claim Justice Olney used that petition signed in 1881 by forty-two men residing on 'Maloga', a mission station, as the date on which the Yorta Yorta had 'abandoned native title rights'. He concluded that the paragraph, which stated that 'all our land within our tribal boundaries has been taken possession of by government and white settlers' was enough evidence to provide the hook for the determination saying, 'the tide of history had washed away all native title rights'. If one were to read further into that petition it also states 'that our hunting grounds are used for sheep pasturage and the game reduced and in many places exterminated, rendering our means of subsistence extremely precarious, and often reducing us and our wives and children to beggary'. My mother would say, 'We hate the system that makes us beggars in our own land'.

We were going to do a case directly through to the High Court, similar to *Mabo*. But because of the cost and the nature of litigation, ATSIC told us to use the native title claims process, which of course is a very narrow view of what the determination was from *Mabo*.

By 1970, 1 per cent of our country was all that was left uncleared. Barmah-Millewa and those forests, it's like our heartlands: our remaining places of where our relationship to country, our acknowledgement of ancestors, the time before whitefellas that was available. Always the elders spoke about the need to preserve and protect our remaining country. That was the paramount reason for going for the native title.

We knew that native title was very limited, that it was really about having to talk with non-Indigenous people about their enterprises and basically it's all about financial interests, it's a commodification of the environment. Even today when environmentalists speak about 'the environment', they have a specialist area and they can't talk about it as a whole. That's the dilemma we're at. Much of my work since the 1970s asks: 'How do you actually talk with the dominant invaders or people who have taken over country and divided it up, put laws and structures in place, and eventually those structures extinguish native title and any connections to country?' I still get frustrated; I still believe that we're talking in the terminology of the invader, and of the introduced regime. No matter how much they try to make a path for us, it is always brought in their language.

Including, you seem to be saying, the terminology, the language of the environment groups?
For everyone who talks about country or land – farmers or anybody. What I've found with environmentalists is they're accommodating and they're quite happy to work with us, I've worked with the [Australian Conservation Foundation], and also the Friends of the Earth – they are probably the ones that will die for you. But even then, they are always mindful of the status quo, and it's not the fight to the death for the land, it's really about accommodating areas so that species can still survive in areas: it's always about a subset. And looking at the list of the most vulnerable and

categorising things and not understanding the whole. It's very, very difficult for our people, and we've lived with whitefellas for nearly 200 years and yet we can't seem to get through. There is a different talk, different thinking, different everything. I find it very frustrating.

The Yorta Yorta native title claim had over 500 respondents, essentially opposing the claim – did that include conservation groups?

Not one conservation group was allowed to become a respondent. It was all people who had a financial interest in the land, even down to the beekeepers. Even the beekeepers, who were interested in talking [with the Yorta Yorta] finally said no: every one of them, whether they run a cow or they cut a tree or they put bees or whatever. The shooting party were allowed to be a respondent. And they always regressed back to being quasi-anthropologists.

In what sense?

'You are really only "half-caste", you don't really come from here'. And they would use whatever references they could, whatever bullshit documents that they found. Even down to, 'You're only a second wave of blackfellas'. So we had over 200 respondents at the first point where you do mediation, under Justice Grey. At that point you sit down and try and share what your thoughts are. This was our land and it's never been dealt with that it is our land. The status quo was continually used, 'We have used; we have done this; we have developed this land: how are *you* going to fit into it now?' Even at that point, where we were supposed to share, they were coming in with their own anthropological and genealogical and archaeological arguments, they were becoming quasi-experts. The mediation crashed, because of that.

Then we went to court because the mediation had no outcome.

Five hundred respondents, and it was all about trying to prove extinguishment. Not to listen, not to learn, not to allow our voices to come through. It was about how to counteract and how to prove extinguishment. Throughout native title we said, 'We keep our connection to our country, we keep our connection with each other'. The family lineages, intermarrying and no separations at any time. Native title was not to be. During the time of our claim, the League of Rights were meeting in Yorta Yorta country. We had Ku Klux Klan events in our country. Those racist elements are still there, they are still there as we go about our daily lives.

What became the focus for Yorta Yorta aspirations after that?

The aspirations never changed. That we be acknowledged as the First Nation People and as traditional owners; that we have a say on our country; and we have full protection around our forest areas – that we remove practices such as tree cutting, and cattle grazing, because the wetland systems could not sustain it. We commenced a negotiation process with the Victorian government prior to the native title determination being reached. We had an aspirations document which set out clearly what we'd like to commence doing. Foremost was that all Crown lands be converted to national parks, that we have the management and ownership over those and that we share that. That cattle and timber and everything be removed. That there be a better process for watering of our country, because of course it's heavily regulated.

We also talked about teaching non–Indigenous people about country. That's why we have the Dharnya Cultural Centre, having places for our own people. The elders kept the same consistency around families, and this is the main thing about having Cummeragunja: family groups can have their own country and their own land, make a financial interest for themselves in their own land, whatever it is. We wanted our own land, so we're able to grow our food, as well as participate in our culture. The family group structure and the call for each of the family groups to have either land or enterprise or whatever it is that they liked, and that our cultural heritage was paramount. We have rights to look after all our cultural heritage, our stories, our places of importance, including language. That was set about.

The most important thing that we learnt from our ancestors such as Uncle William Cooper, Uncle Doug Nichols and Aunty Margaret Tucker and many more is how to lobby and talk with not just government but also non-Indigenous supporters. Trade unions became important, environmental movements became important. They became important, the local environmental groups from the Goulburn-Murray, the national environmental groups. Relationships with people who shared the care for country became very important. The lobbying of trade unions, the lobbying of the Labor Party became very important to get us to a point where we were able to, in Victoria, get the new Labor government's cabinet to finally endorse a process for addressing the aspirations document for the Yorta Yorta Nation.

The policy that came out of that agreement was joint management in forested areas, in Victoria [in 2007] and New South Wales [in 2010]. We have national parks [across both sides of the border, since 2010] and even the ability to be able to have Aboriginal protected areas in NSW. So logging has ceased and cattle has ceased. There is lots to still go and there's lots of non-Indigenous people around the sides, traditionalists who believe that they have the right to be able to use Crown lands for their own means. We've got that ongoing battle.

We have picked it up again since then because we're not happy with the joint management – it's not working correctly. So we're actually entering into new dialogue with the Labor government in Victoria. There's talk about treaty in Victoria. And our highest aspiration is to be recognised as the sovereign owners of our country. We'd have liked to be able to negotiate treaty or something that is square with us being equal. We've actually worked our way to that point and developed our own organisational and traditional structures to be able to represent us as a Nation and get to that level.

I think native title, if anything, provided an important opportunity, because we talked to country and recorded our stories. Some old people are now gone, but we have their stories. We consolidated our views and knowledge about what we were here for and what our rights are and what we wanted for the future. I think that we encircled the remnants of Yorta Yorta Nation, because of course, pre-Cook, we were thousands and by 1860s we were reduced to tens. And that meant that we had to live with the fact that much of the traditional practices would be gone. That's not what we were about. We were saying that the very act of survival and living and maintaining ourselves in our own country through all that adversity, that land rights, itself, and treaty, for our people, over our country, is not based on just this archaeological, anthropological need to be the same as your ancestors from 1788.

But I think when it comes to the environment we have a long, long way to go.

Let's focus in on that. You talked about people who 'share that care' of country. I wanted to know to what extent do Yorta Yorta people and these environmental actors share in the same understanding of these issues?

My elders who campaigned from the 1970s through to 2007, they are direct descendants of leaders including Uncle William Cooper and Uncle Doug Nicholls, Aunty Marge Tucker – leaders who had already been very clued up and had talked to trade unions, because trade unions were quite important in this whole process, and other groups. The groups, aside from the trade unions, the other groups were more Communist party, Christian groups and others the kind of 'smoothing of the dying pillow'. Well our new generation of people who came out of the Black Panther era, the black pride, black power and the tent embassy: they were much more militant. We expected a degree of maturity, both politically and morally and in worldliness about Indigenous Peoples, from the cattleman's associations or the Shire Council, the Murray Darling Basin Commission, and other government agencies.

We also knew that Yorta Yorta – particularly with regards to our rights in water and our river – that we could not do it alone: we needed to join up with other First Nations. We formed the Murray Lower Darling River Indigenous Nations [MLDRIN], which is very important. I think that was because the Murray Darling Basin Commission [now the Murray Darling Basin Authority] were one of the main respondents [to the native title claim], and they were about extinguishment, to promote the water industry's rights.

[Later] I think there was an understanding particularly with agency heads in NSW that we had a right to participate in what was going on with the water plans for NSW. We set up MLDRIN – all the way from the mountain to the sea and the tributaries of the

Murray River. We all agreed to our autonomy, our sovereignty, but agreed to work together. This was based on the old traditional knowledge that those above you would protect your interests in water and those below you – you had a right to protect their interests, to keep it clean as it flows from mountain to sea.

In doing that we decided to become part of the Living Murray [initiative]. I myself was heavily engaged in that process and went on to sit on the Living Murray River community advisory committee. They had their structures up there and the Murray Darling Basin Commission, National Farmers' Federation, people representing a variety of interests – Tim Fisher of the Australian Conservation Foundation [(ACF)] was also on there. I was able to ensure that we had our own stream of consultation. We were just pushing the boundaries as far as we could. That was very helpful and then in the meantime we had a localised campaign. Because of course unless the water comes through in a proper manner, it doesn't matter how much you free up your land from cows and all the weeds and whatever is going on in country, you need the water at the right times. Many supporters, including the Goulburn Murray Environmental Group and Friends of the Earth all came on board, we had a huge meeting. We had a meeting with ACF.

We didn't do as much with the ACF: they're very conservative, very much about sticking to their own agenda. In the end the ACF actually wanted to compromise on the amount of water needed in the watering plan. I found during that time that to a lot of them it is political and it is about compromise. They seemed to just have to go in piecemeal for the environment, which was very confronting for me to see that.

With the local environmental group – the premise that we set with them was that when you come in and work with us, and we protect country, it's on the knowledge that Yorta Yorta are traditional owners first and that you have to acknowledge that. Basically it was about saying that our rights to be able to preserve and manage country did not just involve environment. It was a deeper level than that and it goes back to inheritance and inalienable rights in land. We were quite forthright in saying that if you do business with us, you do it under that acknowledgement that this is our country and that when we negotiate for management of this place, you sit there with everybody else, but you help us because you're a part of the mainstream white society.

One of the things we learnt was that it doesn't matter how much – and I don't want to be confronting to you – but however much non-Indigenous people really say that they are committed in the long run, they're committed to their society. They will side with their own. I think it's ingrained within the education; it's ingrained with their thought patterns that they concede and they'll work within a status quo. And I think our rights are seen in that way as well.

How did people react, some of these people that you were setting out these terms to?
Well of course, we all talked about informed consent. The Friends of the Earth, Goulburn Murray Environmental Group, they signed on, WWF couldn't, ACF couldn't. Many green groups are playing within the system that they're a part of, and when you play within the system that you're a part of, you go between those lines. Always our people were forever saying, 'Well we don't recognise your system but we acknowledge it's there'. We tried to push the boundaries and lay down, 'This is who we are and this is what we think, based on our traditional knowledge'.

Whether in the end you are going to agree with it or not, it's entirely up to you. Of course they never did. What we have been able to learn through this history, since white people coming into our country, is that we have to push and push. I think all First Nations People in Australia have that knowledge that we just have to keep pushing those boundaries. There are always going to be conservatives amongst us too, the ones who are educated ones, sometimes, try their hardest to compromise to be able to meet that other side. I'm very, very pleased that we have such radical groups of our people that say, 'No, that is not correct, that is not the way it should be'.

Our spirit, our love for who we are and where we are is grounded and rooted in the land that we come from. The fight always continues.

You seem to be saying that there are important differences between some of these styles of environmentalism, some more institutional, some more grassroots. Could you elaborate on their different perspectives on Indigenous issues?

I think there is a real passion amongst environmentalists but sometimes they lose their compassion for humanity in that. The further they get into a species of snail for example, they more they lose the essence of why we protect country: that humans and particularly ourselves are no different than the fish, the trees and everything else. That without Indigenous peoples or First Nation Peoples in country, then that is extermination.

You can't look at country, particularly over [the] last 50,000, 60,000 years – since the beginning – and say that First Nation Peoples are to be taken out of the equation when you look after land and water.

As you can see, I don't fall into the trap of talking about my spirituality. That's there, but it belongs to my people, I will no longer use it as a leverage with non-Indigenous people. Because unless they understand the place of First Nation Peoples in country, and that is as important as that rare fish, then they don't understand the interconnection between all those things. That's a separation that's there.

The problem with Olney was he reduced down the Aboriginal component of when we talk about country [to be] about whether we can still sing and dance and do those type of things. Not the fact that we've survived and maintained ourselves and we feel that connection with our country. That whole 'vanquished peoples', that is what we got through to us all the time. 'You need to concede. The foot is on your neck. Concede; yield. The status quo now prevails'.

Having said that, we will utilise white man's structures until the cows come in, to advance our rights but not our responsibility for country. That's where that whole concept of 'cultural flows' comes from. Cultural flows came out of the Aboriginal Community Engagement process through the Living Murray. Our mob articulated with each other what the importance of country and water was, but how do you then interpret that to non–Indigenous people? Well you're not going to be able to. But what you're going to be able to do is incorporate necessary elements from that white structure/mechanisms. The concept of 'environmental flow' came about from previous struggles to get water for country. Environmental flow is so alien to our understanding – the whole bloody flow is an environmental flow. Once we were able to say, 'Well this is how whitefellas see things'. They see the water in different compartments: this goes to the town, and this goes to the farmers, and what goes to the forests and wetlands, of course it's political leverage who gets what and the environment, of course, gets the least.

We had many non-Indigenous people who are quite open to the concept of allowing us to speak to them of our interests and concerns. They would say to us, 'Now tell us what you want'. But we couldn't tell them about those intangible things – that when this flow happens this water grass is released and we know this is the time the swans' eggs are ready – they couldn't understand it. Fancy trying to tell an engineer why water is important for cultural activities or hunting and gathering. The concept of 'environmental flow' was there, so we developed a concept of a 'cultural flow'. Well they've got environmental flow, why can't we have a cultural flow to add to the environmental flow and provide it when it is needed for cultural reasons and hunting and gathering? We weren't talking about a commodification of water, we actually were talking about the living need of water, as our mob were back in that 1860s: they said we can't catch a fish anymore, the fish are dying. It is about use and maintenance of natural flows of the rivers.

Many of the mob down the river were saying, 'The Murray cod is sacred'. It was the creator of the river for us; it is sacred to us. You can't tell them whitefellas because they don't understand that. If you say to them that it has a financial means, because we catch cod to have a feed, it sustains our family: they understand that. When we were going around our country, all our mob would say, 'Well this is where we used to fish but we can't now. This is where our mob camped and had ceremony and did everything but the water and the mussels and everything that we used to celebrate are gone now. The brolga and the magpie geese used to come here but the water has changed now and so they don't come. And that's my totem but it has not been in my country for near a 100 years'.

We developed these concepts that would fit into the psyche of the white mind, that's where you've got to go. Many of our old people resisted those kind of things and said, 'But now we are thinking like the environmentalists who categorise everything and not in a holistic way'. Well let's see what we can get to protect what we've got and maybe advance it.

When it came to the Living Murray, we went for the optimum watering option, with the hope that they'll come back to the middle. The environmentalists went with the middle, hoping to compromise but were left with the lesser option. This is where we fell apart.

Could you tell me more about these tensions with environmentalists?

The relationships have fallen away, because they've gone on to other things. Even with our Friends of the Earth, they were very strong about Indigenous peoples' rights and the holistic view of treaty and those type of things, and now they themselves work with Indigenous peoples in areas that they choose to advance their own causes. It will be anti-nuclear, then they'll go to a place and there's an Indigenous group so they'll work with them. They move on and we're very much aware of it: we understand they've got to live within their society. No matter how passionate young people can be and mindful, they will move on, they'll get married, they'll have children and need a better paying job. You would hope that they would hold on to some of that learning. I suppose we just become a good learning environment for young people to get their teeth into, and later on, when they become part of mainstream, it might have some effect in their everyday work. We still have to work within the confines of the system, it's very much about commodification, very much about financial interest, very much about political groups.

What are your priorities right now?

Ultimately, it has to be respect for the sovereign nature of our Peoples' rights, and to get to a point that there can be a proper treaty put in place for each First Nation. We will move inch by inch, and it's difficult to keep our own people on that path because there are so many distractions. Because when they reduce you to advise them, regulator to regulator, stretch by stretch, species by species: you lose your holistic view of country. You can get drawn into fights such as the fight about whether water should be traded or owned by Aboriginal people and traded in a financial means. People say: what hell have you got these 'cultural flows' for? What the hell does that deliver? Well it was really just to deliver some water to country that needs it.

I might leave you with a couple of thoughts. My mother was very important, like all our elders, in this struggle. These are my mother's words: 'We don't set the conditions, mother earth sets them, only that we can survive'. Then she said, 'We hate the system that makes us beggars'. That goes right back to that petition in 1881. If you're going to make us beggars in our own land where we can't even procure our cultural economy... We need to have land so that we have got a base place and we can continue and be proud. We need land that we can also live off. We need to protect our environment, our land and country, so that we can fish and hunt. What if that wasn't there? We have nations that come from the city, they've still got beautiful places in there that they go to. We don't want to be beggars.

11

STUCK FOR ILL OR GOOD IN THIS BEAUTIFUL COUNTRY

Dave Sweeney (with Eve Vincent)

Since 1996, Dave Sweeney has been the Australian Conservation Foundation's nuclear-free campaigner. Our conversation focused on the uranium issue in Kakadu National Park.

In 1975, a commission was established to inquire into the environmental aspects of a proposal by the then Australian Atomic Energy Commission in association with Ranger Uranium Mines, to develop Northern Territory uranium deposits. The Ranger Uranium Environmental Inquiry, under the direction of Russell Fox, held public hearings around Australia. It issued two reports, in 1976 and 1977, recommending uranium mining proceed only under strict regulations, as well as recommending the granting of Aboriginal title to a substantial part of the region and the creation of a national park. Development of the Ranger deposit in 1980 proceeded on the basis of the 'Fox Report'. A controversial 'agreement' for a second uranium mine at the Jabiluka deposit was concluded in 1982, but in the same year the Australian Labor Party, which came to power in 1983, agreed to what was then known as the 'three mines' policy. When John Howard's Coalition government moved to proceed with mining at Jabiluka in 1996, traditional owners mounted an international campaign, which was ultimately successful.

The Olympic Dam mine at Roxby Downs in South Australia opened in 1988; here uranium is mined alongside copper and gold. Another Kakadu deposit, Koongarra, has not been developed. In 2014, the federal government finally agreed to traditional owner requests and formally included the Koongarra Project Area in Kakadu National Park. In addition to these scenarios, we discuss the 2007–14 campaign against the proposed national radioactive waste facility at Muckaty Station in the Northern Territory.

How did your involvement in these questions come about?
I was born and grew up on a small farm in country Victoria, which has now been chewed up – small farms chewed up by large houses as the urban sprawl took hold. And that landscape has changed utterly. From creeks and paddocks to the fussy furniture fella and concrete drains. This began happening when I was six or seven. Gone by twelve. [I have] strong, sharp memories of it going. And when going, going so utterly. So that gave me a real sense of the fragility of place, and how things can get lost.

[There were no] Aboriginal people in my life growing up. But at school I was always interested in reading history. And I just never understood why there was this whole fiction that it started with Captain Cook. I still don't get why we don't just say: 'Yeah, there were Aboriginal people here and we came and occupied the country by force. That was unfortunate and here we are now'. So, I always questioned that.

Then in my early twenties I took a year or eighteen months off uni, did the 'hitch-hike around Australia thing', met lots of Aboriginal mob, had lots of stories. Had some frosty receptions, some welcoming receptions. Some good drives in country South

Australia. So put those things together and it brings me to a sort of sensitivity to that issue. I was always interested in and aware of mining politics in Australia. I was cutting my student political teeth in the early 1980s – Cold War time. Reagan and Thatcher; people for nuclear disarmament; Labor changing its uranium policy amidst massive protests. I engaged in that. I went to the first Roxby blockades. Got arrested, got flogged, got involved.

The Howard government got elected in '96. They had a strong policy position to break the sacred cow of uranium, and end the three mines policy, and to get another uranium mine up in Kakadu. And I started to get, again, more and more involved, and took a position, a long time ago now, October 1996 – a 'short-term' position to work on anti-uranium issues.

Prior to 1996, what kind of involvement had environmental groups had in the Kakadu uranium issue?
There were a lot of environmental interests in the 'Fox Inquiry', the Ranger Uranium Environment Inquiry – presentations, submissions and attendances at all of the hearings around the country. There were definitely more urban protests, political protests and processes than there were on country discussions with Mirarr. There was some of that. 'Dirt Cheap' was filmed at the time. [Filmmaker] Ned Lander and people were spending time in that area and having contact. There was Willie Warbeke, Dick Borton and Strider, older activists who have since passed on, who were living in Darwin, or commuting to the Park regularly and talking to people. So there was a connection. It was probably less regular, and less developed than it has subsequently become. And I think there was much more of an assumption, perhaps, that because 'they' were opposed to uranium and 'we' – the greens of the time – were opposed then we were all on the same side and 'it's all okay'.

319

For my part, my closer connection with traditional owners in Kakadu around uranium issues was in the early and mid-1990s. It was initially with Bunitj, the adjacent clan to Mirarr, and that old man, Big Bill, was around. And there was a lot of concern. Ranger has always had problems with water management. And there was a lot of concern about a proposed direct release of contaminated water from the mine site into the Majela Creek. I was approached by people representing that man. We had a series of conversations and that was the beginning of a longer-term connection.

What were people asking for?
This mine was going to dump water, and people were concerned about the impacts of that water, what it means downstream, for water quality and for bush tucker and for people's health. They were really clear that they didn't want that to happen. And they were looking for avenues and supporters to amplify their voice. So we had a set of discussions about what might be possible. And then had a pretty short, sharp effective campaign: the company didn't release.

At that time [the Country Liberal Party] were rusted on and born to rule in the Northern Territory: it was their fiefdom. And the mining company, ERA, owned by North Limited, they could do no wrong. They didn't need permission: 'we are just grateful to have you there generating economic activity' was the approach of government. And so it shocked a few people. And I think it also gave some people a sense of agency.

That relationship grew from there. That formed the basis for more understanding and more connection with people, which was obviously particularly helpful at the time Jabiluka came under intense pressure.

Before we get to Jabiluka, how would you map out the landscape of interests in somewhere like Kakadu? How do you engage with a range of actors?

Kakadu is such a layered and complex set of jurisdictions: Commonwealth land, national parks, traditional owners in various parts of what is the overarching Kakadu, the Northern Land Council, Jabiru Town Development Authority, there's a whole range of players. In relation to the Aboriginal landscape, it's not like there's a set template. We ask, Whose country is it? What's the largely agreed...um, nation? Who are they? Who's the rep body? There's the land council, there's the prescribed body corporate. And also, Who is seen in the region as a significant voice? Who do people listen to? And that is seen through two lenses. One is, Who is seen as a community leader? Who do people on the ground listen to and look to? And then, Who is seen – more externally – as a leader? So you might have the NLC [Northern Land Council] as the agency, as the rep body. You might have Galarrwuy Yunipingu, for example, as *the leader* and you might have on-the-ground leaders like that old man, or like, Toby Gangele in his time. Yvonne Margarula in her time.

As much as is possible, we have a respectful engagement, an initial engagement with traditional owners of the country. Explain who you are, what you are, and what you're seeking. Explain how you see the world, and why their country intersects with that part of the world. Listen then to see if that is in any way shared or reflected. 'Yeah, good to hear someone talking about that, we've been worried about that mine', whatever. If it is, then there's the basis for starting to explore whether there might be more cooperation. And if there's not, then making an assessment about whether or not you pull back from that, *in toto*, or whether or not you respectfully explain why you are going to pursue this course of action and then pursue it in a way that is as least divisive and as least damaging or embarrassing or hurtful as possible.

In your answer there's an awareness of the potential for fostering or exacerbating division. Has that always been there, or has that come through experience?

A bit of both. Aboriginal people have a multiplicity of views on issues, too. There's not like a pan-Aboriginal view, 'This is the black view on everything'. So it's acknowledging that there is that complexity within a community. But it's basically also knowing that if you look back, and you look at pastoral colonisation, frontier wars, and if you look now at particular extractives and resources: the fundamental tactic of the forces of power is 'divide and rule'. And it works. There is a real desire, both on a personal front but also ethically within the organisation, that you don't replicate that pattern. Doesn't mean that you get it all right.

When there's division, what we try and do first is back off, a little bit. Just let a little bit of heat dissipate. Certainly not engage in some kind of social media or media slanging match. Really disrespectful and unhelpful. Back off, let a bit of dust settle. Try and have a quiet conversation with the main proponents that we are in conflict with. And say, 'Look we have real concerns over this project. We have a responsibility to prosecute a case against it, in the wider interests. We don't want to do that in a way that will [cause] further division in the community'. And what happens then is one of three things. One, there's no response. Or there's a response that's hostile, 'You have no right, fuck off'. Or there's a response that says, 'Yeah, fair enough. Understand you've got your job to do. But you've got to understand that...' And then you have a discussion. The outcome of the third one can actually be quite constructive. There might be shared bottom line concerns about transparency, accountability, oversight. With no response, we generally re-establish activity. But we are very cautious to keep our primary target either the state or federal government or the company. The company will say, 'Well Aboriginal people will be the beneficiaries'. We try and avoid buying into that and just instead say, 'Look in every project there are winners and losers, but the losers in this project outweigh the winners and they outweigh them over a period of thousands of years'. And where it is really hostile and we've been told to go, that poses a real challenge. And then we need to sit down and discuss how we best respond to that. It's often much less of a challenge for our Aboriginal partners. They just say, 'Well, he's a dick...he's always done that...she's always been like...I could tell you some things about them...'

We keep coming back to the fact that there's a whole lot of people in the white world that do not agree with what environmentalists are saying, on a whole range of fronts. That doesn't mean that you stop what you're saying because it might offend. We keep coming back to: there's an ecological imperative, there's a thousand species who can't speak for themselves, there are intergenerational and international implications of [Australia's] involvement with the nuclear trade. So, we don't seek to override. But it's fair to say we hold that we have, too, a strong and legitimate imperative for action.

A clear example of that is Muckaty. We engaged actively. We had a very hostile response from the Northern Land Council. The overwhelming majority of both traditional owners and wider communities of Aboriginal interest were strongly supportive: 'C'mon, greenies, help us. We need, we want'. But there was a group of Aboriginal people who didn't want that, and wanted to see the project and particularly the benefits for their family group advanced. We didn't pull out of what could be seen as contested territory because there were some people with that view. We felt that there was enough community support, there were enough procedural irregularities, there was enough bigger-picture environmental and Indigenous justice issues, as well as responsible radiological management issues, that actually required us as a national organisation to engage. And the engagement is then shaped by, 'How do you do that in a way that doesn't divide further the community?' Or put pressure on one faction or group, as if they are in some way less credible or have in some way 'sold out'. I think at Muckaty we managed to do that really well. First order target was where it should have been: the Commonwealth government. Second order target, when it came in occasionally, was the Northern Land Council. We never publically, privately, in written or spoken form criticised Aboriginal people on land who wanted to see the Muckaty project go ahead.

When you do collaborate with Indigenous people, is the understanding of the issue the same? Is there a shared understanding?
I think there are some really fundamental underpinnings that are the same. Like there's an underpinning that country, 'country', land or sea, shapes us, defines us, sustains us. We are part of that web. For Aboriginal mob, it might be: 'We are linked to the earth, it's our mother, it's part of Dreaming stories'. And for the environmental mob, it might be: 'This is a living network, this is an ecosystem of which we are part, we're all part of "Gaia"'. So I think there's a sense of the sustaining aspect of the natural world. And not just, 'It provides our crops'. It's also a spiritual or a value-based sustenance. Meaning, as well as fodder. The importance of keeping that runs deep. And intergenerational importance is really deep, and a sense of fragility: those things can be lost. I

think where things can be really different is short-term versus long-term.

Environmentalists want to see a result. So, if we could stop this, start that, protect this, have its status changed from that…it's result-orientated. Whereas often with Aboriginal people it's more: 'This is the right way to do the thing, you do the thing'. There can be a really fundamental difference sometimes – not so much about the goal but how you get there. Tactics and strategy.

How do you effect change? I think the environmental mob have a sometimes vague, but often a pretty sophisticated answer. 'These are the people that are going to make the decision. This is how we can influence them. This is the level of threshold of awareness or on-the-radar or pain that they need to feel to affect the decision. So let's step out the campaign'. Who do they know, who do they like, who do they dislike? And you map out a campaign. Whereas for Aboriginal mob it's sort of like, 'Well, we own the country, we are the country, and we've said "no"'. And there's often a point where you go, 'Yeah, that's right, that's good. But they're not gonna listen. So we've got to do a whole set of things. We've got to say "no" 58 times'. And mob sometimes say, 'Well, we've said "no". That's that'.

I remember once, years ago, Yvonne Margarula gave this really fantastic interview. I'm sitting off to the side, really pow-erful interview. And then she turned to me: 'Well why can't he just share that one now? Because I've said it now'. And I remember saying, 'Look I'm sorry but you're gonna have to say it one thousand times until you're sick to death of it. That's what's finally going to get through'. 'Well why can't that one just send it to everyone else who is ever interested in the Jabiluka story?'

325

What then are the primary goals of shared undertakings, for you?

What started as primary and what remains primary is the cessation of uranium mining in Kakadu. We want to get that industry out. And that's been something that's been shared by the Mirarr, and other people too – like Jeffrey Lee at Koongarra and others that we've worked with over many years now. What's grown on our side is the awareness – it's sort of self-evident – but it has materially changed our view, which is that you can't just say 'no'. What happens next? Okay, so we stop the mine, we clean up the mine, that's a really big job, great. But then what happens? So that there's an income stream, so that there's service delivery. And that should happen in a way the community own and drive. Or, if that's too much, they at least shape, and are fully at the table. They are not bit players, and leave it to us as levels of government to now decide a restructuring plan.

Recently the ACF and Gundjeihmi Aboriginal Corporation, celebrated and noted fifteen years of the Kakadu Charter. And I am quite proud of that thinking – Jabiluka was a hot battle, and most of the charter is about what will happen after we've won. Most of it's about building a mine-free, vibrant, Aboriginal-controlled regional economy. And I remember at the time some people going, 'Well, this is so far down the track, what are you doing this for?' And we were like, 'Well, this is pivotal'. It was almost cockily assuming and stating, 'We're gonna win. And after we win, we're going to consolidate the win, so that that sort of crap never happens again, and it's done differently'.

So did Mirarr put that on your agenda? A beyond-the-campaign future vision?

Absolutely. And that was a sharp learning curve on our side, you know. This is long-term, and this is two-way. It's not just, 'Here's the platform and can someone stand up with a black skin and say "we don't want uranium mining in Kakadu, we love that place and ERA's no good"'. And then everyone claps and they sit down and then we talk about how we're going to do it. There was that. But it wasn't just that. There was more than that.

We did explain, 'These are the theatre bits. We will go to Sydney, Melbourne and Canberra. In Canberra it will be politicians, they're really busy, it needs to be short and sharp. In Sydney and Melbourne, it will be people who don't necessarily really understand a lot that's going on, but they're really sympathetic. They're really supportive. And they would really like to meet you, and hear about what your life's like: what you eat, what you do, why you're worried about this mine'. Sometimes that was spectacularly good, sometimes that was spectacularly...oh God. You know, [testily], 'We can't go outside and have a smoke now, and then come back in, and do all the security palaver again, because in seven minutes, for twelve minutes, we've got the minister. The minister. So let's stay right on track and we can have two times as many smokes in half an hour, so let's just nail this'.

What happens when you deal with someone who says, 'Don't cast me in your play'? Is there pushback against that?

Yes, yes. And it is really difficult, and it happens heaps. And one of the keys is to explain, beforehand, be as clear as possible what it's about. So it's not just, 'You're going south for ten days'. It's, 'Here are the separate components, there are separate parts of it, these parts here are full on, really critical, no big night the night before, no this, no that, no shopping, no mucking around. This one here, these politicians, they can make a real difference'.

That's just the reality of it. We – white Australian male activist blah – are much more in the world of setting up a meeting at Parliament House, talking to a staffer to confirm it, getting through security protocols, getting to the room on time, than crew who are living in the bush. So it's not like you are more powerful. You've got more of a skill set. If I was walking around country with them then I would be completely lost, adrift, and defer to their superbly superior skills. I'm not saying mine are superbly superior but it's a shrunk-down light version of the other way. They're now out of their depth in a patch you're more familiar with: step up, help it, facilitate it, make it flow.

Is there not though a colonial aspect to the relationship you describe? Does that critique arise?

It arose then, it has arisen ever since. And it will arise, I am sure, for the rest of my engaged life. Absolutely. I've had lots and lots of harsh, sometimes 'yeah, hard but fair', and sometimes 'just unreasonable, and where's that coming from' critiques, assessments and vitriol. I've, fortunately, had much more acknowledgement and support and solidarity. But no shortage of the other. It still hurts – there's no question about that. But over time I've become a little bit more resilient. As they say in Tennant Creek: 'It goes with the territory'. The space is an emotionally charged space. And it is a space that has a profound power imbalance. And as you go further down the track, not because you're wiser or anything, but just because you're a year older, rounder and greyer you realise that you're a privileged white man, you can talk, you expect people to at least listen, you sometimes pull a bit of rank – not all have this agency, and with that comes a responsibility to use that.

Cornish and Indigenous author Bruce Pascoe, in *Convincing Ground* wrote, 'The blacks didn't die, and the whites aren't going away'. And I read that and thought, 'In Latin, on a tattoo: maybe'. It makes profound and continuing sense to me. There's no smoothing of the dying pillow. The swag is full and growing. And whites aren't leaving. So sometimes I find aspects of the sovereignty debate, and sometimes I find aspects of the whole framing, on both sides of the discussion, to lack that fundamental matter-of-factness. We're now stuck, for good or ill, in this country. It's a beautiful country. You had it, we took it. It was by force, without consent. Okay, sorry about that. Now it's 2015. Where does that leave us?

There's a massive structural imbalance that needs to be addressed on the white side because we're the victors of force. We're the beneficiaries of crime. So that brings with it the responsibility to actively address that. It also brings with it the requirement to suck up stuff even when it's unfair, because there's a bigger picture. At the same time, I don't reckon it does an individual or a nation or a movement any good to just say 'sorry' all the time. Those environmental activists, those who are locking on at Jabiluka, those who are doing stuff to try and actively make a difference, did not poison waterholes. They are the inheritors, they are the beneficiaries, but they didn't do that stuff. And they are actively, in their life, trying to undo that stuff.

Environmental activists shouldn't make the mistake of getting burnt, saying sorry, or, the opposite, saying 'get lost, that's unfair' and withdrawing. And on the other side, Aboriginal people generally are amazingly generous of spirit and continue to slap us around a little bit, continue to jerk the chain, remind us of that power imbalance. But don't have it set in cement that you cannot or ever be otherwise than a colonial thief. Otherwise we're in a frozen, no-good zone.

We're getting into these difficulties now, so let's talk more about when these relationships get tested. What of the conflicts that unfolded around Australia in 1998 and into 1999 about the direction and control of the Jabiluka campaign? Could you revisit some specific moments?

At the blockade, it was reflected through lifestyle- or anarchically-minded activists who were like, 'I'm not signing a code of conduct, be that from Aboriginal people or not'. Because there was a Mirarr passport: a protocol on country, as a condition for being on country. And some people had enormous issues with that, and that was one tension.

The style of action was a tension at Jabiluka – timing and style. Sometimes traditional owners didn't want anything that could lead to risk or someone being hurt. Some areas were no-go areas: 'Take that banner down, that's a special spot, you should never have been there'. Actions involving the spraying of animal blood to show the blood on the hands of the nuclear industry went down like a lead balloon, and caused tensions. And then there were the urban-based Jabiluka Action Groups: Who controls them? What's their primary focus, is it to stop a mine, or is it to build an awareness of stolen country in a massive pan-Aboriginal way?

What are the sources of these kinds of tensions?

I reckon one is that Aboriginal people and communities feel that their role is tokenistic rather than key. They feel they are being used to support a fly-in fly-out short-term campaign rather than a longer-term one addressing a whole set of grievances.

I think another is miscommunication. People just don't hear the same words.

And another variation on that is unreasonable expectations – on both sides. The greenies expect that Aboriginal people will be there at the drop of a hat because there's an important media or political opportunity. And the Aboriginal crew often think that the greenies are rich. Greenies have lots of money because they live in cities that have lots of money. And they can do this, and they can do that. If it's put up really early, 'Hey, we haven't got enough money. And the two people you are working most closely with are working one day a week each, that's what they get paid for'. 'True?!' Then generally it works out really well, and people are really good. If that isn't done, because either people are a bit shy to say that, or because people really want to see it happen, and because 'that's what they've asked for, and they're the traditional owners, and we need to honour that' – for whatever reason, it comes apart at some point. So I reckon expectation is a big thing.

Cultural protocols, or lack of awareness or lack of sensitivity to them: that can be a really big thing. A difference in speed and need. Like, 'We need you to sign off on a media release by 11 o'clock or we'll miss today's news cycle. And if we catch today's news cycle we'll get a really good hit on this, we'll be front page of the *Sydney Morning Herald*. And 150,000 people will see it. So can you just get the mob together – it's two paragraphs. You've already sort of agreed to 95 per cent...can...you...just...' 'Ahhh. Maybe'.

Often activists come into contact with an Aboriginal reality that is slightly different to what is hoped for or expected. At Jabiluka blockade, because of a history of missionary activity, and contemporary Christian beliefs, women were advised to dress more conservatively. And greenies didn't go to Kakadu to meet Christianity, in the guise of a traditional owner...

Yes, yes. And it can be Aboriginal people eating crappy food, and wearing clothes with a whole bunch of American sport teams, or 'earth-destroying' corporations' logos on them. And it's a long way from, 'Come with me and we'll walk together and learn the old knowledge'. Sometimes the aspirations of Aboriginal people are the aspirations of a whole bunch of non-Aboriginal people in Australian societies. 'I reckon one of those HSV Holden Commodores. That would be the best thing, man'. And you're there expecting that to have been, 'The protection of my country, and being able to pass on my stories'. But it's the HSV Holden Commodore. And it doesn't mean that the other one isn't important but it's the perception, the expectation.

A lot of Aboriginal people are really cautious about the environmental mob. They think that they'll force them to eat tofu, that they'll growl them for all sorts of things. That they're not funny. They're all really serious, and they'll get in trouble all the time, they pick fights and look to draw attention to themselves. And, 'I'm a quiet person, I'm a peaceful person, I don't want my family mixed up in those arrests'.

Were those tensions, at the blockade and within the JAG groups ever resolved, in your view?
They were never really neatly and comprehensively resolved. And I still sometimes run into non-Indigenous people whose scar tissue hasn't healed. I think people made their own resolution – peace or non-peace with it. And then the time moved on. I remember once saying to a Melbourne-based Aboriginal activist involved in all of this, 'You're like a World War I general, you just keep marching them up'. And he said, 'Yeah, well, I want the ones that

can come through the fire'. That's not the norm in the environmental movement. We tend to be more, 'How are you feeling, do you feel supported? Let's debrief about that because it was a really confronting time'. We can overdo the circle work!

So I seesaw between the real importance of reflection, and then, 'Don't over-reflect, don't overcook'. Talk and do. I haven't found easy recipes or formulas, and I don't think there are. Without trying to sound too cheesy about it, I really do think that authenticity is key. You might be on a comparable path or you might even be – from the perspective of an Aboriginal person or community person on the wrong path – but at least he/she is fair dinkum about it. I think a real key is not to surprise. In the sense that, 'I thought you were on our side, and then I realised you're not'. And then I think another real key, and I've learnt this from hard experience too: don't over-promise just because you wish it were so. I've been party to that in the past. Because I've really wanted something not to happen on people's country, when I've been speaking with people who share that desire that that thing won't happen – you talk like it's three-quarter time. And you may have created expectations beyond what you can deliver. That's a danger.

What are the strengths of Indigenous-environmentalist engagements, and what are your hopes for future engagements?

The strengths, I reckon, can be seen really clearly with the Kakadu experience. In 2001, we were looking in Kakadu at the expansion of one existing mine, the opening of two new ones, and an extension of uranium mining in the Kakadu mineral province through to 2050. And we are going to be over and out – mining's finished now. Koongarra's in the [National] Park, Jabiluka's not going anywhere and Ranger's stopped digging and they're just processing. And that processing will be finished in two years. By 2020, it will be over, and we will be in advanced rehab of the one messy mine. That is extraordinary. And it's happened because of a black-green alliance.

Other strengths? The Australian Nuclear Free Alliance – the power of that network, ragged around the edges, sometimes frustrating because of an appetite greater than capacity and all that sort of stuff, but it has delivered consistently. Seventeen or eighteen years of meetings, materials, relationships. Really important. Unfunded.

Muckaty is a classic. Little, little mob against the NLC but above all against the Commonwealth government, with full override powers in law, and beaten. There's no Muckaty dump, never will be a Muckaty dump. But mob on their own would not have been able to carry that. Greenies on their own would not have been able to stop that. One gives a moral authority, a sense of place and time. One gives an amplification and a sense of pressure points and momentum. And when they work together, they're a very, very powerful and positive combination.

And apart from site-specific case studies, I think it's really pivotal for the future of this nation that the twin strands of the world's oldest culture and the protection of the country that sustains and shapes that culture, are linked. My hopes for the future are that that happens, that those connections grow, that they're consolidated.

I want to personally see the environment movement find – we are so scantly resourced but I would love to find – some resources that ensured Indigenous people who wanted to see how the game plays in our world, could do internships and placements. And a bit of vice versa, so that people see the pressures that exist in communities, and it's not just, 'You clock on at nine and you do your stuff and you clock off. Oh, it's a late night, I'll go through to six-fifteen'. There are demands, constantly, and the environmental movement is one of the demands. And I suppose I'd like to see more reflection on what works and what doesn't, what's complex and what's not. Not making an easy road map, but capturing some things that have worked. I want to see things documented.

I'd love to get the funding for a piece to screen on the ABC and SBS – an eight-minute piece on the Jeffrey Lee/Koongarra story. Guy offered multiple millions of dollars, says 'no'. Looks after his country, and says, 'I'm a richer man for looking after my country'. In the time we're living in, irrespective of black-green, people need to hear that those things aren't just an aspiration, or some sort of happy-clapper hope. It's actually happening.

12

NEVER SQUIB THE RIGHTS ISSUES IN FAVOUR OF CONSERVATION

Anthony Esposito (with Timothy Neale)

Anthony Esposito has been an activist for over three decades, working in multiple environmental organisations and with traditional owner organisations. He ran the Native Title and Protected Areas project under the auspices of the Queensland Conservation Council, encompassing regional, state and national environmentalist organisations operating in Queensland. After this, he was the manager of the National Indigenous Conservation Program for The Wilderness Society. Through his roles in these organisations he was engaged in major campaigns and collaborations in northern Australia, including Cape York Peninsula, the Gulf, Channel Country and the Kimberley; and in south-west Australia, including the Great Western Woodlands and the Nullabor.

For the past several years, Anthony has been involved in strategic efforts to prevent the opening up of the Galilee Basin to coal mining, and works with the Wangan and Jagalingou Traditional Owners Family Council in their opposition to the proposed Carmichael mega-coalmine and in their 'defence of country'.

We discuss the context in which we first met — the Queensland Wild Rivers Act controversy — and the challenges and opportunities for environmentalist groups in engaging with Indigenous groups and their country.

To start off, could you describe how you came to be involved with Indigenous groups as an activist?

For me it goes back to the mid–1980s when I lived and worked in a couple of remote communities, Papunya and Kintore, in Central Australia. That was the foundation experience for how I later thought about questions of traditional owners' land rights, conservation and peoples' economic and community development needs. It was a pivotal period for me, but also in national political terms: the year I was there was the year of the Uluru hand back, a milestone in conservation and Aboriginal rights. It was also the year when the Pintupi from the outer Western Desert walked into Kiwirrkurra outstation; and that was their first 'point of contact', if you like, with Australian settler society. In that situation, I wasn't seeing colonialism as an abstract idea of the past. I was confronted in reality by that process.

Were you there as a community worker?

I was there because of my relationship with a woman who was a teacher in the schools. As a result of that I became engaged with the community in various ways: housing projects, community work, school nutrition programs – things that are part of being present in that space and making a contribution. Papunya was absolutely a product of the assimilationist era and had the hallmarks of a ghost town with a tragic past. By contrast, Kintore was a product of the homelands movement of self-determination and an assertion of connection to country. Despite its relative impoverishment in conventional terms, it was a very happy place at the time.

How did you come to be involved in environmental organisations?

When I returned to my home on the east coast, those experiences had broadened my outlook on the continent. I could see through my travels how devastating the impacts of colonisation were, not only in terms of the landscape but also in terms of social and economic processes that had torn, and were continuing to tear, the place apart. I just had a deep visceral response to the destruction of the land and this strong awareness of the original people. Therefore, what I had to do was consider *my* place here, and what I could do with the rights I enjoyed as a free Australian, someone who was essentially in a globally and historically advantaged position. So, I simply looked for avenues to develop that perspective, and, getting into the late 1980s, my impression of some of the environment groups was that they were attempting to engage with Aboriginal rights and protect country, though it wasn't true of the entire movement by any means.

What do you think was motivating those environmental groups that didn't engage or were not interested in engaging with Indigenous groups and rights?

I wouldn't say just 'not interested in' but also, at times, actively opposed to. What was motivating it, I'd say, is the wider misunderstanding of Australia's history, the nature of the colonial project, and, also, an attachment to inherited forms of conservation. National parks, of that previous era, belong to a different worldview and people were deeply attached to that worldview and their achievements. Some felt threatened by Aboriginal claims to those lands or Aboriginal uses of the resources of those lands. That's where it stems from and it was a catalyst, in my view, for changing the movement and the policies of the movement over a period of time.

But was there a golden era of the 'green–black alliance'?
I don't think there's a golden era of *anything*. What I think is that there were progressive phases in which it became apparent that there were grounds on which Aboriginal people and conservationists could work together to mutual benefit. They were the black–green alliances. They were positive in many ways, at various times, and I think that things like the hand back of Uluru were part of that willingness to try to bring about some measure of land justice. But many people assumed that to be the natural order of things – that Aboriginal people are somehow proto-conservationists, and they therefore automatically line up with the worldview of non-indigenous conservationists. That simply wasn't true. The complexities of the real issues played out over time and 'black–green conflict', if you like, came to the fore at a certain stage of development. I think that was the maturing of the relationship, so that now we actually have to treat these issues with much more depth of thought and come to terms with a whole set of issues that hadn't really been dealt with in the context of those early alliances, when we had the euphoria of achieving good ends together.

You've said elsewhere that the idea that Indigenous people necessarily prefer conservation is a 'contemporary nonsense'. Where do you think that idea comes from?
I think it comes, in part, from an unreconstructed romantic notion of Aboriginality. It has real currency as an idea, because the fact is that Aboriginal people did evolve an incredibly intricate system of land management, embodied in which was a knowledge

of the way country worked in terms of its ecological processes. They didn't define them in the contemporary scientific language, but defined them in terms of their cosmologies and their economic realities. So, they had, and have, a complex worldview in their relationship to country. The idea that it was harmonious, based in this spiritual hovering above the landscape, is just a romantic notion of those relationships, and the robustness, the durability and longevity of them. Where I think it transitions into contemporary ideas is that it was a system that was managed for so long to be sustainable, to have this intricate balance in a dynamic system. It's a fantastic model of conservation in that sense. Then there's this fundamental question of 'what is conservation?' In my understanding, conservation is a learned thing, it's a process of evolution of knowledge as human interaction with our environments transcends natural limits and then discovers and responds to that fact. So, the question in the Aboriginal context, which is unanswered, is 'did they, at various past points, exceed the limits of their environment and develop a response to that which you might call conservation?' That's unanswered, in my mind, and it doesn't really matter. Today, we are in a situation where we absolutely know we collectively have exceeded those limits, that conservation is an imperative for all of humanity. By virtue of who they are and where they come from, and what they've witnessed – having seen that destruction of lands and waters and species – Aboriginal peoples have reacted against that from a deep land ethic. And I think that's what people are trying to bring out in what we have termed 'Indigenous conservation' in recent years.

The implication then is that there are Aboriginal people who do not have that conservation worldview. They do not want to continue those practices.

Yes, that's fair enough. This is part of the complexity, because they're just emphasising something else, in a sense, that's in accord with their needs and values today. In a contemporary world of economic imperatives that includes the need to use the natural resources of the land to sustain themselves, their families, and to build livelihoods. But we all have this dichotomy to deal with – this notion of economic development over conservation. The fact is we must actually implement conservation as an organising principle because the global economic development model is exceeding the carrying capacity of the planet. It may be that the planet will adjust around the scale and intensity of human impacts – but it's also indifferent to our fate. The conservation imperative is about our own sustainability and the duration of our kind. This is about conscious choices we need to make. But then if we do these things, if we stop certain forms of development, the question arises as to who is disadvantaged and who is advantaged? These are equity issues. They're not questions of economic development-as-such or conservation-as-such, they're questions about the allocation of resources in the system we have: Is it just for people? And does it sustain the essential processes of life?

Does that not put you in the situation where what you contend is sustainable is different to some Indigenous groups?

For me personally, yes, and for the environmental movement, yes. But it also puts me in the same position with some Indigenous people, as well. I just treat this as a live debate. We all have to engage on those key topics, on a serious level, with matters of justice and equity in mind. I happen to acknowledge that there is an environmental crisis and that climate change poses a significant threat that we all have a stake in addressing. It's not a middle-class urban parlour game. It's a serious confrontation with the realities of our existence. And I chose to engage in that, bringing something to the table – some willingness to learn and to think our way through these problems. This involves social and political interactions. It's how we proceed in that space that is the important ethical consideration.

Was there a trigger for the change from the 'alliance' framework to the 'conflict' framework?

Like a lot of these things, when the trigger 'trips' it looks like things happened suddenly, but these were inherent tensions for a very long time. Inherent in the relations between Aboriginal and conservation groups and inherent in relations between First Nations and settler society peoples. But also between certain policy ideas, particularly those articulated by Noel Pearson around welfare reform and Indigenous economic development needs and rights, and conservation initiatives that were extending beyond the conventional models of protected areas into whole landscape conservation. In cases like the *Wild Rivers Act* or World Heritage on Cape York, the intent of conservation was to manage whole landscapes or whole catchments in these extensive areas of Aboriginal-owned or claimed lands, where there was a majority population of Aboriginal people. Conservation came very much into confrontation with questions of land rights and how those could or would lead to economic development as a path out of dependency and welfare. Wild Rivers really did become the trigger for that debate. There were skirmishes along the way but the Wild Rivers policy was the development of conservation into a new model – from the protected areas idea and the 'CAR' system of comprehensive, adequate and representative sampling of bioregions – into scientific modelling of landscape conservation of whole systems. That environmental science trajectory met the Aboriginal rights movement when it was achieving the consolidation of large parcels of land and looking towards economic development opportunities for Aboriginal communities.

In such cases it could be said, then, that environmentalists were attempting to speak for Indigenous peoples' country. How do you respond to that?

I'm not simply a product of the environment movement and I don't, especially these days, speak for it. But as a representative of environmental organisations over a considerable period, and someone whose role it was to build the policies and frameworks to enable the movement to meet Aboriginal people on a respectful level, I have a particular perspective. First, there can be Aboriginal environmental organisations. SEED, a young climate activist network, is an example where Indigenous people are taking the environment agenda as their own and building into it their own worldview. Second, I think people just have to be clear about their standing in the world. So, if you're an environmental NGO, based predominantly on the support of non-Indigenous people, playing a role in public policy and advocacy in the mainstream political system, you cannot speak for Aboriginal people. It's obvious. You should work with Aboriginal people in the appropriate contexts and carry on a dialogue, and if you are able to build agreements and alliances and shared policy positions then that's a good thing. My role was to try to enable that to happen.

In those cases where you cannot, though, do you absent yourself? Should others?

You can't absent yourself. That's a cop-out! You really have to show up for that stuff and it's the conflicts where we really have to do the work. I showed up for the Wild Rivers debate because I believed it was important and I took on board personally the stresses, strains and intellectual and moral challenges of trying to resolve those issues. We don't always get to resolve them in the first go, and between the first, second or third go might be a space of twenty years. Real purpose and real commitment are essential to the task.

You've worked on campaigns from within and without NGOs (non-governmental organisations). What are some of the challenges of working within one?

The challenges are numerous. Probably the first is that you have a responsibility to the group you work for and its objectives. If those objectives come into conflict with Aboriginal peoples' view of their rights, then you've got to deal with that. I found it difficult if you don't have an organisation-wide policy that's up to the mark in dealing with it – then you end up trying to manage between these conflicting but important values to craft some new understanding, but all the while in a conflict zone. That's extremely challenging. One of the things I regarded as important was the need for time inside those organisations to reflect and do some deep thinking, get the approach sorted out so they can proceed with real conviction and integrity. It wasn't always possible because on both sides of that 'fence' – the organisational knowledge issues and the human relationship issues – the dialogue with Aboriginal people is not always advanced enough to accommodate all this. It's not particular to environmental organisations; it's a feature of living in

Australia and having to confront the realities of our history. We mostly do a fairly mediocre job of that task as a society in relation to Aboriginal First Nations.

In campaigns where you've worked with Indigenous groups, are there shared understandings of the issues?
I think there can be, but I don't think there's simply two distinct and dichotomous worldviews. There's a spectrum of understanding and as human beings with human rights and a common origin we can understand each other. There can be better understanding. In terms of the people I've worked with, I've been lucky to be involved in campaigns where I shared more understanding of the world and the landscape with Aboriginal people than with people on the non-indigenous side. I have as many differences, possibly more, with people who are non-Indigenous in Australia. I think it's entirely possible to build shared understanding. If you want to create a wider benefit, we all have to understand each other, put some effort into dialogue, and not react at the first sign of difference, difficulties or conflicts.

What, for you, are the common primary goals of shared undertakings?
This is where my value set is fairly clear. They are in land justice and protection of country. The management of natural resources in a way that can sustain people and that can allow us to reconcile our existence here.

What do you mean by 'land justice'?
I mean a couple of things. One is that we have to attend to the question of Aboriginal land rights. It cannot be ignored. It also means we have to, all of us, treat the land with respect. Bringing a

just measure and equilibrium to it means not allowing destructive processes to be the accepted norm. We actually have to craft a system over time that can be both equitable and sustainable, but we're moving dramatically away from that. The devastation of lands and waters is the collateral damage of an unjust economic system, which is the product of imperialist, colonialist and industrial and technological forces. And, in one sense, all of that is accelerating. We no longer have the old empires, the old colonies, or the old economic order – they've become these transnational rapacious systems of exploitation. There's an order in which destruction takes place and over a long developmental period, over hundreds of years. The first displacement, the first destruction, is to remove Indigenous people from their lands and to take possession of those lands and start carving them up for natural resources and property rights, and on it goes, to where we build a system of exploitation of the life system that has reached a point of danger at a global scale, and a point of profound economic disparity.

Another figuring of 'land justice' would be Indigenous sovereignty – that it would be just for Indigenous people to determine what is right for their land. Do you agree with that?
I think there's some first principles around that question of sovereignty. There were and still are self-governing Indigenous people and they have the right to govern their own affairs and use their lands. They're the sort of principles embodied in the UN Declaration on the Rights of Indigenous Peoples. I think we start from that. It's a first principle. From that flows the question, in an Australian context, of how do you bring about some compact between the settler society, which is essentially a colony that came and stayed and is not going away, and the Indigenous peoples?

That's a serious political question, one inadequately addressed in ideas like 'recognition' and the Recognise campaign. Then, you do what you would do in any other context where sovereignty between nations is the rule, like the United Nations system, and ask the question of what powers and rights of decision-making does a sovereign group have? What responsibilities do they have to their own peoples and to the wider world? That's the debate we have to have. So, if Aboriginal people are in control of lands and waters – which is atypical in Australia today – and have the power, resources and capital to exploit them to the degree that non-Indigenous industrial society exploits those things, then the issue is one of: Is that acceptable harm? Is that good? Is that something we have concerns about? I simply think that if digging up uranium is acceptable to you then I'm going to have a conversation with you because I do not. That you could harm others is probably the key issue here. Where do we draw the line? How do we adjudicate?

Then let me put a question to you. If an Indigenous group want a mine or gas hub on their country then, in campaigning against it, aren't environmentalists limiting their sovereignty?

I don't believe that's necessarily true. Say I happened to campaign against human rights abuses in Saudi Arabia or China, am I not entitled to that view? And, in what sense am I harming their sovereignty by doing so? Their sovereignty is embodied in the power to exercise sovereignty. This is the problem when trying to discuss Aboriginal sovereignty: they don't have that power. The settler society has that power. And most of the time these issues become arguments amongst different parts of the settler society about what view they take on Aboriginal people. So, when we get to a position of Aboriginal sovereignty again I'll happily engage that debate, and I'll be very mindful not to harm their sovereignty, but I also won't forfeit my own human rights and democratic rights. This is a challenge and definitely something I think about a lot. I think we all have to confront the meaning of being someone who finds themselves in Australia – whether they're born here or arrive here – but are not of the first peoples. We can have connections with Aboriginal people that are mutual and respectful but still have to come to terms with the fundamental realities of who we are and where we are and how the dominant society came about.

Can you think of examples where you or organisations you were working for changed your goals through your relationships with Indigenous people?

I think the work on Cape York was an example of change over time. That was really about trying to negotiate agreements that were acceptable to all parties. The early days, the mid-1990s, was one of those landmark moments where people realised things had to be done in a different way; a new order of things. The advent of native title was the driver, and that spurred a whole bunch of work and thinking about different ways to deliver conservation outcomes. New models of national parks were created that were Aboriginal-owned, land returns were made. It was leading edge in its day though by today's UN standards I'd say there were some shortcomings. Nonetheless, they are examples. The project that I managed in the 1990s was about shifting environmental groups' goals and policy positions in relation to Aboriginal people's rights and to protected areas: that is traditional owners claims over those areas, their right to management, and evolving different models of management. The Indigenous Protected Areas program and its massive expansion is another good example. It came from some people trying to find a solution to a policy driver, being that you had to get these representative samples of bioregions and there were places where the old national park model – taking land out of the so-called 'public land estate' and converting it from one tenure to another – wouldn't work because those were Aboriginal-owned lands. So, a whole new concept emerged and, instead of simply staying as a response to one policy driver, it rapidly transformed into a whole new approach to land management and conservation in Australia, especially in the big remote landscapes. In the last twenty years conservation is quite different to what it was.

And what about the inverse: can you think of instances where Aboriginal groups changed their goals through their contact with you?

I would actually say Wild Rivers was one example, because what was really going on from the inside was a genuine attempt to shift the model. The Wilderness Society was supportive enough with the policy that the Queensland government had, as conservation, but it was not happy with the way it proceeded with it and implemented it, in the first instance. The government had to be dragged to a new negotiating position, to take the opportunity to build a new conservation model based on partnership with Aboriginal people and a clear recognition of their rights. Governments are typically quite slow when it comes to conservation but in this case, from the initial advocacy to the adoption of public policy was a short time frame, and all the policy issues we put up at that time were not answered before the program proceeded.

Now, a number of Aboriginal groups, such as those who made their way to Canberra in 2010 and started changing the nature of that debate, they didn't start from saying, 'we want Wild Rivers'. They started from engaging on it and saying, 'what's going on here? We are concerned about our rivers but we're not sure what this is', and then working together with us and getting information. They became advocates for that protection, so long as – and this was the change – the government addressed a number of key issues for them around rights, equity and participation. So, the government's work shifted over that time and things like the [2007] *Cape York Heritage Act* were the product of trying to reconcile economic development needs and conservation needs while confirming native title rights. No rights would be extinguished or the legislation would have to cede – all that was progressive work and it was driven from two directions: non-Indigenous conservationists who wanted that level of protection *and* were supportive of Aboriginal rights, and Indigenous conservationists who were prepared to take legislative protections because it would give some guarantees around the protection and management of their country and defend it against mining. That was a good – and largely unnoticed – product of that exchange.

When things go askew or there are problems in collaborations, what tend to be the causes? Can you think of an example?

They're many and varied, and I hesitate to keep talking about Cape York but it is such a fertile field for all these issues. I think the Kimberley has some parallels, particularly the James Price Point campaign, and the east coast gas fields. Where there are good relationships, or they start out well, they can falter on different understandings of objectives. The fact that Aboriginal people come into it with their whole rights agenda, so to speak, and conservation groups come into it with their conservation agenda – that's always a fault line. Where the issues are narrowly issues of conservation, then it's easier to manage, but where the wider issues around economic need or impoverishment or inequity are present, it's much harder. It need not be acrimonious, but there are limitations to 'black-green alliances' and it's not really possible for environment groups to exceed their mandates. They end up being agencies amongst a set of others within non-Indigenous society who are implementing a variety of policies in an uncoordinated fashion. For Aboriginal people, in my experience, what frustrates them and buggers things up is this multitude of different policy lines, and agencies, and often contradictory and conflicting approaches. Their need for a coherent interface with the non-Indigenous system to deliver a set of outcomes over which they have self-management and self-governance, some control and can give consent, that's something that will always throw up some difficulties. That was true in Cape York, it was true in the Kimberley, and it's true on Stradbroke Island and other places too.

Are environmental groups unwilling or unable to look at those broader issues?

There are plenty of people that are willing to, and hence some effort went into things like the notion of a conservation economy. There was serious advocacy and collaboration that went into building ranger programs as a way of encapsulating Aboriginal land management imperatives in a job-creating system. The reviews of those ranger programs tend to point to very positive social, economic, and environmental outcomes by fusing that set of issues with a conservation objective and proper resourcing for real work. We spend hundreds of millions, if not billions, of dollars every year through public budgets in natural resource management and this is one aspect of that. So, ranger programs are a really important and constructive example of how environmental groups are open to, willing and able, to advocate more widely. But they're not all open to it, or they don't all necessarily see it as their responsibility. That's a barrier and an unnecessary limitation on conservation options.

One of the criticisms that has been levelled at environmental groups is that they devote resources to particular Indigenous groups and not others. How do you respond to that criticism or debate?

It's not debate but a political contest in which people are, often, trying to justify their own standpoints by some claim to moral superiority in relation to Aboriginal people. It's also, often times, insulting. But that's politics and if you want public policy and historical initiatives then you have to engage and there's no point in whinging about it. It seems simple enough that Aboriginal groups are going to forge relationships with others in accordance with their interests and others are going to do the same in relation to Aboriginal people. So, you're naturally going to get alignments and flows of resources where environmentalists and Aboriginal people are working together. You'll also get the same, and with a much higher degree of resourcing, where mining and development interests find Aboriginal groups to work with. I don't see what the real issue is. If that work is done in public view and there's openness, transparency and it's done fairly then so what?

Have collaborations you've been involved in ever come to a breaking point? And if so, over what kinds of questions?

Maybe not necessarily 'breaking' but ending points, yes. I think they most often come about around issues of representation. This is probably one of the key areas for environmentalists still, which is to make the distinction between themselves and others in the campaign space. I don't want to denigrate anyone here, but there's now a willingness to take up Aboriginal environmental causes into the movement as though it belonged to and was a part of that movement, and therefore to represent them. Or to front environmental campaigns with Aboriginal people. I think we have to be careful around that. It's a conscientious process of building real relationships and negotiations, and I don't think we know fully how to manage that tension properly. There's a tendency, because Aboriginal voices are generally excluded, that environment groups may think they need their assistance to be heard. But, it's not that Aboriginal people can't and don't represent themselves, it's that the system is often stacked against them. And there are systemic racial barriers that make it harder for their voices to be heard.

But Aboriginal people must get to speak in that space, and I think there's a concern that they may not speak the language of environmentalists. That's the thing – they won't speak it and they don't want to, in my experience, unless they happen to work for environmental organisations – and there are very few Aboriginal people working in and for environmental NGOs. That's where you're dealing with two different things. The language needs to be around partnerships, or support, or mutual benefits, where they exist, but those things can't be fused unless they actually have been fused, and I don't think they will be nine times out of ten. It's been a source of tension in other places, like in Canada there's that sense – it's the difference between extractivist or instrumental relationships that an organisation might have with an Indigenous group, where that Indigenous group would serve the purpose of the campaign, and a relationship where everyone's goals and rights and interests are clearly articulated.

What are your hopes for the future of these engagements, for yourself but also for the environmental movement?

Again I want to draw a distinction because I don't feel like part of the wider environment movement or that I can speak for the wider movement. My current involvements are in working directly with Aboriginal groups who are seeking to achieve certain justice and defence of country goals. What I'd like to see the movement do, as someone with a history of involvement it in, is to keep taking up these issues and work really hard to develop them up to the next level – and the next level means coming very clearly to terms with things like the UN Declaration and shifting their policies to align with that. I'd like to see them never, and I mean *never*, squib the rights issues in favour of conservation. Have the courage to measure up. I would hope that people would continue to use their influence to help shift the policy framework so that the conservation goal can be achieved with an advance in Aboriginal peoples' rights. That was the official position of the groups I worked with, but it's unfinished business, long-term reform, and the challenge for these NGOs is that indirect long-term policy work doesn't sit easily and comfortably when the conservation imperatives they deal with are immediate and critical. I'd like to see the movement invest in both so that over the next ten to twenty years we've seen genuine and substantial progress.

Your own experience suggests one response is to leave the movement and support the defence of country.

That's a personal choice, and for me it's because I'd reached personal and political limits. I needed to find a new place for my work. It's not a criticism. It's just simply a natural progression, for me, after spending a couple of decades doing this work. There are plenty of other people to continue that work inside the environmental

NGOs, if the organisations are willing. For me, being able to work with traditional owners and help remove the barriers to Indigenous peoples' agency in that space is what's important.

13

CLIMATE CHANGE, RECOGNITION AND SOCIAL PLACE-MAKING

Tony Birch

Introduction

Recent scientific studies in Australia have reached alarming conclusions regarding climate change and the rapid acceleration of unpredictable and damaging weather events. A joint University of Queensland and Griffith University study found that Australia is on track to reach a 2°C average temperature rise by 2030, a date a decade or more earlier than previous predictions.[1] The figure is also above the 1.5°C rise in temperature agreed to as 'the preferred limit to protect vulnerable island states' at the United Nations global conference on climate change in Paris in December 2015. As a consequence of the predicted temperature rise, the authors of the research have warned, 'we have a choice: leave people in poverty and speed toward dangerous global warming through the increased use of fossil fuels, or transition rapidly to renewables'.[2]

A similar study, analysing temperature rises in the Northern Hemisphere over a similar period, produced an equally dire prediction. A 2°C rise in temperatures, the research concluded, would result in the planet 'breaching a terrifying milestone':

As of 3 March [2016] it appears that the average temperatures across the northern hemisphere breached 2°C pre-industrial levels for the first time in recorded history, and probably the first time since human civilization began thousands of years ago.[3]

The research, while not dependent on scare tactics or apocalyptic narratives to get its point across, produced alarmist media headlines that will likely elicit increased levels of anxiety and fear amongst people – itself a condition likely to foster a sense of hopelessness amongst some. In order to allay fear, or direct it productively toward the *hopefulness* of action in response to climate change, frameworks supporting knowledge exchange, community education and connectivity between individuals and communities must be developed. Likewise, places or sites of connection where productive and ethical dialogues can be nurtured are also necessary. The manner in which information about climate change will be presented, discussed and shared within communities will be a key component for action and change. While the current situation we face at both a local and global level may legitimately be described as urgent (as it often is), a state of desperation will be counter-productive. Ironically, a perceived or genuine sense of *urgency* may produce panic and an inability to respond.

Strategies to deal with climate change require both immediate action and long-term policies. Although it may appear to be a counter-intuitive statement, it would be a mistake to rush to action in some instances when more thoughtful consideration and *time* are actually required. This is not to underestimate or disregard the dire situation that some communities face right now. It is self-evident that particular nations and communities are subject to catastrophic weather events *now*, and face the immediate realities of environmental degradation, the destruction of human life, species, habitat and physical and social dislocation. Across northern

Australia and throughout the Pacific, Indigenous communities may soon be displaced from country and suffer forced relocation. The loss of country will have a devastating impact on the spiritual, physical and social wellbeing of affected communities.

Vulnerable communities able to remain *in place* will not escape the dramatic disruption to life. Rob Nixon, in his influential book *Slow Violence and the Environmentalism of the Poor*, makes the point concerning the impacts of climate change on those subject to such violence, reminding us that economic, social and cultural displacement will also occur *within* homelands, producing dire outcomes for many:

> I want to propose a more radical notion of displacement, one that, instead of referring solely to the movement of people from their places of belonging, refers rather to the loss of the land and resources beneath them, a loss that leaves communities stranded in place stripped of the very characteristics that made it inhabitable.[4]

A leading environmental activist and thinker on climate change, George Marshall, has in recent years turned his attention to the communication – in lay terms – of the physical and social science underpinning climate change and our collective inability to face its consequences and address the changes we need to now make as a global community. His recent book, *Don't Even Think About It: Why Our Brains Are Wired To Ignore Climate Change*, attempts to challenge the dilemma underpinning the title of the book.[5] Marshall begins his book with a deliberate provocation:

> How is it possible, when presented with overwhelming evidence, even the evidence of our own eyes, that we

358

can deliberately ignore something – while being entirely aware that this is what we are doing?[6]

There is no simple answer to Marshall's question, of course. The human species is more than capable of refusing logic and common sense via a range of intellectual, political and economic inhibitors. Additionally, external to our emotional and intellectual inertia, capitalism itself is a seemingly unstoppable force driving our reliance on damaging fossil fuels.[7] There is some optimism that so-called 'market forces' will eventually shift from fossil fuel energy to renewables. But we can hardly rely on or trust the market to budge us from our state of collective psychological paralysis. The more coal and other fossil fuels that remain in the ground, the better off we will be. While a move to renewables is welcome, it will not produce the necessary shift in our social or psychological relationship with the planet required to live more equitably with each other and non-human species. I agree with Jedediah Purdy that 'changes in consciousness are a necessary precondition for big and material changes in the human relation to the changing world'.[8] I also agree that such changes are of themselves insufficient. Purdy is asking something more of society, with a provocation of his own:

> What kind of world to make together – should be taken as a challenge to democracy. The test is whether citizens can form the kind of democracy that can address the Anthropocene question, the question of what kind of world to make. A democracy that cannot do this will have marked itself as inadequate to its most basic problems.[9]

Western 'first world' democracies must accept the necessary changes required to confront a looming environmental and social disaster of our own making and accept responsibility for the severity of the impact of climate change on communities that have produced the smallest carbon footprints on the planet. Indigenous communities in Australia are currently dealing with the injustices of such impacts. Ironically (or not), recognition of the challenges faced by Indigenous people as a result of climate change offer a beneficial outcome to the wider Australian community. Innovative strategies to deal with climate change must engage communities maintaining knowledge and experience capable of assisting a shift in mindset sought by thinkers such as Marshall and Purdy.[10] 'A stronger presence for Indigenous peoples in ecological protection and ecological management' is acknowledged as a central component for equitable 'agreement-making' between Indigenous people and government more generally.[11] For Deborah Bird Rose, an anthropologist who has collaborated with and gained an education through her association with Indigenous communities in Australia for more than thirty years now, new conversations, framed through humility, are required to shake Western discourses from a sense of arrogance and apathy:

> The really scary thing about the idea that our past is now racing toward us from the future is the way in which it forces us to abandon the illusion of immunity, and confront seriously the processes we have been triggering...with western mainstream time concepts losing their hold on reality, perhaps the hubris of modernity will falter enough to allow us to open new conversations about time, place and action.[12]

Caring for Country

> [I]f Will Steffen's predictions about dire and inevitable
> species loss associated with climate change prove cor-
> rect, then surely deploying the precautionary principle
> we should recognise the extraordinary importance of
> Indigenous estate to the nation's ecological future.[13]

The relationship between colonialism, capitalism and environmental degradation and a consequent link to climate change is
unambiguous. In Australia, the usurpation of land not suited for
wide-acre agricultural farming had led not only to the appropriation of Indigenous land, but also the destruction of local ecologies
and the wasteful use of natural resources such as water and soil.[14]
Jon Altman's assessment that 'the brutal colonisation and political
marginalisation of Indigenous Australians can be understood as a
conflict over land and resource rights' accurately reflects the extent
of violence utilised by colonial forces in an effort to dispossess
Indigenous people of country.[15] This is not a conflict located in
the past. The consequences of colonialism reverberate in contemporary Australian life. Inequitable socio-political and economic
structural frameworks dominate relationships between Indigenous
and non-Indigenous Australia, entrenching the marginalisation
and disempowerment of Indigenous communities:

> Operating in an environment of considerable socio-
> economic disadvantage, of extremely recent colonisation
> and displacement, and where the invading and now
> dominant culture's language and world views are so
> vastly different presents enormous challenges.[16]

The degrees of incursion of colonisation into Indigenous nations and country in Australia varies, dependent on factors such as where and when 'first contact' occurred and the strategic geographical location of the site of occupation, including the material and/or strategic value of country to the coloniser. In parts of the north of Australia, particularly the Northern Territory and 'remote' sectors of Western Australia, sustained contact between Indigenous people and white Australia did not occur until the twentieth century. As a result, relative to other parts of Australia, more Indigenous communities in these areas continue to live on country, while continuing to deal with difficulties of external interference that often prevent communities 'from undertaking their responsibilities to care for country, and in many cases unable to enjoy being on their country'.[17] The legacy of colonisation also continues to foster 'inequitable power relationships between Indigenous people and government agencies', stifling or extinguishing Indigenous autonomy.[18]

These same Indigenous communities maintain a wealth of knowledge of ecological systems invaluable to the development of our collective understanding of the historical underpinnings of the current phase of climate change. Such knowledge is invaluable, also, to understanding how national and global environmental challenges might be dealt with in both a contemporary setting and the future. In recent years, informed engagements with Indigenous communities by outside interests have attempted to address the historical impact of colonial imposition on those communities, including disruption to and, in some instances, the destruction of local ecologies. Simultaneously, Indigenous communities are increasingly articulating a desire to link aspects of cultural, economic and social wellbeing with environmental issues generally and climate change specifically. As Roston, Campion and Namarnyilk argue:

> We are all facing some big challenges with the changes in the climate. Over the last few years in particular we have seen how the changes to animals and plants in our country are not happening at the right times…this is a big worry for us. Rain is changing, wind is changing and the life of our country is changing.[19]

This assertion, expressed within Indigenous communities, that *we are all facing challenges* is a generous offer to strengthen conversations and connections with other communities across Australia – Indigenous and non-Indigenous – in the interests of ecological and environmental maintenance within a changing climate. We could use the terms such as 'equitable dialogue', 'cross-cultural awareness' (or 'exchange') or 'two-way learning' to describe these conversations. In basic terms we need to find new ways and places to talk, to give recognition to the wealth of knowledge of climate, local ecologies and the environment more generally held and practised within particular Indigenous communities. While the richness of this knowledge and the potential for productive relationships is evident, unless cultural and intellectual exchange is genuinely equitable, strategies for dealing with climate change within the wider Australian community will remain limited.[20]

The experience of Indigenous people 'caring for country' in partnership with non-Indigenous interests offers a cautionary tale when considering the models for collaborative relationships required if the impacts of climate change are to be mitigated in the future. Such a shift will require an additional *change*; a shift in the collective psyche of white Australia will necessitate an acceptance of, and a subsequent ability to embrace the realities of living on and *in* Indigenous country. Contemplating this challenge, I am (perhaps surprisingly) attracted to a simultaneously innovative, naive and practical 'thought experiment' recently suggested by the environmental humanities scholars Stephen Turner and Timothy Neale. Turner and Neale propose that *we* (being *them*, settler societies in Australia and New Zealand) need to re-imagine *our* own place *in place*, open to the provocation that 'there is no outer settler space. There is only *someone else's country*' – Indigenous country.[21] They explain that their thought experiment is no frivolous act of '"wishful thinking", or an *Avatar*-like affection for indigeneity'. With climate change described by the authors as 'our shared (global) endangerment',[22] they are attempting to nudge the collective thinking of nominally postcolonial societies, not through a utopian proposal (although the idea may appear as such) but through a refreshing proposal that makes ethical, intellectual and common sense. Living *in* Indigenous country rather than attempting to assimilate both it (country) and Indigenous people into a Eurocentric model of occupation could produce a realisation of what both *care* and *country* mean in a dynamic sense; one that is both educative and achievable. As Kerins, an anthropologist with extensive experience with Indigenous ranger programs, states:

> Caring for country constitutes something far greater than a person, or group of people having a job and physically managing a geographic area by dealing with problems created by weeds or feral animals. Caring for country encompasses being spiritually bound to country through intimate connections with ancestral beings still present in the land and waters.[23]

In his analysis of state-funded 'Caring for Country' programs within Indigenous communities, Altman reminds us of one of the unexpected benefits of colonial expansion in Australia: the lack of material attraction to particular country by settler communities has protected an asset of benefit to Indigenous people and the wider Australian community.[24] As a result of certain tracts of Indigenous land 'having low commercial value' in the nineteenth and twentieth centuries (hence their availability for land claims), the same land now yields 'high environmental, fresh water, carbon abatement and biodiversity conservation values'.[25] Country referred to by Altman as 'the most ecologically intact parts of the country [being] Aboriginal owned', offers a shift in approaches to ecological maintenance in an intellectual and physical environment where 'Western scientific expertise alone was failing to deliver outcomes'.[26] An opportunity for the due recognition of Indigenous ecological and cultural knowledge of country is obvious. Non-Indigenous society has failed to fully grasp this value, and build relationships based on mutual recognition and trust. As is often the case, Godden notes, 'partnerships' between Indigenous and non-Indigenous interests are contingent on burdensome bureaucratic frameworks and outmoded colonial models of service delivery that undermine change:

> While there have been strong calls to create more participatory frameworks for Aboriginal and Torres Strait Islander people, many trends to involve Indigenous peoples within mainstream environmental and NRM management regimes have been criticised as occurring within an assimilationist framework.[27]

If such partnerships are not limited enough in their ability to recognise the potential for genuine cross-cultural knowledge exchange, the notion of *care* in relation to country took on a new and unfortunate meaning as an outcome of the federal government's 'Intervention' in the Northern Territory in 2007.[28] Altman expresses understandable regret that a 'brief policy era of self-determination' has been replaced with a 're-imposed and paternalistic regime of normalisation or recolonisation by the state'.[29] As Indigenous communities are drawn into government-initiated, legally enforced and regressive programs (as is the case with the Intervention), autonomy and the value of Indigenous cultural knowledge is replaced with governance and the imposition of metrics. Anthropologist Eloise Fache argues that:

> Community-based natural resource management programmes are a locus where rationales of empowerment and neoliberal principles, although distinct or even mutually exclusive in appearance, are intrinsically entangled, and that these entanglements can be described as a phenomenon of 'bureaucratic participation'.[30]

As a direct result of the Intervention, 'Caring for Country' programs have shifted from a cultural and intellectual focus to the bureaucratically controlled and instrumentally informed slogan, 'Working for Country'. This is not a subtle shift in language. It is, rather, a linguistic disguise masking a more profound shift. Sean Kerins informs us that with the removal of a single word and its replacement with another, an underlying intention becomes a dominant motivation. As Kerins explains, *caring* for country is a multilayered and complex expression of Aboriginal English, whereas *working* for country is an externally enforced bureaucratic and restrictive definition. It is also purposefully narrow in scope. The use of neo-colonial language inhibits Indigenous self-determination and, consequently, the potential for a genuine exchange of ecological/environmental ideas and strategies. Kerins writes:

> By defining what is possible to think [through discourse] and suppressing others, those with institutional power – like Government agencies – do not need to draw on coercive force to change people's behaviour because the dominant discourse has established a framework, or 'rules of the game', that individuals and groups must 'play to' in order to be recognised and participate.[31]

A Difficult Space

Deborah Bird Rose has written of the 'difficult space of simultaneous critique and action' with regard to the environmental humanities as an academic discipline.[32] I want to borrow the concept of *difficulty* she raises and consider it in relation to conversations around climate change in both a general sense and the specific context of the potential for an ongoing dialogue between Indigenous and other communities in Australia. But first we need to recognise the risks at stake for Indigenous people entering into these conversations. Not only are Indigenous communities subject to knowledge appropriation, the concept of *inclusion* itself, however meaningful, can be debilitating and disempowering for Indigenous people. Gilbert Caluya, in a critique of the recent Anthropocene discourse writes of 'concerns with the universal conception at the heart of the Anthropocene because it has the potential to be used to reinstall the white liberal human subject of the Enlightenment'.[33] The enlightened white liberal concerned about the environment is also likely to harbour an unhealthy attraction to 'the native'.[34] He/she desperately wants to *belong* in Australia, and in the spirit of reconciliation, needs Indigenous people to give recognition to this desire for attachment. In situations where Indigenous people refuse to give *recognition* to 'enlightened' Australians, the likely outcome is a sense of rejection. The concept of belonging, along with that of reconciliation (bureaucratically endorsed with a capital 'R') became a populist and intellectual buzzword around the year 2000 (the year of the lauded reconciliation marches). But the notion of belonging itself is also a projection of white privilege. As O'Gorman summarises:

> [Australia] is a nation with a long history of problematic conceptualisations of belonging. Belonging is still mobilised, often in violent acts of exclusion, and means life and death.[35]

Andrew Schaap persuasively argues that governmentally driven reconciliation strategies are integral to 'anti-political movements' enacted to maintain order and moderate conflict.[36] He cautions not only against the formation of populist reconciliation movements in 'divided societies' such as Australia, but also 'the risk inherent in the politics of recognition' itself,[37] which is likely to further disempower Indigenous communities. In consideration of such a view, the recognition of, and genuine respect for, Indigenous ecological knowledge that could form the basis of new and enriched relationships between Indigenous and non-Indigenous communities remains hampered by colonial baggage. Regardless of, or perhaps as a response to, this legacy we could offer ourselves another challenge, our own thought exercise, being that difficulty, or even impossibility, is as good a place as any to begin a new conversation. If we truly desire to commence what Rose calls 'an ethical dialogue' between Indigenous and non-Indigenous people – if recognition is to carry serious weight – it will involve risk for all parties.[38] Rose values the concept of risk, channelled through open conversation:

> One does not know the outcome. To be open is to hold one's self available to others: one takes risks and becomes vulnerable. But this is also a fertile stance: one's own ground can become destabilized. In open dialogue one holds oneself available to be surprised, to be challenged and be changed.[39]

Rose is one of several non-Indigenous scholars in Australia who have, through proactive social and intellectual engagement over many years, produced a template for connectivity, mutual respect and knowledge exchange. She has worked closely with Indigenous communities for several decades, from the position of *student* as much as the university-trained researcher and intellectual. In her research she refers to her Indigenous *teachers* with no trace of paternalistic affection. Her *place* is informed by social interaction and learning through experience, rather than white deference to the 'native', either feigned or self-flagellating. Subsequently, an open dialogue, with all the risk involved, is the potential reward. Her approach refuses dominant models of engagement with Indigenous communities, located within a 'western critical theory and philosophical analysis' that Rose refers to as:

> A monologue masquerading as conversation, mastur-bation purporting to be productive interaction; it is a

369

narcissism so profound that it claims to find a universal knowledge when in fact its violent erasures are universalizing its own singular and powerful isolation.[40]

In contrast to a position of Eurocentric narcissism and ignorance, humility offers us a starting point. And it is not as if we do not have working models where 'outsiders' have given due recognition and respect to Indigenous knowledge. In Jonathan Lear's important work, *Radical Hope: Ethics in the Face of Cultural Devastation*, a study of the life of the First Nations Crow chief, Plenty Coups, Lear begins with the guiding and universal 'principle of humanity: that we should try to interpret others as saying something true'.[41] He asks that contemporary (North American) society seek out and hear 'a new Crow poet', not only as an ethical gesture, but as a challenge to a history of colonisation that relies of the comforting mythology of total conquest; an unstable psychic confidence predicated on unhindered acts of dispossession and extermination. Lear's aim is to undermine this fragile confidence, for the better, within the energy located in the 'vibrancy' of the poetic voice of Indigenous culture:

> Here by 'poet' I mean the broadest sense of a creative maker of meaningful space. The possibility for such a poet is precisely the possibility for creation of a new field of possibilities. No one is in a position to rule out that possibility.[42]

It is neither surprising nor coincidental that particular scholars working with Indigenous communities in Australia have located the creative/intellectual potential and principle of ethics in a similarly broad definition of poetry. Nor is it surprising that the same scholars have developed mutually beneficial and trustful relationships with Indigenous people due to a sustained commitment to an ethical cross-cultural dialogue.

The year 2014 witnessed the celebration of the book, *Reading the Country*, written in 1984 by Stephen Muecke, in collaboration with the Moroccan-born artist, Krim Benterrak, and the late Nyigina elder, Paddy Roe. Muecke has written many books since *Reading the Country* and his association with the Roe family continues. In 1984, Muecke's introduction to the book stated that 'it was Paddy Roe initially who had this desire to speak, to tell the story of his country once again'.[43] The occasionally nomadic Muecke had gone in search of a particular sense of poetry that would productively challenge and unhinge the status quo of colonial authority:

> One cannot imagine that the book is guided by any poetic unity or harmony. On the contrary, the poetry is of a different sort, one that responds to our times. It is a poetry of fragmentation, contradiction, unanswered questions, specificity, fluidity and change.[44]

Concepts such as fragmentation and contradiction may not immediately conjure the optimism that one might hope for with relation to the pressing issues of environmental degradation and climate change. But it is only through an energetic acceptance of the risk inherent to shifting from the restrictive framework of colonialism to genuine postcolonial relationships that change will materialise. In a similar manner to Muecke, Rose came to understand that pre-determined cultural barriers required a fresh approach if she was to begin a dialogue of understanding. In *Dingo Makes Us Human*, she recognised the necessity for new ways of interaction and learning; 'Coming to Yarralin took me out of the indirect world of books, and brought me straight to one of the most basic of all human questions: who are you?[45] After living at Yarralin for two years, Rose left the community and took with her an education delivered through a principle, both direct and profound, that could serve contemporary Australia well when thinking about developing collective ecological values:

> My primary purpose is to bring clarity to a set of issues which I understand to be those which most concern the Yarralin people...[to] understand that life is a gift, and that respect for life's manifestations is the only form of reciprocity worthy of such a gift.[46]

The Essentialism of a Bush University

In order to accept the place of human society *in place*, Jessica Weir suggests 'an expanded connectivity is needed to (re)position humans *within* a web of life sustaining relationships'. She further argues that a possible framework for a more informed sense of connectivity to place is utilised by Indigenous communities in Australia. Within country aligned to the Murray River, Weir writes, 'the traditional owners speak of a connectivity that encompasses, and goes beyond, food web dependencies to include stories, histories, feelings, shared responsibilities and respect'.[47] While Weir advances a practical and philosophical way of thinking and acting that could shift our relationship to non-human species and the planet, we must question white Australia's collective psyche and its capacity to listen to Indigenous people, particularly when the nation has shown itself to be culturally deaf in the past. And while Weir is certainly not suggesting so, we must also caution against Indigenous ecological knowledge being branded and packaged as a quick fix solution to climate change by retro-fitting it to suit Western society.

The challenge to white Australia is to address a question. How does the nation move from a state of colonial anxiety that refuses genuine recognition and engagement to a concept of locating 'Indigenous theories, methodologies, and methods at the centre, not the periphery' of our society?[48] While such a shift could ultimately produce 'an ecological philosophy of mutual benefit', getting there will be a serious challenge.[49] This political and cultural mind-shift would appear seismic, perhaps beyond realistic expectations in a nation where the shrillest voices continue to dominate popular discourse on Indigenous/non-Indigenous relations.[50] Colonial denial, manifested in a variety of forms and locations, is at the heart of cultural ignorance in Australia. With climate change a crisis that can no longer be *denied* (regardless of the worn-out mantras of denialists) both illusion and elusion must become redundant, if the inherent damage of denialism is to cease. Ghassan Hage suggests that:

> The more a colonizing nation can shield its citizens from realities, carving out spaces where they are not exposed to the colonial conditions of their good life, the more civilized it appears.[51]

Hage (among others) articulates a clear link between 'colonial and ecological crises', in particular 'how the two experiences work together to accentuate the feeling of colonial besiegement and to give it its particular intensity today'.[52] Settler colonialism, 'in which outsiders come to make a new home', is dependent on the expropriation of Indigenous land and culture, followed by targeted forms of denialism and amnesia 'designed not to consider place – to do so would require consideration of genocide'.[53] A thoughtful, ethical change of consciousness is too difficult a challenge for those for whom the cost would be the dismantling of a colonial fantasy. As Tuck and McKenzie argue:

> Turning toward place necessitates acknowledgement and reparations based on these histories: of settler colonialism, capitalism…separations of mind from body, body from land. As humans make our planet increasingly toxic, unlivable, and at the same time increasingly inequitable, at what point might these cleavages be sewn back together, might we account for our pasts and to future generations?[54]

A second colonial legacy inhibiting the value of something like mutual recognition between Indigenous and non-Indigenous people in Australia is an essentialist view of what constitutes a legitimate Indigenous identity in the colonial mind, manifested in both a physical/biological identity, in addition to a narrow view of what constitutes a legitimate connection to place and country. An understanding of what constitutes 'country' is too often essentialised by white Australians. It therefore disenfranchises both the land on which the majority of Indigenous communities live and Indigenous people ourselves. If there is legitimacy in the belief that 'according to geographers and environmental psychologists, questions of "who we are" are often intimately related to questions of "where we are"',[55] most Indigenous people are rendered suspect at best, living overwhelmingly in suburbs, cities and regional towns. *Where we are* has a negative impact on how outsiders perceive *who we are*. The consequence of such a view also impacts directly on the legitimacy of the intellectual and cultural knowledge held in urban Indigenous communities. Engagement and consultation on ecological and environmental matters with the 70 per cent of Indigenous people living in urban areas is typically given little attention.[56]

Despite being a relatively large population, Indigenous people living in cities 'have historically been afforded little visibility'[57] except as the dependent, threatening or tainted (with the menace posed by the 'half-caste menace' remaining self-evident, even if the language has changed over time). According to the Indigenous scholar Larissa Behrendt, 'the non-indigenous imaginary' remains fixated on a connection between Indigenous people and 'nature'.[58] Those of us not attached to this concept of 'nature' are of little value beyond relationships fixated on welfare, criminal and various social dependency industries.

The collective action required to deal with climate change must dispose of such ignorant views. A shift in mindset is required in order to produce meaningful and valuable interactions between Indigenous and non-Indigenous people, regardless of where Indigenous people live. Key thinkers in the area, such as Rose, ask that non-Indigenous people begin a conversation that respects Indigenous self-determination while considering the value of relationships built on 'connection' rather than 'unity'.[59] For Rose 'unity' is too often code for assimilation and appropriation. A leading educator and thinker linking education and ecological concerns, Chet Bowers, argues that a framework of 'eco-justice', incorporating a philosophy of mutual recognition, is necessary in order to deal with the environmental concerns we face. He defines eco-justice as:

Understanding the relationship between ecological and cultural systems, specifically between the domination of nature and the domination of oppressed groups; addressing environmental racism, including the geographical dimension of social injustice and environmental pollution; revitalizing the non-commodified traditions of different racial and ethnic groups and communities, especially those traditions that support ecological sustainability; re-conceiving and adapting our lifestyles in ways that will not jeopardize the environment for future generations.[60]

Conclusion

In her recent book, *Decolonizing Solidarity,* Clare Land writes that 'the paternalism and tension in relationships between non-Indigenous and Indigenous activists are, at heart, generated by colonial conditions'.[61] If the Bowers manifesto, linking environmental and social justice, were to gain traction in settler societies such as Australia, the colonial conditions that continue to both haunt and influence relationships between Indigenous and non-Indigenous people must shift, dramatically so, both within defined localities and communities and on a national scale. While a shift in attitude, behaviour and dialogue should not be afforded undue optimism in Australia, considering the levels of racism and xenophobia that continue to infect the nation, the opposite, of journeying forward with blindness and ignorance is untenable for all of us, human and non-human.

In the future, ecological and environmental maintenance will require collective thinking, commitment and effort on a global scale. Solutions to climate change will remain elusive without such an undertaking. Solutions will not come from a reliance on government. In fact, progress on climate change will remain stifled if governments dominate discussion. Gatherings of the 'world leaders' of politics and business have delivered limited outcomes (at best), with discussion rarely moving beyond non-committal communiqués that provide little more than a media opportunity. Rather than wait for governments to act on climate change in a sustained manner we could do worse than invest in the old slogan, 'act locally – think globally' and translate it into meaningful and sustained outcomes. Through an intellectual, cultural and, for some, a spiritual attachment to place and country, we can produce productive outcomes.

References

Altman, J. C., 'People on country as alternate development', in J. C. Altman & S. Kerins (eds), *People on Country: Vital Landscapes Indigenous Futures*, The Federation Press, Sydney, 2012, pp. 1–25.

Aly, W., 'Why Australia Lies To Itself About Indigenous History', *The Age*, 31 March 2016.

Barbour, W. & Schlesinger, C., 'Who's the boss? Post-colonialism, ecological research and conservation management on Australian Indigenous lands', *Ecological Management & Restoration*, vol. 13, no. 1, 2012, pp. 36–41.

Benterrak, K., Muecke, S. & Roe, P., *Reading The Country: Introduction to Nomadology*, Fremantle Arts Centre Press, Fremantle, 1984.

Birch, T., 'Climate Change, Mining and Traditional Indigenous Knowledge in Australia', *Social Inclusion*, vol. 4, no. 1, 2016, pp. 92–101.

Caluya, G., 'Fragments for a Postcolonial Critique of the Anthropocene: Invasion biology and environmental security', in J. Frawley & I. McCalman (eds), *Rethinking Invasion Ecologies from the Environmental Humanities*, Taylor and Francis, Florence, 2014, pp. 31–44.

Daley, P., 'It's not "politically correct" to say Australia was invaded, it's history', *The Guardian*, 30 March 2016.

Dixon, J., & Durrheim, K., 'Displacing place-identity: A discursive approach to locating self and other', *British Journal of Social Psychology*, no. 39, 2000, pp. 27–44.

Fache, E., 'Caring for Country, a Form of Bureaucratic Participation: Conservation, development, and Neoliberalism in Indigenous Australia', *Anthropological Forum: A Journal of Social Anthropology and Comparative Sociology*, 2014, pp. 267–86.

Fredericks, B., '"We don't leave our identities at the city limits": Aboriginal and Torres Strait Islander people living in urban localities', *Australian Aboriginal Studies,* no. 1, 2013, pp. 4–16.

Godden, L., 'Native Title and Ecology: Agreement-making in an Era of Market Environmentalism', in J. W. Weir (ed.), *Country, Native Title and Ecology,* ANU E-Press, Canberra, 2012, pp. 105–34.

Gruenewald, D. A., 'The Best of Both Worlds: A Critical Pedagogy of Place', *Educational Researcher,* vol. 32, no. 4, pp. 3–12.

Hage, G., 'Etat de siege: A dying domesticating colonialism?', *Open Anthropology: a Public Journal of the American Anthropological Association,* 2016, pp. 1–19.

Holthaus, E., 'Northern hemisphere temperature breaches a terrifying milestone', *New Scientist,* 7 March 2006 <http://www.newscientist.com/article/2079775>.

Kerins, S., 'Caring for Country to Working on Country', in J. C. Altman & S. Kerins, *People on Country: Vital Landscapes Indigenous Futures,* The Federation Press, Sydney, 2012, pp. 26–44.

Land, C., *Decolonizing Solidarity: Dilemmas and Directions for Supporters of Indigenous Struggles,* Zed Books, London, 2015, p. 7.

Lear, J., *Radical Hope: Ethics in the Face of Cultural Devastation,* Harvard University Press, Cambridge, 2006.

Malm, A., *Fossil Capital: The Rise of Steam Power and the Roots of Global Warming,* Verso, London, 2016.

Marika, M. & Roeger, S., 'Dhimurru wind bringing change', in J. Altman & S. Kerins, *People on Country: Vital Landscapes Indigenous Futures,* The Federation Press, Sydney, 2012, pp. 119–31.

Marshall, G., *Don't Even Think About It: Why Our Brains Are Wired To Ignore Climate Change,* Bloomsbury, New York, 2014.

McGaw, J., Pieris, A. & Potter, E., 'Indigenous Place-Making in the City: Dispossessions, Occupations and Implications for Cultural Architecture', *Architectural Theory Review,* vol. 16, no. 3, 2011, pp. 296–311.

Moore, J. M., (ed.), *Anthropocene or Capitalocene?: Nature, History, and the Crisis of Capitalism,* PM Press/Kairos, 2016.

Muecke, S., 'Ngapartji Ngapartji', in V. Castejon, A. Cole, O. Haag & K. Hughes (eds), *In Turn in Turn: Ego-histoire, Europe and Indigenous Australia,* Australian National University Press, Canberra, 2014, pp. 259–69.

Nixon, R., *Slow Violence and the Environmentalism of the Poor,* Harvard University Press, Cambridge, 2011.

O'Gorman, E., 'Belonging; Living Lexicon for the Environmental Humanities', *Environmental Humanities,* vol. 5, 2014, pp. 283–6.

Povinelli, E., *The Cunning of Recognition: Indigenous Alterities and the Making of Australian Multiculturalism*, Duke University Press, Durham, NC.

Purdy, J., *After Nature: A Politics for the Anthropocene*, Harvard University Press, Cambridge, 2015.

Robertson, J., 'Dangerous global warming will happen sooner than thought – study', *The Guardian*, 10 March 2016 <https://www.theguardian.com/environment/2016/mar/10/dangerous-global-warming-will-happen-sooner-than-thought-study>.

Rose, D. B., *Dingo Makes Us Human: Life and Land in an Australian Aboriginal Culture*, Cambridge University Press, Cambridge, 2000.

Rose, D. B., 'An Indigenous Philosophical Ecology: Situating the Human', *The Australian Journal of Anthropology*, vol. 16, no. 3, 2005, pp. 294–305.

Rose, D. B., 'Anthropocene Noir', in P. James, C. Hudson, S. Caroll-Bell & A. Taing (eds), *People and the Planet 2013 Conference Proceedings*, Global Cities Research Institute, RMIT University, Melbourne, Australia, 2013 <http://global-cities.info/wp-content/uploads/2014/05/Anthropocene-Noir.pdf>.

Rose, D. B., 'Dialogue', in K. Gibson, D. B. Rose & R. Fincher (eds), *Manifesto for Living in the Anthropocene*, Punctum Books, Brooklyn, NY, 2015, pp. 12–131.

Rose, D. B., van Dooren, T., Chrulew, M., Cooke, S., Kearns, M. & O'Gorman, E., 'Thinking Through the Environment, Unsettling the Humanities', *Environmental Humanities*, 1, 2012, pp. 1–5.

Rostron, V., Campion, W. & Namarnyilk, I., 'Countrymen standing together', in J. Altman & S. Kerins, *People on Country: Vital Landscapes Indigenous Futures*, The Federation Press, Sydney, 2012, pp. 162–73.

Schaap, A., 'Political Reconciliation Through a Struggle for Recognition', *Social & Legal Studies*, vol. 13, no. 4, 2004, pp. 523–40.

Scott, R., & Heiss, A. (eds), *The Intervention: An Anthology*, Griffin Press, Salisbury South, 2015.

Tuck, E. & McKenzie, M., 'Relational Validity and the "Where" of Inquiry: Place and land in Qualitative Research', *Qualitative Inquiry*, 2015, pp. 1–6.

Turner, S. & Neale, T., 'First Law and the Force Of Water: Law, Water, Entitlement', *Settler Colonial Studies*, vol. 5, no. 4, 2015, pp. 387–97.

Weir, J. W., 'Connectivity', *Australian Humanities Review*, vol. 45, 2008, pp. 1–8.

Weizman, E. & Sheik, F., *The Conflict Shoreline: Colonization as Climate Change in the Negev Desert*, Steidl, Brooklyn, 2015.

Notes

1   J. Robertson, 'Dangerous global warming will happen
     sooner than thought – study', *The Guardian*, 10 March 2016
     <https://www.theguardian.com/environment/2016/mar/10/
     dangerous-global-warming-will-happen-sooner-than-thought-study>.

2   ibid.

3   E. Holthaus, 'Northern hemisphere temperature breaches a terrifying
     milestone', *New Scientist*, 7 March 2006 <http://www.newscientist.com/
     article/2079775>.

4   R. Nixon, *Slow Violence and the Environmentalism of the Poor*, Harvard
     University Press, Cambridge, 2011, p. 9.

5   Marshall also presents a 'live' version of the book, via power-point, to
     public audiences, both physical and virtual, using the world wide web. For
     an example of his presentation see 'George Marshall "Don't Even Think
     About it" – with George Monbiot' <https://youtu.be/JdAifpWgh4g>.

6   G. Marshall, *Don't Even Think About It: Why Our Brains Are Wired To Ignore
     Climate Change*, Bloomsbury, New York, 2014, p. 1.

7   For a history of the historical relationship between fossil fuels and the
     rise of capitalism see A. Malm, *Fossil Capital: The Rise of Steam Power and
     the Roots of Global Warming*, Verso, London, 2016. For a concise discussion
     of current debates around climate change and capitalism see J. M. Moore
     (ed.), *Anthropocene or Capitalocene?: Nature, History, and the Crisis of Capitalism*,
     PM Press/Kairos, 2016.

8   J. Purdy, *After Nature: A Politics for the Anthropocene*, Harvard University Press,
     Cambridge, 2015, p. 260.

9   ibid., p. 267.

10   T. Birch, 'Climate Change, Mining and Traditional Indigenous Knowledge
     in Australia', *Social Inclusion*, vol. 4, no. 1, 2016, pp. 92–101.

11   L. Godden, 'Native Title and Ecology: Agreement-making in an Era of
     Market Environmentalism', in J. W. Weir (ed.), *Country, Native Title and
     Ecology*, Australian National University E-Press, Canberra, 2012, p. 104.

12   D. Bird, 'Anthropocen Noir', *People and Planet 2013 Conference Proceedings*,
     Global Cities Research Institute, RMIT University, Melbourne, Australia,
     2013, p. 7.

13   J. Altman, 'People on country as alternate development', in J. Altman
     & S. Kerins, *People on Country: Vital Landscapes Indigenous Futures*, The
     Federation Press, Sydney, 2012, p. 2.

14   See: Malm, *Fossil Capital*; Moore (ed.), *Anthropocene or Capitalocene?*;
     E. Weizman & F. Sheik, *The Conflict Shoreline: Colonization as Climate
     Change in the Negev Desert*, Steidl, Brooklyn, 2015.

15 Altman, 'People on country', p. 7.
16 M. Marika & S. Roeger, 'Dhimurru wind bringing change', in J. Altman & S. Kerins, *People on Country: Vital Landscapes Indigenous Futures,* The Federation Press, Sydney, 2012, p. 129.
17 ibid., p. 119.
18 W. Barbour & C. Schlesinger, 'Who's the boss? Post-colonialism, ecological research and conservation management on Australian Indigenous lands', *Ecological Management & Restoration,* vol. 13, no. 1, 2012, p. 38.
19 V. Rostron, W. Campion & I. Namarnyilk, 'Countrymen standing together', in J. Altman & S. Kerins, *People on Country: Vital Landscapes Indigenous Futures,* The Federation Press, Sydney, 2012, p. 173.
20 Birch, *Social Inclusion.*
21 S. Turner, & T. Neale, 'First Law and the Force Of Water: Law, Water, Entitlement', *Settler Colonial Studies,* vol. 5, no. 4, 2015, p. 390.
22 ibid., p. 391.
23 S. Kerins, 'Caring for Country to Working on Country', in J. Altman & S. Kerins (eds), *People on Country: Vital Landscapes Indigenous Futures,* The Federation Press, Sydney, 2012, p. 29.
24 For a thorough analysis of the conceptualisation and delivery of 'caring for country' programs in the Northern Territory, see J. C. Altman & S. Kerins (eds), *People on Country.*
25 Altman, 'People on country', p. 6.
26 ibid., pp. 2–3.
27 L. Godden, 'Native Title and Ecology', p. 111.
28 For a wide-ranging and informed discussion of the Northern Territory Intervention see R. Scott & A. Heiss (eds), *The Intervention: An Anthology,* Griffin Press, Salisbury South, 2015.
29 Altman, 'People on country', p. 18.
30 E. Fache, 'Caring for Country, a Form of Bureaucratic Participation: Conservation, development, and Neoliberalism in Indigenous Australia', *Anthropological Forum: A Journal of Social Anthropology and Comparative Sociology,* 2014 <http://dx.doi.org/10.1080/00664677.2014.939576>.
31 S. Kerins, 'Caring for Country to Working on Country', p. 26.
32 D. B. Rose, T. van Dooren, M. Chrulew, S. Cooke, M. Kearns & E. O'Gorman, 'Thinking Through the Environment, Unsettling the Humanities', *Environmental Humanities,* 1, 2012, p. 3.
33 G. Caluya, 'Fragments for a Postcolonial Critique of the Anthropocene: Invasion biology and environmental security', in J. Frawley & I. McCalman (eds), *Rethinking Invasion Ecologies from the Environmental Humanities,* Taylor and Francis, Florence, 2014, p. 41.

34 E. Povinelli, *The Cunning of Recognition: Indigenous Alterities and the Making of Australian Multiculturalism,* Duke University Press, Durham, NC.

35 E. O'Gorman, 'Belonging; Living Lexicon for the Environmental Humanities', *Environmental Humanities,* vol. 5, 2014, p. 284.

36 A. Schaap, 'Political Reconciliation Through a Struggle for Recognition', *Social & Legal Studies,* vol. 13, no. 4, 2004, pp. 524–5.

37 ibid., p. 530.

38 D. B. Rose, 'Dialogue', in K. Gibson, D. B. Rose & R. Fincher (eds), *Manifesto for Living in the Anthropocene,* Punctum Books, Brooklyn, NY, 2015, p. 129.

39 ibid., p. 128.

40 ibid.

41 J. Lear, *Radical Hope: Ethics in the Face of Cultural Devastation,* Harvard University Press, Cambridge, 2006, p. 4.

42 ibid., p. 51.

43 K. Benterrak, S. Muecke & P. Roe, *Reading The Country: Introduction to Nomadology,* Fremantle Arts Centre Press, Fremantle, 1984, p. 15.

44 ibid., p. 15.

45 D. B. Rose, *Dingo Makes Us Human: Life and Land in an Australian Aboriginal Culture,* Cambridge University Press, Cambridge, 2000, p. 26.

46 ibid., p. 41.

47 J. W. Weir, 'Connectivity', *Australian Humanities Review,* vol. 45, 2008, pp. 1–2.

48 E. Tuck & M. McKenzie, 'Relational Validity and the "Where" of Inquiry: Place and land in Qualitative Research', *Qualitative Inquiry,* 2015, p. 4.

49 Rose, *The Australian Journal of Anthropology,* p. 294.

50 For instance, witness the recent debate around the term 'settlement' versus 'invasion' and how Australian history is taught in schools as only one instance of ongoing colonial anxiety. For media coverage of the issue see: P. Daley, 'It's not "politically correct" to say Australia was invaded, it's history', *The Guardian* (Australia), 30 March 2016; W. Aly, 'Why Australia Lies To Itself About Indigenous History', *The Age,* 31 March 2016.

51 G. Hage, 'Etat de siege: A dying domesticating colonialism?', *Open Anthropology: a Public Journal of the American Anthropological Association,* 2016, p. 8.

52 ibid.; see also E. Weizman & F. Sheik, *The Conflict Shoreline.*

53 E. Tuck & M. McKenzie, 'Relational Validity and the "Where" of Inquiry: Place and land in Qualitative Research', p. 4.

54 ibid., p. 3.

55 J. Dixon & K. Durrheim, 'Displacing place-identity: A discursive approach

to locating self and other', *British Journal of Social Psychology*, no. 39, 2000, p. 27.

56 B. Fredericks, '"We don't leave our identities at the city limits": Aboriginal and Torres Strait Islander people living in urban localities', *Australian Aboriginal Studies*, no. 1, 2013, p. 4.

57 J. McGaw, A. Pieris & E. Potter, 'Indigenous Place-Making in the City: Dispossessions, Occupations and Implications for Cultural Architecture', *Architectural Theory Review*, vol. 16, no. 3, 2011, p. 297.

58 ibid., p. 300.

59 D. B. Rose, 'Anthropocene Noir', in P. James, C. Hudson, S. Caroll-Bell & A. Taing (eds), *People and the Planet 2013 Conference Proceedings*, Global Cities Research Institute, RMIT University, Melbourne, Australia, 2013, p. 5 <http://global-cities.info/wp-content/uploads/2014/05/Anthropocene-Noir.pdf>.

60 Bowers in D. A. Gruenewald, 'The Best of Both Worlds: A Critical Pedagogy of Place', *Educational Researcher*, vol. 32, no. 4, p. 6.

61 C. Land, *Decolonizing Solidarity: Dilemmas and Directions for Supporters of Indigenous Struggles*, Zed Books, London, 2015, p. 7.